Realizing the Dream of R. A. Kartini

This series of publications on Africa, Latin America, Southeast Asia, and Global and Comparative Studies is designed to present significant research, translation, and opinion to area specialists and to a wide community of persons interested in world affairs. The editor seeks manuscripts of quality on any subject and can usually make a decision regarding publication within three months of receipt of the original work. Production methods generally permit a work to appear within one year of acceptance. The editor works closely with authors to produce a high-quality book. The series appears in a paperback format and is distributed worldwide. For more information, contact the executive editor at Ohio University Press, 19 Circle Drive, The Ridges, Athens, Ohio 45701.

Executive editor: Gillian Berchowitz
AREA CONSULTANTS
Africa: Diane M. Ciekawy
Latin America: Brad Jokisch, Patrick Barr-Melej, and Rafael Obregon
Southeast Asia: William H. Frederick

The Ohio University Research in International Studies series is published for the Center for International Studies by Ohio University Press. The views expressed in individual volumes are those of the authors and should not be considered to represent the policies or beliefs of the Center for International Studies, Ohio University Press, or Ohio University.

KONINKLIJK INSTITUUT
VOOR TAAL-, LAND- EN VOLKENKUNDE

Realizing the Dream of R. A. Kartini
Her Sisters' Letters from Colonial Java

Edited and translated by Joost Coté

OHIO UNIVERSITY RESEARCH IN INTERNATIONAL STUDIES
SOUTHEAST ASIA SERIES No. 114
OHIO UNIVERSITY PRESS
ATHENS

KITLV PRESS
LEIDEN

© 2008 by the
Center for International Studies
Ohio University
United States of America
www.ohio.edu/oupress

Published in Europe by:
KITLV Press
Koninklijk Instituut voor Taal-, Land- en Volkenkunde
(Royal Netherlands Institute of Southeast Asian and Caribbean Studies)
P.O. Box 9515
2300 RA Leiden
The Netherlands
website: www.kitlv.nl
e-mail: kitlvpress@kitlv.nl
ISBN 97890 6718 313 0
KITLV is an institute of the Royal Netherlands Academy of Arts and Sciences (KNAW)

All rights reserved

19 18 17 16 15 14 13 12 11 10 09 08   5 4 3 2 1

The books in the Ohio University Research in International Studies Series
are printed on acid-free paper ∞ ™

Library of Congress Cataloging-in-Publication Data

Realizing the dream of R. A. Kartini : her sisters' letters from colonial Java /
edited and translated by Joost Coté.
  p. cm. — (Research in international studies. Southeast Asia series ; no. 114)
Includes bibliographical references and index.
ISBN-13: 978-0-89680-253-7 (pbk : alk. paper)
ISBN-10: 0-89680-253-1 (pbk : alk. paper)
  1. Indonesia—History—1798–1942. 2. Nationalism—Indonesia—History. 3. Nationalists—Indonesia—Correspondence. I. Coté, Joost. II. Series.
DS643.R38 2008
320.5409598092'2—dc22

2007045856

Contents

List of Illustrations		vii
Note on the Text		ix
	Introduction	1
ONE	Letters from Roekmini	50
TWO	Letters from Kardinah	184
THREE	Letters from Kartinah	214
FOUR	Letters from Soematri	238
APPENDIX	Documents Relating to the Establishment of the Wismo Pranowo School	303
Notes		311
Glossary		381
Bibliography		385
Index		391

Illustrations

Kardinah, Kartini, and Roekmini, c. 1900
Kartini, Kardinah, and Roekmini, 1901
Kartinah and Soematri, c. 1902
Ibu Ngasirah, c. 1900
Raden Ayu Moeryam, c. 1900
Raden Mas Adipati Ario Sosroningrat, regent of Jepara, c. 1900
Jacques Henri Abendanon, 1903
Rosita Manuela Abendanon-Mandri, c. 1912
Home of Jacques and Rosita Abendanon, 1896
Interior, home of Jacques and Rosita Abendanon, 1896
The three sons of Jacques and Rosita Abendanon, c. 1895
Kartini and her husband, Raden Adipati Djojoadiningrat, regent of Rembang, 1903
Kartini, Raden Adipati Djojoadiningrat, Soematri, Roekmini, and Kartinah, 1903
Raden Mas Singgih, Rembang, 1904
Roekmini and her husband, Santoso
Kartinah, 1909
Soematri, c. 1910
Soematri and her husband, Achmad Sostrohadikoesoemo, 1911
Soematri and her son Soearto at three and a half months, 1912
Jacques Henri Abendanon, c. 1925
Rosita Manuela Abendanon-Mandri, c. 1925
Three sisters with friend, 1935

The illustrations appear after page 220.

Note on the Text

The aim in presenting this material has been to rescue the narrative of what till now have been largely unknown women from beneath the shadow cast by their more famous sister. This publication aims to reinstate—or perhaps, rather, to position appropriately for the first time—the story of Kartini's siblings in their own right. In the commentary to the current volume, it is largely assumed that the history preceding these letters is already generally known. An extensive commentary on Raden Ajeng Kartini as person and as phenomenon in Indonesian history already exists, and selections of her correspondence have been available to an international audience for most of the twentieth century and into this one. Inevitably, however, in a discussion of her sisters' lives, references to Kartini have been necessary, if for no other reason than that the correspondents themselves so fulsomely refer to their sister throughout their writing. Therefore, some discussion of Kartini and references to her correspondence will be found in both the introduction and the endnotes.

This correspondence forms part of the same archive that includes Kartini's extensive correspondence, which has been in the public domain for some time and has also been translated by the present writer and published previously. It is possible, then, to read these letters and Kartini's as a single archive of correspondence which, according to the inventory, numbers 235 letters in total. The original correspondence is held at the archive of the Koninklijk Instituut voor Taal-, Land- en Volkenkunde (KITLV), now known by its English name, the Royal Netherlands Institute of Southeast Asian and Caribbean Studies. The KITLV also holds a range of correspondence surrounding the publication of *Door Duisternis tot Licht*, the original volume of Kartini's letters, as well as the photographs used in this volume. This extensive archive was initially presented to the Institute by the descendants of Jacques Abendanon in 1986. I wish to acknowledge the Institute, and in particular Dr. Gerrit Knaap, the former head of the Department of Documentation and Archive (now Department of Collections), and his successor, Dr Rosemarijn Hoefte, for their readiness to support both translation projects over the years and for readily granting permission for the use of the photographs in this publication. For facilitating the inclusion of the photographs, I am indebted to the friendly support from the KITLV Special Collections Coordinator, Jan van Rosmalen, and the librarian of the Special Collections Department, Jaap Anten.

In 2005, I was also able to meet with descendants of Jacques Abendanon, Mr. Dolph Abendanon and Mrs. An Stork, who freely gave their time and access to further personal data. Several photographs and some information used in this volume, as indicated, are the result of their generosity. I am grateful for their time and support for the project. Much more was offered than I was able to take advantage of.

In this exercise in translation, every effort has been made here to faithfully represent the intended nuances and feelings as expressed by the individual writers through their chosen medium of the Dutch language, but also, by judicious footnoting, to point to and clarify contemporary references of significance. Specific historical references as they appear in individual letters are highlighted by endnotes and referred to in the general introduction only in as far as they form part of the broader discussion. Specific note references to letters by Kartini refer to those included in Coté, *Letters from Kartini* (1992; letters to Rosita) or Coté, *On Feminism and Nationalism* (2005; letters to Stella Zeehandelaar). No further citation is provided in the notes.

Apart from several early letters that have been excluded and in one case, abridged (but that have been previously published with Kartini's letters), no excision of the extant documentary material has been made. This means that not all content will be of immediate historical interest, and that the letters remain what they are: a personal correspondence across geographical, cultural, and social distances, recording a range of issues, events, and concerns their authors wished to communicate.

The introduction is intended to provide a general and wide-ranging gloss on this correspondence. It aims to draw out and generally background the historical significance of the events, persons, and ideas referred to. A separate introduction has been provided to each set of letters. Because each of the four women lived well into the latter part of the twentieth century—Kardinah to 1971, Soematri to 1963, Roekmini to 1951, and Kartinah to sometime after 1963—the letters themselves provide an account of only the first part of their adult lives. The introduction has not attempted to provide complete biographies, which would constitute a separate project. Nor has any attempt been made here to investigate, comment on, or imply observations on matters of a more personal or family nature.

This is a translation of many pages of handwritten letters, generally written in a uniform and, after some familiarity, quite readable style, and almost without exception in impeccable Dutch. Only in some rare cases have individual handwritten words challenged attempts at deciphering; where this may have contributed to rendering the meaning of the text doubtful, this has been indicated in an endnote. Stylistically, the original texts vary one from another and reflect an older, and some might say a specifically "Indisch," or Javanese-influenced, Dutch. As much as possible of such characteristics and awkwardnesses has been retained in translation where this did not overly disrupt an English-language reading. In the interest of flavor, all Javanese and Malay (Indonesian) terms used in the original have been retained, as well as some Dutch terms. These are listed in a glossary toward the end of the volume. These words formed part of the version of Dutch that had evolved in the Indies and still appears in the vocabulary of a Dutch generation that has had any association with the Indies.

The terms "Inlandsch" and "Inlander" occur throughout the correspondence, and after some consideration it is been decided to translate them here as "Native," a term that has obviously attracted some opprobrium. The use of these Dutch terms by the authors, who, it is argued in the introduction, espoused firm nationalist convictions, tends to follow a discernible pattern. Generally the terms are used when referring to colonially marked institutions or categories, or when the subject identifies herself in terms of such institutions or categories. When speaking from their own position, however, they almost always refer to "Java" and "Javanese." Leaving "Inlandsch" and "Inlander" in Dutch was considered, but for non-Dutch readers this might have helped disguise the sharp colonial divisions they implied.

Since this translation was first made, an Indonesian translation of the letters has appeared, edited by the late Frits Jaquet, long-time researcher at the KITLV and the person responsible for the initial publication of the complete letters of Kartini. The English translation of these letters, together with the contextual notes and introductions will, it is hoped, ensure an even wider readership for this remarkable archive.

The original spelling of personal names has been maintained, but for ease of identification the modern spellings of place-names have been substituted. Hence: Soematri, not Sumatri, and Jepara, not Japara.

Finally, I should like to acknowledge the person who first set me on the trail of Kartini and her sisters, Dr. Ailsa (Thommy) Zainu'ddin, for whom the history of Kartini and her sisters continues to be a life-long interest and the many (unnamed) friends who continue to teach me about Java.

INTRODUCTION

Introduction

The name of Raden Ajeng Kartini (1879–1904) is well known in Indonesian history. It is a name inextricably linked to the history of Indonesians' struggle for political and cultural independence. Her name has also traveled beyond Indonesia and holds a celebrated place in the history of international feminism. In a series of voluminous letters written in Dutch between 1899 and her untimely death in 1904, Kartini described in detail her ambitions to extend her own formal education in order to be of service in the cultural development of her people. In particular, she wrote of the importance of the modern education of women—the mothers of the future nation—and of the need for the emancipation of Indonesian women from their entrapment in feudal patriarchal tradition.

As is often the case with iconic historical figures, the attention they receive tends to obscure the lives of those around them, people in and through whom their influence was articulated and who may have been essential to their emotional and intellectual well-being. Such is very much the case with Kartini's siblings.

This volume is devoted to the correspondence of her sisters: Roekmini (1880–1951), Kardinah (1881–1971), Kartinah (1883–?), and Soematri (1888–1963). Even among those familiar with the history of Kartini, little is known about these women, largely because their letters have not been made public.[1] The present English-language collection therefore aims to complete a half-told story by situating Kartini's sisters in their own right within the more famous Kartini narrative—and, indirectly, situating Kartini herself in a broader narrative. By expanding the public record of this extraordinary figure, it also aims to contribute to the history of women and the narrative of nationalism in Indonesia.

Kartini was one of a family of eleven children, six female and five male. Two sisters in particular, respectively one and two years younger, formed with her a closely bonded trio of brave "revolutionaries" who attempted to change their world. Two younger sisters, forming as it were a second generation, followed in their wake. With the departure of the youngest of the trio and, two years later, of Kartini herself, as a result of arranged marriages (and with Kartini's untimely death soon thereafter), it was the third of this trio who in fact sustained "the cause," as they themselves had described their determination to achieve a vision of the future. While Kartini had thus defined their place both in history and contemporaneously, it was the sisters who had to assume the burden of attempting to fulfill the dream. Who these sisters were, how they separately lived out this dream, and what characterized their separate pathways through a society that they themselves had been instrumental in disturbing, is a story yet to be told. It is hoped that making this extensive correspondence available for the first time will ensure that the sisters also achieve a place in history.

This correspondence by four of Kartini's five sisters (one older sister never becomes part of this narrative of a cultural revolution), which stretches from 1901 to 1936, is of interest for more than its intrinsic value as the life histories of four women. As the product of four female writers, it has particular significance as an almost unique primary source record of this period in the history of Java. This was an era that saw the emergence and articulation of an Indonesian nationalist movement, but equally it was an era of significant cultural change and social upheaval. It was the beginning of a period in which the characteristics of what can be called "modernity" became increasingly apparent. These women were active participants in both the political and cultural domain. The protagonists against whom they vigorously took up arms in their correspondence were colonial officialdom and its enactment of colonial policy; colonials and their *mentalité;* the traditional *priyayi,* or Javanese aristocratic class, and its attempts to maintain the traditional values of a feudal patriarchal society in the midst of change; and, it needs to be said, "the stupid people," those masses unable to recognize their own best interests. The sisters' own lives, which they describe in some detail, reflect those of a small segment of Javanese society, but reflect upon a much broader narrative of cultural change shared by increasing numbers of their compatriots. They form part of what one might describe as the cultural revolution of modernity.

Like the 105 previously published letters written by Kartini,[2] the letters of her sisters are written in near-perfect Dutch and mainly to Rosita Abendanon-Mandri. The collection, donated to the Institute for Southeast Asian and Caribbean Studies by descendants of the recipients,[3] also includes letters by three of the women's husbands, who each held significant positions in the colonial bureaucracy. These letters, most of them addressed to Jacques Abendanon, the former director of colonial education, provide a more critical insight into the developing nationalist politics of the times and are clearly inspired by other motives than is the correspondence of their wives. They also provide an indication of the extent to which the sisters, as adults, wives, and mothers, remained interested and involved, as Kartini was, in the broader political framework within which they sought to achieve their more specific aims for women.

Although the bulk of this correspondence deals with the period after 1904 and thus after the death of Kartini, in each case the earliest letters included here were written together with Kartini. The dramatic last years of Kartini's life, then, were not just a prelude to, but represent the beginning of, their own separate narratives. Moreover, the sisters saw themselves as continuing a correspondence which they had already begun to share with their older sister, and they continued to write with the conscious reference to ideals and ideas they had come to share with their late sister. An adequate appreciation of the account of the lives of these four women, then, inevitably needs to begin with a recognition of their link with their more famous sister.

The Context

The sisters' father, Raden Mas Adipati Ario Sosroningrat, was a descendant of an old and extremely influential East Javanese dynastic family, the Tjondronegoro. The family, which traced its origins to the regents of the illustrious Majapahit empire of the thirteenth to fifteenth centuries,[4] had established its social position well before the arrival of the Europeans. Under colonialism, the Tjondronegoro dynasty had benefitted from the dependence of the colonial administration on traditional rulers. While less significant under late colonialism than they had been during the period of the Dutch East Indies Company (VOC), outside the European-dominated colonial cities "Native" rulers such as Sosroningrat still exerted considerable influence over their Javanese subjects.

At the beginning of the twentieth century, when this correspondence begins, Sosroningrat had been regent of Jepara since his appointment in 1880, when he replaced his wife's late father. Jepara had once been a prominent administrative and port town for the VOC. In 1513, when it was the seat of a small kingdom, its residents provided a naval force led by its king against the Portuguese in Malacca.[5] By the late nineteenth century, it had been reduced to a minor colonial post. Its Javanese ruler, under the colonial practice of "indirect rule," had become a colonial appointee heading a

Native administration but supervised by a parallel European colonial bureaucracy. The rank of the colonial representative in Jepara had once been *resident,* but was now *controleur,* the lowest level of the *Binnenlandsch Bestuur,* or colonial civil service. Jepara had been bypassed by the extensive train and tram network that radiated out from the city of Semarang, the burgeoning economic and administrative center of Central Java. It was to this bustling city, with its mixed-race population of over 100,000 inhabitants, that the inhabitants of Jepara had to travel, as Kartini and her sisters did, to experience "modernity."

The Tjondronegoro family had become of particular interest to the colonial administration in the latter part of the nineteenth century because of the commitment of Pangeran Ario Tjondronegoro, the sisters' grandfather and Sosroningrat's father, to Western education. As regent of Kudus, he came under the influence of a noted Dutch intellectual, A. J. W. van Delden, secretary to the then Dutch resident of Jepara; and in the 1860s he employed a Dutch tutor, C. E. van Kesteren, to educate his children.[6] This commitment attracted particular interest because the city was a center of Islamic study and had a reputation as an important Islamic holy city.[7] As Kartini made clear in her correspondence, she was proud in the knowledge that her own father, following the example of his father before him, was a progressive and conscientious leader of his people, one willing to step beyond formal traditional custom in allowing his daughters to receive a Western education.[8] On the other hand, her uncle, the regent of Demak, the product of the same education, features in the letters of both Kartini and Roekmini as the main obstacle to achieving their feminist goals, in particular, access to further education.

The maternal lineage of the sisters was equally influential and important. Following a recognized and religiously sanctioned tradition amongst the Javanese aristocracy, Sosroningrat had two official wives: his *padmi,* or formal consort, and his *selir,* or "secondary" wife. His padmi, Raden Ayu Moeryam, mother of Roekmini and Kartinah and the older sister Soelastri, was a descendant of one of the royal houses of Madura, an island off Java known for its Islamic orthodoxy, and the daughter of the former regent of Jepara. His selir, Ibu Ngasirah, the mother of the other eight of his eleven children, including Kartini, Kardinah, and Soematri, was the daughter of an influential local Islamic leader or *kiyai,* whose wife, Njai Haji Siti Aminah, had, as her title indicates, undertaken the pilgrimage to Mecca.[9]

It is clear from the extensive early correspondence, primarily that between Kartini and her Dutch friends from 1899 to 1904, that the apparent contradictions in the cultural and intellectual influences that surrounded her and her sisters—traditional aristocratic and feudal, liberal Western intellectual, pious Islamic—created some confusion in the *kabupaten,* the official home of the *bupati* (regent). At least as seen from the perspective of this correspondence, the oldest children—two male and one female—were largely in conformity with traditional Javanese society. Kartini, Roekmini, and Kardinah, however, felt closest to the liberal leanings of their father. It was his support they constantly sought, and it was his protection (up to a point) of their aspirations that was crucial in allowing them to break—but only to a degree—from the traditional life path set out for Javanese women of high birth. Their mothers, however, represented the traditions, both religious and aristocratic, against which the daughters rebelled most strenuously, and it was their steadfast opposition that the daughters attempted to modify, eventually with success. Kartinah and Soematri, whose mature lives began after the death of their father, appear to have been largely liberated from the tensions created by the intersection of these different worldviews. The subsequent histories of the sisters would not have followed the paths they did, however, had it not been for the intervention of several influential Dutch women and the access to Western education and literature that their father gave them.

Beginning with Kartini

In the period from about 1895 to 1899 (the latter date marking the beginning of Kartini's archive), Kartini, Roekmini, and Kardinah engaged in an intensive reading and discussion of Dutch books, journals, and newspapers. They also had regular contact with Marie Ovink-Soer, the wife of the local Dutch colonial official. In her correspondence, Kartini pays high tribute to this woman, who, apart from familiarizing her with the Dutch language, a Dutch lifestyle, Dutch painting, and Dutch domestic order, was also the person who introduced Kartini and her sisters to contemporary Dutch feminist literature and indirectly to the progressive Dutch circles in the colony. The extent and depth of this reading, extending to key English writers in Dutch translation, can be ascertained from the references Kartini provides in her later correspondence.[10] This early period culminated in the three young Jepara women contributing exhibits to the National Exhibition of Women's Work (1898), an exhibition organized by the Dutch women's movement and held in the Dutch city of The Hague. As a result, Kartini became known to a small group of Dutch feminists in the Netherlands, which in turn led to one strand of the correspondence that ensued.[11]

There is no doubt that Kartini took the initiative in this project. From her letters it is apparent that she was the most precocious, confident, and outgoing of the three sisters. It was her letter to the organizers of the Dutch Women's Exhibition that made its way to the Dutch queen. It was her letter to a Dutch women's journal requesting a Dutch pen friend that resulted in an extensive and informative correspondence detailing the condition of traditional Javanese culture and colonial oppression.[12] It was her attention to maintaining a wide-ranging correspondence that attracted Dutch progressives to their cause. It was her active interest that made possible the rebirth of the Jepara woodworking industry, which became, in the subsequent decade, the center of attention of an infatuation, in both the Netherlands and the colonies, with Javanese craftwork. But, as she herself states, in all this the three sisters acted as a trio, a cloverleaf, as she liked to describe it.

While Kartini was alive, the three sisters truly formed a sisterhood, bound together in common defense against the forces of tradition, which nevertheless eventually peeled them apart, one by one, forcing each to confront in her own way the implications of their dream. The correspondence collected in this volume begins at that point, when the twenty-year-old Kardinah, the youngest of the three, was being prepared as a bride in an arranged marriage. But the real narrative begins slightly later, in the middle of 1902, with the plan developed by Roekmini and Kartini to study in Europe. This "outrageous" idea, that two Javanese women could imagine wanting to undertake higher education and to study overseas, shocked and excited influential circles in both the colonial and Javanese societies.

For many readers of the Kartini correspondence, the events surrounding the failure of the plan to study in Europe and their subsequent proposal to train as teachers in Batavia—which had to be aborted due to Kartini's sudden arranged marriage—represent the primary event in what has come to be seen as the "tragedy" of Kartini. Often overlooked, however, is that this sequence of events also determined the future of Roekmini, and indirectly that of her other sisters. It also provides a spotlight on cracks that were gradually beginning to appear in the traditional colonial and Javanese world at the beginning of the twentieth century.

Colonial Intrigue

In July 1902, Roekmini wrote to their colonial friend and mentor, Rosita Abendanon, rejecting her advice against the sisters' proposal to study in Europe. Kartini, perhaps perceiving that this bold idea would not find support, had only belatedly written to tell Rosita of the plan after it had been made public in the daily press.[13] Made more determined by the events surrounding Kardinah's marriage earlier in the year, Roekmini explained:

> And what you have advised us, to stay in the Indies, we have discussed with others, thought over carefully ourselves, and now that we have found so much support, also for instance from a powerful organization like Oost en West, which will be a wonderful support in the future for the development of the cause, that we have decided to choose Holland. We thank you very much for what you had recommended to us, which forced us to sift and search and to come to a specific conclusion. It will be Holland despite the difficulties. And if this is also agreed to in the office of the Resident, then we already have someone with whom we can stay, and that is Mevrouw Glaser.[14]

Had Kartini and Roekmini undertaken their plan in 1903, they would have been the first Indonesian women to have traveled to the Netherlands to study, at a time when only a very few Indonesian males had done so.[15] But as Roekmini makes clear, their decision required not just parental approval, but also general acceptance by the community and, ultimately, the approval of the colonial bureaucracy. The revelation of their "outrageous" plan by the colony's leading daily paper, *De Locomotief,* ensured that it became the subject of widespread public gossip. In October, Kartini reported that their plan was receiving strong opposition within her family's circle, unnerving her parents.[16] Reports of family and community opposition continued till the end of the year, until, on the evening of 24 January 1903, Jacques Abendanon made a special trip to Jepara to meet with Kartini to convince her to change her mind. In this moment, colonial bureaucracy and traditional community were in agreement.

Kartini acknowledged her acceptance of the change of plan in a letter to Abendanon the following morning, giving no indication whether Roekmini, whose future was thus also sealed, had been present. In her letter she concurred with the logic that suggested that going to Europe would alienate precisely those whom they had aimed to attract and educate—Javanese mothers and their daughters. Their parents, who had only reluctantly agreed to the European plan, were relieved and as a consequence were now firmly supportive of their daughters' idea to study closer to home, in Batavia.[17] Even this was still a novel, pioneering, and ambitious plan, but it was one that Abendanon and Rosita had been suggesting and were thus prepared to support.

Thereafter all opposition from all quarters apparently evaporated. With the sisters' acceptance and parental support, Abendanon now arranged for government approval of funding to allow the two women to study in Batavia. Kartini sat down to write another lengthy statement on the importance of education for Javanese women.[18] Colonial bureaucratic procedure required that all petitions to the government proceed via the local colonial official; only thereafter could Abendanon, as director of education, provide his official advice. In April, Kartini and Roekmini traveled to Semarang to discuss their plan and petition with the resident of Semarang, Piet Sijthoff, to convince him to support it.[19]

In his memo of 27 April 1903, Sijthoff praised their petition, supported their proposed plan to study in Batavia, and dismissed their earlier plan to study in Europe. The supporting memorandum was brief because, as he noted, the petitioners had already discussed their plans at length with the director of education. But he nonetheless provided his own recommendations: "The picture they paint of the unbalanced nature in the way that children are raised is correct, and if they were able, in their future careers, to warn future mothers against this, then for that alone the public would be grateful and the awarding of any eventual subsidies would be fully justified."[20]

Commenting on the plan to study in Europe, he was just as definite in his view: "The majority of impressions they would receive there would only confuse them. Moreover, they would only meet people in circles where etiquette would be more important than personal culture, and, given the charmers that they are, they would be so feted that they would lose their sense of inner confidence." The argument he used against the European plan seems incongruous in an official memorandum, but as Kartini had several times intimated to Rosita how she had had to experience Sijthoff's attentions, he presumably knew what he was talking about![21] According to Kartini, however, it had been she who presented this argument to Sijthoff, not the other way around; it had been Sijthoff who, Kartini asserted, had suggested that instead of studying she should marry, after which she could shine in European circles.[22] Abendanon showed that he also had listened to the two sisters, identifying in detail in his longer supporting memorandum what he considered the appropriate courses, costs, and accommodation required by the two sisters. Their futures were now clear:

> In my view, the best preparation for preparing Raden Ajeng Kartini as teacher would be gained by placing her in the course connected to the private girls' secondary school with residential facilities. This would

also suit her sister, Raden Ajeng Roekmini, who wants to take a course in drawing and needlework and in health, nursing, and first aid. For the former, lessons can be provided in the residential facility mentioned; training for nurse can be obtained at the Institute of the Association for Nursing of the Poor here in Batavia.[23]

Abendanon, however, was slow to act, writing his memorandum only on 26 June, apparently only after an urgent plea from Roekmini to Rosita in a letter of 22 June asking her to beg her husband to hurry as "there was something in the wind." He excused the delay by saying he had spent time checking costs and ensuring that the arrangements were acceptable to both the institutions involved and the two sisters. Indeed, as the letters indicate, coming to a definitive recommendation for the government that met the sisters' requirements had not been a straightforward process. It was only on 30 June that the Council of the Indies received the necessary documents, enabling the advisory body to the governor general to make its recommendation. Finally, on 7 July, in this typically protracted process of colonial decision making, the formal approval for the subsidy was given, making Kartini and Roekmini the first "Native" women to gain financial support to undertake further study. In the meantime, Kartini and Roekmini had commenced operating their school in one of the vacant buildings of the kabupaten. This had also been a suggestion by Abendanon to fill in the time profitably while they were waiting to begin their teacher training course.[24]

On 9 July, Kartini wrote to confirm that she had received Rosita's telegram informing her of the government's decision made two days earlier. But the day before the government decision arrived, her father accepted a request he had received to marry his daughter. On 10 July, Kartini wrote to Rosita to indicate that the resident had accordingly changed his mind about supporting her petition and that the regent of Rembang, from whom the marriage proposal had come, would soon visit to arrange the wedding. For a few days Kartini nevertheless still hoped she might still be able to study in Batavia, but on 15 July Roekmini indicated that, as it was now clear that Kartini would be unable to go to Batavia, she too would now have to withdraw from her study plans. On 24 July, Kartini asked Rosita to suggest to her husband that someone else might be able to profit from the financial allocation that the government had just approved. This was Agus Salim, the future leader of the Islamic nationalist movement.

The historic moment that might have been, already heavily modified from its original design by the intervention of the combined colonial and

Javanese communities, had now been thoroughly quashed. It was in the subsequent careers of the four remaining sisters that the threads of this project were only gradually reassembled. Reading the account of all this by Roekmini, the sister on whom all the responsibility would now initially fall, the reader can begin to appreciate the resilience with which she went on to face the difficult years of her later life, and the awe and reverence she and her siblings had for their courageous sister, Kartini.

But while essentially personal, the entire saga also throws a spotlight on a complex historical moment at the beginning of the twentieth century, in which the upper layers of both the colonial and Javanese societies were involved and had their established values challenged. The episode reveals its main protagonists, Kartini and Roekmini, Jacques Abendanon, as well as Sosroningrat and his wives, as pioneers within their respective domains in a changing world. There are no doubt many other sites in which such initial stirrings can be examined, but rarely with the aid of such extensive and revealing documentation.

A Sisterhood

Within a large family of eleven siblings, Roekmini, Kardinah, Kartinah, and Soematri, together with Kartini, formed a close grouping of sisters separated psychologically and culturally both from two older brothers and a sister and from two younger brothers. Another brother, Kartono, considered a "spiritual equal" and in some senses Kartini's twin, and who may well have formed part of this set, was separated from them throughout this time by his long absence in the Netherlands.[25] Despite the death of Kartini in 1904 and that of their father the following year, and the gradual dispersal of the women through marriage, the link between the four sisters continued to be maintained physically, through visits and letters, and spiritually, through their shared recall of the memory and ideals of their sister. It is thus charming to read, at the end of this correspondence, of the women being again reunited, with their two mothers in their midst. It is this constant common reference point, as well as the existence of a common recipient, that ensures that this scattered correspondence can be regarded as a single archival and literary oeuvre.

That this group of siblings came to form a separate set was as a result of the decision taken by Kartini, the oldest of the group. As she modestly explained in a letter to her Amsterdam pen friend Stella Zeehandelaar in 1899, it was she who took the decision that the traditional feudal honorifics owed to her by her younger siblings would cease:

Amongst us beginning with me we ignore all forms, we let our own feelings tell us how far our liberal tendencies can go. It is really terrible, these conventions amongst us Javanese. . . . Just to give you an idea of how difficult our etiquette is I will give you a few examples. A younger sister or brother of mine may not pass by me except by crawling over the ground. Should a sister be sitting on a stool and I pass her, then she must immediately slide onto the ground and stay there with bowed head until I am completely out of view.[26]

Within their set, the three older girls formed a separate grouping. In 1901, when the younger sisters first wrote to Rosita, Kartinah and Soematri were only just beginning to be drawn into a discourse in which the older three had become thoroughly involved. It was the older three who had over the course of some years finally come to recognize that the ideals they had talked about had first to be experienced and fought for within the family household and in their personal relations. In this they paved the way for their younger sisters. Thus, with Kartini's departure from Jepara and her subsequent death, it was Roekmini who became the pivotal figure linking the older and the younger siblings, and indeed linking the two halves of the entire body of correspondence.

The unusually close bond between the three closest in age, Kartini, Roekmini, and Kardinah, reflected in the letters of 1901–2, had evolved through a series of shared experiences over at least six years, from about 1894. The nascent ideals that emerged from their discussions had been confirmed by their participation in an exhibition of women's work held in the Netherlands in 1898. Already in 1899 they had declared a pledge, a commitment to a cause, to work for the improvement of the condition of Javanese women. Then, in 1900, they had traveled together to the colonial capital, where they met the governor general and other high colonial officials. They had experienced on a daily basis the domestic environment of a nearby European household, that of the colonial official, Ovink, read voraciously from a regular supply of contemporary Dutch-language periodicals and books, and participated in or witnessed the visits of a steady stream of Europeans to the kabupaten, who expressed interest in their development and that of their society.[27] After Kardinah's departure in January 1902, Kartini and Roekmini had the further challenges associated with applying for government scholarships and the excitement of setting up and establishing a classroom.

In the light of Kartini's own accounts of the strictly hierarchical relations within a typical priyayi household, the bond that developed between this filial group of young Javanese women seems remarkably modern, all the more so given that it linked the children of two mothers of different status. In this Javanese household no strong distinction appears to have been made between the children of the padmi and those of a selir. Kardinah, the third-youngest of the group and the daughter of the selir, was the first to be married. In the absence of any male heir from his raden ayu, it was the selir's second son who followed his father as regent, while her third son, Kartono, was given the privilege of studying in the Netherlands. Privately the household appears to have operated much like a nuclear family, with the selir largely responsible for its domestic operation while the raden ayu took charge of the family's formal public and social interaction.[28]

The modern and the traditional were thus apparently blended in this family. Certainly the special privilege they were allowed in attending a European elementary school set them apart from their society as women and as Javanese. Even at the end of the first decade of the twentieth century, only 57 Javanese girls are on record as attending a public European elementary school in the whole of Java from a total of 3,427 "Native" students attending such schools across the whole of the Dutch East Indies, a figure which hardly increased over subsequent decades.[29] In the parallel system of vernacular "Native schools," a total of only 133,425 indigenous pupils were enrolled across the whole of the colony.[30] Unlike their younger two siblings, who went on to further studies, Kartini, Roekmini, and Kardinah appear not to have completed their elementary education.[31] Nevertheless, they continued their reading and education informally and were imbued with a shared sense of privilege and aspiration that their education provided them. According to Kartini, this privilege was made possible by the extraordinarily liberal perspective of their father, whose own sisters had experienced a similarly progressive upbringing.

The three sisters had also experienced intensely the suppression of their ideals and hopes, the "cold hand of tradition" as Roekmini describes it in her account of Kartini's life. The letters of Roekmini and Kardinah, like those of Kartini, reveal the depth of the psychological suffering that they experienced as they anticipated their forced reabsorption into the traditional Javanese priyayi female role and fought to transform their marriages into a new model for Javanese women generally. Arguably, the suffering and personal humiliation Kartini and Kardinah experienced and expressed resulted from their close identification with a modern Western discourse.[32] This would explain the long gap in Kardinah's correspondence with Rosita after her marriage and, in contrast, the triumphal announcement by Roekmini that she had arranged her own marriage. Kartini's initial announcement of her own arranged marriage in 1903 had been similar to that of her younger sister two years earlier: "My crown has fallen from my head. My golden illusions of purity and chastity lie shattered in the dust. It was my pride, my glory that I was a pure, proud girl loved by my Moedertje as if I were her own child. Now I am nothing more than all the rest. I am like thousands of others who I had wanted to help but whose number I have now merely come to increase."[33]

In the course of the correspondence, the personal agony of these two women becomes transformed, to inspire a broader project of social transformation. More importantly, perhaps, marriage required them to transpose their Europe-derived discourses into a recommitment to their Javanese heritage. While Roekmini, Kartinah, and Soematri avoided undergoing the same experience as their two sisters, the social outcome was the same: as wives of high-ranking, progressive Native officials, they committed themselves to implementing in practical ways the new feminist ideals the three had previously discussed so intensely.

In contrast, the two youngest women, Kartinah and Soematri, respectively three years and eight years younger than Roekmini, already reflect a different age. They had been directly inducted by Roekmini and Kartini into the school project, and had no doubt sat through and overheard the hours of discussion that had taken place. Soematri, who was almost ten years younger than Kartini, had perhaps already regarded her as a distant model. They benefited from the pioneers, assumed attending school as a right, enjoyed extra postelementary classes, and gaily flaunted their learning of languages and geography without feeling, as their older sisters did, the heavy weight of the privilege and of the battle between tradition and modernity they had fought. In particular, although only eleven years separate her formal public statement on the condition of Javanese women (1914) from that by Kartini (1903), Soematri seems to represent the modern age in a way that consigns her older sister to a much earlier era. Extending to just a few years before the end of colonialism, Soematri's correspondence in particular allows us to follow the trajectory of this long narrative of gender and national consciousness, stretching back to approximately 1890.

Roekmini, whose life we can trace here in some detail, is in a sense a transitional figure between the era of Kartini and the era of Soematri. In this history of rapid cultural change in Java at the beginning of the twentieth century compressed into a chain of private letters, Roekmini's correspondence links the first challenges to the old with the more confident expression of the new. Together with Kartini, Roekmini declared her challenge to both the Javanese and colonial patriarchal traditions in the privacy of her correspondence, but equally and more dramatically she shared with Kartini the public glare of the pages of the colonial press in 1902 and, no doubt, of the gossip in the corridors of both the colonial and metropolitan governments. She shared everything with Kartini: the correspondence, the pioneering passion, and the burden of disappointment. While continuing to look up to her sister, she steadfastly managed to pursue her own goals, and in the course of the subsequent quarter-century can be said to have achieved them, despite great personal suffering, losing, as well as her sister and father, both her husband and two children prematurely.

The Writers

This correspondence begins with the dismantling of the cloverleaf as the youngest of the three, Kardinah, is "married off," a circumstance which each deplores because of their joint personal and public commitment to their ideological cause, but which they can do nothing about: "Let us forget what there once was. . . . I already do so as do my sisters but, oh God, how hard it is to walk over the ruins of what were once my beautiful ideals with my head held calmly and proudly erect and at the same time not to lose my senses. But I want to and shall do so and I will apply myself with all my strength to do what I intend."[34]

It is the same courageous conclusion her older sister Kartini makes two years later: an outward accommodation to tradition in concurring with her parents' and tradition's requirements to accept the worthy husband they had selected for her, but with the determination that within the limitations imposed, she would yet undertake the goals she had envisaged. By contrast, when the other three sisters eventually married, they could proudly report that they had chosen their husbands themselves.

In continuing the story that begins with Kartini, the letters by Roekmini, Kardinah, Kartinah, and Soematri are important in recounting the narratives of four socially active women in a world that changed rapidly after 1904. The correspondence reflects, and reflects upon, a time that Shiraishi has so aptly labeled "an age in motion."[35] A new social and political culture was emerging, as Java, and Indonesia as a whole, began to awaken to a modern national consciousness. While the letters do not describe cultural change in detail, they do provide an insight into the experience of some of the participants in it. Further, while they do not cover the entire period of the late-colonial, preindependence period of the first half of the twentieth century, the lives of these women were inextricably entwined with the history of this transformation of Indonesia into a modern independent nation. Although it is not covered in this correspondence, the four women lived to carry their dreams and hopes across the historical divide to participate in the birth of the new nation. In 1964, Kardinah and Kartini's grandson were present when Kartini was formally recognized as a *palawan nasionale,* hero of the nation.[36]

The women who wrote these letters formed part of an admittedly tiny minority elite and of an even smaller number of Javanese women who, at the beginning of the twentieth century, had experienced a Western education and were in different ways associated with the European colonial establishment. They were not representative of the Javanese masses, who remained largely rural and who lived in more or less traditional (although also rapidly changing) environments, and their lives were not indicative of how the masses may have experienced the last decades of Dutch colonialism. What they did have in common with a growing proportion of Javanese was the experience of an urban life and of the new, modern, and largely exogenous influences that were beginning to penetrate further into the Javanese landscape as the twentieth century progressed. As indicated above, the Tjondronegoro family was among the first to appropriate such influences.

The women authors and their families all resided in towns (one briefly in the capital, Batavia) and thus came to be associated with some of the more significant episodes in the cultural history of early-twentieth-century Java, which took place in cities and—not purely by chance—with some of the leading public figures of the period. The survival of this archive of letters thus provides a unique insight into the inexorable changes wrought by global technological, cultural, and political trends introduced to Java by Western imperialism via these urban settings. Urban centers remained the primary domain of Europeans (three-quarters of the European population of Java in the twentieth century resided in towns) as well as of a relatively large Chinese commercial population.[37] But the urban space was also shared by a significant core of westernized, Western-educated and employed Indonesians, and a larger number of manual and low-skilled Indonesian workers.[38] Officially at the beginning of the twentieth century, only about 4.5 percent of Javanese were registered as urban dwellers, that is, resident in settlements with populations of more than 10,000. By 1920 this figure had increased to 5.5 percent, and by 1930, to 6.35 percent, total numbers rising from 1.4 million in 1905 to about 2.6 million in 1930, out of an overall indigenous population that increased from about 29.7 million to about 40.9 million over the same period.[39]

The writers of these letters cannot be regarded as constituting Gayatri Spivak's mute subalterns—the invisible individuals, women, who form the anonymous masses of history—since, as the letters demonstrate, these women did speak. Although their social and cultural position located them within an elite, it was precisely women of this class who historically had been most thoroughly silenced by traditional expectations, as Kartini herself made clear. Nevertheless, once they had rejected these traditions, their social position did provide the necessary conditions that allowed them to proceed to enter the pages of history. It was their location as Javanese priyayi, and as members of a significant dynasty that had the ear of colonial reformers, that ensured their subsequent ability to speak across historical and cultural boundaries. Jacques Abendanon, husband of the main recipient, Rosita, was, as will be outlined later, a key actor in the ideological and political debates on colonial policy of his day. Beyond Abendanon, there existed an array of advocates of a colonial "ethical policy," who saw the sisters' plans and ideas as the translation of their own vision of a colonial project. Kartini also secured a place in history by being taken up by the Dutch women's movement, and later by the international women's movement, for whom she came to be seen as emblematic of what they had been striving for. While it must be assumed that writers of such voluminous letters as these must have written many more and to a wider range of people,[40] it is specifically their association with those in power that has ensured the survival of at least this correspondence. At the same time, partially because of this international recognition, a new Western-educated Indonesian intellectual elite also came to see Kartini's vision as exemplifying a model for the new society they aspired to.

If Kartini, as a woman in a colonized society geographically, if not ideologically, isolated from the center of power, was able to secure a place in history, it is ultimately her iconic name that pulls the four women who are the subject of this volume into history as well. Kartini was immediately catapulted beyond the small circle of her correspondents into being a historical figure by the 1911 publication of extracts of her letters in the volume entitled *Door Duisternis tot Licht* (Through Darkness toward the Light) and by the wider political discourses and events that surrounded it. Kartini's sisters contributed to this "beatification,"[41] and, as this collection of their letters shows, they remained consciously in touch with the ideas of Kartini. They were thus conscious of themselves, because of Kartini, as historical figures with a historical responsibility. The letters they wrote, then, despite the genuine emotional attachment to Rosita Abendanon-Mandri that they suggest, cannot be considered entirely private. Their public nature is underscored by their husbands' intervention in the flow of communication. They explicitly recognize the public-political significance of the relationship with the recipients, Rosita and Jacques Abendanon. This public dimension is also highlighted by the contrast represented by the series of "girlish" letters that Soematri and Kardinah wrote to their friend Lien, in which the "special relationship" that always hovers over the correspondence with Rosita is absent. These letters can thus be seen to have been written in the constant shadow of the writers' consciousness of the colonial context that they recognized themselves as inhabiting.

These letters describe how the four women (and their spouses) responded to this period of rapid cultural change psychologically, intellectually, and physically. The letters reveal them as not merely reacting to change, but in fact participating in the process of change and, to a certain extent, perpetrating that change. The women are representative of a new Javanese generation born of the twentieth century and are in that sense true representatives of what their contemporaries defined as the *kaum muda,* the young generation. The letters reveal intelligent and politically aware women (and men) living private lives on the edge of changing political and social environments, into which they attempted to initiate incursions on their own terms.

The Medium

This collection of correspondence draws attention to the significance of the art and the medium of the letter itself. The letters are of interest to us later readers as much for what they tell us about their writers' private lives in a historically significant moment as for what they reveal about the social and political changes in which they participate and to which contribute. As letters, they are perhaps of greater interest than, for instance, contemporary narratives or historical reconstructions, in that they freeze the present moment in all its personal, emotional, and psychological detail. For Kartini, who begins this stream of correspondence, the letter made possible her virtual mobility. Despite constructing an image of herself as enclosed in a gilded cage in the isolated Oosthoek of Java, she was relatively free in her movements. Beyond Jepara she had traveled to Batavia, where she stayed with the Abendanons, and several times to Semarang, making use of the modern transport systems of tram and train. But it was specifically through letters that she felt she was able to take herself out of her confines to envisage and even participate in activities in far-off places. Through letters she had all but physically participated in person in the triumphal Dutch feminist project of the Women's Exhibition in The Hague.[42] And Kartini was not alone among the colonized Javanese in dreaming of the West as a place of progress, of learning, of personal reconstruction. But, like her male contemporaries who actually did go to Europe, it was not where she would have wanted to remain. Europe provided a temporary refuge from which a new Java could be envisaged.[43] Metaphorically, through letters, she envisaged herself in a modernized Java where she could share the company of fellow Indonesians (and Europeans), of other women as well as men. This was the Java that she conjured up in her correspondence

Letters, then, allowed Kartini to inhabit a world that did not yet exist, to which she could transport herself during the long nights in which she composed communications twenty to forty pages long. A decade later, however, actual mobility was far more possible; her sisters physically inhabited the makings of a world that Kartini could only have envisaged, and their letters, in consequence, report more and more frequently on physical journeys rather than standing in for journeys that could only be imagined. There is also a quickening evident in the process of writing and receiving, a greater felt urgency in the need for this technology to make possible the proper conduct of life, not just the imagination. There is therefore, perhaps, a lessening of emotional intensity and imagination in the later correspondence. The impact of World War I, in this context, represented a problem in interrupting not just the exchange of ideas but also the physical movement between colony and metropolis (both Kartono and Soewardi Soerjaningrat had to stay in Europe, for instance) and of physical documents embodying those ideas.

The tone of the post-1904 letters of Roekmini and Kardinah, as well as that of the correspondence of Kartinah and Soematri, is noticeably different. Much of the supplicatory character that can be noted in Kartini's letters gradually disappears, replaced by an increasingly confident tone, less "colonial," more self-consciously and proudly nationalistic. The change can be traced most clearly in the more or less uninterrupted sequence of Roekmini's correspondence between 1902 and 1920. This begins, very much as Kartini's had, with much gushing sentiment. Roekmini quickly assumes Kartini's form of address for Rosita, rapidly switching from a formal "Mevrouw" (madam)—addressing a person of high social position—to the more familiar "Moedertje" (a sentimentalized diminutive of "mother"). In so doing, she also initially positions herself as a dependent child in relation to a loving and loved adult. The sentimental style may be annoying for the postcolonial (feminist) reader for the way it may be seen to doubly demean the writer, as female and as colonial subject, but it is more a matter of nineteenth-century literary style than it is of politics. And a careful reading of Kartini's letters reveals how she was able to use the poetic literary style strategically as artifice and as a tool. She was able to forge the emotion-laden language into a strategic new political medium, manipulating the foreign European language to accommodate the elliptical style of traditional Javanese etiquette and to manage issues of real or potential conflict in this colonial relationship without disturbing its more positive aspects.

A transition from the old to a new writing style, as it were from the nineteenth to the twentieth century, soon becomes apparent. In Roekmini's correspondence, within the sequence of letters expressing with cloying sentiment a long-winded farewell to Rosita, Roekmini's letters had revealed moments of much sharper language when concerned with "real" issues. Soon thereafter, the tone of the writing changes, marked by the style of address changing from "Moedertje" to "My friend." This change coincides with her marriage at the fairly advanced age of twenty-eight. The same confident tone and form of address are adopted by Kardinah when she resumes writing in 1911, and by the very "modern" Soematri. "My friend" then becomes the common form of address between nascent nationalist and sympathetic colonial progressive. It expresses the growing confidence, not just of these women as married females inhabiting significant social positions, but of a nationalist consciousness. It is not a form that Kartini could have used, even when elevated to the position of raden ayu. It neutralizes the implications that once dominated the relationship, as is further emphasized when the men in this sequence use it too, although they remain more conscious of the colonial yoke—the humiliating environment within which they must nevertheless seek to direct their personal and national ambitions.

While this shift in tone is apparent in the body of correspondence directed to Rosita Abendanon, several letters by Soematri and Kartinah to an age-mate provide further evidence of the role of stylistic artifice in this correspondence and of the women's facility in adopting a variety of voices depending on the relationship they have constructed. Like the obvious difference in tone reflected in letters Kartini writes to her pen friend Stella,[44] Kartinah's and Soematri's correspondence with their former Jepara girlhood confidante Lien demonstrates not just the freedom of expression that this same-age, cross-racial friendship guaranteed, but also their shared social, cultural, and political awareness. The butt of the delightfully chatty series of letters to Lien, so full of gaiety and gossip and—dare it be said—naughtiness, would seem to be the Eurasian community of the town. Lien, young, white, and Dutch, could appreciate the emerging antagonism against this colonial community, shared by both Javanese—as Sosrohadikoesoemo later emphasizes—and *totok*, or immigrant Dutch. It is the colonial, Indies-raised European community, rather than the new generation of educated, urbane Dutch officials such as "our friend" Mühlenfeld, that most exemplifies the encrusted values of the colonial establishment.

Javanese Nationalism

Strategic, literary, and personal characteristics of this correspondence aside, ultimately an appreciation of its historical significance must take account of its authors' awareness of the colonial relationship that frames it. It was their insight into colonialism that ultimately motivated these Javanese correspondents and that continued to inspire the correspondence over the three decades after physical contact with the recipient had ceased. And it is the evidence of the growing political consciousness of its Javanese authors, and, to a lesser extent, the insight provided into the activities of some key "progressive colonials" who are specifically netted in this correspondence, that give this correspondence its wider historical significance.

These Javanese correspondents can be defined as members of a modern, nationally conscious, Western-educated generation close to, and associating with, the progressive elements of the colonial regime. On the other hand, although clearly from privileged backgrounds and clearly conscious of their priyayi origins, they saw their privilege and social role in ways that distinguished them from the older generation of Western-oriented bupati. They remained optimistic of achieving progress by associating with progressive colonial individuals, but they were already pessimistic about the outcomes of an officially reformist "ethical" colonial bureaucracy, both Dutch and Javanese.

Roekmini, Kartinah, and Soematri were among the first members—and among the few first female members—of the first Indonesian nationalist organization, Budi Utomo, or "uplifting endeavor." They were present at its first public rally in Yogyakarta in 1909. This was a momentous event. Indeed, the correspondence reveals that the sisters quite possibly preempted the male students of STOVIA, the medical school in Batavia, and themselves had envisaged the formation of such a body. These young men were already aware of the sisters' public call to young Javanese intellectuals with similar beliefs, their "Oproep aan Jong Java," and had invited them to participate in their plan. In a letter published in newspapers in Java on 23 July 1908, Soewarno, on behalf of the STOVIA students, explained: "In the last few days some newspapers have featured interesting articles on the activities of the three Raden Ajeng of Jepara and the Regents of Jepara, Temanggoeng, Karanganjar and Koetoarjo.... We have immediately informed the three Raden Ajengs of Jepara about our association and its objectives and we have requested them to establish a local branch, while at the same time we made it known that we also supported their own efforts."[45] After attending the first meeting of Budi Utomo, however, the sisters soon resigned, as did other young male intellectuals, when they recognized that their vision of a new Java was about to be taken over by their more conservative elders. One such disillusioned contemporary was Soewardi Soerjaningrat, who was later exiled following the banning of a more radical political entity, the Indische Partij, of which he was co-leader.[46]

In the following decade, the correspondence reflects a growing eagerness among this circle of Javanese to assume a greater degree of autonomy, and at the same time a growing suspicion of a Eurasian usurpation of such autonomy should it be offered. It gives no evidence, however, that this growing national consciousness extended to the archipelago beyond the shores of Java. In as far as the correspondents seem conscious of, or interested in, what were generally referred to as the Outer Islands, they see such communities as having parallel, but not common, aims. In terms of ideology and social class, the correspondents defined themselves as secular and, in a real sense, as a modern middle class, below a recognizable elite that, as Roekmini complains, continued to dominate and suffocate the kaum muda, but separate from and superior to the new urban masses. This also ensured they would remain outside the largest of the organized protonationalist movements of the day, Sarekat Islam, which increasingly attracted the working and unemployed urban and rural masses, although it too was established by modernized urban elements of Javanese society.

For this middle class, the colonial regime was a government they complained of but could not do much about; the status quo they depended on but wished would change. They were, however, optimistic that there were individuals both within and outside the system who could be depended on to modify the worst excesses of the regime. They have been largely unrecognized by history because of their in-between stance—too close to the colonials to be recognized as nationalist and suspicious of mass or radical action, yet seeing themselves as working towards national emancipation. They were representative of a relatively small but significant middle Indonesia, the historical product of a cultural revolution.

Similarly, apart from some key figures, the range of colonial representatives mentioned in the correspondence has also not been the subject of much historical investigation. They too are recognizable as a group as proponents of the "ethical policy," a contemporary slogan for a colonial policy of increased support for Native welfare advocated by the conservative Christian government in the Netherlands in 1901. Clearly, however, the correspondence provides little evidence of reform emanating from Batavia. What is apparent are the efforts of individuals to modify the status quo. Although it is outside the scope of this volume to do more than footnote these figures, the individual actions of a number of prominent colonial officials and political actors are documented here. These demonstrate how close these women writers were to the center of an influential element within the colonial establishment, but also suggest how the correspondence can be used to track currents within what is otherwise often seen as a monolithic institution.

Key among the better-known political figures referred to in this correspondence are Henri van Kol and Conrad van Deventer. These nineteenth-century colonials turned twentieth-century Dutch politicians have traditionally been closely linked to the history of reformist colonial politics. Van Deventer in particular is recognized as one of the architects of the reformist colonial policy, following the publication of his political landmark 1899 publication, *Een Eereschuld*. In this article, he calculated the "debt of honor" imperial Netherlands ought to acknowledge and pay back to its colony to begin to rebuild it after years of neglect. He was also the major propagandist for the establishment of Kartini Schools. Other lesser colonial figures also play a role, including the educators G. A. J. Hazeu, a director of education, and J. E. Jasper, author of a major report on and proponent of the development of Native arts and crafts; N. Adriani and H. Bervoets, both progressive in outlook and associated with the influential Dutch Protestant Missionary Society, the one as linguist and Bible translator, the other as medical doctor; A. Mühlenfeld, initially a lowly but ambitious colonial official who became closely involved in the Javanese cultural movement and eventually head of the colonial civil service; regional agricultural experts Lawick van Pabst and M. C. Brandes; and Charlotte Jacobs and Nellie Stokvis-Cohen Stuart, both influential Dutch feminists and medical practitioners who devoted themselves to improving women's health in Java.

Several significant Indonesian figures also make an appearance, including R. M. Koesoemo Oetoyo, regent of Jepara, and R. Sosrohadikoesoemo (Soematri's husband), both progressive Javanese but politically conservative nationalists; Admodirono, a trained architect and influential Semarang municipal councillor; and two of the most prominent of the early advocates of women's education, Siti Soendari and Dewi Sartika, the latter recognized as one of the earliest and most successful of the Indonesian women educators.

Other prominent historical figures are referred to, including D. J. A. Westerveld, a Semarang teacher, leading socialist, and municipal reformer; E. F. E. Douwes Dekker, the leader of the "Indo" movement; and Noto Soeroto, early leader of the Indonesian student movement in Netherlands and the leading spokesman for Javanese cultural revival. Finally, key institutional elements in the history of the early Indonesian nationalist movement, such as Budi Utomo, Sarekat Islam, the Indische Partij, the Indies Social Democratic Party, and the Indische Vereeniging in the Netherlands, also receive some attention from perspectives not normally found in the historiography of Indonesian nationalism.

The central colonial figure portrayed in this correspondence, however, is Jacques Henri Abendanon, Rosita's husband and co-recipient of many of the letters in this archive. Throughout the letters one is made aware of the activities of this former director of Native education, religion, and industry, who was a major influence on the early years of the development of moderate nationalism, mainly among Javanese students and primarily in the Netherlands, but also, more directly, in the development of girls' education in Java—and the promotion of the Kartini legend.

The Recipients

Unfortunately, history has left us with a one-way correspondence. While for almost a century the letters received from Kartini were carefully preserved (presumably from a sense of history), apparently no thought was given to keeping copies or drafts of the letters written to her. For some, notably Annie Glaser, the sisters' one-time teacher, preservation meant preserving a memory *from* history. But in the case of other recipients, notably Rosita and her husband Jacques Abendanon, it is not an unrealistic expectation that the return correspondence might have been saved. This was a household that had long been at the center of a bureaucracy renowned for its meticulous record-keeping, and Abendanon was very clear as to his historical role both as colonial official and, perhaps more significantly, as a private individual after his retirement. On the other hand, perhaps the fact that copies of replies were not carefully preserved confirms the extent to which this was a spontaneous and private correspondence, intended, in Abendanon's case, to be conducted beyond (or below) politics and away from the public eye, and in Rosita's case, as a correspondence between women, beyond the intervention of men (male interventions in the correspondence, when they do occur, are overtly political and do indeed jar). In this, perhaps unintentionally, lies the historical significance of these unique documents.

ROSITA ABENDANON-MANDRI

Rosita Manuela Abendanon, née Mandri (1857–1944) (still referred to in the family as just Rosita),[47] was the inspiration for a correspondence which altogether spanned thirty-seven years and of which this is the second part to be published.[48] She was also certainly the nurturer of the project to publish the correspondence of Kartini, an idea first mooted in 1905, some months after Kartini's death, as the Abendanons were returning to the Netherlands. Its publication in 1911, referred to several times in the correspondence in this volume, gave rise to the international recognition of Kartini as a pioneering feminist.

Rosita was clearly no bureaucrat: all family references to her suggest that she was "Latin" in her nature: enthusiastic, jovial, empathetic, and unpunctual. As the original correspondence by Kartini and its continuation by Roekmini and her sisters make sufficiently clear, the Javanese women were responding to a remarkably warm person, who, in no more than two visits, had inspired sufficient trust and emotional response to generate many pages of confessional writing.[49]

Rosita was the second wife of Jacques Abendanon, who met and married her in Barcelona in 1883 after the death of his first wife, Anna Elisabeth de Lange. Abendanon had taken a two-year furlough in Europe for health reasons. The loss of his wife, the burden of his three young children, and the stress related to his position no doubt aggravated a chronic illness that continued to plague him for the rest of his life. Rosita was from Puerto Rico, but had an English upbringing. Little is known of her activities between arriving in Java in 1884 and 1900, when she first met Kartini. Family history recounts that, although fluent in Spanish, English, and other languages, she arrived knowing no Dutch, Javanese, or Malay. She had no children of her own—perhaps surprising given that she was only twenty-six when she married—but dedicated herself to raising her three stepsons. Initially Abendanon, who worked in the city but had spent his formative years in the colony in Pati, Central Java, installed his new wife and children in an old VOC *landhuis* outside the capital. Her friendly nature ensured that she quickly integrated into social circles, although family accounts suggest that the children took some time to adjust to their new Spanish stepmother. The Dutch nationalist history taught in the boys' school represented the Spanish as the enemy, and her attempts to teach them Spanish songs did not ingratiate her to them at first. She must also have felt isolated in their large country home, which, according to family accounts, she always thought haunted by Javanese spirits.[50] She may well have spent much time sketching, as it was her sketches of landscape scenes from West Java that later decorated the publication of Kartini's letters.

In 1895, on a second furlough, Abendanon took his family to Europe. When he and Rosita returned the next year, they left his three sons in the Netherlands to continue their education. That this may have been a difficult separation for Rosita is suggested by numerous sympathetic comments by the Jepara sisters about her far-off stepchildren. Back in Java, the couple moved, because of his work but possibly also because they were now childless, to a more prominent residence in the city center, in Kebon Sirih.[51] Here the cosmopolitan Rosita must have been a welcome addition to what is often described as an inward-looking Indische colonial society. By this time Rosita would have not only mastered Dutch and Malay (although not necessarily Javanese), but also become well acquainted with the colonial establishment, in whose circles her husband moved. She must have had quite a presence, as a vivacious lady who played piano, painted, and sketched, was fluent in English, and expressed firmly held feminist ideas. She was decidedly modern and "uncolonial" and had direct access to the English-language feminist literature that she and Kartini discussed in person in 1900 and to which Kartini subsequently referred in her correspondence. Committed to modern ideas in relation to women's education, child-rearing, and education, Rosita would have participated in the discourse of the capital's progressive circles and may well have been the inspiration for Abendanon's campaign to promote the education of Javanese women.

In any event, as the correspondence suggests, much of her time in her last years in Java and in the decades following in the Netherlands was devoted to an expanding circle of young Indonesians. Given the emotional, artistic, and intellectual qualities this woman appears to have possessed, one can only guess at the emotional energy she expended on the Javanese women, who for her may well have substituted for the children she never had and the stepchildren whom, after 1895, she was parted from.

JACQUES HENRI ABENDANON

Jacques Henri Abendanon (1852–1925) commenced his career in the colonies in 1875 at the age of twenty-three after completing legal studies in the Netherlands. He was himself of colonial origins, his family, which was of a Jewish Portuguese background, having settled generations earlier in Surinam, in the Dutch West Indies.[52] His family's wealth—his father was a successful Netherlands-backed banker—allowed Jacques Henri to be educated in the metropolis, after which he decided on a career in the East Indies colony. Java, following the liberal 1870 reforms, which officially inaugurated a new era of colonialism, was just then transforming into an attractive opportunity for Dutch civilians. Following a similar political shift in the Netherlands,[53] these reforms heralded the end of old-fashioned colonialism characterized by government monopoly over economic activity, and the beginning of the growth of a European civilian population and a Western-educated indigenous elite. Abendanon dedicated himself to judicial reform, soon reaching the top of his profession within the colonial bureaucracy. In 1876, he married the twenty-one-year-old Anna Elisabeth de Lange, daughter of a substantial Batavian family, who rapidly produced three children before dying of cholera in January 1882 at age twenty-six, leaving behind three boys aged two, four, and five. Two of the children were born in Pati, within the then administrative district of Jepara, where from 1878 to 1881 Abendanon served as chairman of the *Landraad,* the chief district legal officer.

When Abendanon left his sons in school in the Netherlands, he was following a normal practice for colonial-born young men; Abendanon himself had experienced the same separation as a young adult. Further education in the Netherlands prepared such young men from the colonies to take up positions of influence in the colonial bureaucracy or the emerging private economy. The schools had a tradition of close association with the East Indies: John, the eldest, followed his father and enrolled in law at Leiden University before returning to Java; Eduard, whose later important career as a colonial geologist was rewarded with a professorship, studied engineering in Delft Technical College; and the youngest, Gandolph, after completing his secondary school (HBS), did the same.[54]

On his return to Java in 1896, Abendanon was appointed Raadsheer at the Hooggerechtshof (law councillor of the supreme court) of the Netherlands Indies, the highest legal position in the bureaucracy. In 1900, he was appointed to head the politically sensitive and, in the new political climate, key policy position in the colonial bureaucracy as director of Native education, religion, and industry. Here he attempted to implement a number of reforms, in particular the expansion of the provision of Dutch-language education and girls' education, most of which was frustrated by a conservative bureaucracy but which attracted sympathetic interest from young Javanese intellectuals as well as suspicion from the conservative Javanese elite.[55]

While Abendanon is not the direct recipient of many of these letters, most of the matters of public and historical interest in them revolve around him, both before and after his retirement. In one way or another, he was involved in most of the public issues that touched upon the lives of this priyayi family. It becomes evident in the correspondence that the male correspondents recognize the networking opportunities that their wives' connection with Abendanon gave them for chasing promotion in the colonial bureaucracy (as in the case of husband Santoso and brother-in-law Tjokrohadisosro), or his value as a sounding board (as in the case of Soematri and Kardinah's husbands). Soematri's husband, Sosrohadikoesoemo, had a direct connection with Abendanon via their mutual involvement in the organization and administration of the Semarang Kartini School and the associated Kartini Fonds. Thanks in part to their wives, the husbands were also able to draw on the influence of other progressive colonial figures, such as Henri van Kol and Conrad van Deventer, in their attempts to advance their positions.

Kardinah, in her extensive correspondence about her school (which is effectively addressed to Abendanon), seeks not his political support but his technical advice. Roekmini also directs much of her correspondence in effect to Abendanon for both personal and financial reasons. As Abendanon supported Roekmini, her stepsons, and her brother Kartono financially for a lengthy period after the death of her husband, there is a significant debt of gratitude underpinning her correspondence. But her correspondence also reveals the extent of Abendanon's role as mentor for the growing crowd of young Indonesian students studying in the Netherlands.

While Abendanon's thirty-year career as a colonial official ended in 1905, it came to form, like the careers of his contemporaries and fellow progressives Henri van Kol and Conrad van Deventer, merely an apprenticeship for a lengthy post-colonial career as colonial reform advocate in the Netherlands.[56] Many colonials, and some Indonesians, finding the political, legal, and cultural climate in the colony too restrictive to allow them to exercise any modifying influence, worked for change in the more liberal and democratic climate of the Netherlands. Although, as the twentieth century progressed, the "colonial lobby" was increasingly dominated by capitalist interests,[57] within its broadly based membership were also a significant and influential number of experienced colonialists. Abendanon was a key member of a "reformist lobby" of ex-colonials, largely supported by an academic cadre (many among which also had had some colonial experience) that was responsible both for the training of a colonial civil service and for providing the scientific research upon which colonial policy was ostensibly based.[58] This group also remained in contact with, and attempted to influence, the group of Indonesian students studying and organizing in the Netherlands and, via a network of official and personal links, serving colonial officials. While such active progressives were clearly not in the majority, the letters provide clear evidence of the existence of an interlocking circle of these older, Netherlands-based reformers—such as Abendanon, van Deventer, and van Kol—and a new generation of idealistic, educated colonial officers who retained close contacts with progressive Javanese and who constituted what has been referred to as the *ethici,* or supporters of an ethical policy.[59]

Given the poor reception of all his big plans as director of Native education—the rejection of his attempts to develop girls' schools, expand Dutch-language education, and promote Native welfare by developing indigenous craftwork—it is apparent that Abendanon did not represent mainstream colonial thinking. The bureaucracy's counteradvice to the minister of colonies in response to Abendanon's proposal to expand Javanese access to Dutch-language European schools and develop education for girls was that "this proposal is simply foolish! Where will the theories of this utopian director lead us?"[60] His 1904 report on the economic advancement was "so extraordinarily wide-ranging and divergent in its proposals"[61] that it was simply ignored in favor of a set of reports produced by, among others, Conrad van Deventer, a much more astute politician.[62] In 1919, a year that, according to some historians, marked the end of the reformist period, another ethici, Hazeu, the advisor for Native affairs and later director of education, was similarly branded a "well-meaning idiot," "mad ethici," and "dangerous fanatic."[63] However, at least in the period to 1920, Abendanon—despite long periods of illness and a constitution that required him to leave the Netherlands each winter—worked energetically behind the scenes in the interests of his vision of the developmentalist direction that colonial policy should pursue. He remained, therefore, a valuable and respected contact, and, as a consequence, most of Abendanon's postretirement career is documented in these letters. At the same time, the personal connection this particular family had with Abendanon indicates how this representative element of the Western-oriented Javanese elite continued to base its hopes on the progressive colonial lobby and acutely follow the Dutch press for signs of the direction its political rulers were taking.

Abendanon's activities in relation to colonial reform operated at three levels: privately, nationally, and internationally. Privately, as the letters record, Abendanon's home was a center for regular *kumpulans* (social gatherings) of Indonesian students. Out of this informal activity emerged the Indische Vereeniging, the forerunner of what, after several transformations, would become, in 1924, the Perhimpunan Indonesia, one of the key training schools of Indonesian nationalism. Under the moderate influence of Abendanon and Noto Soeroto[64] (and, less significantly, of the sisters' brother Sosrokartono), the early Indische Vereeniging did begin to shape, if not a political agenda, a more systematic cultural nationalist consciousness. Privately, the Abendanons in the Netherlands continued their support and care for the Sosroningrat family, which began with his diversion of teaching staff and colonial funds in support of Kartini and Roekmini while he was director of education.

Nationally Abendanon remained preoccupied with colonial policy, directing two enquiries into colonial education, initiating a fund for the establishment of girls' schools in Java (the Kartini Fonds for funding Kartini Schools), publishing numerous articles on colonial education policy, and participating in international conferences and debates. Underpinning Abendanon's continuing influence was his long, if not always successful, international career. A long-time member of the International Colonial Institute, he remained in touch, and contributed to, an international imperial discourse.[65] Apart from the International Colonial Institute, he regularly attended the Universal Races Congress, the first of which was held in London in 1911, and this international involvement allowed him to maintain a comparative perspective on the direction of Dutch colonialism, which he considered to be well behind that of English and French colonialism.[66] All this, together with his own extensive experience of colonial government and continuing involvement with a stream of visiting Indonesian students—an extensive contact of which this correspondence represents only a fraction—provided him with the resources to write regular informative and strongly opinionated articles for colonial and Indonesian-oriented journals and audiences and deliver influential speeches, to which the correspondents here regularly refer.

Abendanon's influence on the narrative recorded by this correspondence was considerable, but looming over all was his effective control over the legacy of Kartini. Abendanon was more than merely the recipient (or over-the-shoulder reader) of these letters: he was responsible for giving the 1911 publication of *Door Duisternis tot Licht* its political focus. With this publication—containing an introduction by Abendanon and a selection of carefully edited letters by Kartini[67]—he was attempting to shape not only colonial policy but also the responses of its Javanese readers.[68]

The Issues

As well as referring specifically to individuals, institutions, and events, the correspondence sheds light on a number of broader issues important to an understanding of late colonialism in Indonesia and the emergence of an Indonesian national consciousness. These letters reflect on the contested vision of a modern Indonesia and the nature of an emerging modernity in Java, dealing with themes such as the question of education, specifically women's education; on the importance and development of Javanese traditional arts and crafts; on the interaction between colonial policy and Indonesian nationalist goals; the career opportunities and attitudes of Western-educated Indonesians; the psychological impact of modernity and Westernization and the effect of the rapid disruption of tradition; the growing (nationalist) antagonism expressed toward Chinese and Eurasians; and the nature of urban life in the early twentieth century. Beyond this, the letters can be read as a discussion of the nature of modernity: of the nature of modern consciousness; of the emergence of an "imagined political community"; on gender consciousness; and on the effect of technological development on the spread of national consciousness, communications, and mobility in Java.

COLONIAL POLITICS

Because this correspondence involves a personal relationship between colonized and colonizer, an immediate issue is the nature of the broader political debate surrounding this relationship. Within Indonesian historiography, the advocates of cooperation in this protonationalist period have been termed "associationist." Associationism was a position that colonial officials such as Abendanon, Dutch political aspirants such as van Deventer and van Kol, and academic colonial policy advisers such as the Islamicist Snouck Hurgronje had begun to advocate at the turn of the century.

Abendanon, as already suggested, was clearly wedded to the idea of association between "enlightened" white colonials and educated Javanese. For him and the other associationists at this time, however, this idea did not include any clear sense of Indonesia as a whole or as a polity, nor imply a timeline for independence. Moreover, in their visualization of an ideal, modernized society, neither the Dutch associationists nor their Javanese supporters saw a place for the Eurasian or for a hybrid Indische culture, which had been the "modern Java" of the nineteenth century. Nor was the type of government that nineteenth-century colonial policy had produced—dependent, semifeudal, and hybrid Indische—acceptable to the transnational capitalism that was fast transforming the economic environment of both rural Java and the more distant jungles of Sumatra. The meeting of minds that took place in educated circles in urban Java and Dutch cities at the beginning of the twentieth century was part of an idealistic moment in history, in which "civilized" Europeans who "understood Java" and "forward-thinking," Western-educated and Dutch-speaking Javanese aristocrats found it stimulating and inspiring to engage in discussions about Java's future.

But it was not all talk. Abendanon was a major force in the multifaceted organization Oost en West, which brought together most "friends of the colonies" after its founding in 1898. It promoted the exhibition and sale of indigenous arts and crafts; promoted the welfare of Indonesian students in the Netherlands by arranging accommodation, organizing supervision, and raising support funds; provided information for prospective students and their families; and constituted a lobby group advocating various colonial reforms. Its activities were coordinated by a network of members in both metropolis and colony and by a mixture of serving and private colonials and influential Europe-based well-wishers. It was an active, practical, and influential advocate for progressive colonialism, connected closely with Javanese who inhabited similar in-between social, cultural, and political positions.

This correspondence documents a central element of this interlocking network. The sisters' brother Sosrokartono, one of the earliest of the new generation of Indonesian students in the Netherlands and from the beginning closely linked to the Dutch academic circles underpinning the colonial reform movement, was not only a founding member of Oost en West in 1898 (he had arrived as a student in 1897) but also a regular adviser, a recipient of support, and one of the links that enabled it to operate effectively in Java. Abendanon, while he was director of education in Batavia, was, along with Rosita, a key link for the organization, probably from its foundation. The sisters were well integrated into this network, not just because of Kartono (although he possibly initiated the idea), but directly through the work they had undertaken in relation to the 1898 women's exhibition and thereafter, from 1900 to at least 1910, in supplying the gradually expanding European arts-and-crafts market that Oost en West had fostered.

This was, of course, only one of the overlapping points of contact between the sisters and Abendanon, one of Oost en West's most prominent members,[69] and between Abendanon's membership in that organization and his other activities directed at what in colonial parlance was referred to as "uplifting the Native." This included his encouragement of Kartini and Roekmini to train as teachers; his arrangement for a teacher (Annie Glaser) to be appointed to Jepara to teach them; his encouraging them to establish a schoolroom in the Jepara kabupaten; his detailed arrangement for the women to study in Batavia (and his discouragement of their plan to study in Europe); his support for an application for a subsidy for their school; and of course his support for their application for a scholarship. Later, apart from his continuing interest in their personal welfare, there was also the publication of Kartini's letters and the establishment of the Kartini Fonds, Kartini Vereeniging, and Kartini Schools. The discourse that came to surround the name of Kartini ensured that the women attracted the attention of colonial authorities, at least for the duration of the "ethical period," while Abendanon's active involvement in these matters made it possible for their menfolk to attempt to exploit this connection (and the iconic significance of Kartini's name) to advance their own careers. It gave Roekmini and Kardinah direct access to subsequent directors of education, ensured Roekmini of a position at the Kudus HIS (Dutch medium Native elementary school) and a school subsidy for Kardinah's school; it undoubtedly ensured that Soematri was invited to contribute to the *Mindere Welvaart Onderzoek*.

KEMAJUAN

While the flow of influence might appear to have been in one direction, in fact it was Abendanon (and Oost en West) who initially came to Kartini, not vice versa. Indeed, Abendanon and Kartini were participants in a colonial linkage between the Javanese elite and colonial progressivism that stretched back to an earlier generation. The sisters' grandfather, Tjondronegoro, as noted earlier, established a family reputation for progressivism, a reputation maintained and extended contemporaneously by their father and uncle, R. M. A. A. Hadiningrat, the bupati of Demak.[70] There is thus, in a sense, nothing surprising about the way Kartini and subsequently her sisters were drawn into the center of a progressive colonial network whose core focus was education.

This is not to say that the significance of Kartini and the publication of her letters or the establishment of Kartini Schools (and the promotion of girls' education generally) was entirely a colonial construct, as the late Harsya Bachtiar controversially maintained.[71] While Kartini and others such as Dewi Sartika and Kardinah who went on to develop more permanent schools did become, in a sense, exhibits for the advocates of colonial reform, they were among a growing group of early Indonesian advocates of *kemajuan* (progress) in their own right.[72] They attracted the attention of colonial reformers because their vision of a Javanese future appeared to parallel that of the colonials, who often failed to recognize the powerful nationalist sentiment these Javanese expressed.[73]

The vision advocated by indigenous advocates of kemajuan expressed their own agenda for emancipation from the oppression of feudalism, access to the promise of modernity and progress, the right to personal and political autonomy, and the possibility of national greatness. It was a vision shared by a growing number of Indonesian intellectuals, many of whom had hoped that it could be achieved in association with their "elder brothers." This early optimism could not be sustained in the face of the obvious refusal of the colonial government to honor the contract implicit in an associationist politics, and this vision was gradually displaced by a more independent and proactive political position.[74] By early in the second decade it was being challenged by more radical elements, the advocates of political action criticized by Soematri and her husband—Indonesian students in the Netherlands and urban masses in Java were increasingly looking elsewhere for leadership.

Best known, most coherent in his views, and most persistent in his commitment to a nationalist-associationist position was Noto Soeroto (1888–1951).[75] Related to the royal house of Yogyakarta, in numerous articles and publications he articulated what the sisters and their husbands were also groping towards, and he appeared to be speaking for many compatriots in Java located in the same cultural, social, and political location as these women.[76] In 1911, Noto Soeroto wrote strongly in support of Kartini's "thoughts for and about the people of Java," which were widely heralded in both Javanese and colonial progressive circles as "the signs of the times." Noto Soeroto saw that this publication of letters by a Javanese colonial subject—and more dramatically by a woman—reiterated much of what he had previously expressed, but that the appearance of these ideas in a form more accessible to a Dutch-reading audience might elicit greater Dutch support, as well as influence among a Javanese elite. Others, such as the outspoken Javanese journalist Tirto Adhi Soerjo, considered that the fact Kartini wrote in Dutch was the problem in itself.[77] This objection did not overly concern the influential Javanese journalist, politician, and aristocrat Soewardi Soerjaningrat, who in 1916 interpreted Kartini as advocating in Dutch (as he in turn did in expressing his more anticolonial stance) the expansion of general education in Javanese for national progress. Little wonder that the appearance of the book was also an exciting and stimulating experience for the sisters, each of whom had earlier been excited and stimulated in a similar way by the Dutch feminist publication *Hilda van Suylenburg*.

Noto Soeroto, in any event, continued to publish prose and poetry in Dutch that advocated and, as he saw it, represented the flowering of modern Javanese culture. Equally significant was the role of his close friend, the Solo Prince Mangkunegara, who as Soeriosoeparto was briefly a student in the Netherlands. On his return to Java he was briefly chairman of Budi Utomo in 1915 after which, as Royal Prince Mangkunegara VII, he became the center of an influential mixed European and Javanese intellectual group advocating the revival of Javanese culture and civilization. In 1917, he was the key instigator in the establishment of the Comité voor het Javaansch Nationalisme (Committee for Javanese Nationalism), which published the periodical *Wederopbouw* (meaning literally "rebuilding" or "reconstruction," but with overtones of "rebirth" and "renaissance"). The Dutch name, as well as the use of Dutch language, provide an insight into its philosophical and political orientation and its apparent optimism about being able to gain colonial support for the revival of Javanese national and cultural consciousness. It did have the support of many sympathetic colonial intellectuals and educated officials, not least because it appeared to support the traditions of a hierarchical Javanese society against the growing radicalism of an Islamic popular movement.[78]

EDUCATION AND NATIONALISM

Much of the correspondence in this volume revolves around the issue of education. This is not surprising, since these letters form part of the sequence of letters that commenced with a conversation about the education of women between these Javanese women and the colonial advocate of girls' education Jacques Abendanon and his wife. The letters presented here are a natural continuation of that conversation, separated only by a publishing decision from those that have previously appeared.[79] These letters should also be regarded as one half of a two-way conversation in which the Javanese correspondents are equal partners and in which the initiative in writing about and defining the content is not monopolized by the European recipients.

As this correspondence makes clear, education was far from being a politically neutral subject. Whether at the explicitly political level, at which Sosrohadikoesoemo approaches the question, or at the more practical level, at which Kardinah critically compares the principles of her school with those of the European-sponsored Kartini Schools, educational discourse stood for a broader, though still embryonic, nationalist debate. In the age before the formation of Indonesian political parties and distinct political discourses, it acted as a vehicle for representing a political position. The sisters' brother Kartono, their uncle R. M. A. Hadiningrat, regent of Demak, and their father, Sosroningrat, had each made demands for access to Dutch-language Western education.[80] Calls for the expansion of Dutch- and Javanese-language education both carried strong nationalist overtones, but calls for Dutch were more explicitly code for association politics and had been associated with the interests of a Javanese male elite. But that oversimplifies the case somewhat. Sosrohadikoesoemo was no less nationalistic in arguing for Dutch-language education, as his reference to Japan suggests. He saw in the insistence by his political enemies that Javanese be the language of instruction an attempt to "keep the Natives down." The sisters also clearly expressed their concern that those Javanese (male and female) who had the need, the means, and the motivation should not have their access to Dutch-language education limited.

On the other hand, Sosrohadikoesoemo's insistence that Javanese women continue to be mindful of their role as the carriers of tradition—which he admitted may have sounded conservative—was, as has been often pointed out, the standard position of modernizing (male) nationalists in Asia. As Chatterjee has suggested, this ensured a distinctly patriarchal tone in the nationalist position on progress.[81] In his iteration of this view, Sosrohadikoesoemo was distinctly and forcefully but politely expressing a nationalist view in his letters to Abendanon: your science, yes, your culture, no. He fully supported the development of girls' schools (he would have been in terrible trouble with his wife had he not!), and little separated him from the opinions of Kardinah on the content of women's education. Both also agreed that Kartini had not intended the education of Javanese women to be limited to those of the upper classes, or that it should be an exclusively Dutch-language education. But on the other hand, categorically limiting "Inlanders" to a vernacular-language education, as suggested by his political opponents, was to him no different than what the colonial bureaucracy had always stood for. He saw education as a battlefield of political agendas, in which colonial, Eurasian, and Javanese advocates were each attempting to extract an advantage.

As reports of the Eerste Koloniaal Onderwijs Congres, arranged by Abendanon, trickled back to Java, Sosrohadikoesoemo found, not surprisingly, that he and Abendanon were on the same side. As director, Abendanon had long argued for more Dutch-language education and the expansion of educational opportunities for girls. This was a progressive position that was implicitly critical of existing colonial practice. Also not unsurprisingly, in consequence, Sosrohadikoesoemo found himself on the opposite side from Soewardi Soerjaningrat, the exiled radical former co-leader of the Indische Partij, who, in Indonesian historiography, is normally regarded as the first to advocate the iconic Indonesian nationalist slogan: a national Indonesian language for Indonesians. Soewardi's politics, far more radical than those of most Javanese, were already distinctly antiassociationist by 1913. In opposition to Abendanon and indeed many of his fellow Javanese intellectuals both in the Netherlands and in Java, Soewardi insisted that the people of the Indonesian archipelago should be provided with education in their own regional language rather than in Dutch, while pointing to the importance of Malay as a lingua franca, a national language that would allow all indigenous inhabitants of the colony to communicate. A foreign language, not necessarily Dutch, remained necessary to allow access to Western knowledge. In this he claimed he was in full agreement with Kartini.[82]

The language issue was also what distinguished Kardinah's school in Tegal from the Kartini School concurrently being established in Semarang, with which her sister and brother-in-law were associated. In her correspondence with Abendanon, Kardinah gently but firmly maintained the importance of providing practical modern education to ordinary Javanese women in Javanese, against the preconceptions of the Kartini Vereeniging and the Kartini Fonds. She saw herself as thereby implementing the practices that Kartini and Roekmini had commenced in Jepara. Dutch-language education, as for Kartini and Roekimi, would be available, but only for those whose vocational ambitions required it. In her appeal to have the Kartini School, and the later Van Deventer Teacher Training School, established in Tegal under the care of the most senior of the Kartini sisters, Kardinah failed to appreciate the politics of the Kartini Vereeniging. Neither the decision to locate the school in Semarang nor that to include Sosrohadikoesoemo on its committee had anything to do with the whereabouts or interests of the Kartini sisters.

The facts that Soematri happened to be a resident of Semarang and that Sosrohadikoesoemo was on the board of the Kartini School were incidental. Sosrohadikoesoemo was a leading Western-educated colonial civil servant who had previously attracted the attention of both van Deventer and van Kol during their respective, parallel visits to the colony to consult with representative Javanese interests. Both parliamentarians had pleaded his case for an appointment in the colonial bureaucracy more appropriate to his qualifications. As a municipal councillor, a key figure in the organization of Javanese colonial officials, and an influential local opinion maker in a town where Marxist and revolutionary rhetoric were most concentrated at that time, he had become a useful protégé of van Deventer and those advocating associationist politics.[83] The Kartini School was to be a private Dutch project, a monument to private Dutch philanthropy, and Semarang had a much larger Dutch population than Tegal. Semarang had also been the home of Conrad van Deventer, the Kartini Vereeniging's most active member; he may also have seen it as his contribution to the city where, as a partner in the leading law office, he had worked for almost two decades. It was also where van Deventer had learned his politics before composing the article that was to make his political career, "Een Eereschuld."[84]

Among numerous other indications of nationalist consciousness scattered throughout the letters, one recurring theme is the sharp criticism directed against the Chinese. This provided another context against which a sharper Java-centric nationalism was registered. Initially expressed here as concern about Chinese appropriation of an iconic Javanese symbol—the creation of model gamelan instruments[85]—expressions of concern about Chinese economic exploitation became increasingly explicit. The young Soematri voiced her concern for the Jepara woodworkers who had "to try to compete with the Chinese who are always after making a profit, it's really shameful"[86] (1910). More explicitly, the raden ayu of Tegal, that is to say, Kardinah, in the context of discussing colonial education policies, gives voice to an evidently widespread concern of Javanese on the north coast: "But is it not dreadful and irritating that we indigenous people are so put down while the Chinese, by contrast, the foreigner, is raised above everyone? Yes, the Chinese here get everything and for them even the Chinese schools aren't good enough for those foreigners, they are even going to get Dutch Chinese schools. Bravo!"[87] One can sense here a taste of the widespread anti-Chinese feeling that at around this time supported the founding of Sarekat Islam, initially as a Javanese merchant guild to protect Javanese commercial interests, but which rapidly became a vehicle for a form of nationalist expression that these sisters explicitly rejected.

MODERNITY IN JAVA

For all this, an Indonesian identity was never articulated by the sisters, who remained Javanese nationalists. Education as discussed in this correspondence, either in the colonial or vernacular language, had everything to do with what all sides were agreed was the need for the modernization and progress of Java. In the early 1920s, there was as yet little recognition among these correspondents of the archipelago beyond. Only vague references appear, as in the case of the letter to Etty Wawu in far-off Minahassa (Sulawesi); the reference by Kardinah to the enrolment of the Acehnese "princess" at her school in Tegal; the reflection by Soematri that in Batavia one was increasing likely to meet people from elsewhere; or the possibility of her husband being posted to Bali.

The term "modern," often used by Kartini, can be found throughout the writings of other Indonesians of this period in a variety of Netherlands- and Java-based publications.[88] In his selection of "the ideas of Raden Ajeng Kartini for and about the Javanese people," Abendanon purposefully positioned the term to appear on the first line of the first sentence of the first page of the 1911 publication: "I have so often wanted to meet a 'modern girl.'" At best, with the notable exceptions of the journalists Abdul Rivai and Tirto Adhi Soerjo, one a Sumatran and the other a Javanese who did envisage a broader nation, "modern," in the first decade of the twentieth century, tended to be linked with a parallel development of separate ethnic nationalisms.

In the circles embraced in this correspondence, the association of "modern" with "Java" remained a dominant theme into the third decade of the century. It was reinforced in the writing of the expatriate Noto Soeroto, to whom the sisters make reference, and it emanated from the cultural circles around the Solo palace of Mangkunegara VII. The latter, in responding warmly to the receipt of a new edition of *Door Duisternis tot Licht,* thanked Abendanon for his contribution to "the redevelopment and repair of the Native society on modern foundations," seeing his publication of Kartini's thoughts as reinforcing the aims of the Javanese Dutch-language publication *Wederopbouw,* of which he was a major driving force.[89] Even the radical nationalist Soewardi Soerjaningrat, on his return to Java from the Netherlands in 1922, expressed his nationalism—as he had in the 1916 education congress—in terms of the modernization of Javanese culture in establishing the Taman Siswa school system. Within Java, this did not reflect competition among ethnic groups and regions; rather, it expressed opposition to competing visions within Java, not just Marxist, Indo, European, or Chinese but also what some perceived as the foreign influence of an Islamic revival.[90] Unlike the other rivals to a Javanese modernity, registered in this correspondence as potentially or actually hostile, Islam is notable here for its absence.[91] Ricklefs concludes about the ideological situation in Java in the mid-1920s:

> Some important patterns had emerged, but they had only increased the sense of disunity among Indonesians. Instead of a vague sense of a shared Islamic identity, it now mattered what kind of Muslim one was or, indeed, whether one wished to be a Muslim at all. Instead of an unspecified opposition to Dutch rule, it was now a question of what kind of anti-colonial doctrine one supported, or, indeed, whether one's interests really lay with the colonial regime. Instead of a general belief that Indonesians had something or other in common, regional identities were even clearer as a result of the growth of ethnically based organisations. Instead of an assumption that various classes in each region were brothers of a sort, the bureaucratic elites and their subjects were very clearly warned of the interests that divided them.[92]

Letter writing, while not itself "modern," played an important role in this process of defining alliances in what would ultimately emerge as what Anderson has so succinctly identified as an "imagined political community." As this correspondence exemplified, Dutch language was for many the vehicle in which a discourse of modernity could be conveyed, and not only, as here, in terms of a cross-cultural dialogue. Kartini, it seems, conducted correspondence with many Javanese contemporaries, likely in Dutch (although such correspondence unfortunately has not survived). One other set of correspondence specifically alluded to here is that initiated by Kartinah. Busily attempting to establish a network of young women with progressive ideas—her own challenge to the elitist Budi Utomo, from which she and her sisters had just resigned—Kartinah perceptively remarks on the wonder of the medium in linking in partnership people she had never seen. "We would very much like to do something together to help our sisters in general. But what? Actually, I already have an idea but I first need to consult with all my Native girlfriends for advice. Oh, this exchanging of ideas with all these girls is such fun! I haven't ever seen any of my correspondents. What do you think of that?"⁹³ Letters—and modernity—broke through the significant obstacles of both geographical and social distance separating recipients in the still quite traditional world of Central Java. Among Kartinah's correspondents were the royal princesses of Yogyakarta, sisters of Noto Soeroto whom she would have been unlikely ever to meet, let alone address directly, in person. Although the language was likely to have been Dutch, rather than being merely a colonial language, this foreign medium had become central to a nationalist movement, essential at this stage in linking a disparate political community that crossed racial, regional, and social boundaries, and in providing and conveying a shared vocabulary of modernity. It was this that Sosrohadikoesoemo had argued for.

As this collection of correspondence shows, letters could include, at one extreme, the communication of specifically political sentiment, and at another, the thoroughly chatty exchange of gossip between the young girlfriends; could vary from the intensely personal, seeking emotional and moral support, which characterized most of Kartini's and Roekmini's early letters, to the more matter-of-fact information exchange of the later letters. Envelopes carrying the one could also include documents reflecting the other, such as the sisters' historic "Call to Young Java," Kardinah's school documents, or Sosrohadikoesoemo's speeches. But whatever its character, the subject matter of such correspondence was, in one way or another, an interrogation of the colonial situation and, as were its authors and recipients, totally ensnared in a politicized social structure.

MOBILITY

In an age when physical mobility was still limited, the letter stood in for mobility, allowing one to travel, at least with one's ideas, anywhere one wanted to. But increasingly people were moving about physically as well. Kartini's uncle, in the 1860s, had written the first Javanese travelogue, a journal of observations of two tours through Java, which represented, in literary terms, a transformation from traditional pilgrimage to modern tourism. It was the increasing mobility in Java and the archipelago, as well as the literary representations of travel in Dutch publications, that had motivated Tjondronegoro to undertake such a journey himself, reflecting an intellectual transition that he had himself made.⁹⁴ The expansion of train travel, to which each of the sisters alludes (the first railway line out of Semarang had opened in 1867), was having a dramatic impact on the towns that the trains serviced, Semarang in particular.⁹⁵ In 1900, Kartini,

Roekmini, and Kardinah had traveled to and from Batavia from their isolated town of Jepara, as any colonial official might have done. Three years previously, their brother had been one of the first Indonesian students to sail to the Netherlands to study. Kartini had once spoken of her wish to escape an oppressive Java—which had become too small for her!—to join Dr. Adriani in isolated Central Celebes, while Soematri considered the possibility of a posting to Padang to be with her old Jepara friend Lien, or even to Bali—but definitely no farther afield!

In the second decade of the twentieth century, the sisters regularly traversed central Java, enjoying visits to each other's homes, visits that, because of the distances, often stretched to weeks. Java was also increasingly open to international tourism,[96] while study abroad, as well as "internal furlough," were becoming increasingly popular, also among a growing group of Javanese officials. Soematri followed her husband's postings from Semarang to Batavia, to Tegal, and back to Semarang in the course of a decade. The correspondence reports an expanding colonial bureaucracy and a growing civilian European population that added to the regular flow of Indonesians and Europeans traveling to and from Europe, to which the First World War would bring a major disruption. It was, as Shiraishi has so effectively phrased it, "an age in motion" in more than one sense.

New locations now took on a new significance. Recuperation in the mountains was well established as a colonial escape from the oppressive climate of coastal cities and the stress of the office, but it now became common for higher Javanese colonial officials as well. Roekmini recuperates in Salatiga; Santoso gets to like traveling; Kardinah, like any modern urban nine-to-five employee, remarks how refreshed and ready to resume work she feels after a three-week vacation in the mountains away from the demands of her school. Travel also created expectations and comparisons. Kartini was already in the habit of traveling from Jepara to Semarang, where she would regularly have photos taken. Roekmini regrets being unable to send Rosita a photo of her child due to good photographers being unavailable "in the village," where, moreover, little could be attempted by way of education because the women were still so backward. The city, travel between modern urban locations, and the contrast that modern urban life bestowed on the rural become crucial to the conduct of life. Even the susunan of Solo, for the first time in history—that is, in the modern era constructed by the colonial presence—traveled by train to Semarang, where the sisters were presented to him in a dramatic meeting of tradition and modernity.[97]

Education, reading, and travel, all fundamental activities in modernity, were not just personally enlightening but were already contributing to creating new, or redefining old, social, cultural, and racial divisions. The new colonial residents of Jepara about whom Kartinah and Soematri gossip altered the familiar social landscape of the town as Kartini had known and described it at the turn of the twentieth century. But that sense of the familiar was already a new tradition, since Jepara was no longer the seat of a colonial resident and the social busy-ness around the *sos,* the racecourse, and the street associated with such centers no longer existed. The departure of those familiar faces—including, soon thereafter, the Sosroningrat family themselves after a presence that stretched back at least to the previous generation—left the town socially dead, complained the younger sisters. On the other hand, newly arrived from the country, Soematri was struck by the rudeness of urban people in Semarang and could sigh for the rural peace she had left behind: "The people, at least those whom I have met to date, don't impress me greatly, they are noisy when they speak and the women especially are so coquettish, they saunter more than they walk. No, then I would prefer to see my simple *desa* women with their *kain loerik* up to their knees, revealing their muscled calves, with which, in energetic strides, they have managed to traverse the many long roads."[98]

MODERNITY

By the end of the second decade of the twentieth century, Kartini's sisters could enjoy the modernity of Java. Soematri describes this in her account of contemporary Java for Rosita:

> What I wouldn't give if you could just see these young Native households, headed up by young women, unselfconsciously contributing to the advancement of their people by the new atmosphere that they have brought into being in the Native world. Among my friends there are lots of young housewives from all parts of Java, East, Central, and West Java, where, oh, it is such a pleasure to see this personification of Kartini's wise words; as young mothers I can admire them because they are so doing their best to be good mothers. If in the past, it was usual to have a baby tended by 2 or 3 *babus,* this practice has now been almost completely abandoned. The baby now finds itself in a baby carriage or box with the little mother sitting beside it doing her sewing; didn't that use to sound like a fairytale? And this is now the case in almost every household. I even saw a wife of a regent with her child in a *slendang* getting into a train. Friends, when I saw that I was moved to my very

soul and I felt like kneeling down in front of her, not because she was the wife of a regent but because she had felt and come to understand the message of what it was to be a mother, even as wife of a regent.[99]

In describing the regent's wife, she is intentionally making a stark comment on the nature of modernity; she is distinguishing herself and the object of her focus from any trappings of a traditional cultural framework. It is a rejection of the pseudomodernity that marked the Indische urban culture of the nineteenth century and an expression of a new modern morality. Earlier, in her account to Lien of her vacation at the home of the young Mühlenfelds and her allusions to her own "affair" with Mad and a previous crush on a local European boy, Soematri could not have sounded more modern—in a "modern" sense. Class and culture, tradition and race had disappeared from Soematri's narrative.

Not only was the letter an indispensable vehicle of modern communication, but in a more physical sense, it explicitly allowed the representatives of a new generation to bypass, if not entirely subvert, tradition. Roekmini's courtship was undertaken by letter, accompanied by all the romance of "postillons d'amour." Soematri's description, as well as her actual avoidance, of a marriage ceremonial—admittedly caused by illness—contrasts dramatically with the ritualistic meeting of the families that preceded Kartini's wedding (as described by Roekmini) and the slow, ritualistic journey undertaken by Kardinah and Kartini to their respective new homes.

Life had certainly changed in the five years since Kartini's marriage, and not only because the head of the family, Bupati Sosroningrat, had died, although that no doubt did help to weaken the rigorous application of ritual. The earlier marriages had been formally arranged, with appropriate regard paid to the position of each of the brides' fathers and of the grooms and their families. By the time Roekmini married, the family was no longer part of the colonially maintained hierarchy, although her mother still retained the title of raden ayu.[100] It had obliged, but also allowed, Roekmini to employ a friend of the family—in this case a colonial official—to negotiate symbolically on her family's behalf with the family of the groom, a lesser Javanese bureaucrat, about a marriage to which the couple had already committed. After Kardinah and Kartini, each sister could triumphantly claim that she had chosen her husband herself; that she had experienced a courtship equal to that in any European novella; and that she had achieved that meeting of minds that Kartini had only been able to imagine—although she too claimed to have found such a partnership after her marriage.

But these changes were already in motion in 1903. Despite the traditional accoutrements, Kartini had demanded and received acceptance of conditions she believed would secure her modern freedoms to act within the confines of marriage. She refused to dress in customary style or to enact the customary symbols of female submission. Western influence had also already seeped into the rituals that were still observed, evidenced by, among other things, the sending of European-style marriage announcements and the inclusion of prominent Europeans among the wedding guests.

The changes produced by modernity opened up many new possibilities. While Kartini's story was overwhelmingly a sad one of fighting against and ultimately succumbing to the forces of tradition, since then the sisters had been able to win many small battles. Their view of a changing world was more positive:

> One good sign is that there are now more young Native people who have completed their education; even though they may not be participating in all those political goings on, their own education and broader view of life will definitely have an educative influence, in the first place on their own families and later on, on wider and wider circles. If you were able to take a look at the family life of young people in our society now, you would be surprised at what great changes for the good have occurred! One can feel that spring is in the air; everywhere one can already see the buds forming which will later transform everything into a beautiful blossoming field. But, at the same time, one still feels the cold and the chilling winds of winter. Dear Friends, do not turn away from us when you see excesses increasingly occurring. We Javanese also are seeking the right direction, but the way there is still very unclear.[101]

MODERNITY'S VICTIMS

Modernity, however, also had its negative aspects. It defined new criteria for existing social divisions, and it created new divisions. New leaders were interposing themselves between the traditional elite and the people. A sophisticated and now socially well-established Soematri—adopting here the familiar-sounding position of the traditional priyayi—wondered whether the people of the city were so stupid as to be misled by the (modern) Marxist leaders of the local urban branch of Sarekat Islam. While each of the mothers was able to take pride in her children's school achievements, Roekmini, in a series of letters, reveals the problem that these new expectations represented for her stepson, Soedjono, who, unlike his older brother, refused, or was unable, to conform to them. He, like Kartini's own child,[102] appears to fall through the tentative structures that modern society was creating.

But throughout the pages of correspondence it is the tragic saga of their brother, Kartono, that haunts the narrative of modernity in the same way that the death of Kartini provides a constant echo of the cruelty of tradition. As Roekmini wisely remarks of her slightly older brother, "If only he had been better prepared for what life in that far-off, foreign land would present to him, the temptations and all that extravagance that he did not know about. Now, from the original personality, which did show some evidence of weaknesses, there remains only a set of rather confused character traits that now so embitter his life."[103]

Throughout the correspondence, reports on Kartono's alternating behavior indicate the material and psychological pressures that had entrapped him in the modern Netherlands. At first, after his arrival there, he was widely paraded as a trophy by his academic mentors,[104] but his academic career quickly became bogged down in a drawn-out saga that eventually concluded with his acquiring a degree but not a doctorate. Similarly, his important role in helping found the nascent Indonesian political association the Indische Vereeniging in 1908, and in contributing to numerous publications, failed to lead, despite his long tenure in Europe, much of it as journalist, to a satisfactory career.[105] Returning to Java in 1925, he wrote to an aging Rosita that he had always been committed to the same ideals as his sister, whose letters to and from him he now offered to publish.[106] He saw himself as contributing to this vision by putting into practice a long-held plan to establish libraries "using donated books on science and literature in all languages . . . for compatriots and others who do not have the means to buy books themselves, to maintain and extend the knowledge that they had gained at Dutch schools."[107] He complained to Rosita about the reasons for his lack of success since returning from Europe:

> I have often been ill and, on top of that have had the misfortune of never being able to get a position for the simple reason that from Holland people have continued to accuse me of being a "communist." These are terrible accusations that are made but against which one is powerless because one does not know where they originate from. But, most highly esteemed lady, I swear on the grave of my father and the grave of Kartini that I am not a communist, have had nothing to do with and have nothing in common with that, and that nothing would please me more than to work for the spiritual education for my compatriots in the way intended by Kartini.[108]

Though he was apparently thoroughly at home in the new technological age, modernity had in fact entrapped him. He eventually turned his back on its promises to assume the role of a traditional Javanese *dukun* (mystic and healer) and devoted the rest of his life entirely to spiritual and physical healing and meditation, regularly traveling through Java and Sumatra and living the life of an ascetic.[109] Although he gained nationwide fame, his sisters apparently could not recognize this as an achievement: no reference to his return is made in the correspondence.

Other examples of the agony of modernity litter the correspondence. The anger expressed by the husbands, who are humiliated by the conditions of their colonial employment, reflects the extent to which they felt trapped between their modern aspirations and the limitations imposed on their progress by a colonial regime. The young and modern Mühlenfelds experience a modern divorce, leaving Marietje totally isolated and alone and effectively destroyed, as far as one can tell from Soematri's account. By the end of the second decade of the century, Kardinah and Roekmini were experiencing the difficulties of meeting the increasingly complex demands of modern qualifications and regulations in establishing a school and gaining a teaching position, respectively, while Soematri agonized over a society that was increasingly fragmenting. The romance of modernity had soured.

> The days of peace and quiet have passed. Everywhere there is tension and dissatisfaction. People are finally trying to get to understand each other, but where for hundreds of years people have lived and worked side by side but as two completely separate nations, it is difficult for them now immediately to get to understand each other's way of thinking. This won't happen without some problems, unfortunately. Many have wanted it differently, but what can an individual do against the majority which is still too stupid to comprehend that many of these leaders only get up as leaders out of self-interest. How often, without realizing, do the masses not place the yoke on their necks themselves, such as in the case of those strikes and other protests where they are completely vulnerable?[110]

But perhaps these difficulties were inevitable: "The history of Western peoples tells us, however, that in Europe too, as a result of new ideas, clashes are unavoidable in the advancement of the Indies and her inhabitants; that here too more extensive experience of the meaning of life will result in outcomes that will be of lasting benefit for those now feeling their way."[111]

At the end of this period of change, Soematri looked back with a sense of nostalgia: "The chaos that has resulted from this has led in many cases to the need to reestablish a sense of family life. There are exceptions, of course, but generally it won't be so easy to bind the young people, who have found more pleasure in the cinemas and dance halls than in the calm and peaceful atmosphere of the interior of the home. Moedertje, how happy I feel that I have kept to that which my father and mother passed on to me. How will our children look at these things?"[112]

This collection contains one later letter, written by Kardinah in 1951 following the death of her sister Roekmini. It was written to one of the last remaining Dutch links from the past, Hilda de Booy, née Boissevain. In the troubled times of 1951, Kardinah reiterated the sentiments her sister had expressed two decades earlier. Clearly these women, reflective of the traditional elite classes of Javanese society, remained troubled by the "disorder" that nationalism had brought while remaining committed to its ultimate goal, autonomy of the Indonesian people. Their comfort lay in the fact that their sister come to be recognized nationally as one of the pioneers who had helped bring about the emancipation of the nation.

Conclusion

In the span of this correspondence, we can catch sight of a historical moment. On the basis of the earlier correspondence of Kartini, we can locate each of the women as the product of a culturally transitional household where old tradition and new ideas were kept in careful suspension: Western education was balanced, at least for the older three, by training in traditional women's arts and perfunctory religious training; formal parental love and respect, by joyous and (in the case of Kartinah and Soematri) irreverent engagement with contemporaries; appreciation of modern culture, by admiration of the traditional crafts; appreciation of these crafts, by an urge to modify and modernize designs. Significantly, perhaps, the sisters purposefully suppress their traditional selves. Kartini, in presenting herself as a "modern girl," suppresses information about the extent of her training in traditional values, including Koranic instruction, which we learn of only through Kardinah's later account. Soematri, in presenting herself as a troubled young mother in correspondence with the Christian evangelical Nellie van Kol, also denies having received any fixed religious direction. Soematri, when she declares herself a modern housewife, is chastised by her oldest sister for her lack of traditional domestic abilities. Kardinah transposes old domestic skills into modern new teaching manuals, the sale of which will raise money for her school and, later, a hospital. In their personal and domestic arrangements, therefore, each consciously suppresses the past to achieve the transformation that Kartini at the beginning of the century could only dream of.

The changes reported in these letters were partly the inevitable consequence of social and physical relocation from the tradition-bound kabupaten world following the death of their father. But the narrative of the correspondence reveals how the traditional world, challenged by the older sisters at the opening of the century, had ineluctably succumbed to modernity. After fourteen years of marriage and despite being surrounded by the formal trappings of her social position, Raden Ayu Kardinah had more freedom than she had had in Jepara fifteen years earlier. And the Jepara household, which encouraged its young daughters to be educated, was already much more modern than the households of the thirteen-year-old child brides of polygamous older men that Kartini had described. Soematri's household, even more, becomes the very model of modern Java.

The letters represent in themselves, and in what they describe, indications of the broad changes that were taking place in the way life was lived. They provide an impression of representative members of a newly emerging Javanese society: urban, modern, Western-educated, confident, conscious, above all, of their place in the world, and, though critical of their condition and circumstances, proudly nationalistic. A precise meaning of "nationalistic" was beginning to emerge, as was how such a vision needed to be formulated and pursued. But a large degree of common understanding of what this was and meant already appears. As Partha Chatterjee has argued for India, an integral element in the history of nationalism was the development of "cultural nationalism," which, as he sets out to show, needs to be discovered in domestic as well as public settings and was constructed by women as much as by men.[113] Where traditionally a historiography of modern Indonesia has focused almost exclusively on the more radical and political elements of the national movement, the real story of modern Indonesia is far more complex. As these letters record, modernity was an integral part of nationalism, infusing the political and the cultural, the domestic and the public. New means, as well as new forms, constituted and made possible the national movement.

The narrative of the development of a Javanese cultural nationalism must be uncovered in the intricacies of the cultural, literary, and social activities of the preindependence era as they can be traced at multiple levels of society. The Javanese focus evidenced in this correspondence conducted between Javanese and Europeans is of course only one focus. As European colonial intervention increased in pace and intensity in the early twentieth century, its influence became increasingly important but was accompanied by, and gave rise to, a similar intervention from, and communication with, centers and representatives from an Islamic core, as Laffan, among others, has shown in similar detail.[114] In both centers of cultural influence, Indonesians were active alongside foreigners in defining and directing change, and the shifting balances between exogenous and indigenous actors and influences need careful tracing. As Shirashi has shown, while the contexts and values may have differed, the means and the fundamental discourses that drove them were not essentially different. Certainly in this early period, before the major geographical, cultural, and discursive separations hinted at in this correspondence became more evident, much still linked Javanese and colonial reformer, Muslim and secular nationalist. Many of these embryonic developments, moreover, were taking place alongside each other, as this correspondence explicitly reveals, in the city of Semarang and surroundings.

Chapter 1

LETTERS FROM ROEKMINI

Introduction

Kartini's ideals, marriage, and subsequent tragic death in September 1904 have formed the basis of an almost legendary history, but when we read these events as described by Roekmini we realize that while Kartini was alive she was clearly a partner in this history. Kartini's departure from Jepara and subsequent death constitute the prelude to the life awaiting Roekmini as she continues the trajectory of a future they had planned together. Roekmini appears, in her initial letters, to be vicariously experiencing the events that more directly affected her two sisters, Kardinah and Kartini. In fact she deeply shared their suffering and feelings of disappointment and betrayal, both emotionally and intellectually.

A closer reading of the early letters reveals that while she clearly held her older sister Kartini in awe, Roekmini had her own separate plans for the future. In summarizing their life and future plans in a letter to her Minahassan contemporary Etty Wawo Runtu, Roekmini clearly emphasizes her own role up to that time. By 1903, she had also become a distinct and intimate correspondent of Rosita's, in a sense sharing "moedertje" with her older sister. Roekmini's relationship with Rosita appears to have developed around the emotional time of Kardinah's marriage and in the subsequent process of clarifying her own future hopes and desires. This confessional context provided by the correspondence produced a significant deepening of Roekmini's confidence in herself and in her relationship with Rosita. Symptomatic is the change of address in her letters during 1902, from "mevrouw" to the familiar "moedertje." The growing closeness in the relationship in this period is further indicated by the number of letters (twenty-seven) written by Roekmini to Rosita in the period between Kardinah's marriage and Kartini's death: December 1902 to September 1904.[1]

While this correspondence makes it quite evident that Roekmini was very much an equal partner, it is still Kartini who attracted the attention of contemporary Dutch politicians, journal editors, and feminists and as a consequence has remained the center of historical attention. This may ultimately be explained by reference to their different personalities. An early contemporary observer, the missionary and Bible translator Nicolaus Adriani, after meeting Roekmini for the first time in 1900, wrote several days later to Abendanon, at whose home the meeting took place: "She seems to me someone with a fine and clear perspective on things and someone with an independent mind." Roekmini, he thought, also had a good appreciation of the missionary's aims in Central Sulawesi and compared favorably to her "jolly and lively younger sister Kartini." He was of course mistaken about her age, but his description underscores the different character of the two women.[2]

Roekmini's plans for herself were initially dependent upon those of her older and more articulate sister. She planned to accompany Kartini to Europe and thereafter to Batavia, and when Kartini had to cancel her plans, Roekmini did too. Nevertheless, she had always defined a different program. Her love of and desire to develop her ability in painting remained central and evidently underpinned her interest in Fröbel play and woodcraft. The departure of her two sisters left Roekmini, now the eldest daughter and child in the *kabupaten*, with the responsibility of pursuing those goals alone and providing guidance for the younger sisters. Already in the latter part of 1903 she had taken primary responsibility for projects that she and Kartini had just begun before Kartini's attention was taken up, after July, by preparation for her marriage and her departure in November. It was only because of Roekmini that the Jepara classroom, with which the name of Kartini has always been associated, as well as the craftwork undertaken by the Jepara craftsmen, were maintained.[3]

Roekmini's accounts of the classroom also suggest that she had a clearer and more practical pedagogical appreciation of the needs of the children than did her older sister, who was perhaps more idealistic than practical. Had it always been so in their relationship? It might seem that while Kartini was more outgoing and articulate and attracted the attention, Roekmini provided solid support for her companion. Why, one wonders, had Roekmini twice been overlooked as a prospective marriage partner by her parents? Although not the oldest, she was the daughter of the raden ayu. In 1901 and 1903, it was not initially clear which of the women would be selected. While in 1901 "Kleintje" may have been chosen because she was the least likely to resist, in 1903 both sisters showed equal determination and steadfast refusal to countenance marriage. It is evident that it was Kartini's higher profile that ensured Roekmini was spared.

The death of their father in 1905 represented a clear break between one era and the next. The Jepara family was once again held hostage by the conservative forces that, as Kartini had suggested, he had just been able to hold at bay. Surprisingly, the eldest son was not appointed in his father's place, and so the family was evicted from the kabupaten that they had inhabited for a quarter of a century. The political intrigue behind these events within and between the Javanese and colonial branches of the regime can only be guessed at. One consequence was that the school Kartini and Roekmini had established was rapidly deserted by its pupils once parents perceived that the family was no longer socially significant.

Effectively now sidelined from the colonial circuits of power, Roekmini nevertheless retained valuable cultural capital with which to negotiate a public role, primarily through her direct involvement in the increasingly fashionable interest in Javanese woodcraft. Her knowledge, administrative ability, and contacts—including those with the influential Netherlands-based organization Oost en West—ensured that she continued to be recognized by interested colonials as a key cultural intermediary. Initially this seemed to promise Roekmini employment as well as a prominent cultural role in "modern Java," but it quickly became apparent that the visions of the idealistic reformers would not gain official support. Hopes for a craft shop and later for a school in which Roekmini would play a leading role rapidly faded.

The correspondence also confirms that Roekmini was not simply dependent on such contacts or on her older sister: she demonstrated her own strengths and forged the confidence to assert herself in the world on her own. Her decision to apply for a position (eventually unsuccessfully) with the newly established rural credit bank and her hope of working in a vocational school for girls not only place her at the forefront of new colonial policies but show her as deeply committed to "the cause" on her own terms. It was the colonial system, not any weakness on her part, that ended both possibilities. Typical perhaps of the resolution she expressed, and the negative response it attracted, was her bold proposal to work for the rural credit bank:

> And now I have to tell you that I have applied for the position of administrator at our branch of the bank. The administration thought it was an excellent idea, and with the support of the Assistant Resident, I wrote to the Inspector of Agricultural Credit. But what a disillusionment. This person, after discussion with the Director of BB, thought

that it was better that the position not be filled by a woman because of its perambulatory nature, something which the administration had not even mentioned. Because I am someone who knows the region and its people very well, the Ass. Res. and the others thought the idea of my applying for the position with the bank was an excellent one.

A number of other plans followed—promoting traditional craft, heading a girls' vocational school, establishing a school in Jepara—each with the support of progressively minded individual colonial officials, each one for which Roekmini would have been eminently suited, and each foundering because of the continuing prevalence of conservatism within both the European and Javanese branches of the colonial establishment. Despite these disappointments and the tragic deaths of her husband and children, Roekmini persevered, her optimism apparently unshaken.

One can conclude that the trajectory of Roekmini's intellectual and nationalist development differs from that of her better-known male contemporaries only because of her gender. Her call to Jong Java (Young Java) coincided in both time and sentiment with that of her male contemporaries. Roekmini and her sisters' later rapid disillusionment with the direction of Budi Utomo similarly allows one to locate her in her time: as part of a younger and more radically inclined section of the *kaum muda*, the young generation. Indeed, throughout her correspondence, though her tone remains constrained and polite, one can detect a strong undercurrent of nationalist feeling that of course never expresses itself in the revolutionary terms of the next generation.

For Roekmini and her sisters, the progress of Java needed to be the responsibility of the Javanese themselves; European help would be welcome but should be given without the imposition of a particular ideology or with any presumptions. As she writes in 1904,

> [W]hat wouldn't I give if we were already so far advanced, we Javanese ourselves, that we were able to just stand in their shadow; that we had become conscious of the fact that, aside from the respect that we have for them, we needed to feel more, namely: that we would no longer accept that the task that is ours is undertaken by others with that sense of self-satisfaction, as if it were self evident, indeed even with indifference, unfortunately. I have deep respect for people like the van Emmerit family, Miss Jane, the Bervoets family, Miss Prijzel etc. but at the same time I also cannot suppress a sense of embarrassment, or shame, that I can only observe that they are doing our work.[4]

Even after her marriage—which itself represented a significant victory over tradition—Roekmini remained active in the public domain. However, it was difficult, she noted, working with the women of the village and the wives of lower officials. She also lacked the public authority that her two other sisters had gained via their marriages. Once widowed, she returned to public life as a teacher, building on her earlier experiences with the modern Fröbel pedagogy and benefitting from both her mastery of the Dutch language and her association with the Kartini name, which by then had entered the realm of cultural history. The latter years of her working life thus saw her where she had once imagined herself: as a teacher, serving the new generation. Even after retiring from teaching, as Soematri reveals in her later letters, Roekmini continued to be active in community work and eventually also returned to her love of painting, which she had once planned to study in the Netherlands.

For a brief period, Roekmini also became active in the European-dominated women's suffrage movement, the Vereeniging voor Vrouwenkiesrecht. Possibly she was encouraged in this by one of its more active members, the vice president and a fellow Kudus resident, Mrs. van Overveldt-Biekart.[5] Joining the organization in July 1927, Roekmini remained a member of the executive board until mid-1931.[6] While the journal *Maandblad van de Vereeniging voor Vrouwenkiesrecht* makes mention of a growing number of Javanese members, the organization remained primarily for European women, and its primary objective, the female franchise, realistically only a European one.[7] Its other activities and concerns, however, related directly to the concerns of Roekmini and her sisters: women's health and education, prenatal and child welfare, the abolition of child marriage, and the involvement of women generally in social progress.

In the four years she was on the executive board, Roekmini contributed several reports, although possibly not attending any meetings.[8] In July 1928, she reported on a proposal to establish a Kudus branch of the VVV. While the initiative of the very active VVV vice president, van Overveldt-Biekert, this branch was to be under the patronage of the raden ayu of Kudus and administered by a committee of the wives of Native officials, the local Javanese doctor, and a certified city midwife. Its aim, Roekmini announced, would be to provide Native women with knowledge of hygiene, child care, and first aid, for which courses would be established. This Kudus branch, which would take the Javanese name of Mardi Kamoeljan (Striving for Progress), was envisaged as a purely Javanese women's organization.[9] In December, she was able to report that courses were well attended by married women and girls and supported by the European director of the regional hospital. In that same month, she attended the Indonesian Women's Congress in Yogyakarta, reporting enthusiastically on it in the 1929 February edition of the *Maandblad*.[10] In her reports on the activities of the Mardi Kamoeljan and on the Indonesian Women's Congress, which she attended in a private capacity, Roekmini was articulating her own (or at least a Javanese) agenda more than that of the VVV. This period of public activity seems to have faded quickly, however, as no further formal reports of the Kudus branch (as published each year for the other five branches: Batavia, Surabaya, Sukabumi, Semarang, and Madiun) appeared before she left the executive in 1931.[11] We are left to wonder why none of this was reported to Rosita, or, if it was, why no letters recording her activities in this period have survived—or why even Soematri failed to report to Rosita on her sister's activities.

The detailed account of Roekmini's personal life should be read for its broader historical significance, not simply for its disclosures of her family's private suffering. In the first place, Roekmini's marriage provides a perfect balance to Kartini's. A decade earlier, both women could only imagine contracting the kind of modern marriage Roekmini had. Roekmini's marriage was the first in the family that was not arranged, and so also represented the achievement of the central goal of their combined project. Kartini had not regarded marriage as incompatible with a vocation: in terms of their cause, she had rationalized the value of her marriage as providing the necessary support for undertaking the task of raising socially responsible future citizens and pursuing social reform. What she and Roekmini had rejected, and Kartini had partially experienced, was the singular trajectory that tradition imposed on women's lives and the humiliation and suffering that a traditional priyayi polygamous marriage entailed. And, as Kartini and each of her sisters assured Rosita, they found in marriage friendship, varying degrees of happiness, and the pleasure associated with raising children. In the evolution and articulation of the personal, one can read the evolution and articulation of modernity.

Roekmini's correspondence also details the the career of her husband, Santoso, and the saga of her two stepsons. Santoso's history and concerns can be compared to those of the other men in the correspondence: Soematri's husband, Sosrohadikoesoemo; her older sister Soelastri's husband, Tjokrohadisosro; and her brother Kartono. In the lives of each of these men, located in different levels of the colonial bureaucracy and colonized society, each politically aware and each articulating or experiencing the everyday workings of the colonial regime, we see the anger, humiliation, and frustration that fed into the larger story of an Indonesian nationalism. In reading about these men, we gain some insight into the intrigues within the colonial bureaucracy, upon which Soematri's husband comments quite specifically. The success of one of her stepsons and the failure of the other, and the extended tragedy of her brother Kartono after his initial academic success exemplify aspects of what Frantz Fanon described as the psychology of the colonial subject, replicated many thousands of times during and after colonialism.

Roekmini's correspondence does not reveal her whole life but does, like that of her sisters, clearly define the trajectory not just of one woman but of a whole generation and class of women. The correspondence ends tantalizingly at the beginning of the twenties, when a long, difficult chapter of her life had come to an end and, as other sources indicate, she was beginning a new, productive period in her life. All the issues that had drawn her into a dependence on Rosita and her husband had now been brought to an end. With a paid position, she was financially independent, and her children were settled. While it may not have been so intended, Roekmini's last letter can be seen as a final closing of the account. The abrupt ending of her correspondence, like that of Kartinah's, suggests a symbolic disengagement from the colonial connection.

Roekmini to Rosita Abendanon-Mandri

Jepara, 2 December 1901[12]

Dearest Mevrouw,[13]

May I begin by expressing my sincerest thanks for the beautiful presents with which you have made me so happy. Each of us is so grateful for what we have received, especially the youngest two;[14] for them it is as if you had overheard their prayers that the good old Saint [Nicholas] would not forget them, without letting them suspect that you had sent the presents, and they call you, as we always have, "the good Angel"! Young people here do not celebrate *Sinterklaas*,[15] and with us here at home in the present circumstances, when our heads and hearts are totally preoccupied with such sad thoughts, we could hardly contemplate it and the little sisters know this.[16] They can feel something is not right; can you imagine how great their happiness was when you nevertheless thought of them?

Mevrouw, dearest Mevrouw, I *cannot* write further. Kardinah has come to me with eyes red from weeping and icy cold, to tell me that she has agreed. Poor, poor darling. Oh God, oh God what will happen? They have

pushed her to the extremity like a hunted deer that can find no further route of escape and yet is piteously taken. It will happen! A superior force has conquered, has triumphed, but what matter, it has its victim; what matter if thereby hearts are broken. They have got what they desired, but their consciences will gnaw at them for eternity. Kleintje says we ought not to reproach our Parents, not to protest, and that we should not be sad. Oh Mevrouw, my heart is breaking. It is as if she is about to die, the way she tells this to us. But is it any less than that? It is more, much more than that. She has sacrificed herself. My darling, my darling! Mevrouw, pray for us, we are desperate. We are fated. Away, away; everything is gone, I can no longer think. When you tell Mijnheer, do so softly, because we know how great your grief will be when you both hear it. My dearest Mevrouw, they have murdered our souls, there I have said it. My little one is prepared to die. Oh God, how can it be? You, who are love itself; how can this happen so mercilessly? Do not be too sad, dearest,
  Your despairing,
  Roekmini

Roekmini to Rosita Abendanon-Mandri

Jepara, 23 June 1902

My dearest Mevrouw,

  What a long time it has been since you last heard something from me. Will you forgive me, Mevrouw? I am ashamed of the way I seem to be acknowledging the wonderful friendship which we know we have and without which we could not imagine what our lives would have been; when knowing you forms such an important part of it. Your love for us is so deep, so great, and possessing it, we will always feel rich, even if the entire world should turn away from us. And this is what I have given so little recognition of, even though in fact my whole being is filled with a deep gratitude. I so hope that your feelings for me will never lessen as a result. Light of our lives, we love you so much, continue to be for me the same beam of light that you were before. Do give me this: point out and light my path for me.

  When you receive this letter, Annie Glaser[17] will already have been to see you; we have followed her in our thoughts up to the time she would have visited you. How we wished that we could have accompanied her. We would so love to see you again, to be with you for a long period of time, to hear once again your voices which can so excite us and bring us such joy. We have a very strong desire to stay a while in an atmosphere like that which surrounds you, far removed from the mundane, in the world of your home, where one only breathes in a superior air, that would uplift us, revitalize us. Here in our world, people have found something new to gossip about which we merely shrug off and try to treat as a joke but which nevertheless has almost caused us some difficulty.[18] Of course it concerns us. They regard us as such impossible creatures because we continually show our desire not to want to walk sedately and normally like them in the featureless plain which constitutes their world totally lacking in mountain peaks, but on the contrary to prefer to climb mountains and to shout with excitement when we have reached the top.[19] Their cries from below, disapproving of what we do or what the consequences will be, their attempts to prevent this, are in fact less the gestures of friendly advice to perhaps warn us of dangers, than of envy because they are not able to participate or are too lazy to do so.

All this would not concern us in the slightest were it not that this has affected our Parents' trust in us, they who have always been so indulgent towards their children who have never caused the slightest problem. By hiding their falseness behind an appearance of friendship, these people have nearly convinced our Parents and have caused their faith in us to waver, and that is what has angered us, has made us long all the more to be near you, indirectly to feel your presence in order to recharge ourselves. Fortunately, oh, I don't know how to express it, we have now for three-quarters, or almost completely, won them over to us again.

As you will have learned from Kartini, we have set out our plans for Mr. v. Kol during his stay here and he was not unimpressed.[20] His Exc. promised at that time to do all in his power to ensure our attempts succeeded. We told him everything and in our innocence we thought that that this would remain confidential, just between Mr. v. K. and us. But then, a coeditor of *De Locomotief* who at the time was traveling with Mr. v. K. through the Semarang Residency had presumably taken his task as a journalist too literally to heart. Even though it may only have been a matter of eavesdropping, he also poked his nose into this matter, which after all was private, and this might not have been an issue had he done it properly! But, by his doing so only partially, the result is that the plan has been given an entirely incorrect explanation which puts it in a much less attractive light.

This gentleman, then, has written in *De Locomotief* what he heard, but in such a way that it seems to us that he did not understand half of our conversation. Indeed, he wrote quite favorably about what we were striving for and he expanded on it by saying how fine he thought it was and in the first place because European civilization had brought us closer to understanding our own country and its character rather than separating us from it, or leading us to despise it, in that we had chosen as our ideal to commit ourselves to give our people that which we ourselves had received. But then about the matter of going to Holland! In regard to this he came out with the nonsense that Kartini had sought permission for *all* daughters of regents—permission to live there—in order to expand their perspectives and enrich their minds. And *that* has put the cat among the pigeons! We did think when we read it that it would cause a sensation in this district, but beyond that we did not give it a thought until our Parents stayed with a highly placed Native[21] family, known in the European community as being among the leading families and with whom the country could be proud to identify.[22] When there is talk about true intellectual development, it is these people who are placed at the head of the group of educated sons and daughters, and we were certainly reminded of this by them. Our Parents told us how there was intense gossiping about the idea while they were there, and that Kartini was sharply criticized and we were widely ridiculed and put down.

Actually, it would be a lie to say that we did not expect that it would generate such agitation, because these people seem to be basically perfidious! Anyway, everything which Ma had to say about it was too despicable to pay the slightest attention to, and for our added delight there were also Europeans present who participated. The family then said, and many others there agreed, how they would never permit their daughters to do something like that, to spread their wings more vigorously in order to fly higher in the sky than they had been taught: that was nonsense, it was not proper. And the Europeans ascribed our behavior to our shame that at our age we were not yet married[23] or, perhaps more directly, that it was because a younger sister had married first, because in Holland, or here, they said, the girls who are attracted to the idea of emancipation are also the ones who have no chance (!!!) of getting married. Or are these girls aiming to become attached to Europeans because here they do not think they can find equals amongst the Natives? And then someone said they would make it easier for us. When I heard that, Ma said, I thought a stone had fallen on my heart. (These opinions by Europeans Ma heard later from the family and therefore not directly.) Ma found all this very sad, you can imagine, and it was for this reason that our plans had not found much support from her. To this was added the provocations of the family, who, pretending to be interested in our welfare, did as much as they could to hinder us. But now we have convinced Ma to such an extent about the rightness of what we want to do and that what is being said about it is pure envy—that it is because we dare so much more than they—that Ma is now 3/4 on our side and that Ma's only concern is how we will endure living in Holland, that far-off foreign country, for so long.

Poor Parents, this is how it is, why could it not have been arranged otherwise so they would not have to suffer so in regard to their most beloved possessions?

The letters which Mr. v. K. had asked us to write to provide our names, age, and in short to provide him once more with all the details, have already been sent. So when we received permission we did not wait another day. What our Parents now most want is that when Mr. v. K. has discussed the matter, it will remain confidential and not made available to the press. They would find it so terrible for us if everyone knew all about it and if, in the end, it should be refused. Kartini made this point in the letter to Mr. v. K. We totally agree with our Parents and hope that the press will not get involved, unless the result is favorable and then it can say what it likes. When that moment has arrived, how will it be? Mevrouw, when we received permission to write, we felt we had to yell it out but now we hardly dare assume that something else will go smoothly. But should it eventuate, we will still avoid getting overexcited, as we would have been earlier about a favourable outcome. No, we would not be so naive again in expressing our feelings, we would be too frightened. Haven't we had to pay for each laugh twice over? I hope fervently that Mijnheer will still be able to speak to Mr. v. K. during the last occasion when he is in Batavia, and even more that His Exc. is able to meet you.[24]

You have seen the samples of my talent? Tell me what you think of them; it was for that purpose that I sent them with Annie. It is not much but I do intend to draw a lot by myself as practice and also in case, in connection with my application, some samples may be required to gauge whether or not it was worthwhile to provide me with that training. But above all, they must take account of the fact that I have never had any lessons, at least not specific lessons. I have shown my work to everyone who has some knowledge of drawing for their opinion, and I have received much advice on the basis of which I have trained my power of observation. Previously Mr. Quartero was there to help me, but now I must progress on my own.[25] If only I were able to come to you, what a help that would be! Oh, can you still remember how I could stand before your paintings,[26] especially the one of the landscape with the deer if I remember correctly, refreshing itself by a clear pool of a waterfall from which a small stream flowed which transported the crystal liquid away to unknown places? I can still see the great boulders on which the slender legs of the noble animal rested. Do you still remember with what joy I wandered through the hallway? To stretch out my wings in that domain has always been my aim.

And so my proposal or desire is to undertake training at a technical high school (or arts academy) in order to devote myself later to Javanese art, which is currently undergoing a revival. It has recently become a greater desire than ever. But if it should appear after several months that I have no prospect of studying further with much success, then we have thought of another means for me to follow to reach our goal, and that is domestic science as it is currently being taught in progressive institutions in Holl. I will then take examinations in that area so that I can then establish such an institution in conjunction with K.'s school. In this area also we can see great prospects for our endeavors because would not knowledge about this find immediate support from parents? As a result of such instruction, girls would learn to appreciate infinitely more the value of everything related to domestic economy, in the first place the value of money, for which the government has already provided an example in teaching the Natives thriftiness. Since all these things depend on the woman, how much better would it not be if she had a complete knowledge of this area! Kartini would very much like to see this done, also because of the publicity. You cannot imagine how everything European, especially such things as European cooking, is of such interest to our mothers, how they direct their daughters' attention to it as though it were something which was the very latest in refinement and how that will assist to raise the significance of what we are doing in their eyes.[27] This was also something which Mr. v. K. enthusiastically supported. Should you not yet know what is taught in such domestic science schools, apart from home management and cooking, then I will write to you about it next time. It is a pity I cannot do so now because the mail is collected at night at 3 o'clock so that this letter will have to go very soon. I am looking forward to Annie's arrival. I have just received a postcard from her which gives us so much pleasure. She writes that she has dined with you and so enjoyed your company. We knew that she was with you at that moment. I will tell you about that later.

Oh, how we would have loved to have joined you. How familiar everything will have been to her, you, your home and everything in it, because we have described everything to her and have always spoken about it. It would be wonderful for her if she were to live in Batavia and could come to visit you frequently. Often we feel so sorry for her when we see her as she exists here, where she does not belong at all. And what a joy it is for us to know that she can come to Mijnheer herself with all her concerns. Could Mijnheer not do something about this soon, this year even, dearest Mevrouw? Don't regard this as an interfering request, it is nothing more than that she is very dear to us and that we would wish her only joy and pleasantness in her life. This place which is no different than any other small place in its petty-mindedness is no place for her on her own. Nor will she be able to stay with us, and after the vacation she returns to that terrible hotel, you can imagine how we can allow that only with great distress. We wept when we had to tell her, knowing that thereby we would cause her such sorrow. Then we quickly and emphatically advised her to see you. Now we would rather lose her than that we had her here in these surroundings, as long as she came to live in a better location. For her and for us it has to be the case that she goes away.[28] Poor child, we are so fond of each other. What cheer she brought to our home in those two months. If you should see A. again, will you show her all those beautiful souvenirs from Norway? She knows all about it. Do you have any good news from Didi?[29] How is that child of your heart?

Well dearest, our warmest regards to Mijnheer and a warm kiss for you from your dear,

Roekmini

Roekmini to Rosita Abendanon-Mandri

Jepara, 28 July 1902

My dearest treasure, my sun, with all the love we have in our heart, many, many times over we wish you all the best on 1 August from your Native children.[30] We can say, can't we, Light of our Life, that we are yours. Because of the way you have constantly guarded over us and will continue to do so through everything that threatens and thunders, clashes and dies, as enduringly as only a mother's wings can be spread protecting her young, I can only think of you as our Moeder, where we may find love so rare, so pure, which supports us and keeps us upright, the greatest, truest love, totally unselfish—should we not call her our Moeder, not give her that endearing name? Oh Moedertje, how we thank God for this great comfort in our lives, possessing you; continue to stand guard over our souls, that they may gain some of the paleness of yours.

And now, dearest, we have a small surprise for you, something of little significance but something we ourselves have made with which we hope we will be able to bring you some pleasure. We have been working on this with love during these days when storms and battles were raging at their worst and it was as though we extracted our strength from this each time we sat down to work at it.

How happy your postcard made us, the one you wrote during your illness.[31] It was for that reason that it had double significance for us. You see, the realization that there are people who share with us all that is sacred gives us courage, the courage to go on, ever onwards. And we have found one more, or rather another couple who have given us their heart to extract strength from in order to fulfil our lives in accordance with the goals we have set.[32] Oh and are not our beings, our entire beings completely filled with gratitude for so many blessings received from above? With this permission[33] we are actually standing for the first time at the beginning of life, even though we have already experienced much, but with this heavenly blessing in the form of all the love emanating from you, we have been forced to consider what we have. And when we commence our work it is not only to achieve our goal but as much again, to be worthy of your love and trust. To shame you would be for us like hell is for the rest of the world.

We think it is wonderful that you will be writing to N. v. K.; when we received a letter from her, our first thought after we had read and reread its contents, which were to us like purest water to one dying of thirst, was of you and how wonderful it would be if you also could be in contact with such noble souls. How happy we were when you thought of that yourself. What is more, I could not believe that two such noble beings, living on one and the same earth, with the same views, at the peak of their lives, would not meet each other and embrace each other. And they both belong to us, oh, what a treasure, a treasure greater, richer than anything on earth; it is something of which the Javanese says: "a melati which opens her petals in the depth of a heart." The article about K. by N. v. K. has been reproduced in the ladies' journal *De Echo,* whose editor knows us, has added a further piece in which she focused the attention on us and on the expectation that Native women should all support us as far as they could, as they should, according to her.[34] Such support, how good that makes us feel each time we hear it. Now our plans are known to everyone, so that it is now merely a case of carrying out what is known, of acting firmly, it has to happen, as quickly as possible. And what you have advised us, to stay in the Indies, we have discussed with others, thought over carefully ourselves, and now that we have found so much support, also for instance from a powerful organization like Oost en West,[35] which will be a wonderful support in the future for the development of the cause, we have decided to choose Holland. We thank you very much for what you had recommended to us, which forced us to sift and search and to come to a specific conclusion. It will be Holland despite the difficulties.³⁶ And if this is also agreed to in the office of the Resident then we already have someone with whom we can stay, and that is Mevrouw Glaser. She is a most suitable woman to take in and care for real Indies guests; she has spent her whole youth, not to say 3/4 of her life, here in the Indies and therefore knows the customs of the Indies very well.³⁷ And not only that, but also because through her daughter we have came to know her thoroughly as an excellent, fine woman to whom we will be able to entrust everything that is in our hearts like a mother. She has offered and she would love us as her own daughter who is in our country, she said. Isn't that kind of her? Others will be suggested to us, also fine people, but because we know this person, as it were, personally, we would choose her. I believe it is best to follow one's heart, don't you think, dearest?

Now, my spiritual Moedertje, I will say good-bye. Are you both well? Are you up and about again? Please do not become ill again, it saddens us so to hear that, dearest. Please give Mijnheer our warmest regards, and you are closely embraced by your devoted

Roekmini

Roekmini to Rosita Abendanon-Mandri

Postcard
{PRIVATE}

Jepara, 22 February 1903

Welcome home!
Dear Moedertje,³⁸

I am just writing to tell you that we received your letter, which has made us very happy. How we have been waiting for the moment when we would see that beloved handwriting again.³⁹

This of course is not a reply to your letter, but we just wanted to thank you for it. Moedertje, at the moment Kartini is very busy, so she is unable to write herself.⁴⁰ Concerning all that you have written, there will be a letter shortly. We have also received wonderful news from N. v. K. She wrote that her husband has had lengthy discussions with the Minister about us, that the latter was most taken by our plans as a result of which he (the M.) apparently wrote privately to the G.G., who is more directly involved in the decision on this matter, to support us.⁴¹ Wonderful!

Now, dear, kind Moedertje, once again, welcome home, much love from us all and especially from your loving children.

Roekmini

Roekmini to Rosita Abendanon-Mandri

Jepara, 29 March 1903

Dearest Moedertje,

Because we are so confident in the knowledge of being able to come to you at any time, in whatever circumstances you may find yourself in, as your children who love you, who always share your life with you, I will let nothing hinder me from coming to you now, dearest, at this moment when we especially feel that our hearts more than ever need to be together.

The day before yesterday we received, together with yours, a letter from our dear, good friend and brother,[42] in which he told us that now, with the best will in the world, there would be no chance of us meeting each other, about which we had such beautiful expectations, and that he would also have to leave very soon. What we felt when all this had sunk in, dearest, oh, could I but let you feel how it actually was and still is. We also told Didi this, but not everything, knowing full well how he himself would be grieved by it if we had, that dear, dear boy.

Moedertje, it was a tremendous blow that we felt come down on the structure that we had built from our dreams, it was such a sadness for us when we knew that everything, everything was destroyed, and a question arose from us why it should be that a meeting with him for whom we have such warm feelings would never eventuate. Why then were we given the hope that this would occur which had made us so happy?

Previously, when we had never thought it possible, then it was not so difficult for us to accept that in this life only our spirits would ever meet, but now, now that we so often received the promise that we might meet, not only in spirit but also in person, this capricious twist of fate has *been devastating*.

Yes, dearest Moedertje, it "has been" because I can tell you that we have largely got over it. We have pushed everything deep, deep down into the region of the forbidden, no matter with what sorrow, but, on the other hand, we have had to exercise much energy to remain normal when so many things in our surroundings remind us, things which are closely related with what we had imagined, how near it had been. We are so fond of your darling, dearest. How happy we were to receive such unsolicited evidence that he also has such brotherly feelings for us in that he very much wanted us to come. How grateful we are to you that you had not written about this before, oh Moedertje, how much more terrible it would have been to have known then that it was impossible. We could but sadly smile at your words. Oh, how did we not dream of this possibility of meeting together. Everything was intended for his stay here. We would do everything with him, even if he wanted to go to the borings;[43] in short, to turn those days into moments of pure joy in our lives with our soul brother, and always him between us, everywhere, and often his hand in ours as we did with you: in this way, you see, thinking about it, we can still become sad.

But we promised each other, Tini and I, to be strong. Besides ours, there are other deep feelings of those who are also very dear to us, beside which we should regard our fate as insignificant. And then, who knows if later we will not experience some good from what we now perceive as something cruel and hard. Yes, we *do want* to seek what is good in this because it must be the case that something is intended by fate, so extraordinary have recent events been with everything which has unfolded before us. We *want* to continue to *believe* in *the* Wise Hand which continues to lead us toward the good, even though the road to it passes through darkness as in the depth of a forest. But set aside any idea that hope has disappeared, leave us contented in our spiritual meeting, just that of our souls, above the material world, what after all is more beautiful than this?

Away then with everything by which this world can cause us to grieve over him, we only want to continue to live as we have done in our relations with him, that dear, sweet brother of ours. In our thoughts we called out our farewell to him in the earthly aspect of life because our heart tells us that we will never meet him there, because as things are now, that will be for the best. We pray that it will continue to be so for us all, may the whole rest of his life be where he is going.

Moedertje, we thank you with all our hearts for your confidence, may we continue to deserve it; that people continue to open their hearts to us and especially because it is you, this touched us deeply. May this continue to be a guarantee for others that we will continue to strive for what is good. And when the time comes, Moedertje dear, that we can in reality be with you, then we fervently hope that we may make up somewhat for the great absence that you feel in your life. How much we are already looking forward to surrounding you with our love, as our own, very own Moedertje, when we are finally with you, dearest.

Our Parents have put us entirely at your disposal at that time in the future.[44] It is so wonderful for us to see how, more and more, they are coming to accept the idea of us going to B. and are sharing in our cause: nothing exists in the future any longer as far as they are concerned than our plans. Already when it comes to the point, Father lets it be known that we are going to study, going to Batavia, and Ma shares in this as much as possible in gaining support among officials' wives for our plans and has on many occasions had success. Those dear, kind Parents, how grateful we are to them for this. Now the application will need to be handed in quickly and then we will soon be with you; we are yearning to be there, Moedertje. If all goes well after all, we could be there in July.

We sent Didi everything he asked for straightaway, we gave him everything possible. In Holland we hope that he will get on with our brother Kartono as well as he does with us, he is such a fine boy.

Well, my dear, good Moedertje, your child embraces you in her thoughts and at this moment is with you with all her heart. A warm hand of support to you both and believe in her great love for you.

 Adieu dearest till later
 Roekmini

Roekmini to Rosita Abendanon-Mandri

Jepara, 15 June 1903

Dearest Moedertje,

The day before yesterday I received your letter as well as the regulations for nurse training. Thank you very much for both, dearest, you don't know how welcome this is to us and especially to me, as I now know what I have to do.[45] We think it is so nice of you both not to want to lose any time, and to inform us immediately of what we need to do. And now I won't delay either to tell you what you will both want to know. I have read and reread the regulations carefully and I can say only that the training course appeals to me very much. It encompasses everything that I have always wanted to know when I have been at the side of the sickbed. It attracted me immediately and I promised myself that I would devote myself to it in order to complete these studies successfully. More and more I have come to the realization that this vocation of tending the sick appeals to me, and for that purpose I would gladly do anything that is required of me. But at the moment, since you have insisted that we should consider the matter carefully, the question is whether I would agree to enroll in an institution. Yes, dearest Moedertje, we also think that one would most profit from the education provided as an intern, one would then *completely* exist in that atmosphere; we completely agree with Mijnheer, but nevertheless we think we will follow your suggestion. Kartini has written to you about it and you will now know precisely what we think about our accommodation.[46]

You see, Moedertje, it is as you have said: it would be too great a change for us to *all at once* be parted from everything. We have not been able to entertain the idea (and perhaps never will) of our having to live apart in strange surroundings. We would no doubt feel lonely, and who knows whether that might not have an effect on our work. I read in the regulations that as an intern, one would not have much time to go out. No, that would not concern me, as long as I had Kartini by me in the same house, but if that were not the case, then I would not feel alive, and K. would feel the same. Perhaps this might be possible later, when we became accustomed to that existence, when what is strange to us now was no longer so, but now, in this initial period, when we are as if alone in the world, and we still need to support each other so much, now, I do not think that a separate existence would be good for us. We would have to make too much of a demand on our constitutions, our work would suffer, and then what? Your idea therefore was not unexpected, but yet was a surprise. We are so pleased that you think about this as we do.

Dearest Moedertje, if it is possible, let us then initially stay together and take lodgings with someone who, as you suggest, lives at an equal distance between Cikini and Laan de Riemer (well, the distance is not so important).[47] Certainly you have considered this as a true woman, and you have definitely not misjudged since your protégés are also women, so that naturally a large degree of agreement exists between you and them. What you had thought of has found a complete response in their heart, Moedertje. Yet the traveling to and fro would not outweigh being separated. Now, dearest, will you tell Mijnheer that for the time being, this is our view? But now I hope that it will be possible for me to do my work as well as if I were an intern.[48] I would very much want to be regarded as a good student despite the fact I was living outside.

It is wonderful to know that you will by now have received K.'s letter and that you will now not have to worry so much about our accommodation. And, as you now know, for our dear Parents it will also be much better if we can stay together, we have constantly had to promise this. Let it be this way for the time being, who knows, even they may in time change their mind on this point and if it then has to be, then we will be able to do it more easily. How happy we are with your suggestion that initially we come to stay with you. To tell you the truth, dearest, we had hoped for this, but of course we did not dare tell you. Of course we think it is wonderful to be with you, you did not need to ask us that. That would be the highlight of what was to come. Oh, you do not know how melancholy we became when we read your letter which reminded us how soon we would have to take our leave of everything we loved, and especially when Mijnheer made the suggestion that we should live apart.[49] We could have cried, but fortunately that may now not be necessary—the sooner the time comes to leave, the better it would be for all of us, we would not wish it otherwise.

From the moment that we received your letter we have been preparing our Parents in order to get an early decision. Ma is unable to sleep at night because of it and yet that dear Mother is daily more in favor of our putting our ideals into practice. That is the only future Ma has in mind for us. How empty it will become for our Parents when the two of us suddenly leave. Poor Parents, may it be that their sacrifice will never be in vain, that we will continue to have the energy to do our work *well,* and that Father and Mother will find pleasure in us for as long as possible. Ma now proposes to take us to Batavia herself. What do you think of that? If possible, Pa will, but should it not be possible, then Ma will come with us on her own. For us of course it will be wonderful if she comes. Ma declares that she would be prepared to travel thus far on her own. Once we are here, I do not have any illusions about being able to go home during those three years, because as you know, I will have very few days off in that time. You must not imagine that my first thoughts are of pleasure, but doubtless the time will come when we will want to go home so I can now prepare myself to accept the impossibility of that, which will strengthen me. But then we will find another home which for us will be equally wonderful to enter.

How surprised we were that Didi would return so soon.[50] It will then still be possible for us to meet him? Once, surely, it will be possible for that dream of ours to be realized, for us to be together with the three of you in friendly surroundings. "That darling of us all"—I would not be surprised to hear that said then—he is such a dear, kind boy. I hope our brother met him and has become a friend of his.[51] How we would love to see this happen. How wonderful that things are going so well for him. And Doppie has passed his exam![52] Our congratulations, Moedertje—I hope that apple of your eye will be a source of pride and pleasure for a long time to come. How happy Mary and he will be about it as well. Please pass on to Mijnheer our congratulations and good wishes on the news.

Tomorrow things will be busy again. We will have visitors staying, among whom will be a very intelligent teacher of secondary school French, Miss Bosch, who is also a good storyteller, and another, a very cultivated and artistic woman. The day before yesterday, we returned from Semarang, where we were presented to the Susuhunan. As you know, he has honored S[emarang] with a visit, and because it was such a good opportunity for us to meet him face to face, we could not pass up the opportunity to go.[53] Well, we had a good look at him at the home of the Resident.⁵⁴ Can you imagine, he had had such a pleasant time in Semarang that he is seriously considering coming again in the future and to travel farther, to Batavia. However, when he was on the point of leaving, he apparently became very anxious because of the realization that a Susuhunan had never been outside the boundaries of his princedom before except as an exile. But now that he is convinced that the government means to deal justly with him, now that this trip has pleased him so much, he wants to travel again next year. The sea, which he had never seen before, he thought was wonderful, as were the ships lying at anchor in the harbor which he visited. He would also have liked to have stayed there forever! We also had a pleasant evening on board the warship *Regentes*.⁵⁵ An experience on board such as this, with a wonderful view of the sea, is heavenly. We sailed a long way from the pier in the moonlight, and it was an indescribable delight. How we will miss this in Batavia! Those few hours on the waves, when such a wonderful sense of peace can invade one's body and soul, these have now passed!

But another pleasure awaits us, an unselfish and higher one, and in that our thoughts are now vested! Dearest, if you have anything more to tell us regarding our stay, we are eager to hear it! But Moedertje, you must not make yourself ill. Can you not ignore that life for a while, which you have to live there and which makes you so ill? How terrible it is for you, all those dreadful duties you have to perform, which so wear you out and force you to be so punctual. We can easily imagine how it disgusts you because it is not unknown to us. But take some rest, Moedertje, please, and write to us at a time when you really feel fresh and alert! All is well with us.

Good-bye, dearest, kindest Moesje, give Mijnheer our warmest greetings, and once again, many, many thanks for your letter and for what you have sent us. With a warm kiss from those who love you,

Roekmini and K⁵⁶

Roekmini to Rosita Abendanon-Mandri

Jepara, 22 June 1903

Dearest Moedertje,

Perhaps you might find it very ungrateful of us but I am here to ask you something with regard to our petition. Please do not get a shock, Moedertje, but we suspect trouble is brewing for us both, and when the decisive moment for that arrives, only our independence can save us and this only a positive response to our petition could provide us. We would then no longer be financially dependent either, and this would be an especially good weapon for us. Would you now ask Mijnheer on our behalf if he could not arrange that some haste is made on this matter? We recognize that we are asking far too much but we would never have done so, dearest, if we did not consider it absolutely necessary. We must after all never give in, our work after all must be done, mustn't it, and it is in regard to this that we sense there is a danger that there will be an attempt to obstruct us and we must do everything to ensure our plans are carried out. I am speaking here in riddles, but I am not yet able to explain to you what it is about. You will get to hear about it, dearest. How unpleasant it is for me to be so secretive toward you, you who knows everything about us, you cannot know.[57]

Would you be prepared to do this for us, Moedertje? You would make us very happy and we would thereby be able to continue living, do you understand?

Oh, to discover that everything is almost as far away as ever when we thought we would be able to achieve it, to find again that something else has intervened. But you yourself must not think about it too much, dearest, perhaps the possibility for us to receive a favorable answer is now closer than ever before and this obstacle may then also disappear. You will no doubt ask why K herself is not writing. Moedertje, the poor thing is ill. She has measles with some smallpox as well, which she developed as a result of catching a cold, which caused her severe fevers and headaches. Now she has to remain in a dark room, is bored to death, and suffers much discomfort when both lying and sitting as a result of the smallpox eruptions. If it were not for the eruptions, then she would be feeling quite her old self.

Last week we had a student from the second class of the pol. school staying with us who was taking a trip to visit Dad and Mum during the holidays. Naturally I immediately asked after Dop and his girlfriend. He knows them very well and he spoke[58] very warmly about our friend. I felt so good. I showed him Japara and told him that he, the student, had seen everything which causes this district to make such an impression on so many people. He is the son of the artistic woman about whom I wrote to you recently, that she intended to come. Imagine, these people came especially to get to know the wonders of Jepara in detail. How overjoyed we were in our hearts. Now Moedertje, dear, you will do it, won't you? We thank you very much in advance. Hoping everything will turn out for the best, your daughters kiss you warmly.

K and R

Roekmini to Rosita Abendanon-Mandri

Jepara, 15 July 1903

Dear, kind Moedertje,

Since Kartini wrote to you yesterday, I can no longer contain my urge to write to you again. I had wanted to for a long time but I have been constantly prevented as I became ill and then got smallpox. For a long time, for the entire duration of the illness, I had to wait while so many things demanded that I come to you; you can imagine what I went through being forced to lie still and in a darkened room at that, in which thoughts had even greater free reign.

Now I only wanted to say, do not be so sad any more, dear Moedertje, and nor should Mijnheer. Kartini has told you everything. And I shall not repeat what we have had to put up with in the last days—what would be the sense of it? After all, don't we want to remain strong? But now it must be that we have received God's blessing because we have found peace after the battle. We have been granted the strength to continue in this life, even if along a totally different road than before. Yes, I can assure you, dearest, we still have a great deal of courage to live, and if we have that, we are not entirely lost after all, are we? I wish you could convince yourself that that is the case; it is certainly not said in order to throw sand in your eyes, to deceive you into thinking that everything is all right while in fact we face the opposite, but it is the complete truth when I say this.

The cross which our darling must carry is heavy, and I also feel its burden, but who knows, who knows what good might flow from it for her and me. Both of us, despite the heavy blow continue to search unceasingly for the "light" and I think we have been able to find "it." You are aware of the conditions, aren't you, drawn up by Tini and regarded as natural and reasonable by our Parents? Well, it can still be beautiful, her life. She can still continue to work for "the people" and perhaps she may now be able to do more good because the people will naturally regard her as the one for whom they in the first instance must set aside a place in their hearts as the wife of the one who is their "Father." I hope this can be a comfort to us, dearest, since she is able to retain her Ideal; if she suffers, it is for her "love," and that brings glory. There is so much, so much that we have had to bury, but since we still have a life before us, we now want to find our comfort there. I know how you both, whom we have included in this beautiful dream, are affected, but we pray to you that you will look at it as we do, to live once more together with us, dearest. Forgive us and assuage the suffering that we have unintentionally caused you. It will once more make us happy to know that our dear friends, who are at the same time our Parents, are at peace again. Forgive our Parents; you can place them in the category of "people who want nothing more than the happiness of their children." They acted in good faith. Also with us two, we had to pray and pray, why, for what, we ourselves did not rightly know, but we felt we had to, for everything we received ... It was a rich piece of life for us in all its terrible forms. May it in the end be to our benefit!

Now I also will not be coming to you. My Parents think that for me on my own there are even greater difficulties. And what would it be like for me so completely without Kartini? Where I had considered a separate existence, as we had thought would be the case with K[artini] in L[aan] de Riema and me in Cikim, would be so terrible, how then would it be when I knew she would not be near me at all? Even here at home it will weigh heavily on me, this life without her. We had always been so close.

And here I have our little school, about which you no doubt know a great deal. I will live for that, as much as I am able. I am very fond of the children, and they continue so wonderfully to do their best that there is always a great pleasure in teaching them. Only it is a great pity that I will not obtain that medical and first-aid knowledge. It would be wonderful to possess it. But perhaps I will still be able to learn this.

You know what held us back from going to Batavia in the end, Moedertje, it is no small matter. We continue to get shivers over our bodies if we but read the letter. It is such a crude affair, and given that the man will have had his pride bruised, he will never be able to forgive us, and that is our fear![59] Oh, then how badly were we mistaken in thinking to be completely free through what we revealed of ourselves. We thought we had engendered a distaste for us in the minds of these people in that respect. But alas! We so hope that that person will leave it at this and not trouble us any further.

But there is also a source of comfort for us, dearest. My prospective brother-in-law is *a somebody:* he is no ordinary person.[60] His special qualities, however, are to be found in nothing more than in his heart, which must be made of gold. He also respects quality of intellect: despite his lack of knowledge of European languages, it had been his wish to have no other wife than one who was completely at ease in one, sparkled in its use, who moved in modern circles, because he very much wanted his children to become what life here in Java now demands for society. As the bearer of the future of his children he chose our Tini, he must have been considering the idea for a long time but never really had the courage to take it that far until that particular day. We learned all this from others because his proposal was a great surprise to us. You see, dearest, if we can believe everything we have heard about him, then we can hope that everything will go well. Mijnheer Gonggrijp knows him very well.[61] He said of him that he was someone whom you could respect. "I have such a healthy respect for him, he is extremely *pinter* [clever]!" His people are very fond of him, and when he announced his engagement they apparently greeted it with great enthusiasm. He himself is *so* happy, *that* I can imagine! The official who brought him Father's letter which contained his approval was so warmly welcomed and entertained that he became confused. And what of his language! He is indeed a poet, his letters are poetry, they reveal a soul of pure goodness. What a contrast with that other. Leaving aside everything else, we are sometimes able to simply enjoy it as literature. I hope, I pray fervently, that sister's sacrifice will not be in vain.

Now you know everything, dearest, but only you of all our friends know the real course of events. Only to you we reveal what we are, toward others, our acquaintances, we want to maintain appearances, for them we want to appear totally happy. No one else needs to look into our hearts, only to you is this entrusted. Will you now help us to play this role well, Moedertje? If people ask you about us, smile and tell them a story. After all, not everything is lost, is it? After this letter to you, I want to write to Annie, whom I still owe a long letter and to her we want to write a letter full of enthusiasm, for her we plan to be the "lucky ones." Will you assist us in this, dearest, and when she speaks to you about this also give the appearance that you share in our happiness? We ask a lot from you, but after all you are like parents, and we hope that you will continue to value such confidence. Oh, we thank God for such support as that from you and Nellie v. Kol. What would our lives be otherwise.

We received the [government] resolutions, may we keep them, or what should we do? How we would love to keep them as a relic, a reminder of our beautiful past. We already have the telegram; that belongs to us.[62]

Well, dearest Moedertje, may our letter bring peace to you both as well as faith in us regarding the rest of our lives. If you do have that, write and tell us, it would make us so happy.

The engagement has been public for 4 days, the people are happy, they have prayed for God's blessing for the couple. May the prayer be heard, which is also mine. How will Kartono receive it, poor boy? It will be such a terrible contrast to all the good fortune he has received. Poor, poor boy. And Didi. Oh, why have you only had suffering, suffering, suffering from us?

We so long for a real embrace at this moment from our friends, a kiss, and a few words given in person. Our head longs to nuzzle against the shoulder of our dearest one.

Well, Moedertje, dear, may you write to us soon. To you and Mijnheer we send much love and a warm hand from your devoted daughters.

Bye, we embrace you warmly. K. is beginning to sleep better.

Roekmini

Roekmini to Rosita Abendanon-Mandri

Jepara, August 1903[63]

Kartini has no doubt told you about her own plans for a new life. Yes, she would then love to see that a school is established, but we don't know. I myself have no clear idea yet about the future that now lies before me when she is gone. There will be at least 5 months after the wedding before work can begin in setting up the school. And so, disturbing that beautiful dream of being able to work together again on our ideal, comes the thought of the time that we will have to live apart. That we had not anticipated, even though we had been prepared for a separation of our lives. Yes, *of* our lives, but not *in* our lives.

But I know it is very wrong of me to think like this; I have become weak. Reprimand me firmly, dearest, shake me awake, after all I must not think this way. I must be prepared to bear this part of my life and appreciate the fact that there still exists a ray of light, that it may still be possible to work together with my sister. Be angry with me, tell me firmly what I already know that I must do. It would be good for me if you were here, I would ask you to give me a good thump on my back. Give me a good thump with words, I want to hear from you that what I am thinking is really wicked, wicked. Then I would be woken up. If you knew how I am doing everything as though in a dream, how everything here has become unbelievably indifferent to me, then it will please you, I think, to give me a good clip around the ears if I ask you for it. Oh, I must not be weak, because life still needs me. Help me ban these thoughts from my head.

Three times a week we have the children with us from 9 to 12:30, but recently I have not been able to do much since I have been so unwell. But now that I have completely recovered I want to begin giving myself totally to the children together with my two youngest sisters, who have been doing the work in recent days. Will you also encourage me in this? I wish I could *hear* your words and feel your hand. Oh, we can so yearn for a kiss from you now.

Just before, we received the wonderful news that our brother, the assistant Wedono of Welahan, has been promoted to Wedono and will be allocated the district of Banyaran, in Father's region, a few hours from Jepara.[64] Wonderful, especially for our Parents and for the boy himself, who has finally had his longed-for wish fulfilled, his beautiful dreams realized. "They now stand bathed in light and wish for no more!"

Kartini will begin her new life in three months' time. Yes, so soon already.

As you know, the Regent of Rembang has been here and a decision has been made. We therefore also had the opportunity, Moedertje, of seeing him in person. He has a pleasant manner, only he is somewhat overweight, but apart from that he made a generally good impression on us. Now you must not think we had a meeting with him, we girls, not at all, Moesje. The princesses were not permitted to appear, but whenever there was an opportunity we peered around the corner. And on the evening when there was a formal dinner, to which European people were also invited, we took up our position behind the windows of the dining hall. We had a very good view and could hear everything, but it had to be so secretive, otherwise the people would have heard us laugh, especially when we saw our Regent, like a young girl, cast down his eyes, or blush, or wriggle on his chair, when Mijnheer Gonggrijp teased him.[65] Then we could not contain ourselves.

And the one who had the most pleasure was of course our sister. But more importantly, the conditions that Tini proposed for her new life were accepted wholeheartedly: he would not have wanted anything else because he is like her, constantly striving for the advancement of the welfare of the people. What he now wanted for his children was a mother with a beautiful view of life under whose guidance they could grow into honest people, and it was only of her that he could have such expectations.[66] Well, I am so happy to know that the future for Kartini appears so good.

Oh, my sister, sister, doesn't she deserve every good fortune, she with such a noble, noble heart!

Moedertje, it pains us that Mevrouw Pauline regrets that we are not coming. Thank her for her support of our cause. How grateful we are for the interest she has taken. But Moedertje, I can only say, like you, that for the time being there is no hope of my going to Batavia, at least with plans such as those.[67] We must not count on it. Last week we had a midwife to stay who had also studied at Mojowarno. But, Moesje, what a lovely girl she is. She is just 19 and is already known for her ability in her chosen vocation. We came to know her through Dr. Adriani, who had met her in Mojowarno and thought her very nice. We are really taken with her. Well, when I met her and spoke with her and heard her speak about her work, then everything came back to me. Oh, oh, how I was filled once more with a desire to go. I tried to get approval for the idea but unfortunately with no result.

Then I remembered the suggestion of the doctor in Semarang to come to study with him for six months. He would ensure that we would get to know quite a lot. I believe Kartini told you about this. It would mean that I would still be close to home and it would only be for six months. Oh I do so hope I can but I do not dare to count on it. Pray for me Moedertje. And after all, after that I would return home and be able to use my knowledge here! What do you think of that. When K. has left home then I could follow her example but go to Sem. Yes, that would be wonderful! And, when later we came together again, then I would also already have learnt something about what I had planned to do.

Will you be looking for a home in the Priangan? It would be wonderful for you two, it would be the best thing to do to prevent the heat from getting the better of you.

So Didi is doing well? He is certainly allowed to enjoy himself. The poor boy, he deserves all the best things in life. I do so hope that Kartono will meet him often.

Well, dearest Moedertje, until next time. Our dear father has become ill as a result of catching a bad cold. I wrote this letter yesterday. Good-bye, dearest, good-bye! Give Mijnheer warm regards from all of us and receive a warm embrace from your daughters. When will it really happen?

Roekmini[68]

Roekmini to Rosita Abendanon-Mandri

Jepara, 17 November 1903

My dear Moedertje,

Many, many thanks for your thoughts for me on 8 November.[69] You cannot know how my heart filled with gratitude knowing that you were also with me at that moment when so much of significance was taking place in our lives. It was so good to know that at that moment it was as though I was lying in your arms, against your heart, therefore not alone! Also my deepest thanks for your heartening words, dearest. They are such a comfort, such a relief for my heart. I read and reread them.

I wanted, however, to tell you how I felt after everything that has happened. When everything had yet to take place, when I was experiencing merely the "idea" of separation and my sister was still around me, then I felt supremely cool and light-headed about everything that was about to happen. This is what I wrote to you and I thought and believed that this feeling would remain, but when the moment arrived, I was confronted by the actuality in all its detail, then I felt so strange, so strange and debilitated. All the optimism vanished and I no longer had any light shining in my heart. It constantly pained me anew to think that everything was real.

That is how you would have found me, Moedertje, at that moment my heart was dead. But then afterwards I once more felt God's hand above my head and this was because I could accompany my dear one to Rembang, as could the two younger sisters. We were allowed to bring her to her new home and stay there for several days. Oh, how I came back to life, to be allowed to continue to be with her and, while there, to then receive your letter with its comforting words. Then the light in my heart was restored. It produced a complete reversal of my disposition. Once again I thank you. Oh, how could anyone thoughtlessly want to be an egoist? Praised be the hand which in this life from time to time gives us a good prod to ensure we remain a good person, in the best sense of the word.

In my despondency I forgot I had a task to perform, now grown larger than ever, now that I am here on my own, which were I to neglect it, I would despise myself for. I forgot the feelings of others who, like me, also suffered from the separation, and that is now where my duty lies, to bring them comfort. My Parents, my sister, and everyone else here pities me, knowing how attached my sister and I are, but I want to face reality, Moedertje. I must not think that this affects only me. If there is a suggestion of making up for the loss, then they have as much right to it as me, and as oldest daughter and sister, it is now my duty to make this up to them. I will and want to seek my comfort in bringing cheer to those who have just as much need of it.

And yes, thinking about continuing the work which we began also brings relief. We are already looking forward to bringing the children together again; recently they have been on holiday. For this reason also I do not need to feel lonely; there is so much to do which will uplift my heart. How beautiful the words are which you wrote down for me. They so speak to my heart. Oh yes, Moedertje, I would a thousand times rather fill my book with colors as red as blood than that they should remain white and empty, so empty. I have come to learn that through suffering one comes to know real life sooner than through good fortune, of whatever kind;[70] that is the life which offers the widest perspective and the deepest empathy for those who live alongside us. For that reason I open my book to life's experience both in sunshine and heavy rain. Moedertje, I want my life to be constantly active; how else would our existence here be of any value? Give me more of those beautiful verses. They will revive me.

Eight November passed by very simply. Except that there was a reception and an evening for the Native officials, everything took place very calmly. Even the bridal couple was not in bridal costume, as was the case when Kardinah married. Kartini considered it would be too ridiculous for her to present herself as a puppet, and her husband declined because of his circumstances. They were therefore both formally dressed. Kartini was wearing a yellow silk *kabaya* set off with white embroidery and a silk *kain* woven with gold thread and a very few decorations. There were, however, many flowers, *melati*. The wedding took place at half past five and was attended by the Resident. At the formal introduction, that is, when the bride and the bridegroom were brought together, K. did not offer her husband a foot to kiss, and oh, what a murmur that produced amongst the family. However, it did not go beyond that and K. had her way. Nor did she have to bow. It was also a surprise for her husband; he had not expected this, being accustomed to the traditional practices at such weddings. However, being liberal, he quickly realized her intention and, in accepting it, he promptly offered her his arm, after which they walked to their places like two friends. For both of us it was a moment we will never forget. We looked deeply into each others' eyes as she passed me, and recognized in that look our farewell to the past.

On further acquaintance with our brother-in-law we became, as we expected, daily more impressed. He is a man with a spirit one can only call sparkling. His knowledge of the world is extensive, and apart from that he has such broad interests that besides the enormous admiration one is forced to have for him, one also feels affection. The evidence of his generous nature was most apparent when, together with his young wife, he returned to his administrative district. It was as if a royal couple was being welcomed. The whole town was decorated in green and there was not a kampong dwelling without a flag, even on carts which served as hire vehicles. On the arrival of the couple at the station there was already a packed crowd, which included the European inhabitants, who, on seeing the two people who had been so eagerly awaited, joined in the loud "Hooray!" And during the ride to the kabupaten there was music of all kinds barely several paces away from the common people, who as it were formed an escort for the carriage. The Javanese welcomed the couple with gamelan, the Chinese with Chinese music, etc., etc. It was a terrible to-do. The following evening a ball was held at the kabupaten which lasted till 8 o'clock in the morning. The whole residency was in attendance, and the Resident, who in fact was still unwell (he had a nasty fall and had been bedridden for the previous two months) did not wish to let it pass without having attended, if only briefly. It was a nice gesture on his part. He proposed a toast to the couple, of which the only thing we understood properly was that he was very pleased to see that a relationship had been established between one of the best regents of Java and the Regent's family. Kartini also received praise from the regents, including from the younger brothers and sisters of the Regent. It had been such happy news for them when they learned that she was to be the wife of their much-loved brother, and now that this had come about their happiness knew no bounds. Having heard so many appreciative reports about her, about the kind of person she was, they did not now want to regard her merely as a sister but as something higher, a mother, in the same way that their brother had always been for them a father. They would hold her up as an example to their wives and children, and later, after a lapse of time, they would send their children to her to be educated. Then K. would have to reign over them, they would be left totally in her care. What a reward for her struggle to hear those words, wasn't it, Moedertje? That because of their deep appreciation of her, people would be prepared to do this. They follow her everywhere she goes, including her husband. She cannot be separated from him for a moment without him looking for her. The little children are still a little shy with their new Moedertje, but they are already smiling at her from time to time. After a while they will probably be hugging her. The Regent of Pekalongan, who was there as well, spoke similar words of admiration. He said grandfather continued to be held up as an example to all regents, and he hoped that K. could become an example to all regents' wives.

I wish you could see them together, the mutual regard they have for each other. How wonderful it was to hear from Mijnheer, before this event took place, that he approved.[71] Oh, you cannot know how happy such a token of support was able to make us, especially coming from you, our dearest friends. For that reason I would wish that you could convince yourself of the outcome of all this to see this for yourselves. There was so much she had to tear from her heart, but we trust that in the future there will be much that is beautiful which will now grow in her heart.

And now, Moedertje, I have a message from her to give you. She wishes me to thank you heartily for your letter—that first of all. She would have had to keep you waiting for too long if she had to write herself, because she is still too bewildered after all the activity. And then, if you insist that she must absolutely choose a present, then she would most like to have a wooden carving, a screen, for example. Is that all right? What a sweet idea of yours to send flowers. She, and I also, deeply appreciate your thoughts, dear, dear Moedertje.

And now the O en W business falls on my shoulders.[72] I do not know if I will ever be able to handle it as well as K. The mirror frame costs 15 guilders.

Can I also ask you something, Moedertje? Would you be so kind as to order some boxes of Fröbel articles for us here at home? We would like to instruct our pupils in their use, the youngest ones of 5 and 6. Those that K. had she is so pleased with that she has had them sent on to Rembang to be able to use them immediately with her children.

Now good-bye, Moedertje, this is all for the time being. Thank you once again for our dear letter. How I would love to have come to Batavia had Kartini gone.

Oh yes, Kardinah also visited with her husband. The child looks very pale but is well.[73] How happy she was to be with the old brood again after two years. She immediately became again like a vine wrapping herself around the two of us. Her husband is a fine fellow, good natured, almost superficial but yet with a depth of feeling so that there is certainly some good in him. We got on very well with him. They stayed with us for two weeks.

Now good-bye, Moesje, now I will definitely end. We have yet to visit the Assistant Resident to give him a report on everything.

Give our warm regards to Mijnheer and received a warm hug from your daughter
Roekmini

Roekmini to Rosita Abendanon-Mandri

Jepara, 4 January 1904

Dear Moesje,

Finally here is something from me. I have been intending to write to you for so long. But first of all, has Hassim[74] passed on our regards? Has he already visited you since his return from Jepara, and has he already brought you the *stangi*? Ma thought the opportunity too good to miss to once again send you something which you like so much. We had not been able to talk much with Hassim, however much we had wanted to. We had been expecting him since the beginning of the holidays, but he continued to stay away and he only turned up at the very end. But then it was just in the busy time of *Lebaran*,[75] and apart from that, we were all more or less ill, so that we were not good for much.

Are you both well, Moedertje? I have just experienced such unpleasant days, days of such terrible longing for what was, which now for me must remain buried. I longed for a reunion with my sister so that I could, as of old, daily show her tokens of my affection. But Moedertje, you must not think that I encouraged this feeling; it was because I had been ill. I was experiencing an unpleasant time, suffering a bit of everything because I had caught a cold which had forced me to keep to my room, and for days I have not been able to enjoy the fresh outside air, so I began to think about things which can no longer exist. Now, however, I have recovered but continue to have this roaring in my ears which can sometimes drive me mad.

Kartini has written to you, hasn't she, Moedertje? Was her letter not completely filled with an account of her new life? We write to each other a lot, but always on the understanding that on her part it is what her circumstances allow her. We have therefore also still to get used to this: that despite the correspondence, a lot remain unsaid between us.[76] You know what comforts me then, Moedertje? The poems of De Genestet,[77] Oh, perhaps they are regarded as old-fashioned, but in the writings from his pen I continually find refreshment, regardless of my mood. I will never tire of reading these poems, they revive me so, I am so grateful that I can understand him. In recent days I have had no desire to read any other book. They do not please me. If I have to take up anything in the way of literature now, my heart has to find sustenance immediately, and that I can only find in the poems of De Genestet, they are so simple and yet they find a way directly to the heart.

The same applied to "Grains of Corn from Nellie's Store." This is a collection of thoughts of hers, of Nellie van Kol's, collected in book form. N. v. K. gave Kartini a copy as a present. It contains such fine sentiments, in fact everything that it contains is beautiful. I take these thoughts with me everywhere in my heart, and whatever mood I am in they are such a wonderful comfort for me. Do you know the work, Moedertje? If you do not know it, let me recommend that you do.

I am no longer familiar with what contemporary literature has to offer (except that by N. v. K.). Now I want to steep myself in such literature again—it doesn't seem to want to let me go. The books pull me toward them, and hold me, but I am not lingering there. We divided our books, and most of them went to Kartini.[78] It's sad how everything has to be separated, each volume going its own way. Why are we people so stupid? Don't we know that each hour of the day, each second, contains within it the cold reality of the inevitable separation of everything and everyone; we don't think about that until, all at once, we feel that that hour has arrived, and then we moan and complain. Does Nature not provide us with sufficient examples? Yes, we know all this too well, and yet I believe we will always remain stupid because in everything we only look for "Life." An intelligent person, capable of realizing it, would never be susceptible to all those things which so grieve our breast, and never feel so deeply all that is uplifting, all that which provides us with a glimpse of the wondrous glory which Life has to offer is. But to endure intelligently what weighs on us so heavily, if only we could . . .

Moedertje, now I would like to ask you something. Would you be able to send us some of those Fröbel boxes like those you sent Kartini (without the dolls). Our aim is this: we want to initially *engage* our youngest pupils, who do not yet have any idea of what to do with needle and thread, with some Fröbel work. They would enjoy that so much. They often fall asleep while sewing, which is why I would rather have them play. If we had those little boxes, then we would be better able to keep them busy.[79]

Our little school is going very well, although it is a pity that once again at the moment the children often have to stay at home. We now have a total of 9 pupils, 10 counting the married one. It is such a pleasure to see the children working so earnestly. But among them are those whose parents are not well off enough to provide for their children what is required at school. If, for instance, they want to do needlework, then the children will often have to bring the necessary items from home (that is, those who can) because as far as possible we want to help those who are less well off. But we will probably not be able to maintain this for very long, and these children will then one day have to do without. We would like to see that all children can work equally. Already now some have to watch the better-off ones surpassing them as they are not able to provide for themselves those things which are needed to attain the same standards as the others. This lack on the part of those children concerns us greatly.[80] That is why we wanted to ask you something. When we could see that there was so much that was lacking before we could hope to see a good result from our work, we wondered whether we could not receive assistance from the government. Could we not get a subsidy? Then none of the children or pupils would need to pay anything. But what enrolment would a school need to be entitled for this?[81] Oh, if only I were rich so that I would be able to do everything myself! I don't really like all this asking, even when it is not unjustified. But I have nothing so I must perforce ask. Nothing in half measures, isn't that so, Moesje? But if I am mistaken in this, would you please correct me. I only want what is best.

Letters from Roekmini 83

I wish you could see in person how everything is going here, how beautifully the girls are already able to write in Javanese and Dutch. (There are only a couple learning the latter and they happen to be the most sickly, who consequently miss many lessons, but otherwise they are learning well.) The ones who are only learning Javanese are girls for whom Dutch would be an unnecessary extravagance. If they only master their own language properly, that would already be quite an achievement. Among this last group there are two married women. Don't you think that is nice? We particularly encourage these two since we can well appreciate what it must have taken for them to have made this step, to put themselves on a par with the little ones, and what a thirst for knowledge they must have had. You see, Moedertje, they also belong to the underprivileged, and they in particular must not meet with disappointment since they would feel it doubly compared with the children who still more or less do everything unconsciously and not of their own free will. Oh, if I knew English I would place my hand on my heart and turn to that great philanthropist, Carnegie.

How wonderful it is that things are now so much easier for us Javanese to attend European schools. This year, from January, 9 Javanese children have begun to attend the school here in Jepara and the head teacher had received many more applications which he was not able to accept because he had not enough places. These [extra applicants] are now going to a private school in order to prepare to be the first to be eligible for selection in June. The head teacher thinks he will then get another 60 children [applying]. The thirst for "the light" is very strong amongst us.

Oh yes, I wanted to tell you a little more about the Bervoets family.[82] It was such a surprise for us when we received a telegram in which they announced their arrival, it was so unexpected. We had always wanted very much to make their acquaintance, but we never thought that we would ever see them here. We very much appreciated their kindness. They stayed with us for only one night, but we enjoyed it very much, they were such perfectly wonderful people. It turns out that Mijnheer had just come out from Holland, but when he was in Batavia he had not been able to see you, which I regretted very much. They also attended the little school for a while. They so wanted us to come and visit them for a while. Oh, I would love to so much. The family had already heard a lot about us from the Ovink family and so they also wanted to make our acquaintance. They had already been to Rembang. It was as though God had sent them. It so happened that my brother-in-law suddenly became very ill while they were there, so critically in fact that it was thought we were going to lose him. At that point they woke Mr. B. and his wife, who treated and nursed him so lovingly that all danger passed. They even stayed longer than they had originally intended when they saw how completely on her own Kartini was. You can imagine how grateful we were to them for this, we will never be able to express sufficiently our appreciation for this service of love that they have shown.

And what is the state of things here at the moment? Do you know, Moedertje, that at the moment we are almost without *tukang* here to undertake the work for O. en W. So many men have been engaged for the construction of the Wilhelmina Room[83] that at the moment we have only 5 workmen and one overseer to undertake all the orders that are awaiting completion. We received a major order from Holland, namely the construction of a room (a complete wall) to be made in the style of Pa's office. It will be a marvelous piece of work, and on top of that we continue to get more orders from O. en W. so that we are really put out by the loss of the workmen. But we would not have been able to hold those people, such is their expectation of what awaits them in Batavia. And among them there are those who previously had refused to work there for those wages. What caused them to change their mind now I do not know, but I am terribly disappointed. Recently we sent a large consignment to Batavia. In February, Mr. Zeilinga will come to Semarang, at which time he will no doubt make a quick trip to see us.[84]

How are your children, Moedertje? Are you getting a lot of *kabar* from Didi? And how is Miss Pauline getting along, you dear friend? How I would love to meet her. When she is with you next, would you give her my regards and tell her there is someone here who holds her in high regard? Now, Moesje, I must end, I hope you will give me the pleasure of another letter. Our heartiest greetings to Mijnheer and a firm kiss for you,
From Roekmini

Roekmini to Rosita Abendanon-Mandri

Jepara, 28 January 1904

Dearest Moedertje of mine,

A thousand times a thousand thanks for your letter with the wonderful news about the subsidy and the presents for the children. Oh, you have made us so happy, dearest. About the subsidy, we have even more reason to consider this since the number of children continues to increase. At the moment we have 15 pupils, of whom 4 are new, and in February we will get another 3 from one of the districts of father's administrative region, while a relative of ours (from Pati) will send another two girls. Then we would have 20 pupils altogether. Among the 4 new ones we have at present there is one married woman, 2 are boys of 5 and 3½ years, the youngest of whom cannot even say the letter "r," and one is a girl. Can you imagine what wonderful satisfaction this provides us in the way that our efforts really seem to be appreciated? And especially that a married person has come, that is such a wonderful thing for us. Oh Moedertje, you should see these women, there are now 3 of them working alongside the very young ones, at one level with them intellectually because in their case their parents had never allowed them to learn, they declared to us when I asked them whether they already knew something about reading and writing. How moved we are each time when we see them at work, but at the same time we admire then for their courage and attitude. There is a 6-year-old girl who started school earlier than they did and is of course further advanced, but, and this is also something wonderful for us, despite the fact that the younger one surpasses them intellectually, we have never seen her make fun of them. Old or young, educated or not, our pupils are always friendly and helpful toward each other. There is no difference in status among the children, the daughter of the *Patih* mixes freely with that of the *Mantri,* they know so well that this is what we would like.[85] Often the mothers come to sit in on the lesson and, impressed by what they see, say to each other: "Years ago, when we were young, why weren't there any such avenues open to us to be educated? If I did not have grown-up children then I would certainly come here to learn myself."

We do not demand that the married women attend all the lessons. They come when their household circumstances allow, otherwise they stay home. But yet, Moedertje, they come regularly to classes. When we give the older girls cooking classes, more of the married women come; that happens once a week. We have already tried the Fröbel boxes with the 3 little ones, who had such fun. When they are allowed to put away their slates and take out the boxes, the three of them plunge into the activity together. Did I understand you correctly, Moedertje, that we could get more boxes for them? Oh, dearest, in that case we grasp your offer with both hands, we are grateful to you for your great kindness in making the children happy. Can we have some of the "ring game" and "basket-weaving" activities and a building box? Moedertje, once again and once more thank you for everything. Our little ones get so much pleasure from it. One day I will try my hand at photography and send you some snapshots of the school. Otherwise we would have to wait on someone else, as photographer who might happen to come here by chance. But when that would be? It will have to wait a while, but one day it will happen. I will write to you later about the memorandum.[86]

So you will be leaving Java for a while, Moedertje?[87] It fills me with mixed feelings, knowing this. Should you leave earlier than all of us expect of course we would be happy for your sake but for us, we would all suffer so from the deep wounds which the parting would cause us. What emptiness there would be. We would search for you throughout Java without finding a trace of you. But what a beautiful, wonderful journey it would be, perfectly heavenly. May God prosper all your plans. I hope in that case that when you travel across Java you will not forget our little corner. Please, Moedertje, I fervently hope that you will be more successful than our dear brother Edie in your plan to come here. We were so disappointed, for so long, when he could not come.[88] I can still well remember the way Mijnheer's assistants were constantly buried under the weight of clerical work when they went with him to the office, so I can now imagine how it must constantly fill you with sadness when you see those piles increase.

Yes, Moedertje, when one is standing before the goal one dreams of, one doesn't know how to best make use of the brief time one has in this life to realize it. Then nothing can be a match, can withstand the extraordinary power that drives us . . .

But how are things with Edi? Are you getting much news from him? Here, once again we have had a death. The Regent of Pati, a first cousin of Father's, died on the 23rd of this month. He had no children, and now there is a great to-do amongst the officials who have an interest in it about how they can realize *their* ambition to become a regent. There are of course a great many who hanker after the position. Oh, as long as the honor goes to where it is due, then all the fuss is unimportant, but if that should not be the case, then I hope the people are strong enough to raise themselves above the mere matter of the position, above conventional opinion, and be *themselves*.

Moedertje, do you still hear from Oost en West? Last month we sent a whole load of woodcarving to them, but till now we have not heard whether it has been received or not. Has the chest arrived safely or not? We do not know that here.

Do you get many letters from Tini? She is so busy carrying out her plans. You know that, don't you, Moedertje.

Well, for the time being I will stop. I thank you once more for everything, dearest. Our warm regards also to Mijnheer, and for you a big kiss from the daughter who loves you.

    Roekmini

Roekmini to Rosita Abendanon-Mandri

Postcard

Jepara, 4 February 1904

Dearest Moedertje,

I hardly dare write you this postcard knowing what it involves for you, but because it was so urgently requested I dare do it, although with a beating heart. You must know that our uncle, the Regent of Pati, has died, and since he is childless there are many candidates for this position, among whom are our boys (brothers and brother-in-law). Now my brother-in-law has begged me to write to Mijnheer to put a good word in for him when his application arrives (if he gets to hear about it). I promised to write, but not to Mijnheer, because after all I know he is already, as it were, buried under his own work. I am therefore directing this to you, but if you think it is inappropriate that Mijnheer involve himself in this matter then I request that you do not let him know about it and I will convey this to my brother-in-law.

Oh, you cannot know what this request has cost me, but at least I have fulfilled my promise to my brother-in-law. Why he seems to distrust his own abilities even though he is a respected official in his residency I will tell you later. But he requested me to ensure that this would remain a matter between you and me. He is the Wedono of Undaan (Kudus), and his name is Tjokrohadisosro. He is a very conscientious man.[89]

Dearest forgive me for this request. Be assured that this is only done with an anxiously beating heart. You are warmly embraced by your loving,
Roekmini

Roekmini to Etty Wawo Runtu

Jepara, 12 February 1904

Dear Esteemed Lady,[90]

How can I describe the great joy that your approach to us has given me? To have met you like this on my life's journey is wonderful, like recognizing a familiar face, like my, or rather our, sister. My sister and I share your ideas, and now you also are no longer a stranger to us.

How could I not now approach you with anything less than an indescribable feeling of happiness in my heart and as though with my two arms outstretched welcoming you into my life?

We also knew of you from a sketch by Mrs. ter Horst in *De Echo*[91] and were thus able to gain a glimpse, albeit a superficial one, into your life, as a result of which there arose in us more than once the desire that one day we might get to know you in person. It has taken a long time—circumstances have contributed to this—to conspire to keep us from realizing this plan. We had given up any thoughts of it, our hearts no longer hoped for it, and now, like a ray of light I am suddenly allowed to see it before me, all those longings realized at last.

How can I adequately convey to you that, by your approaching us, you have given me such great, great pleasure? This act of yours toward me has surely arisen directly from the heart. And now, therefore, before going further, I want to say: I thank you for everything. Well, actually more than that: I thank Providence for bringing this about for me. Only it would be even more wonderful if I did not have to savor this pleasure on my own, a pleasure which I once dreamed about sharing with another. I must now have this satisfaction on my own, but at least I am happy that I can comfort myself in the knowledge that only pleasant duties keep those others, my sisters, from sharing my joy with me here at this moment.

You need to know, therefore, that the two of us were indivisible; an existence without each other was unthinkable. That is why, in expressing this joy of mine, I automatically speak of her. Once we had dreamed of it together, so it is better that you come to know me as part of a threesome that together formed the origin of all those ideas of a beautiful life that we imagined and know, and in terms of which that circle "outside," from whom we received so much support, saw us.

We sisters are part of a large family, and at a certain point in time in our lives, when we came to realize what life was all about, we were suddenly brought together by the discovery which filled each of us with the one and the same idea. We immediately made a pact with each other whose aim was to begin the Good Work; that is, to seek "all that was good and beautiful in this life," to be able to supplement that which was lacking in our society. We wanted to stand up for "Our World," to bring to *Her* all that was beautiful that *She* did not yet know, and, once it had taken its place alongside *Her* own fine qualities, we believed that this would drive *Her* forward to unimaginable and wonderful new heights.[92]

This is an aim that you too share.

Full of youthful exuberance, we marched forward and dreamed the golden dream of the single road that would carry the three of us forward *together* to our "Ideal" . . . Youth and "dreams": where in the world don't they go together? And where does Youth not awaken from the dream at a given moment when it becomes too beautiful?

We paid no heed to the cool, stern voice of Reality. But it did come and asked from us more understanding of our aims. We could not continue to dream about it. Reality took control of us. We were allowed to carry out the good work but for this purpose She directed each of us to a path of our own. From the very beginning She sent one of us away out of our circle, and then later one more. And that is how it was when you met us.[93]

And what did our inexperienced hearts feel at this intervention by Reality? It gouged wrinkles in our foreheads. But do you know what these are, what it means in a young forehead when brought on by an idyllic dream? It disappears at the slightest caress of a loving hand that knows how to direct a young heart to see the wisdom of such interruption to her illusions.

We too felt the cold and stern wisdom of our Disturber (our forefathers), and yet She was wise, since She only meant to show us what life had in store for us in giving us the illusion of being free agents. She pulled us out of our surroundings so carefully and pushed us on to prepare us for that which would in fact one day await us, to take up the fate of pioneers ... Now indeed we are separated from each other, but what of that? Our thoughts about *our Goal* remain one, and that, after all, is what is important ...

And so, Miss Etty, with these few words I have briefly sketched to you the lives of three women, since, where they once formed a single whole, a description of one of them would never give you a satisfactory impression of what you would now like to know. Both my two sisters have gone away from me to follow friends who love them above anything else, and who also contribute a strong voice in support of the work they have taken on. The youngest is now in Pemalang in the Tegal region, married to a patih, who is also a full cousin of ours. She was the darling of the threesome, so tender, so fine. And the oldest is in Rembang, as you already know. She was the mother, the *wisest,* the *best.*

And now, as to what our main objective has been? We wanted to establish a position for our sex on the basis of which they could become fully conscious of their role in this life. We wanted to seek their cooperation, which in fact they must contribute, to improve the welfare of the people. We wanted to provide education for women, wherever they have come to feel the need for becoming educated, to bring about an improvement in the moral state of the people, to shape them as a powerful force in general. How else would our struggle ever achieve a good result? For that reason, originally our plan was to set up a school for the daughters of Native rulers for whose spiritual development no consideration had ever been given. This would be one which would also pay attention to their moral development, so that young girls could get the right idea of their own worth as the *carriers* of the welfare of the people. We would offer them what we ourselves knew, the finer things from the West; the language medium would be Dutch because, after all, it is only through that that you (and we) have been able to get the knowledge of the West that we have. Only by that means can our women be brought up to the level where we would like to see them, isn't that so? But to achieve this end we ourselves would first have to improve our own technical ability to be able to teach. We planned to gain our basic teaching certificate for elementary education but then . . . there came that intervening hand and . . . the shape that our thoughts took to achieve our "Ideal" (to improve the condition of the children of the top layers of society) could no longer exist. We could no longer work together. We realized each of us had been given our own road to travel, we had to separate! We had first planned to establish our school in a center where the people could easily reach us from any direction, in Magelang for instance.

And why do I, the only one left, not go on with that idea? I will frankly admit to you that where once the energies of two people were needed, it seemed to me that mine alone would be too deficient, I felt that quite honestly.

Besides my sisters I know others who could work to this end. But I know also that no matter how much they would perhaps like to in their hearts, they would not dare take up this work because, as you know, our task is that of pioneers, isn't it, and that does not suggest to them a very rose-colored future . . . We have never seen any indication of support for our plans. They are in favor of the idea of improving the position of woman but to work for this themselves . . . that would still create too many difficulties for them.

At the moment I am doing the work here with my two younger sisters, but they are not really suited to this work. But they are helping me as much as they can, and I am very touched by this. The three of us now are still running a school for the daughters of Native leaders. Oh, what surprising indications of appreciation we have received for our attempts, it is so wonderful to see, and the best indication of that might well be that *married* women attend our school. That perhaps gives us the greatest satisfaction from our work because that surpasses all our expectations. They give us a living proof of how great their sense is of what is lacking in their lives. Oh, it is so pleasing to see them begin together with the very youngest children of 5 years, but on the other hand we also inadvertently feel a sense of amazement at the energy which they possess.

The children can come to us for free; this is in order that there are no obstacles to anyone to come to us to learn, so that children from all classes of society can come. And we give instruction in two languages, Javanese and Dutch. For the girls of the lowest social classes, for whom instruction in their mother tongue alone is still very much necessary, we give classes in Javanese. Here are also included the married women, while the older children, who already know Javanese, are taught Dutch. These women have a total lack of knowledge of their own language. When we suggested to them that perhaps they were just pretending, they swore by everything they held sacred that they spoke the pure truth and that never in their youth had they been *allowed* to learn anything! Oh, how readily a passionate prayer of thanks to Providence arises in us that She has given *us* the task of being of service to our fellow human beings in bringing them a school because it is such a wonderful feeling.

We also give lessons in cooking and handicraft, in which the parents as well as the children themselves find great pleasure. Oh, in this way we have been able to gain a special place in their hearts. We have two other married women taking these classes, so in total there are four. And parents (the mothers) of the pupils who were also inspired by all this wished that they themselves were still young in order to be able to learn with their children! "Why didn't this exist in our youth?" was the constant cry when they came to see a lesson. We even have girls living with us whose parents did not have the means to educate them, to provide a governess. They entrust their daughters completely to us to make of them what we can because at home they would not be able to provide anything for them. May it be granted to us that we may never, never disappoint the trust these people have placed in us. God save us from that.

[fragment of the final damaged page]

... as I am afraid that you may have to wait too long for a reply to your greatly appreciated letter.... After this I am sending your letter to my sister, with whom I want to share the joy of making your acquaintance.... also for your best wishes for the New Year which I also wish for you, and so let me do so, after wishing you my warmest regards.

    Yours,
    Roekmini

Do you hear from Uncle and Aunty Adriani?[94]

Roekmini to Rosita Abendanon-Mandri

Jepara, 18 February 1904

Dearest Moedertje,

Many, many thanks dearest for the wonderful gift from you both for the little ones. Oh, Moedertje, I had not meant this, it has made me so embarrassed, you don't know the half of it. When I read there were 17 boxes, I could not believe what I was reading. Now we have enough, I think, dearest. The children now have a large supply of toys and so I will now no longer need the rings and ring games. Once again, once more many thanks, also on behalf of the children, dearest! Or rather, all the girls thank you because, big or small, they all take pleasure from it, especially painting the pictures. I just leave them to it when I see they are really getting enjoyment in playing and are not distracting the little ones, then they are free to play. You should know that such a thing is unknown in our "world." All the children get enjoyment from it, and their parents, recognizing the value that the children can derive from such play, are full of interest. They are very pleased for them. The mothers often sit with the children when we are instructing and then they pay very close attention to everything that is being done.[95]

And now the other matter, Moedertje. You wrote about the last consignment sent to O. en W. To my amazement I read that they assert that they had already written to say that they had received it. We never received anything, and really, Moedertje, it could never have been so because it was only this afternoon, the 18th February, that we received such a letter. It was written as though they had only just received the consignment, while, just imagine, it had been sent on 24th December 1903. Better not mention it again. Fortunately it hadn't caused the craftsmen any unpleasantness.

Do you know what I saw recently? A Chinese here thought of the idea to have a whole gamelan orchestra made in miniature. It is very nice—it was brought to our house for us to see it. All the stands have been carved and the *sarons* and the large gong have been made of silver, they look like small lids. The carved figures, of course, are all Chinese, but the idea is very nice. The whole thing cost him one and a half guilders. I would have preferred that everything had a Native appearance as it should, and then I would inform O. en W. to see if that organization was interested in having one.[96] Of course it would not cost so much since the gongs would be made out of copper. Or would you not like one yourself? It is really very sweet, it stole my heart away. Don't you think it would be a nice idea to have one to go with all those other miniature things which you have of Native household items? I wish I could show you.

Dearest, today I am jumping from one thing to another. You asked me for news about Kartini. She has not written to us for a while, but we are thinking of going to visit her in several days' time, in which case you will get all the news. How I regret that you have now had to give up the idea of coming to Jepara again. Will we therefore never see each other again? What a melancholy idea that is when the heart had been so hopeful. Yes, it also surprised me, that news about Didi, and together with you, dearest, I hold my breath. But let us hope for the best, let us pray for him, that dear, fine boy. And yes, what effect might this war also have on us here?

Just before, I received a letter from Hassim in which he told us that he had been to visit you one evening with his friends and how much he had enjoyed being with you. What a pleasure that gives me that he still often comes to visit you because we were most concerned when he had not passed his exams. Moedertje, when he was here I asked him whether he had passed (I did not know then that he had sat the exam). At the time he did not reply to my question and instead told me all kinds of things, including that he had almost brought his downfall by keeping bad company. Ma and I had a serious talk with him and he seemed then to show remorse and promised to ward off anything that could have a bad influence on him. Neither did we know then what was really behind this. Only later did I understand him, and therefore, dearest, when you meet him encourage him to work hard. Be an angel for him, he is basically good, keep him on the right path. We are sorry for his mother, who loves him. He is her youngest son, the most loved of all her children, particularly because he will go further than all his brothers and sisters. She has very high expectations of him. About eight months ago his father died, so that now she is even more alone than ever because her husband was already old then and her other children live far away. She still has one daughter at home who is also taking lessons with us, but this one is not refreshing company for us as she is a spoiled and unpleasant child. Poor woman, when I consider all this, then his loss of a year makes me very sad and I will do what lies within my power to support him on his way. Do not let him notice that I have told you all this, but do talk to him about his loss of one year of study. You will make us very happy by doing so.

Well, dearest, watch over that young heart, will you, by continuing to encourage him to work hard when you meet him. Apart from this he is such a fine boy but still young and very susceptible. I thank you on behalf of his mother for your help, dearest.

You are warmly embraced for that by your daughter
    Roekmini

Roekmini to Rosita Abendanon-Mandri

Jepara, 7 May 1904

Dearest Moedertje,

How are you now? Have you both recovered from the long and tiring journey? I read in the paper that you took the boat from Cheribon to Batavia.

Moedertje, how will I ever be able to express what the meeting with you has meant to me? You simply made me so happy. I went home so revitalized, with such renewed confidence.[97] Just seeing you both, hearing your voices, oh how thankful it makes me to be alive. You are our wise and guiding hand in our path of life, Moedertje.

Do you know who we had here and who has only just left this morning? Kartini, her husband, and a few of their children. Oh, that was such a joy for us. It was the first time since she had left home. It also made her so happy to be in her old surroundings again. She kept wandering to and fro to get the feel of everything again. They left this morning and calm has once again returned, as it had been very hectic while they were here.

And now, Moedertje, reality is imposing itself again. Do you know what I am about to ask you? Would you be so kind, when it is convenient, to ask at the Permanent Exhibition if they have received the woodcarving that I have sent? Father has written to Mr. Zeilinga including an explanatory note on these objects, and now we would like to see that the woodcarvers will soon receive what is owed to them for what has been supplied because it is so demoralizing for them to have to wait for payment while they have done their best to produce good work. Would you do that for me, Moedertje?[98] If they don't like the prices, well then, why don't they just say that? But yet they are the same objects that they received earlier, just as they had ordered. I have asked the headman to sketch the chair—you know the one I mean—for which the beautiful material will be used on the back. I have also passed on all those messages to Kartini from you, and I am doing everything to support the craftsmen in all sorts of ways.[99]

Well, dearest Moedertje, I hope to write more later. I hope you will write me a note to tell me how you are after your trip. You will, won't you, Moedertje?

I received a letter from Nellie van Kol in the mail as well as a few books from her children's library. One of them, *Jong Java,* consists of a series of pen portraits of Javanese children. Very sweet. Now she would like it if we also provide her with some writing. We will give it some thought.[100]

Well, good-bye, Moeke, give Mijnheer our warmest regards and be warmly embraced by your loving
Roekmini

Roekmini to Rosita Abendanon-Mandri

Jepara, October 1904

My dearest,

You have not heard from me for so, so long[101] but that is because each time when I wanted to write to you, the words would not come. Although

I did not tear up the many epistles to you that I had begun, no matter how many circuits of the house I made, I simply could not find the right words to say to you. Isn't it true that what hangs so heavily round my heart is also weighing on yours? And what I am going through you are also experiencing? It is for this reason that I could find no words to speak to you, because everything that I wanted to say was the same that you were also feeling. Your having always been such a dear mother to the both of us, I can now do nothing more than silently carry this burden of suffering in your presence.

I keep imagining how our souls, like two tightly sprung and similarly tuned snares, would spring loose with the slightest contact with such suffering, despite the best of intentions. I had been sitting here in deep thought for so long when I suddenly realized that this had been going on for too long. Surely you had to hear something from me. And I myself, how my heart longed for you, you who could give me what I needed to ease my pain, something that I could hardly find here. Moedertje help me!

Now I want to do my best to tell you as much as possible. How often have I not wanted to be cradled in your arms like a small child and rocked to sleep so that for one moment I would not be conscious of anything. What a relief that would be. Everyone here is burdened with grief, but for you and for me and my dear brother in Holl. I think I can say that that will be endless, since only we knew her intimately and knew her true nature and were the only ones who loved her for that. Do you feel how much I can long for you, to pour out my heart, to feel your heart, to freely give expression to my feelings!

I received your letter. Thank you so much, Moedertje, and although I had not written back to you, oh, I had such a need to stretch my arms out to you.

I will tell you everything that has taken place, Moedertje, but in brief. You will feel with me, see how it still makes my heart bleed to remember what we now realize are serious questions which we would prefer to keep buried in our heart. It will be the same for you, won't it? But for you, Moedertje, who still does not know all the details, I will do my best.

It was a complicated business, the arrival of the little one, and for our beloved it was a time of continuing problems with her health. She did remain strong but only outwardly. In reality she was utterly weak. In the letters she wrote you can find a whole series of complaints about her constant state of ill health. But in the end everything went well. Our beloved herself also thought so because as soon as it was over she asked for champagne to celebrate with the doctor on the successful outcome. For the following days also she was very, very well, even on the morning of that terrible day she was still very alert. Until at midday, when everything suddenly changed. Suddenly she became ill. Just before this the doctor had been with her and found everything in order. But he had barely been gone for 10 minutes when he had to be called back. The illness took hold; she experienced tightness of the chest. What was actually the cause of that we still don't know exactly. It is impossible for us to ask the doctor about it, not that we have anything against him—his assistance was excellent—but it would be too painful to hear. When the doctor returned, there was nothing he could do.[102]

But our beloved left us gently and calmly, still clear in her mind. Her passing was so peaceful that it was barely noticeable for those who stood by her bed. But what a blow it was, because it was so unexpected. I went out of my mind, Moedertje, when I became aware of what had happened.

I was not able to be there with my beloved because I had a patient to care for at home. I was just then feeling happy for her and for her good fortune in becoming a mother, having only just received the good news about it. You can imagine how frantic I became when I heard. At that time I was alone at home with my two younger sisters. Ma had been with her for quite some while and Pa had left just that morning when he had heard of her illness. Oh, I went crazy at the news, and thinking of Pa who had to hear it en route. Pa, all on his own and lately so unwell! Oh, at that moment I could only believe that our lives were ruled by Fate alone.

We left for R[embang] that evening to see and get to know something. The Gonggrijp family helped us wonderfully.[103] Were it not for them it would have not have been possible. We were able to be there the following morning in time.[104] Her last resting place is next to the previous Raden Ayu, under one roof in a small shelter. They seem like sisters, hand in hand. I took some flowers from there, dearest, to give to those who had loved her but were far from her, and I also kissed the place on their behalf. I will send them to you, those religious relics. The place where she now rests is a spot that she thought was beautiful. It is on a hill where her husband had erected a small *pasangrahan* [lodge] surrounded by a beautiful garden. From there one gets a beautiful view of the sea and the land below. It is a spot where the previous Raden Ayu often came and which became her last resting place. Here then our beloved is now laid next to her. Oh God, your power is frightening!

My poor brother-in-law, who loved her so very much, as no other, for whom she had been such a joy, was struck down with grief. Fate had visited him so swiftly again after the last, and this time taking away, as it were, his very life. What will become of him and his other children who had also received enlightenment from her, God alone knows. And her legacy, the dear little one who has to do without so early in its life, the most beautiful thing on earth: a mother's love! But if you saw him yourself you would say: this child is not born to suffer. It is a child that in its first moments has already amazed many of us. Everything that we have noticed about him makes us think that his being will enrich this world. Already on his third day he seems as big as an infant of 14 days, very healthy, with rosy cheeks, a lively little face in which the eyes sparkle like the purest precious jewels. The total impression one gets of this well-built strong little body with those clear proud little lookers is, to put it in words: *veni, vidi, vici.* Through his own willpower he will learn to live his life as it needs to be lived. And his facial appearance is already looking more and more like that of his dear mother. You see, this is all the more reason to believe in what this little one promises.

You know, Moedertje, it was as though our beloved always had the premonition of what had to be. Several times she wrote to me: if it should ever happen that I could not raise my little one, then I would entrust it to no one else but you. No matter how often I told her to desist, she would continue to repeat it and repeat it. And now, see how these words become all too real, that she will not be able to raise the little one. This memory touches me deeply, time and again. Now I don't know what is going to happen, whether we will still be able to have the little one with us. With how much love wouldn't I receive that little piece of her. I would live for him. But my brother-in-law seems to have a different idea. One can understand it: for him it is an indispensable comfort granted him by the wife whom he worshipped. But if my dearest wish to have the little child here with me should not be granted, Moedertje, then I also know that my life will never be anything more than a dead body that must yet undergo the trial of having to live. I already feel that I will never be able to feel young again. Haven't we already lived an entire life in which we have loved, in which we have suffered? As I combed my hair several [hairs] already told me so by their silver color. That did make me feel good, wonderfully good, because my entire being was in entire agreement with it.

And now, dearest, gentle Moedertje, who will be able to provide you with the balm for your wounds in your love for the little Javanese who once formed the beautiful cloverleaf? Who can make up for you the dream that you had for them? Why should they only give you deep wounds? Can you still remember, at this time, how much we loved you? My dear, dear Moedertje, how I long for you. I so wanted to see you both, my poor dear friends. I only have to think of you two and such a deep melancholy arises in me that I briefly forget my own suffering, thinking of yours, that of a mother. How often am I reminded of your parting words when we last met: "Stay well." Yes, dear, good friends, now that I must remain living I shall also live for the sake of those who are still saved for me, albeit with a great emptiness alongside me, a colorless life.

My Parents are well.

Moedertje, how my heart wept yesterday again for the same grief that had overtaken the royal family of Spain and Austria.[105] I read about the Infanta Maria Mercedes and the wife of the likely successor to the Austrian throne, that they experienced the same fate as my dearest, and my head began to spin. I wept with them who had also felt the poisonous arrows of Fate.

Now, my very dearest Moedertje, if my writing is all over the place you will have to forgive me. It reflects the state of my heart, and the chaos in my head. Now that I have written to you, I will feel better. I have also written to tell Annie,[106] I can write to her more quickly because she is someone outside our intimate circle.

Consider yourself hugged by your own daughter and press Mijnheer's hand for me warmly.

Your loving,
Roekmini

Roekmini to Rosita Abendanon-Mandri

Jepara, 6 November 1904

My dear Moedertje,

I embrace you warmly for the letter you have sent me. What a support you were for me, my rescuing angel! For the first time, after I received your very welcome letter, I began to feel better, both my spirit and mind felt lighter. So this is why I had longed for you so much. It was because I felt that only in you could I find this relief for my heart, you, who will doubtless remain a comfort and support for me for the rest of my life, to whom I can cry out my tears of suffering.

I was constantly feeling desperate and rebellious, and feeling that my weakened body could no longer withstand such turmoil in my being. And my spirit also sighed and yearned for this moment of rescue, dearest. Until one afternoon—I was in a light sleep—I dreamt that you were with me and were caressing my cheeks and when, full of emotion, I awoke, oh, how surprised I was to find your letter at my bedside. I pressed it to my heart, Moedertje, and in it I found what I had fruitlessly sought here. Oh, I cannot press it strongly enough on my thirsting heart.

Yes, dearest, from now on I will only think of her as God's specially chosen one who has simply found her greatest happiness. Your words were so true and they drew out all the bitterness within me, to be replaced only with thoughts of kindness. As a result, I felt like a child who, exhausted from crying, feels the tender caress of a mother's hand. An occasional sob welled up within me, but without the emotional turmoil of before, which had now been calmed. And now, Moedertje, although in my heart there is a deep loneliness, the bitterness I felt has dissipated. You have implanted there the only comfort possible. I now no longer think about her, our beloved, as a dead person. For me she has merely gone ahead to a higher, purer place where she will experience only the most complete fulfillment. Yes, I will find comfort in that.

Dear mother of mine, my love for Her in this way has surely only become greater since our separation; giving in to my feelings of sadness would be a denial of that love because then we would be only thinking of ourselves. So you too now live with the same love for her as you had previously, like I also had for her, for her beautiful spirit. Oh, now all we need to do is to pray for strength to raise up our lonely hearts, to enable us to walk the rest of life's journey with that empty place beside us, isn't that so, dearest? Yes, now that She still lives for me it is also possible for me to pray to her with a request to support me as before. I pray for mercy from on high, dearest, so that it may be granted me to remain strong to be able to make this life meaningful.

The work of uplifting the people, that has been begun, and for which She would have been able to do so much, has now been lost. That is to be regretted, but believe me, Moedertje, I will keep alive the vision she left in my little circle. That will now be my life and my future. I will write to you in a later letter about the woodcarvers and what I intend to do for them. If you approve of the idea, I will consider it a sign from Her, my dearest sister, from on high.

What did Hassim write to me? Well, that you are in poor health, dearest. Oh, I would have so loved to have said what your dear friend Pauline said: to have you with me to look after you, to spoil you. To have been able to do just what she did. And now that one possibility that might have brought me to you has also disappeared.

And then, the time is also approaching when retirement in the Fatherland is coming to take you away. Oh, dear friends, if you have to say farewell to our land, I beg you, keep us firmly in your hearts, we who so dearly need you, and who have, after all, already gained a small place in it. Take us with you everywhere, in your heart, that will be such a comfort to us. Even though we will no longer be able to hear much about each other anymore, possessing your love will make up for everything for me. I had better not tell you what this separation will mean for me, I will just ask of you: continue to keep me warm in your heart. For your sake I am pleased with the news that you both will soon find the rest you need. Then I can say, go, go!

I didn't know, Moedertje, that Dr. Bervoets was ailing, but I did hear that a young doctor would be coming to Mojowarno.[107] What a lovely evening that must have been when you had those people at your house. I can never have enough respect for those who give themselves to charitable work, and especially of course if it is for my people. The concern that those people have for our people, or at least for that part of them who are most in need, makes up for their country's failures in their duty to ours. In their indirect, unselfconscious deed in trying to do good, they make up a lot for that. It is only a pity however that in their work they also aim at a specific religious goal. Why could they not, in as far as it concerns belief, operate in a neutral fashion? They are surely of high enough stature, I would have thought, to be capable of that, given how most of them demonstrate a sufficiently high love of humanity.[108]

But now, Moedertje, what wouldn't I give if we were already so far advanced, we Javanese ourselves, that we were able to just stand in their shadow; that we had become conscious of the fact that, aside from the respect we have for them, we needed to feel more, namely: that we would no longer accept with that sense of self-satisfaction as if it were self-evident, indeed, unfortunately, even with indifference, that the task that is ours is undertaken by others. I have deep respect for people like the van Emmerit family, Miss Jane, the Bervoets family, Miss Prijzel, etc.,[109] but at the same time I also cannot suppress a sense of embarrassment, or shame, that I can only observe that they are doing our work. Oh, should you have those people at your house again, please convey to them my gratitude for what they feel for my compatriots and for what they are able to achieve, and my deepest respect for them.

And now good-bye, my dear Moedertje.

Oh, and I also need to sincerely thank you, on behalf of my Ma, for the more than marvelous present that you and your husband have sent. We cannot admire it enough. Ma is extremely happy with it. We will give it a place of honor in the hall, where we most often come together.

I can also send you something that belonged to our darling, can't I, dearest? I have a sarong of hers for you, one that she had worn.[110] Would you also like a medallion photograph of Her, like the one I always wear in a medallion?

Well, good-bye now, treasure, till the next time.

The fondest regards from the family here to you both and a warm kiss for you from your loving daughter,

Roekmini

This letter has lain here for a long time. Good-bye, dear.

Roekmini to Rosita Abendanon-Mandri

Jepara, 8 December 1904

My dearest Moedertje,

I received your letter of 3 December in good order. I thank you very much for it, dearest!

What an unpleasant surprise we had on St. Nick's day, Moedertje. This is what I had to tell you. Two of our pupils, girls who live in with us, have left. It happened so suddenly that we are very upset. They are the daughters of a *mantri guru* (a teacher) who used to live in our neighborhood and has now moved to Ungaran. We have already had the children with us for a whole year, and now that the father has been transferred to Trenggalek, he now thought, for a number of reasons, that it would be better if the children came to live with him. Neither we nor the children wanted it. We had become very attached to each other. They themselves would have very much liked to stay; and we watched them leave with great sadness in our hearts, almost certain how they would grow up in their old environment. They had the kind of characters that you needed to be especially careful with if they were to develop properly. We so sorely regret it, we had advanced so well with them. And how sad they were, those poor little things. They had so wanted to stay with us until they had learned everything. We had also managed to get the former pupil of our darling to come here to us.

While writing to you now, the end of the *puasa* is just being announced.[111] What a melancholy fills our heart at hearing this. It is only just one year ago that we were reflecting together on our childhood years. Our greatest happiness then consisted in setting off marcun[112] and wearing beautiful clothes. Nothing at that time could seem more wonderful. Then we were children without a care. It was then that we, our darling and I, were to be separated for the very first time; to celebrate Lebaran isolated from one another.

And now dearest Moes, this is now no longer a letter, of course, but has turned into just chatter to simply thank you for your writing.

Good-bye, dearest, my best wishes for you both!

Please receive the warmest regards from the others here and a warm embrace from your loving daughter,
Roekmini

Roekmini to Rosita Abendanon-Mandri

Jepara, 17 December 1904

My dearest Moedertje,

I received your last letter in good condition and I thank you for it. I am so happy that you have received those precious souvenirs in good condition. Yes, dearest, things with me are still the same, I can hardly believe it but I do my best not to let such thoughts overtake me any more, because then I become so weak, so powerless. And after all, I must live and I do have you to comfort me, haven't I? She lives for me now as in the past the way heroes in history lived for later generations, and She inspires me as I continue to idolize her more and more, more than She was able to do while alive. She is even more sacred to me now, the Greatest Love in my life, who awakens me, inspires me, and provides me with an example to follow.

My sincere thanks for your good wishes for Lebaran. I also prayed to my Darling for your support.

Now, I can tell you that here, my experience was exactly like yours, the way you were forgetting your body while your strong spirit wanted to stay; that you were neglecting the one for the other. I was not, nor am, particularly ill, but recently I was so weak physically that I attracted everyone's concern; I had severe headaches and suffered from dizziness. I was totally exhausted. Oh, Moedertje, I would not have told you this because I didn't want to upset you but now that I see you as you are, and because I have your absolute trust, I can tell you alone, that I felt the same as you! But be assured, I feel much better now. Now that life on all sides is making its demands on me, you can be assured that I have been faithfully consuming strengthening food. Physically I still don't feel my old self, but the headaches etc. have gone and I feel I have more energy. Kartini was not allowed to tell you about this but now I am telling you myself.[113]

And now, I am so grateful to you that I will have the opportunity of actually seeing you in the flesh. How much sweeter you are now to me. I so longed for this, because I was not at all satisfied about your health. Now I can only think the best about you.[114] Oh, my firm hope is now that good days lie ahead for you, days of rest, rest.

How I am looking forward already to the long letter that you have promised! Even if it should be the last that I will receive from you while you are in this country.[115] I am waiting impatiently for the letter that might bring with it the judgment that means our separation.

We still hear nothing from my brother Kartono. Oh, I am so worried about that poor boy. The last news came from his guardian. Oh God, help him, my poor dear brother. I now long for him even more knowing that there is a very good chance that next year in June he will gain his doctorate, although I now hardly dare to say this any more, knowing what melancholy his fatherland will present him with.

Now dearest, adieu, I don't know how quickly I have to write this letter to get the last from you. I am waiting with great longing.

Receive with this the warmest greetings from my Parents for you both, and for you, a warm embrace from,

Your loving,
Roekmini

Roekmini to Rosita Abendanon-Mandri

Jepara, 7 January 1905

Dearest Moedertje,

I just want to talk to you about the frame for the portrait of the Pope. The sketch for the decorative carving has been enlarged and I emphasized to the workman to ensure that the work is done as carefully as possible.[116]

But since then you have said that you also would agree to allow us to arrange to have the entire frame decoratively carved, like the frame for the mirror. The frame is going to be 85 cm by 71 cm wide on the outside. Won't it become too large with so much decoration on all sides? I would like to know what you think about this.

And is the frame to be as you originally sketched it? Wouldn't it be better if the emblem was of the same wood as the frame itself?

You don't mind this, do you, dearest, because everything does need to be perfect, doesn't it, and that's why I just want to check everything with you again. The men were not able to start on this work any earlier because they had so much to do. Do you know that Controleur Jasper, who organized the exhibition in Surabaya, wants to get into contact with us?[117]

Have you received the tile for Mrs. Mensinga?[118] Would you present my excuses to Her Ladyship that it has taken so long? I just couldn't send it any earlier, as I didn't feel up to doing any of my work.

But don't be concerned about me. I am gradually recovering.

Yesterday we sent you our photos. You can see me in those, Moedertje, as I am now. You will remember my sisters, but that tall boy is Moeljono, the small one in white is the youngest,[119] while the other little one is the son of my oldest sister, and so the oldest grandchild of my Parents.

And how are things with you, dearest? I still have to thank you for the kind words from Mijnheer, that your hearts will remain here, even though you will be leaving our land. I did always feel this but I cannot neglect to say what I think about our forthcoming separation. And dearest, may I know when this event will actually take place? We still have not had any news from my brother Kartono in all this time. We are so concerned about him. Poor, poor boy! If only we could leap across these few months then there would be the possibility that we might have him here soon. How I would encircle him with my love, because you know, Moedertje, he will do his best to graduate this year. Oh, I pray to God that everything goes well!

And now, dearest, I hope to hear soon from you how you are. And should Didi be there, would you then also give him my warmest greetings.

From all of us here warm greetings, also to Mijnheer, and consider yourself warmly embraced by your loving,
    Roekmini

The frame for Mrs. Mensinga's tile will cost $f3$: 58.

Good-bye, dearest

The pupils who have left us are continuing to write to us! In this way perhaps I can still do something for them. Do you have a photo of Singgih[120] already? We have already ordered one for you.

Roekmini to Rosita Abendanon-Mandri

I have something very sad to tell you here

                                            Jepara, 19 January 1905

My dearest Moedertje,

I have just received your long letter, for which I thank you sincerely, oh dearest, and yet you have to know that I have hardly read it properly. It has only been your spiritual proximity that has made me grateful. I have to tell you something for which the courage continually fails me, knowing what it will also mean for you.

Dearest, dearest, my father is *very* ill. So ill that we feel another great tragedy is about to befall us. On Monday morning last, all of a sudden my father collapsed and now he is lying down *without any control over the right side of his body and he cannot speak*. Oh, Moedertje, it is too terrible to name the thing for what it is.

Do you understand how it makes me long for you and yet prevents me from coming to you?

I don't want to despair, I am trying to remain calm but, oh, oh, to have so little hope left. I don't even know from whence I draw the courage and strength to tell you all this.

And we also have to see you leave us as early as 20 March? Help me, pray for me to have the strength to bear everything. As soon as things improve a little I will have your request seen to. The doctor says my father is out of danger but fears . . . Oh God, it is so terrible. Do you understand Moeder? What is father if he should be put out from the service, even if he were to recover?[121]

Good-bye, Moedertje, pray for me. A warm hand to you both from your deeply saddened,
Roekmini
The money order arrived safely

Roekmini to Rosita Abendanon-Mandri

Jepara, 4 February 1905

Dearest Moedertje,

I am still not able to write you much. I am still overwhelmed by everything, but I thank you both nevertheless for sharing in our suffering, once again, also on behalf of Ma and the sisters. Don't however be too concerned that I may become a loss to my surroundings, there is still so much waiting for me to do. And what is it that I am hearing also from Hassim about himself? Poor boy. Truly it's so hopeless. How hard life is! With this I am sending you the box for the painter. I hope it is to your taste. The cost is 17 guilders. The frame for the Pope is in preparation. I saw the notice about Didi's promotion.

Good-bye, dearest, also greetings to your husband and to Didi and especially a warm embrace from your loving daughter,
Roekmini

Roekmini to Rosita and Mr. Abendanon

Jepara, 16 February 1905

My dearest Friends,

My heart wept when I received your letter in which I read of your great concern for me. Apart from my gratitude, I also felt some blame in having left you till now in a state of uncertainty about my situation in these circumstances when I felt that it must have been preoccupying you. Since then I have been reproaching myself that thereby I have been merely adding to your worries, rather than lessening them.

Dear, dear friends, let me thank you especially for so intimately sharing with us in our new great loss, and again for your great affection for us, which shines through every word you have written. Your spiritual proximity has been so good for us. Oh, to feel your love in our hearts, it was where I first turned in my sorrow. Thank you, oh thank you so much, dearest, for everything.

And why have I remained silent all this while? I have been quite well all this time, of that I can assure you. Only, till now, a great battle has been raging within me, between the weak and the strong person. Yes, as long as this struggle was raging, in which the former threatened constantly to overwhelm the latter, it was impossible for me to come to you. No, to come to you I had to be the strong person, hadn't I? And although it's true that not everything is back to normal, and within me the silly child can still be found weeping for what has been lost from its life—those feelings of deep melancholy—the stronger side has finally regained the upper hand through the force of necessity. Nevertheless, even though this is now the case, it can never succeed in raising itself too far above the other.

What a blow it was for us to also lose our beloved Father, it has been almost unbearable.[122] Who could have thought that within that beautiful person lay buried such terrible fate. Until that day, 16 January, everything was still so fine, nobody could have suspected the thunder clouds that were to appear on our horizon, and then all of a sudden everything broke loose. We knew of course, deep in our heart, what Father's illness might mean for us, but yet we lived in hope, in the belief that things would improve. We tried to silence the warnings that whispered within us, and dared not reveal to each other our real feelings. I had written to you about the illness. Oh, it was so hard to see Father in this way, completely dependent despite his physical appearance, and then also, Father had not been able to speak any more. Yet, while the doctor continued to hold out hope, we also held on to ours. Oh, we wanted to believe it, it was impossible to think otherwise. On the fifth day, however, we had to open our eyes to the reality. And the following night everything came to an end, and we had to let go of what was dearest to us.

How was Father himself in those days of his illness? Those days can be considered as being among our better memories. It seems that Father did not suffer at all. It is true that Father could no longer speak and was unconscious for most of the time, but during the periods in which he regained consciousness, the only impression we could gain from his movements was that he was at peace. Father could still stroke his chin in such a genial manner with his good hand, pull our hair, or caress our hand. It always seemed as though Father's mind was at peace, indeed nothing had changed in the appearance of his face. He still looked as he did in his good days. And his deathbed, dear friends, saw Father depart from us in the greatest sense of peace. Oh yes, that is certainly a fine memory of Father in his last days. Most of us (the children) were also privileged to be with Father in those days and until the last moment. My oldest brothers and sister were constantly there with Father, together with my sisters and me. Only our poor Kardinah and Moeliono were deprived of this opportunity. They could only manage to be here in time to be with us at the funeral. They were also totally heartbroken, poor dears!

But now, well, how must it be for our poor Kartono. He, who knew with what longing Father awaited his return, he who had only a little time before made Father so happy with the good news that he would soon be coming home; he who could scarcely realize that joy that his return would bring. How will he take this latest, bitter blow? How will he take this terrible news? He wasn't able to be there during those last days to participate in all those services that we could still perform for our dearest Father. We Natives[123] have the tradition, which I can only describe as a moving expression of the love children have for their parents, that at the funeral the children assist in carrying the coffin out of the house. So when I saw all my brothers and brothers-in-law gathered around my Father, to perform that last duty of love, it broke my heart. It will also probably be a long time before I can write to him. Poor, poor boy, I hope that this terrible blow will not have a lasting effect on him.

The person who stands out most by her strong presence, dearest, you could never imagine: it is our dear Moeder.[124] You can't imagine the half of it, how she approached everything with such strong determination. She has been our constant model for how we should behave. She is a wonderful figure in our darkest days. It is her deep conviction in her belief that provides her with this enviable sense of peace. We often feel ashamed that we younger ones, in whom, as it were, so much youthful energy still exists, are constantly in danger of being overwhelmed by our grief.

From now on, dearest, I will dedicate my life to my Moeder, who is such a shining light for us and whose efforts to ensure our future happiness have become unshakeable, and in whom we have a spur to keep our father's name in honor. May it be granted me to ensure that Moeder will always find in me the satisfaction of having realized her aims. Moeder's motto is: to see that Father's good work for us is continued and not to rest until everything has been realized as Father had wished. All the studies the little ones were engaged in will be continued even though others have advised her to end them. Moeder would hear none of it because that would be in contradiction of Father's spirit. Father had wanted to provide us with much more that he considered necessary for our spiritual development. Moeder is extremely interested in the work of Singgo[125] and our school. Oh, I will never be able to give you a true picture of this mother of mine. It is so beautiful. It is not she who is the weak one here, dears, it is your daughter. For her future happiness was now lost forever with the passing away of Father. For her there remains only an endless grayness.

But now it is Moeder who is the strong one, who goes on despite the despair, strong in her faith in the beauty of life. Can you see how She now constitutes my finest thoughts, how, despite everything, my heart can still be grateful? How blessed I can still consider myself when I compare myself with others, who in their struggle and suffering through life receive no support from those who surround them and only feel alienated from them instead of feeling bound to that beloved core with firm bonds.[126]

The time is now also approaching with rapid strides that will separate you and your child. I can hardly imagine it. My Moeder will have to reteach me how to live through this. Oh, I would love so very, very much to embrace you. Oh, may it yet happen that I can see your dear faces, feel your hand, once more. That would mean so much, so much to me.

And now my dears, for the time being I have to close. There are so many more letters I have to write that I had not yet been able to think about before now but which now must be written.

Have you received the box for the artist? What do you think of it? The workmen did not carve a *garuda* on it even though I had so expressly asked him to remember to do so, but I thought the box was so fine that I sent it any way. The frame for the Pope will also be finished soon. My plan had been to send you a souvenir of that work, something special, but I was so busy and then that unexpected happened and now, regrettably, I will not be able to send it to you while you are here. Shall I send it to Didi later and ask him to send it on? I imagine you would not yet be in Holland then.

And now, dearest, my heartfelt thanks to you for everything, for your great love.

Will you write again, I continue to long for you so much.

    For you, much love from your loving daughter,
    Roekmini

Do you know how Hassim is? What has happened to him actually? I feel that he is surrounded by much suffering.

Roekmini to Rosita Abendanon-Mandri

Jepara, 20 February 1905

My dearest Moedertje,
How long will it be before the judgment upon me will be executed, that I will once again have to lose, lose lose. That once again I will have to experience the loss of someone on whom my soul has depended. How short this sad, sad space of time is which separates me from that moment and hence, oh dearest, how heavily it already weighs upon me. Oh no, during the day I don't feel it, time does not allow me to have such thoughts, but when the evening peace and silence fill my room, when all that ceaseless activity is finally swept away and I am free to let my thoughts roam freely on my own condition, how heavily it all weighs on me then, the thought of what must await me. Sleepless nights follow such periods of activity by my weary soul.

Oh, dear Moeder, it weighs on me so heavily, I feel so deeply that hanging over me again is the pitiless reality of another separation from what remains of the dear circle that I once had. Oh, the child, that happy child, that once lived such a carefree life, always believing in the fulfillment of the dreams that life offers, the child that was always ready to laugh—she will disappear forever with your departure from this, the land of your lonely daughter. That which you once loved so dearly will disappear forever. Oh, Moedertje, your child begs of you, love her twice as much, give her double that which she already has from you, she is convinced that a cold wind will come that, as it were, will numb her. My deepest wish is, you know—I would so dearly love, if only for a moment, to hear your voices, to feel the warm pressure of your hands, to see your dear face, my dear, Friends, who I will never, never see again.

I cannot imagine that you will be leaving our country without having that opportunity. Who knows what that would do for me? Or would I lose my sanity in the face of that reality, were I to find myself in your arms where I would conjure up all that will be lost to me? And then to think again how I must also tear you from my heart. Wouldn't I clutch tightly to you, or would I fall, never to stand again? I don't know, but I so long for it. The tears that are burning in my eyes, I can not bear it.

Oh, if I had a gramophone, that wonderful invention that reproduces the voice, then perhaps that could make up for what I must now do without. I would beg you to have your voice recorded, how I would then be reinvigorated. God knows what the future will hold for me. Oh yes, what I forgot the last time, dearest, may I have a sarong and kabaya that you have worn? You know what this sort of thing means for us Javanese,[127] don't you? And also a lock of your hair? You would make me so happy. Now I still have the ring of yours in which your initials have been inscribed in a golden heart. How beautiful the memory of why you gave this to me. The one that my dearest sister had worn I sent to Holland to dear Kartono, whom I asked to wear it. I am eagerly looking forward to receiving your clothes. I want to press my face on them.

The sentences I have inscribed here are certainly deep and powerful and in my heart are as red as blood, hot as fire. Do you know that, Moedertje? Do you still remember that you sent me that beautiful poem that went: "I once stood there with open book"? I little expected how soon this would be written into my own book with colors as red as blood and then have those pages torn up. Please give me a word, dearest, that will teach me to say: "Go on!" If you have the time, will you do that, Moedertje?

And now, I hardly dare, but I will chance it. I want to ask you one more thing. May I also have something from your home and also from yourselves that will remind me so much of you? It is something that had formed part of your own welcome. And this is, dearest, that I remember a very small painting in your bedroom, a mountain scene. The soft pink of the setting sun provided the background color and the mountains were a deep gray. It was a painting which your threesome once stood in front of, during a wonderful moment, full of concentration. I will give it a place in my room alongside the group photo in which you two are standing with the three boys in front of your house, which I look at so often, and close to where I spend so much time these days, my writing table.

Good-bye now, dearest, dearest darling, oh, if only I could once more feel that warm kiss on my cheek, Moedertje, my Moedertje. Oh, I would exchange my place, if only it were possible, with that of anyone who was now breathing in the same air as you.

Oh, if only you were going to Australia, then I would be able to await you along the coast.[128]

Good-bye, dearest, goodbye, say something to me. Give my regards to Mijnheer and to Didi. And hold me with my arms around your neck.

Your daughter who yearns for you,
Roekmini

The drawing about which you wrote last that you had sent to me I have not received. Could it have gone astray? And how do you like the box and what does Mrs. Meringa think of the frame for her title?

Good-bye, good-bye, good-bye, dearest!

Roekmini to Rosita Abendanon-Mandri

Jepara, 4 March 1905

My dearest Moedertje,

When you receive this you will perhaps already no longer be standing on the same soil as those who love you. Oh, in my mind I have been living with you these last days. Do I still have to tell you how very grateful I am to you for your letter which so clearly confirmed your unalterable attachment and love for me, for what is dear to me, this land and its people, and so much more; for what was contained in the letter which provided me with the will to go on, on my difficult journey? Oh, dearest, it filled me with such a warm feeling, it is such a comfort for me. Yes, Moedertje, my duty to try to do the best for my fellow beings in life before seeking my own benefit, that will constantly weigh most heavily on me.

It is reemerging, it is coming back, that sense of duty. It ennobles, it will rise up from this sleep. Oh, when I presented myself to you, so clearly broken spirited, it was more because of the unbearable grief I felt for not being allowed to see you again for the last time, which was my dearest desire. The thought didn't even enter my head to wish that you would stay here any longer, knowing how much you two need the time to relax. It was just that I longed and longed to see you once more by me, in the flesh. And if, at the moment you are reading what you have in your hands, you are at the point of leaving, oh, my dearest, dearest Moeder, then farewell, farewell, feel how my heart reaches out for you, more desperately than ever, my dearest. My warmest kisses go to you in my thoughts, my thanks for everything that you have been for me here, for us. Press Mijnheer's hand warmly for me and tell him of all my feelings about this moment concerning you both and also my thanks.

Now I seem to have been mistaken. I thought that you would go to Surabaya to meet your sister.[129] But I have just read that it is Sukabumi, which is why I wrote at the beginning that you might not receive this letter while you were still here. Oh, but now it will still arrive in time and I can still reach you and call out my farewell while we are both standing on the same soil.

Oh, Moedertje, how I can feel with you during these momentous changes, what these last days must mean for you. Your heart must be torn, divided into two parts, half for those who must be left behind. But it could hardly be otherwise since your love is so deep, your bleeding heart is the evidence of it, isn't it? How strange it would be, surely, if the heart remained unaffected by such emotions produced by such a parting from what we claimed to love, if we could not. Oh, in this way, in the final resort suffering must be sweet, holy; for our heart's sake, we wouldn't want to miss it, no matter how hellish, how all consuming this grief in us is, without it, how poor we would be, how empty our lives. Isn't that so, dearest?

I received such a sweet letter from Didi that made me so happy. And with it, something . . . a memento. The thought of sending it was so touching, made me so grateful, and at the same time so melancholy, but nevertheless for me it is of great, great value. I have now locked it up in my cabinet of religious icons. I am going to write him my deepest thanks very soon for what he has done, that dear friend. How these days must also be hard for him; if I, who am so far away, already feel like this, how must it be for him?

For you it is a brief meeting, a greeting and . . . separation again. I empathize with you in this so much. But in my mind Didi is still the luckiest of your boys who have to live through this. I can't exactly tell you why but I consider Didi the most fortunate in your love.

And now, adieu dearest, forever adieu. How my fingers, my hand, tremble in writing this. It is as though I am actually seeing you leaving. Adieu, adieu, my thanks once more for everything, everything you had, have and will continue to give me.

You are warmly embraced and greeted and loved by,
Your daughter,
Roekmini

Good-bye, my dearest friends, good-bye. I hardly know how to part and to call out to you. Good-bye, good-bye, please love me still, my best wishes to you.

Roekmini to Rosita Abendanon-Mandri

Jepara, 6 March 1905

My dearest, dearest Moedertje,

When you receive this it will be your last evening, and therefore I could not give up the opportunity to bring you one more greeting, to wish you good-bye, knowing that this will still reach you here. Oh, I still can't accept the fact that I will have to stretch out my arms in vain. How more fortunate your friends here are, even Didi, compared to me. They will see you for the very last moment, till the very last step. They may hold your hands, and look into your eyes, and receive back a greeting from you, a glance full of love. All that is denied me. Oh, Moedertje, when you leave I will see nothing, I can only feel a painful grief. Feel me once more in your arms, around

your neck, my very last farewell. Good-bye, my dearest Moedertje. My very best wishes to you both. I received such a dear letter from Didi and also a memento. How melancholy that made me, seeing that. But yet I found it so sensitive of him to have given me this. I simply can't thank him enough. Now, for the last time, good-bye, my friends. Farewell. My heart goes with you.
    With all my love,
    Your daughter, R.

Roekmini to Rosita Abendanon-Mandri

Jepara, 14 November 1905

Dearest Moedertje,

    First let me congratulate you and also his dear grandfather, on your first grandchild. What a joyous welcome for you in Holl. where there was a new member of the family awaiting you, together with all those others who adore you. And isn't it marvelous to know that both mother and child are doing well. Yet you must have been fulfilled with such happy feelings about the young mother, a daughter whom you had never seen before. Would you also warmly congratulate the new parents from me, Moedertje? I had already heard all the news from Didi when she was still expecting. How wonderful also that Kartono had remembered my welcome greeting for you, Moedertje. I have followed you everywhere although it may have been that only when you arrived in Holl. that you had a real indication to convince you of that. Yes, you heard so little from me, your traveling and my unfamiliarity with the length of your stay at each place you called in to, restrained me.

    I was fearful that the letters might have got lost, but, on Didi's advice, I decided nevertheless to give it a try. And then your wish that I should do so also helped convince me, so I sent it to America, fortunately including with it your address in Holl. That is where you then first received it? Everything you sent me has arrived safely, including the souvenirs. My dearest dear friends, you have made me so happy with them. What a comfort it was for me in my sad loss of you both to be aware of your constant spiritual presence even though there was so much that must have absorbed your attention. With each token of your attention I felt so grateful, even though it first brought on feelings of melancholy. How I enjoyed your many descriptions of all those beautiful things you saw on the way that you enabled me to share with you.

    The total impression on me of all this was tremendous. In my own small, isolated spot your letters opened up to me a new world. What a wonderful country Japan must be with its rich treasure of flowers of which you sent me some small mementos that are now very dear to me, especially because you had worn them close to your heart. Oh, they tell me so much about the heart on which they must have rested in the moments when you were enjoying the beauty of that far-off land. I stared and stared at the small twigs until, dearest, a charming small figure from that land seemed to appear, a sweet little woman in colorful yet tasteful traditional clothing that was flapping in the breeze who in soft voice began to tell me of your love. And I was completely enthralled by it and these flowers have now become holy to me. Do you still remember that young Buddhist priest who gave it to you? Your description of him also affected me greatly. It made me think of that wonderful figure created by Henri Borel in his *Wisdom and Beauty in China*.[130] He himself was also something to behold, wasn't he, Moedertje? And was the "garden party" not like a dance evening? Weren't the ladies dressed in European style? And of course also the gentlemen were dressed up like Europeans. And one of them reminded you of my dear Father? Yes, that amazing energetic life; we Javanese should not just stand and admire it too long but adopt it from that valiant people. Oh, Moedertje, with us here the necessary willpower to do so is still so scarce and, with regard to the question of the advancement of women, there is so very little, so that when they contemplate the great job that lies before them, they often ask themselves: would I be able to bring it about against the opposition of the majority who simply refuse to budge. Is that not the case with all good principles?

About that idea of the missionary with whom you were talking about us, I should tell you that I would have no objection if you wanted to publish our correspondence. I give you our complete authority to do so.[131] In particular to give our dear Tini the opportunity to speak once more through her letters. Let people know once more how indestructible her spirit is. Let Java once more be convinced how a woman once lived in order that they may realize their destiny, their future.

What a beautiful souvenir you sent us from Niagara, and your last letter written on board the "Potsdam" I also received safely. Many thanks for that, Moedertje. I have to read your letters very slowly. Oh, I could hardly follow you in everything you explained to me about what you had seen, experienced, and enjoyed. What an amazingly interesting and unforgettable journey you have had. You should keep your impressions in a more concrete form for you and your loved ones. How wonderful that would be for them, almost as good as having experienced it themselves. What news about the Mijnheer's finger? How unfortunate. I do hope everything is all right now.

Can you yet realize yet that you are now in Holland, Moedertje? That you have had that wonderful experience? That Java has been without you now for almost a year? I find it difficult. Sometimes I can't believe it, that it might all be just a bad dream that we now have come to this. Why should we now have to live an entirely new life, completely separated off from the old dear one we knew? Is it possible that one day a time will come when we will just come to accept that that which almost cost us our lives to give up has passed away?

Yes, everything is so painfully new for us. By now you will no doubt have heard that the new appointment for Jepara has been announced and also that, as a result, a judgment has been passed on us, that from now on we will be strangers in this place that is so dear to us. A stranger has come. Oh, Moedertje, you will be able to understand what that means for us. Was it not enough that we had to tear up so many bonds of love, to also have this thrust upon us as well? One good thing is that my brother has become a regent.[132] And now he has already moved to his place of appointment (Ngawi) with our youngest brother.[133] But Mama and we girls are still here. We still cannot decide whether to leave Jepara, especially Mama, poor Mama.[134] But of course we have moved and now live diagonally across from the house where we spent our best and most beautiful time. But this still may be temporary and we may find something else, which would be for the better because it would be too much for us to stay here much longer.

Yes, in August and September, as a result of having high temperature and nervous irritation all over my body, I went to Salatiga[135] together with my sister Soematri, who was also suffering from fever. Oh, what an immediate effect the change in environment and the cool climate produced. It was so wonderful that occasionally I had the outrageous idea of not returning home again because only there, in that different environment, did I feel I would be able to find healing. I so enjoyed it, that peaceful existence, the life surrounded by nature. Here I could be a child again, climbing hills, splashing through streams or resting in the shadows of the trees. There you felt that you were a part of the pristine environment and that you always, always wanted to remain this way. In next to no time our health had returned. And by the time we had to return home we had regained so much of our former strength that we had the courage to face it again. Now we have been home again for a month. Oh, what if we went to live there, in Salatiga![136]

And Moedertje, in the meantime our little school has fallen apart. Now the girls who have reached the age of 13 are no longer allowed to come, since they are then considered adult and for them the time has come that they are to be considered as being "marriageable." So they are no longer allowed to appear in public. The others have left with their parents to other places and now, now that we no longer live nearby the seat of authority but some distance away (that is to say, a few minutes away), they are also reluctant to send the daughters who would still be allowed to come, because they could not bear to allow the little children to "flâner" up and down the street in this way.[137] I am so upset, and when I see the little ones it cuts me to the quick to think what could have been and what now lies in ruins. We will try once more, try once again to build up our house of dreams

And what now awaits for us to do? Moedertje, I have written to you that the girls were allowed to study.[138] The girls had in fact already begun, but now obstacles are being put in their path that are making things difficult for them to continue. The entire family is against it.[139] If it were only they who were against it, we couldn't give two hoots about their opinion, but they have found a way to bend our Moeder to their view, that poor thing who is now without the support she once had and is often so weak, so that she also no longer likes our ideas and is now also against it. So now here we must again commence our struggle against both friends and foes. In this you will recognize the saying: To defy one's enemies is no effort, it is child's play; but to oppose one's neighbors, one's loved ones, that requires courage. We have only courage to overcome love, as Carmen Sylva says.[140] And against Moedertje, who is now so all alone in her struggle. My heart is gradually breaking.

So now we want to proceed only very gently. Fine, the majority has won over Moeder and Moedertje has become weak and we want to, for her sake, conform somewhat to her wishes, but the outside world will never suppress us as they think they can. You can understand that our respectable family has only our best interests at heart in this matter, primarily to provide themselves with a cover to disguise the fact that their opposition is to prevent us from becoming better than themselves. Even Europeans have conspired with them. Moeder is of the opinion that we are exaggerating. But be assured, we will hold firm. Why else would we have received so much that is wonderful from this life, like the love of our friends, the example of our dear sister and dear Father, were it not for this end, to live for what is the Good.

And now the people have something else to tease us with, that is that there is a regent, a young man and a friend.[141] While he does have a marriage partner reserved for him, he has not yet tied the knot, so that now we must not leave ourselves open to the world by appearing in public, the family says, when they learnt that the sisters were having lessons outside the home and went to their teacher on foot. Moe[142] should not allow this, that her daughters were becoming the subject of public gossip, especially now when there no longer was a father to guarantee their reputation. Oh, what a sensitive issue they have broached there and how it has weakened Ma even more. Now we are even forbidden to go outside much. Oh Father, how much of our free life went with you to the grave, now that you have departed from us? How those hands are even more ready to smash our wings![143]

But now, what is our situation? The sisters are continuing their studies, but at home. They are receiving assignments from their teacher. And now, for Mama's sake, we want to conform somewhat to the wishes of society because we are waiting on better times, that is when Kartono returns.[144] But the world will never be able to claim that it was right, because, no matter how far we seem to depart from our chosen direction, as far as everything else is concerned we are still living our own lives as far as our powers allow us.

If you could only see how we still walk outside, or, to lift our spirits, how we burst out into a hearty laugh or song, how we let our voices be heard so that people would be ashamed, had they heard us, of how absolutely we do not follow the rules of respectability that should be obeyed by young Javanese ladies. Yes, what a halfhearted preparation we have had: we have been given wings on our shoulders but we have been taught that to make use of them is the biggest sin. We can only spread them out in our imagination, and stare into space imagining what we might be able to do if we could. The wings are only to give us an external beauty, they may not affect our character. With our spirit, that has been shaped towards freedom, with our ideals and dreams of the light, we have to come to regard the state of marriage as the only pivot around which everything should revolve. Marriage is the only true destiny for women, I often hear people say, but does our society happen to be able to provide the guarantee for this, that she can without concern live according to this norm? What does the state of marriage tell us, based as it is on traditional foundations formed by our society? Isn't it likely that it provides us with the painful certainty that it will be a damper on our life of enlightenment?

Do you know this poem?

> Its little head buried in its feathers
> so downy and fine

> what is your illness
> dear little bird?

This is also what we now ask ourselves because we are no more no less now than "birds in a cage," who stare sadly out at the freedom we were promised but which will never be granted us.

> Oh if only I could follow them
> into the far distance
> then I could unfold my wings
> I would sing a song

For us all avenues are being denied that could bring us happiness, other than that one. Oh, and now these cages have become smaller because of the departure of our father. But please God be with us now, to continue to provide us with the food we need to succor our spirit so that we ourselves can still make sufficient space for ourselves. And for this reason we must avoid any obstacles, appearing different from everyone else, so that we may still be able to take advantage of any opportunity that may arise to reach the goal that we have determined for ourselves. As if on the part of the gentlemen of the world it is not yet well enough understood that we are the least of the least, and the least able to give them "a life of happiness" as it is generally understood; as if we were not steadfast in our determination to make the best of the opportunities that may befall us, where already too much damage has been done by these interventions in our lives, to that sacred right that has been given us of being allowed to live, how these things are bound to come about eventually; where all too much of it has already been sacrificed and to what advantage of either party? Oh no. It has been too much already. Poor Mama, who we have once again promised nothing but sorrow.

I made mention before of better days to come, if Kartono returns. Yes, then we would have such wonderful support here, and also, for what he would do to turn Ma back to her former self. Only Kartono can help us. We cannot depend on our brothers here. Even though we ourselves realize how it will be for Kartono to see Java again, which will only give him a taste again of his saddest days, we nevertheless long for him to return and the good fortune of seeing him again. Have you already met him, my poor, dearest brother? Will you cheer him up, my fine boy? In John[145] he has found a good friend, as he did in Didi. How busy he must be now. We rarely hear from him any more. But now and then I send him a greeting and then I get a reply. Poor Didi, how lonely he must be feeling. I don't dare to send him long letters now that he is so busy.

And my dearest Moedertje, will you pass my regards on to your husband and to the happy couple and you yourself, receive this embrace from your loving, faraway daughter,
R.

Roekmini to Rosita Abendanon-Mandri

Jepara, 7 March 1906

My dearest Moedertje,

What must you think of me, not having heard anything from me for such a long time? And yet, how many reasons haven't there been lately to do so. I cannot really offer any excuses. All I can say is that, even though I didn't write to you, I have always been thinking of you and that it has pained me greatly to make you wait so long.

First let me thank you so much for the beautiful art pieces which you have sent us, souvenirs of your wonderful travels. We are so pleased to have received them; apart from the fact they are such remarkable objects, we are touched by the fact that your kind thoughts accompany them. All the things were so beautiful, that silk cloth and that strange object made from seeds and shells, and so on. Moedertje, I also have now begun to collect seeds. Mevrouw van Zuylen[146] also wanted examples of the same kind of craftwork for the Paris Exhibition. I am sure we can find all the seeds used to make that here. Only I am not sure whether those black ones which are on the satin cloth are the original color or have been painted. They look like *ketimun* seeds.

Dearest, I am now able to tell you that we are staying in Jepara, which of course I think is marvelous. Only the youngest boys went to live with Boesono.[147] Ma is staying here with us three girls. We are now living opposite the kabupaten, our former house, and where we live now is quite comfortable and good enough for us. Oh dearest, everything is now different than it was before yet we are facing this new period of ours with confidence and optimism. I don't know where we are drawing this from, but if you could see us now you would only see us with hopeful faces. There is still a lot of sadness for what we have lost, and we still lack the confidence to reach out for what should be ours. But dearest, although you do not see us engaged in any activity, continue to believe in us, that we are still the girls you knew before, with fire in our hearts. After all, Moedertje, there is not just one way to reach our goal. So one day you will see us on a new path to achieve our ends. Oh, may God grant us the strength for this. And hold us in your hearts forever, my dear friends.

At the moment or rather, recently, my heart is being confronted by so many strange emotions, which are so occupying my thoughts that I can hardly describe it to another person. And this is actually why I have not been able to write to you all this time, although my heart, in contrast, did want to, and continually reached out to you both. Had I been with you I probably also would not have been able to say much, merely lay my head against your breast. Yet it is not a feeling that depresses me. I am so happy with the flowers you picked on your arrival in Holland and with your thoughts in the postcard you sent me. In this way one could never, ever be alone or feel deserted, however miserable the circumstances that surround one. And so now I feel so rich, so contented, dearest. I hope very much, dearest, that over there you are granted better times and rest, especially for Mijnheer.

Both the newspapers that His Excellency has sent me arrived safely and I have read them with great interest. Please convey to your husband our heartfelt thanks for them. How is it possible that the report could have been attacked in this way?[148] Is this the way for ensuring that the best interests of the Javanese are being met? It saddens us so to see this and we clearly understand the bitterness Mijnheer must feel to see how the system deals with all his work.[149] I did not follow the debates on the Indies budget in the papers, dearest, because it is only now that we are receiving the papers again on a regular basis.

How wonderful that you have now got to know Kartono. He also wrote to me about how he had immediately felt at home at your house and how he would like to share the benefits of your friendship as we do. He would very much like to have a place in your hearts. He is such a dear boy, Moedertje, and in his difficult life that has delivered him such grief in the last years, it was so important for him to meet you and Mijnheer, to be told so much about those he loved by those who loved us. He also wanted to be an element in our friendship and love for each other. He writes to me every week. He knows John very well and he has become an intimate friend. I think this is so wonderful. In this way Kartono is completely part of your circle. Here I also hear occasionally from Edi. Oh, I hold him fast, as it were, since I don't have you any more and regard it as making up for what I am missing when I hear something from him.[150] Poppy[151] and May and the little one of whom you sent me such a sweet picture are already in Arnhem, I suppose. Edi told me that your littlest treasure has been named after his grandfather.

We have also received a photo of our little Singgih. We hadn't seen him again for such a long time and we were so surprised at how that child has grown. He already looks like a child of three in his jacket and with that wise little face of his with those intelligent eyes, like his mother once had. No doubt you have also heard that he has a new mother, a princess from Solo, not young and a real conservative.[152] Poor little boy, my little treasure. May God keep his soul pure and upright in those surroundings full of contradictions.[153] May he have the strength to lift himself out of that environment. Life, life is one long prayer, isn't it, Moedertje. Moedertje, should we be expressing these doubts when we should be grateful, even if this is more a case of clutching at straws? We hope that our little one may grow up the way his eyes suggest he might.

I am still actively involved with *Boeatan*.[154] Mev. v. Z[uylen-Tromp] recently said she would send me some money for woodcarving and some other things. I am still arranging such craftwork for Batavia. And now the people are busy for the forthcoming exhibition (annual market) in Surabaya.[155] You know what? We girls have received an invitation from Mr. Jasper to come over with some workers.[156] Then we could be part of the committee and would travel there at their expense. Well, how this idea appealed to us! We accepted immediately and, if nothing intervenes, we will be going to Surabaya in May. And there are such wonderful carvings being made at the moment, Moedertje.

In the paper we read that your husband received an award. I didn't know it was a watercolor. It must be beautiful, was it, Moedertje?

The other day Edi sent me a poetry collection by Guido Gezelle.[157] Oh, he makes such beautiful verses. But do you know what inspired Edi to send me that present? I had sent him some verses of mine and he advised me to take up poetry writing. Shall I send you some, Moedertje? It just popped up in me one lonely day, when the sisters weren't here, to give vent to my thoughts and feelings.

We would love to meet your niece. It would be wonderful if she could come here to see us. She would find good friends in us.[158]

Dearest, I had almost forgotten to thank you both for your best wishes for the New Year. May it be a better year than those we have just had, those last two sad ones.

And will you read this, Moedertje, to see how well I have done it?

A poem

Black head
with dark, flashing eyes,

poor child
in a world without pity.

What is it you are searching for
with your thoughtful, staring look?
The Almighty
who determines your fate?

My poor one
you feel it, even if I don't say it,
it is you
who has suffered so long.

You were brought
like seed from outside your home.
Oh, little flower
that must still maintain your character.

You must survive
but silently, hidden deep
in an environment
that is dark, deathly, and small in nature

The other
was light, airy, and free,
here you would develop.
Your leaves intensely happy

Like the birds
you were also blessed with wings
that could
not be ensnared in its mighty flight

Then one would see
how you enjoyed the freedom
and would call you
completely immoral

The world
would point you out, and sternly shake its head,
She would forget
that you were once granted that freedom.

Now it holds you
fast in softest leather
and indicates to you
silly things from the past

My little child
how sad and hard is your fate
but don't despair
your spirit, clear and upright is the light of God

After this I will send you some more that I still have to correct. What do you think, dearest?

Once again my thanks to you both for everything what you have done for me dearest friends and forgive me that I have made you wait so long.

With love from Ma and the sisters and much love from,
    Your daughter,
    Roekmini

Roekmini to Rosita Abendanon-Mandri

Jepara, 28 October 1906

Dearest Moedertje,

Many, many thanks for your long letter, which of course was more welcome than I could ever say. No, it never entered my head that we would be out of your thoughts, but I now know that, since your return from such a long journey, you have been fully occupied by all kinds of things and in arranging your permanent settlement in that country. That was the reason we had not heard from you. But then, I have also written so very little, haven't I, dearest?

Our great losses have continued to have significant consequences causing a lot of misery for us. I still just go on with my life, but oh, Moedertje, for a long time I lacked the strength to raise myself up. Given the way I was I didn't dare to come to my friends who expected other things from me. But now I am my old self again. I want to live a fully conscious life again, now that I have my strength back. When I received your letter I was so filled with sadness: everything from the past wafted in front of me so clearly, it was as though you yourself laid a hand on my shoulder. I became melancholic, but at the same time I was shaken awake, to become again as I was. The trust, the expectations of old dear friends awoke a feeling of shame in me. You will forgive me, Moedertje, won't you?

From now on our life will consist of a continuous series of leg irons and traps, and as you said, in that case God grant us then that we can retain the strength that I now feel to cope with it. But we continue to hold to our dream of one day being a support for the work being undertaken here in this country, especially with regard to the woodcarving work. As you will have read, we, or rather our exhibit, won a silver medallion at the annual fair at Surabaya. We went there ourselves on the invitation of Mr. Jasper, who was the head of the craft section of the exhibition. We became members of the subcommittee and so we were able to travel there for free. It was of course a rare opportunity.[159] And at the exhibition we had such indescribable pleasure looking at all the craftwork that our nation produces, which we had never seen before with our own eyes.[160] It was all so wonderful, down to the smallest items. For us it was even more enjoyable that we were also able to participate in setting up the exhibits, so that we could admire everything at our leisure. Oh, it is simply impossible to express in words the skill of the art of our ordinary people. And therefore how praiseworthy are the efforts of those who want to shed light on this work. Only when one has seen everything with one's own eyes does one feel a sense of gratitude for the many people who have helped to bring this to realization.

Next year there will be a similar fair; which will be for the display of the varieties of bird feathers and fruit, and there will also be an opportunity to exhibit again. We also have an invitation already. But according to the reports in the paper, next time it will be supported by private citizens. The financial support for the previous fair was not a subsidy but an interest-free loan. Had it been otherwise, Mr. Jasper had planned to use the profits, if he didn't have to return them, to establish an industrial school for girls. Then he would have appointed us to head it. But now, now that it has become clear that the government wants its funding back, we don't know what will happen.[161]

We were not able to send a contribution to the fair in Krefeld[162] because we are always dependent here on advance payments when we have large orders to fulfill. We simply can't do otherwise because the craftsmen do not have any business capital. Our Regent did receive some money, but only 50 guilders. I don't know what he could have done with that. Yes, it's very awkward that despite the fact that there is much that we have in common intellectually, etc., the Regent and we do not have contact with each other. We would like nothing better than that, to have some interaction with him, but it seems that he is still rather conservative when it comes to women. He would prefer them not to be too emancipated, even though he is not unfamiliar with the modern times.[163]

I was saddened not to be able to do anything for the exhibit [in Krefeld], especially because your husband had worked so hard for it. We received the circulating letters. Are you going or have you been to the exhibition yourself? How wonderful that your Japanese collection receives pride of place in your house. And that all your treasures have been to be well displayed so that they can properly represent the region from which they originate.

What a beautiful house you have, the arrangement of the rooms and the furnishings are wonderful, especially the latter, not too many but all artistic pieces. I can well imagine how beautiful it all must be and how you have given it your special cachet. And that climbing plant, what a lovely symbol that is, Moedertje. But you must have forgotten to send me a leaf from it, Moedertje, I didn't find any although you wrote that you would include one in your letter. I would still love to receive one. You will send me one next time, won't you?

I also received a lovely letter from your husband from Blaren. How is he? We read in the paper that he had also been at the exhibition in Krefeld. Yes, I can imagine how concerned you must be when your husband is ill and still won't rest. That's the way these important personalities are in Europe, and in the case of your husband, his spirit will constantly be in conflict, even more so than here in the Indies. Yes, like you, I am also worried about the effect of these unavoidable situations, of which your husband continues to experience too many. A man surely cannot limit himself when driven by his spirit. But how is he now? Has the cure at Schwarzwald helped any?[164] And has Edi really resigned from his government position, Moedertje? That really surprised me because I did not know the reason for that. I had still written him a letter addressed to the Office of Mining, but it seems that the letter never arrived. I heard from Hassim that he will be going to Holland. I would very much have liked to send him a farewell greeting, but now I don't know where he is. Now there really is no one here anymore who is in any way related to you, but the ties that bind remain strong, don't they, but still a pang of regret always goes through me when I think that one by one you have all left this country. Will you tell me later why Edi has left? He had once written to me from Kapahian, his last location.

With us here everything is fine. Have I written to you before that we have such nice friends here in the Controleur and his sister?[165] They are two young, kind, dear good people whom we have become very close to. We are now practically doing everything with them; they are such a boon in our lives. We are practicing modern languages with them, Moedertje, and my sisters are now also learning to play music. And these days I am also writing a bit. A ladies' journal has now been established in the Indies, and I have written several articles for it.[166] And I have been engaged as a permanent contributor to write Javanese legends, for which I receive an honorarium.[167] I think that's a good use of my time. I sent my brother the first piece, entitled "Evolution of Native Girls," and have asked him to send it on to you. A novel should also be published soon.[168] I will have them send it to you.

What you wrote concerning batiking Mrs. van Zuylen has also already written to me about.

15 November

Tomorrow I will send to *Oost en West* over there the craftwork they had ordered. Prices are really starting to go up for the beautiful things people are ordering, so that, before I knew it, the sum of money that Mev. van Zuylen sent me as a deposit had all been used up, merely for the carving. She also asked me to try batiking on silk, to make ties, tea cozies, etc. It is certainly a very good idea and it will undoubtedly be very popular.

Do you remember, Moedertje, that you gave me a few lengths of material (Pekalongangsch batik[169]) for covering a chair? Should I return it to you at some convenient time?

In the meantime it is now almost the end of November and the letter is still lying here. It is shocking. We have been very busy because of the *Lebaran Puasa*. In another week everything will be over. And so now Edi has also left for Holland. I regret that I was not able to greet him before he left.

Well, I had better send the letter now, dearest, although I really haven't finished telling you all the news. Say hello to Mijnheer for us and imagine that from me you are receiving a kiss,

From your faithful and loving daughter,
Roekmini

Roekmini to Rosita Abendanon-Mandri

Jepara, 6 January 1907

My dearest Friends,

First of all let me thank you, Mijnheer, sincerely for your lovely letter from Schwarzwald in which you included a postcard. Your kind attention cheered me up so much, but yet it is only now that I could send you my appreciation for it. I feel a deep sense of shame about this; it is terrible the way that my attention to letter writing has so deteriorated lately. Well, one would love to write down for one's friends everything that one felt within one's heart, but that is not possible, not even allowed, so that the desire to write like that, spontaneously, is lessened, even though one feels a strong urge to do so.[170]

I also have not yet sent you greetings and good wishes for the New Year, dear friends. May it especially bring you much good health, dear friends! How are things with you, Mijnheer? In the daily papers there was a report that you had attended the exhibition in Krefeld as well as given a speech there. That must have been soon after you had returned from Schwarzwald. Didn't it tire you too much? But what a success it was! And what a mountain of exhibits there was from Java. We also received a similar circular requesting contributions, and it saddens us that we did not enter anything, but not having any means to do so, there was nothing we could do. Fortunately woodcraft was well represented. I don't think our Regent sent anything, or did he?

I also received a copy of "Führer durch die Niederlandisch Indische Kunst-Ausstellung" from Krefeld. My thanks also to you for this. It is still not very easy for us to read German but there are some things we understood. Going by the booklet (I am just looking at it again), there was no woodcarving there. I thought in Holland there would have been many people besides you who would have had examples to offer; Mr. van Lawick,[171] for instance? The overall impression we can get, however, is how much of the priceless art of almost the entire Indies is now known by foreigners. That is so wonderful for us Natives to realize, and we can't thank enough those who have lent their support for this. This year there will be another annual market in Surabaya, but this time Mr. Jasper will have to find private sponsors. Advances will no longer be offered for the exhibition contributions. But for many workers who do not have any capital, it will be simply impossible to provide samples of their work without receiving an advance. Mr. Jasper thought he might still be able to get a subsidy from the government. We have already received an invitation to go. But now I think that we won't be going because around that time we will have to go to Ngawi for a while, although not permanently.

And now, you asked for information about whether they could make furniture for you here with carvings. It was unforgivable of me that I did not provide you with the information about this as soon as I had found out. The man who works for me, the head of the *desa*, declared he was not capable of doing it, especially not if it had to be made of *sono* wood.[172] But I think the real reason that he does not want to take on any significant jobs is that recently many of his workers have left the area in order to work for traders. (Many have gone to live in Sem[arang] as well.) He definitely said that it was not possible. They are indeed very busy because there is still a strong demand, although mainly for the smaller objects. Also they are not yet as far advanced in furniture making as they are in Kudus. I hope that the Regent of Rembang will be able to help you more in this.

We have recently enjoyed some wonderful days. Dr. Adriani came to visit us. Yes, remarkable, isn't it? We never thought it would be possible and for that reason we thought it doubly nice of him to have done so when he had the opportunity. He was on his way to Holland to see his wife, who is sick and needs him. What sad feelings his visit induced, since, after all, it was at your house that we had met him.[173] But it seemed to me that he had changed considerably, he was older and thinner so that I hardly recognized him at first. Now already it seems like a dream that we had him here, but the days we spent with him were truly unforgettable. Once again I learned so much. And I was so pleased about it because he will soon be coming to visit you and then he will be able to tell you all about us. We have given him a *box dessa* to give to you.

What a pity that we have not yet met your niece, Mientje. She must have continued traveling through to Winangan. And now Didi must be with you already. His resignation surprised me very much and it really pained me that I was not even able to say farewell to him since the letter I wrote him I know never reached him. I was in doubt as to where to send it.

Hassim asked me to pass on his regards to you. His address is c/o Dokter Djawa School, Batavia.[174] The poor boy carries his terrible fate bravely now that he has given himself over to religious contemplation. In that he has found some comfort. He is also progressing well with his drawing, he says. He says he will write you.

And now, dear friends, I hope this letter finds you in good health. From your children here please receive our warmest greetings, and for you. Moedertje, imagine you are receiving a warm embrace from your loving,

Roekmini

Roekmini to Rosita Abendanon-Mandri

Jepara, 21 December 1907

My dearest Moeder,

How will I begin? There are so many things I have done to you over all this time that I have to make up for. None of this was worthy of me, who calls myself your daughter. My dearest friends, only God knows how much I myself have suffered knowing how I have shamed you so in your faith in me. I still love you both as much as ever and the thought that I may thereby have alienated you from me is the least thing I can bear. Can you still forgive me?

Till now, my life has been one of running and climbing and struggling in an attempt to achieve that which one much stronger than me had aimed for. And all this time you two and my other friends, whose friendship provides me with the energy to go on, have never been out of my thoughts. But yes, it is now high time that I gave you some tangible evidence of this. What would you think of me otherwise? But to do so has been so difficult because there are too many sad things that I have to tell you. And because of this I have terribly neglected you both, as well as the Adriani family and Mev. van Kol, my very dearest friends, for the sake of the problems of this world. Forgive me for this again, and again. I am guilty.

I received in good order the copy of *Eigen Haard*[175] that you sent me, which contains a picture of a room of the Queen that has been furnished with the craftwork from the Indies, and I thank you very much for that. At the time I was in Ngawi with Ma and my sisters for my youngest brother. In August we were there again for the wedding of Boesono, who is Regent there. At that time I also learned from Kartono that he often came to your house, which made me so happy, Moedertje, knowing what a blessed influence you two and your home would have on him. You know he has suffered very much, has been surrounded by so many problems which seem almost insurmountable. He has told us everything and so we cannot be more grateful to you knowing that he has come to our friends who will continue to give him encouragement. He has such need of warmth in that strange land where he himself has ruined much, and feels completely isolated because of his feelings of guilt. My poor brother. We here are also very saddened by it of course. Physically, he is also suffering as a result. Can you tell us anything more, Moedertje? When he writes with such feelings of desperation, we too become desperate. Does he still come to visit you often? He has also been to see the van Kol family. You know that he cannot expect the least bit of support from Boesono. Boesono is also acting very strangely toward us, continually trying to distance us from him, and we have had enough of it.[176]

It is still unclear to me how long Kartono is going to stay in Holl.[177] Had he been able to sort himself out then we would be able to accept it, but our mothers, who have in the meantime grown quite old, are continually asking about it, about when they will see him again. They are becoming more demanding by the day, and well, we can never pluck up enough courage to tell them about Kartono's situation. They are still under the impression that he is studying with the support of the Studiefonds and they don't know the pressures he is under.[178] It would make them ill, because they know they would feel unable to help him, to save him. Our mothers have become gray, but, thank God, in many other respects still maintain a youthful fire in their hearts that makes them powerful figures.

And how are things with you, Moedertje? Had I ever replied to your last letter, Moedertje? Oh, I ask this only with great shame and sorrow. I reread it and was overcome with sadness. At the top it states April 16. It is more than a year ago. Don't ever think that your Javanese daughter has no heart any more, keep offering me your trust, dear friends, my struggle still exists and it will continue.

How is Mijnheer, has he now recovered completely? I heard from Kartono that Edi and John are traveling abroad. And Dop and Mary have another little one. How wonderful for you to be surrounded by them all, especially the latest. Don't you have any photos of them? I would so love to see them, those little ones. I can hardly imagine, because it's as if I actually know him in person, that he is now already a father of two. How are you now? Have you not become even richer?

You asked me last time about batiking on silk, as Mev. [van Zuylen-] Tromp had. I enquired about it but none of the Native women here dares to take it on. It is more what Chinese women do. But I will send you a sample, just as I did to Mev. Tromp. The well-known Mev. Jans and some other ladies who concentrate specifically on batik work are also unable to tell me. I still have some silk from Mev. Tromp. I received a request from the Director of the Museum van Land en Volkenkunde in Rotterdam for some samples of *plangi* cloth for which only coloring derived from plants may be used. This year, oh no, I am wrong, in 1908, there will be two exhibitions of Native art and craft, one in Sem[arang] and one in Surabaya. In Surabaya one will be held every year. We have already received an invitation to participate in the committee for the Sem[arang] exhibition.[179] This promises to be a lot of work for us. I am getting busier and busier here looking after the woodcraft work, which, also because of the activities of others, is becoming increasingly more known. And the workers are still able to undertake the work. For them the establishment of the credit bank has been a great boon because it is always ready to provide an advance. The bank takes their work as guarantee, and the great thing also is that when the items are eventually sold and make a profit, this is returned to the workers. It is truly a wonderful creation for the Native in general to save them from the claws of the foreign orientals.[180]

And now I have to tell you that I have applied for the position of administrator at our branch of the bank. The administration thought it was an excellent idea, and with the support of the Assistant Resident, I wrote to the Inspector of Agricultural Credit. But what a disillusionment. This person, after discussion with the Director of B[innenlands] B[estuur], thought that it was better that the position not be filled by a woman because of its perambulatory nature, something which the administration had not even mentioned. Because I am someone who knows the region and its people very well, the Ass. Res. and others thought the idea of my applying for the position with the bank was an excellent one.[181]

In the meantime Controleur Jasper has engaged us, my sisters and me, to work at the domestic science school that he is planning to erect after the exhibition in 1908. It will be for Native girls and, in the first instance three skills will be taught: batik, weaving, and plaiting. The school will be built from the profits of the exhibition. It would have been established last year except that Mr. Jasper had to repay the interest-free loan that he had received to the government so that too little remained, which made it impossible. The exhibition will now be put on a commercial basis, and since Mr. Jasper now has some experience in doing this sort of thing, he has already been able to calculate that this year it will really be possible to set up the school. You can imagine how our hearts are totally filled with the prospect, and how we are in complete agreement with him. However, we are not yet entirely sure if all three of us can go, since Mama would prefer not to live anywhere but in Jepara and the school is going to be established in Surabaya. In any event I have offered my services.

How wonderful it would be if we got to that point for which we have been constantly aiming so that our once-broken dreams could be revived.[182] Oh, Moedertje, I would not want to disappear from the world stage, no matter how often circumstances might suggest to us that this would provide a welcome solution for our battling souls, before I had redeemed myself in your eyes and, in my mind, in the eyes of our beloved Tini and Father; before I had fulfilled my promise to make myself useful. Let me achieve that first and then peace can come to me when it will.

How close our two spirits must have been: just as I sat down to write this letter, Moedertje, I received your so most welcome letter. I was thinking so much about you, I could find no rest while you still had no news from me.

Moedertje, I am still so affected when I receive something from you. On those occasions I am filled with joy, although never totally, since that feeling is always struggling to come to the fore against the feeling of melancholy, memories of another time, of living together with that fine spirit, which, in turn, more than anything else, brings you to my mind.

A letter arrived from Kartono at the same time as yours saying he had come to see you. It's wonderful to know that he is now looking much better; let us hope that the claws which have him in their grip at the moment will eventually be cast off. His letters are still filled with such a sense of desperation and we can't do anything other than sit here with our hands in our laps. Will it last much longer? Couldn't he try other things to get himself out of this position? Here we can only have such a limited idea of what is happening, simply because his capacities are so much greater than ours. Poor boy.[183]

Moedertje, at the time of that great moment in our lives when our dear Tini left us, did you then, like us, feel that this could well bring in its train other causes of grief? But yet we all feel, dearest, that our unforgettable loved one has left behind an expectation, that the glow she had once ignited in our lives would not die out, and that we now feel a deep sense of responsibility for that legacy and will never lose sight of that life struggle. One day the time will come when, if she can, she will look down on us with satisfaction. Oh, Moedertje, it rages within us, it burns inside us, it cries out, but then something else comes to the surface: her love and her belief in us. Since you have shared everything with us, we also feel that your belief in us, your belief that we will make something of what she left behind, is gaining strength. So you are right, it is impossible for this bond to break.

Have you been so ill? Kartono also once wrote to me that you were busy writing me a long letter. That must surely have been the letter you wrote while staying in the mountains. I was so excited in anticipation. Moedertje, in that letter you wrote how you thought it was so strange that I had never seen your family. Yes, that's right, yet the existence of you all has become so much part of my life that I can often forget that. If there happens to be a photo, then I would love to have one. Has John recovered yet? And are he and Didi back home? Yes, Didi and his special personality—I share your thoughts about him that one day we will see him make a name for himself in society. Kartono has also always written so enthusiastically about his abilities, he regards him very highly.

I had never doubted that all of you still hold in your hearts warm thoughts about this country. We know that about each of you that you will all always do your best for anything to do with the welfare of the Native on this island of Java.

What awful news I received from you about Hassim. It's terrible, isn't it? Only a few months ago he was here, although he didn't look us up, but it was not his fault and we both regretted it very much. He occasionally writes to us, but alongside his deep suffering that is almost destroying him there, there are some signs that his spirit is trying to fight back but does not seem strong enough against that other. Poor boy, it's heartbreaking to think how a human being can be tortured in this life, and it will always remain a mystery to us why that should be.

You asked me whether I was tied to a journal. Yes; but at the moment it would be better for me not to do so, because it requires me to produce work quickly and after a while that will have a bad effect on what I produce. So I pulled out of that. I prefer to first read more of the standard works, such as a history. It was only writing for a newly established paper, *Het Damesweekblad van Indië*, that had not yet been too demanding of its contributors. If you have never read what I have written, I will send you some. Now I think that the piece could well have benefited from lying around for a while to mature; as it is I am not really happy with it myself.

I heard from Kartono that you were planning to publish the letters of our Tini. We here think that's an excellent idea, nothing less, especially so that she will live on in the memory of all those who knew her and loved her. We enthusiastically applaud the idea. Where will they be published, Moedertje? We are dying to know. We have just received a photograph of her little boy, a recent one, showing he is already a big *boy*.[184] He is looking more and more like his mother, and our most earnest prayer is that he may become totally like her. We only rarely receive news from his father. But the Gonggrijp family is now in Rembang[185] and so we will hear about how the little fellow is going from them.

My sisters and I live our lives now very much as when I was with the other two. We will also do everything to try to keep that glow alive. There is much in our daily lives from which we can draw inspiration for our spiritual needs. The Ass. Res. family here, or [rather] the Controleur, who it so happens knew Kartono very well in Holl., are very nice people.[186]

But now, Moedertje, before I knew it, I have already filled 9 pages. Next time more. I want to try to answer your questions if I can. Regards to your husband, to John and Didi, our best wishes from us and a warm embrace for yourself from

Your daughter.
And best wishes for the New Year
Roekmini

Roekmini to Rosita Abendanon-Mandri

Jepara, 8 March 1908

Dearest Moedertje,

In the first place many thanks for the beautiful calendar you sent me. What a kind thought of yours, Moedertje. Of course it came in very handy. But how I have let you wait on any news from me. Please forgive me, dearest.

In the meantime I have received a letter from Kartono in which he wrote that he had visited you, driven by problems which have now been averted. What a terrible existence, surely there must come an end to this soon. But I thank you so much for all the help you have been able to give him, Moedertje. The future looks so bleak for that poor boy. And yet he writes constantly, for us to continue to trust him and to believe that one day all of this will come to an end. Yes we do believe and trust him and also believe that he is doing his best to get himself out of the nasty and difficult circumstances in which he finds himself, to keep his promise to us; and in our letters we can't express sufficiently to him our love because that gives him so much comfort. Physically of course he is also suffering from this. I feel quite desperate in the knowledge that in the foreseeable future there is no other prospect for him than having to endure further this uncertain, difficult existence.[187] May God grant that later he will have the power to go through life with sufficient confidence in himself. My poor, sorely tried brother. If only he had been better prepared for what life in that far-off, foreign land would present to him, the temptations and all that extravagance that he did not know about. Now, from the original personality, which did show some evidence of weaknesses, there remains only a set of rather confused character traits that now so embitter his life.

But how are you yourself, dearest? With us everything is fine. Perhaps I had already written to tell you that we have such a nice controleur family here. They are both such extremely polite and well-educated people and still very, very young, so that we have become very close. We do so many things together. At the moment we are thinking about organizing a Dutch course for Natives who are most in need of a European education, such as less well-off young *magangs* clerks etc. who will have very little chance of a reasonable career if they haven't mastered the Dutch language. We already have several students. Mühlenfeld has his magangs and I have the magang and the clerk of the Regent. And then we also have some girls and young women of the Native officials. Besides that, we are also practicing foreign languages and Javanese with that family. The sisters are now having piano lessons again. I will send you some newspapers that include some articles by Mühlenfeld on the education of Native girls. The uncle in Demak has written to me about it. Uncle is of course against us.[188] You will be interested in reading it, naturally.

Mev. van Zuylen has written that she has sent someone to the Indies to study the arts in its many forms and that he, a Mr. Duero,[189] will probably also be coming here to Jepara. I have once again so much to do for Boeatan.

And now, dearest Moedertje, lots of love to you and your husband. With a loving kiss,
  Your,
  Roekmini

Roekmini to Mrs. and Mr. Abendanon

[*Letterhead*] Raden Mas Adipati, Ario Sosro Ningrat, Regent van Jepara

Jepara, 17 June 1908

Dearest Friends,

The letter that I have always been meaning to write to you remains unwritten. I really wanted to thank you as quickly as possible for your kind thought in sending me the picture of Holl. but even in that I did not succeed. At that time we were very busy moving (to another street in the city) and after that we received, for the umpteenth time, such dreadful news about Kartono from someone who had just come from Holland with specific information about him. We were so depressed about that, dear friends, we felt so powerless in the face of this dreadful situation. Of course we don't just depend on the news from one source, it could well be biased, but we have received more or less the same information about our brother from many more people whom we can trust, and the only conclusion we can draw from everything we have heard is that he is in a very unpleasant situation.[190] He himself also writes about this from time to time but not about why he actually does not get himself out of it and try something else, to be more active. It seems he may have to wait a long time yet before he can graduate because he is now completely without means. Why does he not try something else that would put him in a position to get something, something that might in the longer run enable him to bring his studies to a successful conclusion? Many people have advised him to return to the Indies, and one of our friends has asked me to write to him to say that he would gladly help get a position if he would just come home. I wrote this to Kartono but he never replied.

What I now regret most is that he has broken with Mr. van Deventer and a prof. who had always been so friendly to him.[191] Who knows who else he has broken off contact with. Last week he wrote that he had dined with you. That was such a comfort to us knowing that from time to time you are able to have him with you, that perhaps you are keeping an eye on him. Would you know whether it is true that he spends too much time with the Solo princes? Recently we received a photo which showed him with these young Javanese, the Paku Alam and Solonese princes, a Batak person and a former chief justice officer of Solo.[192] How Kartono has changed. We are so saddened seeing him in this condition. I hope the other young people are faring better than he is. It is so terrible what our brother has to endure. Who knows whether it is not just as well that our father and Tini have passed away? You are right, Moedertje. He also wrote that you were busy organizing the letters of our dearest sister in order to publish them.[193] We are so looking forward to reading them. How time flies. It is now almost 4 years ago that our Tini passed away.

Do you know that the Regent of R. has again become a widower a month ago? She also died as a result of giving birth, although this time the baby also died. What an unfortunate man he is. We haven't heard any more about him, he must be quite devastated. We also hear very little about Singgih, but in a little while we hope to meet him in person to ask him how he is.

And now, dear friends, I must tell you something serious about myself. I have become engaged and my future husband is the *Wedono* of Mayong, a district less than two hours from Jepara.[194] This great change in my life only occurred a month ago. I was able to have total freedom in this matter and he is therefore, as it were, my own choice. He is not of high aristocracy (against which the family would have had objections in any case). Indeed he is of quite lowly background, yet well educated and cultured and pure enough of heart to be able to make me happy. He is a *self-made* man, dear friends, someone who has worked himself up from nothing to what are now his not inconsiderable capabilities.[195] He is a widower, 35 years old, and I will become the mother of a girl and two boys.

Everything went the way I had always wanted it. We have regular contact with each other through correspondence. We hit on this *akal* because personal contact is forbidden. But of course so is every form of contact against *adat*, whether mental or physical. So the correspondence has had to be carried out very secretively. Well, in this we had some good luck: our Controleur and his wife, both young people themselves, with whom my husband-to-be is a friend and via whose intermediary we came into contact, are both part of the conspiracy, as are our sisters. The Mühlenfelds in fact are our *"postillons d'amour"*! My letters are included with the official correspondence, and those from Santoso, that is the name of my fiancé, are addressed to the family. So it couldn't be better. We write to each other daily and have now the best guarantee that we will have a happy life together. How often don't I have to think of my two sisters, and how my heart is gripped with sadness when I think that they were not able to do the same. Dear friends, please give me your blessing, please wish the best for me. I don't know exactly yet when the wedding will take place, probably as soon as September because he does not want to wait longer than necessary. Then we will work together for the public good. He is so very liberal in his beliefs and can only be a great support for my work.

As far as the plans for the domestic science school in Surabaya are concerned, the idea that we might be appointed teachers there is not going to go ahead, although the school itself will be established after the exhibition, which at the moment is in full swing. The reason is that here in Jepara it is becoming recognized that a school for girls is just as important as that for boys, and the Native administrators themselves have taken the initiative to request that a school for Native girls be established for us here. Now we are working with the Mühlenfelds for this. He will look after the education of the Native officials and she will give lessons in needlework and similar things. At first we will be teaching from home, but later it will become a government establishment. The main subjects will be Javanese, but Dutch will also be taught, although, because not all the children will have the opportunity to go on with that (for instance the girls from the desa who will also be admitted), Dutch will not be one of the required subjects. At the moment, through the intervention of Mr. Mühlenfeld, a desa girl has received permission to be trained as a pupil teacher, and after her exams she will be attached to our school and come to live with us. Don't you think that's nice? The school will be opened on 1 July, and while I am still free I will also give it my full support.[196]

And then there is something else, an idea I want to circulate among the young Javanese. I will make you a copy of a letter inviting them to join us that will publicize this idea.[197] It is really wonderful to have people around you who share your ideas and feelings. The Mühlenfelds—he especially is a very intelligent and noble man—are doing everything together with us. Apart from that he is also a true blessing for the people, for whom he feels great affection. He is a disciple of Buddhism whose prescripts he follows to the letter, so that he is necessarily a friend of the Javanese, who, deep in their heart, are still entirely attached to this belief. He is also a vegetarian. And what wonderful books they have, and she plays and sings beautifully.[198] Kartono knows him very well. Do you know he was also the person who delivered the official answer from Ma? With us Javanese the practice is for a marriage proposal to be brought by family members of the groom, who are also required to take back the answer from the woman. It was Mühlenfeld who offered to undertake this transaction because he felt so much a member of our family. And on the 14th of this month he went in grand style on our behalf to Mayong. So it was not until the day before yesterday that it was publicly announced.

And now, just as if you had guessed that I would be in the middle of writing you a letter, the mail has brought me a letter from you and one from Kartono. Many thanks for that, dearest Moedertje. What a lot of interesting news it contains for us, dear, for me and my sisters. We are longing for you to complete your work in sorting out the letters of our dearest Tini.[199] Kartono also wrote about this. May this ensure that thereby she will continue to be remembered. We also want to do everything we can to this end, because what we are now is due to her, and her strong and noble soul. And I am also so happy to hear so much good news about Kartono. Thank you so much. What a relief that was, and in his own letter he himself was also full of self-confidence. How easily people upset us with their news. But now we know from the best of sources. It's wonderful that you care so much for him. And for himself that has, of course, been invaluable. I will soon write him a cheery letter.

As far as your question is concerned, as to whether I am having too much work to do in relation to the woodcarving work, I can assure you this is not so. No, I just think it's wonderful because it provides evidence of the increasing appreciation for this craftwork. But I will heed your advice. Things are also improving with regard to the problems associated with it. The Ass. Res. of Central Celebes would also like to introduce this craft there.[200] He has requested that a selection of tools be sent. I sent an especially fine example of woodcraft to the exhibition in Surabaya. It was a screen measuring 2½ meters tall and 1½ meters wide cut out of *one* piece of timber (teak). Should there be anyone interested, it will be sold on the spot. It's a beautiful piece. I will write to you later in detail about all the other things in your letter about the crafts. There is so much else I want to tell you first.

We like the idea that your niece, Nellie, and her husband will be coming to look us up.[201] I would like nothing more than that we get to know more of your family, especially because they are such extraordinary people. We will make them really welcome. Who knows what we may be able to do together for our people, she with such capacities. We could get girls to take advantage of the opportunity to learn from her about some of those things that are so important in our world of women. How wonderful it is to read that so many Indische, or rather Inlandsche [Native], young people, are coming to your house.[202] How enjoyable those meetings must be. The lecture by the Tehupeiory brothers we also read with great interest.[203] Yes, we feel so much respect for that clever trio, and especially that girl. I didn't know that Asmaoen[204] also frequented your house. I was also amazed that he had converted to Christianity. Doesn't he also still have a brother in Holl.?

It is possible that this year a son of our Patih, Achmad, will be going to Holl. to study to become a OIA (*Oostindische ambtenaar*).[205] We will certainly be recommending you to him. I hope you will like him, because he is very pleasant, if a little quiet. It's marvelous to see that things are finally happening for us in the East.

I will send you the articles by my uncle and by Mühlenfeld to read. Yes, you will see in the one by my uncle what a confirmed conservative he is. He constantly goes out of his way to stifle everything we do, although till now he has not been able to succeed. And now I could not have found a better way to tease or irritate him than by becoming engaged to Santoso, who not only is not someone of the aristocracy but is someone who will support everything I do to bring about progress.[206] It has certainly not made him happy, but he has resisted trying to place any obstacles in my way because he feels powerless against our determination.[207] How strange it is also to see that Oetoyo, the Regent here, is also more or less against the advancement of the Javanese. We would never have thought that of someone who has always presented such a different view of himself.[208]

We are looking forward very much to receiving your photo. What sweet children those two of Dop and Mary are. How are the others going?

Next time I will write to you about all the other things you mention in your letter. Give my regards to your husband and children and I squeeze your hand,

    Roekmini

Attachment

A Call to Young Java[209]

For a long time we have regretted that amongst Young Java (that is, those amongst us interested in progress to a new age and, where necessary, in freeing ourselves from the old *adat* in as far as this might hinder us from applying enlightened ideas) there existed no association through which we could express ourselves more powerfully and establish a movement which would have to be listened to.

Several daily newspapers, especially *De Locomotief,* often carry articles which warmly support our cause, but these are mostly by Europeans, even if Europeans with fine intentions toward us. They are not written by Javanese themselves.

But are there among us enough who can express themselves and speak on behalf of the people? If there are, why don't they speak up? Why do the voices of men like "Djono" or "Native" in *Het Weekblad voor Indië* remain as sole voices in the desert?

It is because there is no association, because no communication exists between us. We do not know each other sufficiently, we do not even know what talents there are lying dormant among our people.

Arise then, let us form an organization under the banner of "Progressive Java," which, if it attracts sufficient support, could publish its own journal through which we could work for our own holy cause, the goal of the development of our people; in which we could discuss our weaker aspects to indicate the means by which we could improve; to take up a position against those published statements which we find in newspapers that are less than friendly towards the Javanese, such as the opinion which is so offensive to our nationalist feeling, that the Javanese are untrustworthy.

Whoever shares this aim with us and would like to work with us for the success of this endeavour should inform the first of the undersigned so that if there should be a large enough response, we can begin to work toward this goal.

In order that as many Young Javanese as possible will get to know of our intention, we ask you (and for the important cause this is surely not asking too much) to transcribe this announcement three times and send it to three of your friends of whom you know that they are sympathetic to our views and request these in turn to send out three copies, etc.

    Signed: Raden Ajeng Roekmini
                  Raden Ajeng Kartinah
                  Raden Ajeng Soematri

Roekmini to Rosita Abendanon-Mandri

Jepara, 26 September 1908

Dearest Friends,

My sincerest thanks for your warm best wishes to Santoso and me for our future together.[210] I am really moved to read your words, which are so important to me and reflect such a deep friendship, of love, of sharing with me this important step in my life.

I cannot describe what thoughts went through my brain with all this. On that day itself, 17 August, I especially thought so much of you, my dears, so far away in the West, intuitively knowing how you were also then thinking of me. You were the first witnesses to what lay behind the former threesome, who would know most clearly what that day meant for me.[211] As far as possible the day was celebrated according to the way we wanted. Apart from my two sisters, Soelastri and Kardinah, and my youngest brother, Rawito, the whole family was there, even my brother from Ngawi.[212] Totally unexpectedly, and as if in a dream, Mr. and Mrs. Bervoets also came to the reception, which was such a surprise to us and made us so happy. Yes, they had heard of my plans and, happening to be in the area, made use of the opportunity to see me. It was a kindness on their part and I couldn't appreciate it enough. Your niece and her husband were also going to come, but it was not to be because Mr. Stokvis[213] would have had to take off too much time.

Yes, I did write to Nellie after I received your letter in which you wrote about her and through which I had therefore been able to make her acquaintance. The plan is now for them to stay with us during the vacation. It is so pleasant to have someone again who brings with her something of the good old days. And I think it's wonderful that she is a doctor. Who knows what I might learn from her that could be useful to our situation. I am already looking forward to her coming. What a lovely idea of yours to arrange for Kartono to spend the day of the 17th to celebrate the wedding with you. He wrote me all about it, how he felt seeing the photo of the two of us there, decorated with flowers. I thank you so much, dear friends, that was something that only you could have thought of, something that touches all of us to the core. What mixed feelings Kartono must have had, poor boy. On the one hand happy for the happiness of his sister, for the friendship of people such as you, but oh, how melancholic when thinking of himself. His writing again is so sad. Yes, you are right, Moedertje, it is clear now that Kartono has told us everything, how less hopeless everything appears and how very inconsiderate people have been of our feelings in what they have told us. And I am even more comforted than ever now by the fact that he comes to visit you so often. I think it's a wonderful idea of yours to encourage the young people living there to get together at your house, to discuss the important news of the day and to act on that where appropriate. I assume this has now already started.[214]

I have also received a very nice letter from Didi. Is it possible that we may never meet him in person? It would be beyond words were we to be able to see one of yours here again. Together with this we are sending a photo as souvenir of the 17th August. That will also let you see what Santoso looks like. I receive so much support and attention from him, we are very happy together. How my thoughts often fly back to the past, when we could never have imagined that it would ever be possible to experience a life such as this, given our adat and so on, which, while leaving our minds free held us imprisoned by our feet; that one day I would break those bonds with my very own hands and thereby enjoy such privileges? We will ensure that this beautiful happiness will remain strong.

I have now moved to our new home with my children. I am so enjoying my life with them because they were so friendly and immediately regarded me as their Moeder, especially the youngest, a boy of 5 who had been without maternal love for so long. He just clings to me, and as a result I feel so happy in my new life and it is no effort at all to have the little ones learn to see me as their mother. My husband leaves their upbringing completely to me; it is so nice to be immediately confronted with the real thing. We had to close the school that we had begun in Jepara because of the malaria epidemic during the months of July and August, but the sisters will recommence it after the *Puasa*, that is, after October.[215] Among the Native officials the need to educate their daughters is increasingly widely recognized, despite the declarations to the contrary of my uncle.

And also, the Bond der Jong Javanen will be holding a congress next month in Jogya.[216] That is surely a first brave step, isn't it? Finally the much-dreamed-of moment has happened, to establish a Union among us Natives, a concordance through which we can energetically get to work for all those things that are of importance to us. We have also joined with them, and there are also many other girls who have become members.[217] Don't you think that is marvelous? The idea of the union is just like the plan we had. Our plan had also always been to form such a union, and as a result we immediately got in contact with the organizers, those clever young people.[218] It would be wonderful if we could also get your support. We will write more about this later. Your efforts to set up an association among the young people there is already a great support for us.[219] Because we were so busy with the wedding we were not able to go ahead with this, and it is only now that we are getting to some of the things we had planned, about which we will write to you later.

Moedertje, you asked me in your last letter whether Kartinah might not want to learn to batik on velvet. She would like to very much so that she could later teach this to the girls here.

And now, dear friends, once again our heartfelt thanks for your good wishes for us, also regards from my husband, who already regards you as his friends, as well as from me, who loves you still,

Roekmini

Roekmini to Rosita and Mr. Abendanon

[Letterhead] *Santoso*

Mayong, 28 March 1909

Dear Friends,

Until now it has been impossible for me to get around to writing to you, although there have been so many reasons for me to have done so. In the first place we thank you for your kind attention in sending us that calendar, the scrapbook for the children, for the copies of the articles and the card that all of you had signed on the 17th of August, which is such a wonderful memento for me. For this I can't do anything else but express my absolute appreciation.

But there is another reason that demands that I come to you as quickly as possible to express my deepest gratitude to you, and that is for everything that you have done for our brother so that he has now finally arrived into a safe harbor. That is such a great joy for us all. We know what your friendship and guidance have meant to him, how much this has protected him from further danger and how much this has contributed to his better fortune. You cannot imagine what impact your news had on us. We were so surprised and at the same time that sudden and good news made us so happy and yet also sad. And how must Kartono himself not be feeling? What are his plans now? Will he be coming to the Indies soon? Or does he have to stay in Holl. still? We of course are all longing to have him in our midst again, especially Mama.

As far as the Ver. B. O.[220] is concerned, you will no doubt have read in the papers that it has already spawned many sister organizations. It is really a definite sign of our times, and of the as-yet unarticulated desires we have for a new life. It is a great opportunity for our people. We sincerely hope very much that these initiatives may continue to receive the support of the government and, in time, win the hearts of the conservative Native officials. There is also an organization among the regents whose aim supposedly is to advance the interests of the Native people, but it is feared that it will be more concerned with maintaining its own position.[221] Hopefully, in time the B. O. and that organization will join together, and that would be the finest thing that one could imagine. The young organization, whose highest ideal is unselfishness, will then attempt to hold them to account, it seems to me, rather than anything else. We can imagine how your hearts are beating strongly in support of the movement, which is entirely in accordance with your ideas. The future of our country, as you imagined it, will surely now come into being since the means available to bring it about now largely exist and will now only continue to increase.

The appeal we made some time ago is now no longer necessary because the B. O. organization, which is so well supported, was established almost at the same time, and already well provided for. All we needed to do was to join them, and we have done so.[222]

And how are things with you, Moedertje? How happy I am with your promise that I will be getting a photograph of you both. I am looking forward to seeing whether or not you still look the same as you did.

Very soon we will also be able to send you a photo of the grandchild who is on the way. Hopefully all will go to plan. I am confidently looking to it.

What a tragic ending Dr. Tehupeiory had. We were all so upset when we read about his sudden death.[223] What a great loss he is to society. Do you also know his sister? What a blow it must have been for her and her other brother. We were also very saddened to hear that the very promising son of the Regent of Kutoarjo had to give up his studies because of illness.[224] How strangely things can turn out in this life. What a hard blow this must be for the poor boy. Hopefully in time he will find some comfort to compensate him for this disappointment. Didn't he return to the Indies together with

Didi? I thought that Didi had come here and had already even returned to Holl. We saw his name in the list of returning passengers not long ago.

We have still not met your niece, but we hope to be able to do this shortly. There is much she still has to do first if she is to lead our women in the area of health, for which she has apparently already gained the help of Raden Kamil.[225] And she has first to make a lot of progress in her study of the Javanese language. I am enormously interested in hearing about her plans.

In the course of the following month we have a very good chance of meeting Dr. Hazeu,[226] who will be traveling throughout Java and Madura to give Native officials the opportunity to get the correct information about the latest plans for the establishment of a Native law school.[227] We also would love to have an opportunity to discuss this with him.

And now, dear friend, receive with this our love,
  Remaining your loving,
  Roekmini

[The following two letters from Santoso were attached to the preceding letter from Roekmini]

R. M. Santoso to Mr. and Mrs. Abendanon

[Letterhead] *Santoso*

Mayong, 20 March 1909

Most Esteemed Mijnheer and Mevrouw Abendanon,

It is a great privilege for me to now also enjoy your friendship, and I feel obliged to express to you my gratitude for this.

I have already heard much about you from my wife and also have myself got to know via the newspapers what you have done for our country and our people—and what you will still do—for which I, like many of my countrymen, feel a great sense of gratitude.

We continue to follow with keen interest everything that you are doing for our country far away in the West, and I thank you for your concern to keep us abreast of these activities by sending us your printed articles.

The future that you see for our country is also for us forming an image that is gaining a distinct shape, in connection with which the unexpected establishment of the newest organization among us Javanese can be considered an important contribution. And we will continue to do our bit to maintain the pace of this important development, in as far as my position allows us.

For the time being I am not able to write you as much as I would like because my official duties prevent it. I propose to write to you more often as opportunity allows.

We are very well.
>My appreciation for your much valued friendship.
>My sincerest regards,
>Respectfully,
>Your obedient servant,
>Santoso

R. M. Santoso to Mrs. and Mr. Abendanon

[Letterhead] *Santoso*

Mayong, 28 March 1909

Highly Esteemed Sir and Lady,

Respectfully I wish to inform you that on this day, the 29th, a daughter was born. Mother and child are in excellent health.

I also make use of this occasion, also on behalf of my wife, to offer you my sincere thanks for the garment that you have sent us for the little one—it will be very useful.

>With respectful greetings
>Respectfully,
>Your obedient servant
>Santoso

Roekmini to Rosita and Mr. Abendanon

[Letterhead] *Santoso*

Mayong, 11 November 1909

Dear friends,

Finally I can thank you for your felicitations with the birth of our daughter. As you can well imagine, we are very happy about it, and especially because I had always longed to have a daughter. It had always been my dearest dream to have a daughter, to be able to bring her up in my own way as we had so furiously always dreamt of doing. I would like to give her that which we ourselves received, but then much more, as much, as it were, as her arms can carry and as will benefit her character. Oh, till now a woman has had to become a child to be able to begin to learn, to change from how she has been and still is. Oh, that she may, as one of the rising generation, be able to achieve that which for me, as one of the older generation, is still difficult. I am still uncertain how to raise my daughter, dreaming all the while about what would be best for her future, to enable her to make a contribution for what is still lacking in our world.

We will send you the photo as soon as we have one. Here in the village one cannot get hold of a photographer so easily. She is now five months old and a lovely photo could already be made of her. She is developing well and will soon be able to wear the dress that she received from you, Moedertje. If only she could toddle off to see you to give you a kiss. But still.

I thank you for the beautiful photo in which Doppy and Mary's pride and joy are displayed. You both have not changed much, dear friends, perhaps a little grayer, but in my opinion you look much the same as you did. But what big chaps those two grandchildren of yours have become, those boys of 3 and 1½ years. They look like boys of 5 and 3, and especially the eldest with his serious face, he definitely looks much older. You daughter-in-law also looks well, as does her husband. Is Edi still in the Indies? I had so hoped to see him in our house, but that was just an idle hope. Is it true, as the *Locomotief* reported, that Mr. van Kol will be settling in Java?[228] Could it be possible? And will we be fortunate in the new Governor General and the new Min. of Colonies?[229]

How are your monthly meetings with the Javanese friends going in Holland?[230] You will have read in the papers that this year the second Congress of the Young Javanese was held, but that it didn't go as well as the first one.[231] And there is another thing, which is a great pity. An energetic worker for the young movement has left the executive and has been replaced by the Regent of Jepara, who, although he is educated, gives no indication of being able to make use of his brilliant talents, purely because, despite his education, he has remained totally conservative.[232] In this the Association has made a serious mistake. Why did they have to choose someone like that? If the Association wants to stay on course, it will not be able to get rid of the newly elected member fast enough; if it allows itself to be fooled like this, it will be a great pity, because it will be dangerous for the entire movement. As long as it does not become an association for the regents, this would be precisely more likely to suppress the movement than anything else. No, that surely won't happen. These mistakes will be recognized soon enough and removed pretty quickly.[233]

How are things with Kartono? When is he coming? We have not received anything from him for a long time. Is his thesis not yet finished?

My husband will write to you soon.

Receive with this much love from us all,
I remain your loving,
Roekmini

Roekmini to Rosita and Mr. Abendanon

[Letterhead] *Raden Ajoe R. Santoso*

Mayong, 10 August 1910

Dear Friends,

Your letters of March are still lying here unanswered, for which I ask your forgiveness. It is more than terrible. Given the information they contained, in the end perhaps your letters were just what we needed since we had never really known Kartono's true situation before, while we really did want to know. But you can imagine how your news deeply affected us, and how that the information about Kartono caused us a lot of pain. We can imagine how this had prevented you from informing us about the true circumstances.

How K. has wrapped himself up in mystery. We simply don't understand him anymore. What can his intentions be in doing all this? And what has led him to it? He was so different when he left the Indies. What dark forces have taken hold of him that have caused this aboutface in him? With our limited knowledge of his circumstances (the real ones), we cannot comprehend his situation and can only feel great sadness for him, especially remembering how much is lost in him and our dear departed ones who were so fond of him. What can have gotten into that boy? Now there is nothing also that we are able to do for him since he has not written to us for a long time; it seems that he also wants to cut himself off from us. We receive absolutely no news from him anymore. So now we can hardly express to you the gratitude we feel for what you have done for him; for how tirelessly you have worked to put him back onto the right path; for the depth of your friendship shown to our family which this demonstrates. Oh, it was with great emotion that we read each of your communications. What you have done and no doubt will continue to do could only come from a rare and generous heart, and that is all done for us. We are so grateful, so grateful to you, and let us hope that one day our poor Kartono, led astray by false forces and now prevented by a false sense of shame from showing his face, will be struck by your constant, well-intentioned intervention. Our fervent prayer is that he may return to his old self and that you may one day have the satisfaction of seeing the fruits of what you have done for him.

Now we ask ourselves, what is Kartono living on? What means does he have to enable him to live according to his status? That he is now opposed to the idea of returning to the Indies after 14 years in another environment when he has not yet succeeded in his chosen path, we can very well understand. This we can understand. But that he has made it so difficult for himself, has, as it were, detached himself from all support, how will he survive now? Oh, our heart and head are in turmoil when we think how far he has sunk, he in whom we had such confidence, and loved; who could have been so brilliant and who could have helped all of us as well as his land and people; he who surely did once love us too. It is so strange. We could not believe it when others (before you) had told us that things were going wrong with him. We could not believe it until we had heard it directly. No, it was difficult for us, even if it was something we wanted to know. And now, if it were necessary, we could also not even support him financially. The only one who is in a position to do so is Boesono (Ngawi), but relations between them are not so good so that Mama and we would not dare to rely on a positive response from B. I don't know what will happen. In our view only a change of heart in Kartono himself can help him. What use would a thousand hands be if he persists in his stubbornness? We have seen this in relation to your own noble deeds, where His Exc's kindness towards K. was only met by resistance. If it has come so far, let us hope that his wrong behavior may soon come to an end.

And are you both well, dear Friends? With us things are excellent! I should tell you that in June we made a big journey to Batavia. The purpose was to bring our oldest son, a boy of 12, into the care of the committee there that Mr. Hazeu has set up to supervise young Native students whose parents desire it.[234] Because we live here in a desa, where opportunities are not too good to study, especially for boys (that is to say, to get to a school easily without the child suffering too much), we have decided to let him board in B[atavia] in conditions as good as any that parents could wish for. And so we brought him away ourselves so as at the same time to have the opportunity to meet Mr. Hazeu. We were shown a boardinghouse by the Committee, through whose good offices the boy will also be going to a first-class school. The people with whom the boy will be living are a very nice young couple well able to look after the children who have been entrusted to them. Besides our son, there are two boys from the Maharaja of Deli.

Unfortunately, we could not stay in Batavia very long because my husband's leave was far too short, we later realized, so we did not see much of

B[atavia]. Nevertheless the whole trip was a marvelous break. We also went to Kebon Sirih to visit Mr. Sijthoff, the former Resident of Semarang, but I could not recognize where in the street you used to live, where we spent such a glorious week with you.[235] B. seems to me to have totally changed after all these years. On the way back we again traveled via the Preangan and then via Magelang, and Ambarawa, in other words, largely through the mountains as it was in the old days, which we also enjoyed greatly.[236] My husband has caught the taste for traveling, to relax in this way, and is planning to do it more often.

Unfortunately, we were not able to catch Mr. Hazeu at home, although we did meet his wife, which was no less pleasant for us. We had already met Mr. Hazeu the previous year, however, when he was traveling through Java to try to gain the support of Native officials for the law school. At that time he also came to Jepara and took the trouble to pay us a visit. Of course we were very honored by that, it was such a friendly gesture. Now we are thinking to also steer our boy in that direction (law studies) should he possess the requisite abilities. In B. we stayed with Annie Bruyn-Glaser,[237] who was actually on the point of leaving for Holland, but she was so kind as to receive us anyway. Yes, and from her I know about your plans to let Kartini's name live on, to make her eternal. She asked us our permission with regard to the letters that she had, and of course we had no objection as long as she herself thought they would be suitable.[238] What a wonderful idea it was of yours to do this. We are so happy about this and are looking forward to more news about it.

I am so happy to have a daughter that I can raise all by myself to adulthood in the way we had always wished, and hopefully one day she will resemble her beloved aunt. In these times it is so wonderful to have a little daughter, who carries within her what we could only dream of. I hope our little girl may enjoy life more than we did, and that everything around her will contribute to her happiness. She is such a dear little thing. She is already 14 months old and still you don't have a photo of her. I wanted to get a good studio photo, but there is no good amateur photographer in the vicinity. Can you wait a little longer, dear friends? And can I also thank you so much for your kind thoughts for her first birthday? It was such a surprise for us. Yes, and soon our household will become busier because we are expecting a little brother or sister in November already.

Also my sincere thanks to you for the calendar that you sent me, now already so long ago. I feel ashamed that I have been silent for so long, continue to forgive me dear friends. I have no excuses. Is all still well with

you? And the grandchildren? No doubt they have grown steadily? Mr. van Kol will soon be in the Indies. How we would love to meet him.
Please receive lots of love from us all,
Thinking of you always,
Your Roekmini

Roekmini to Rosita and Mr. Abendanon

[Letterhead] *Raden Ajoe R. Santoso*

Mayong, 5 May 1911

Dear Friends,
What a long time since I have written to you. Will you forgive me? My husband has been getting busier and busier and he therefore apologizes for not having written to you in the meantime. Your letter arrived just when my youngest was born, another girl, and we thank you sincerely for your kindness in sending us your felicitations in advance. It is a very healthy child and is already 5 months old, and full of life.

But in the meantime I have been very poorly and even now I am not quite my old self yet, which is the reason, dear friends, why you haven't heard anything from me for so long. Nonetheless, with each letter we receive we share with you your experiences. We have received everything in good order and we thank you very much for it.

How happy we were, initially, with your news about Kartono's change of heart. But now we have again received painful news about his reversion to his old ways. Oh, it hurts us so, but mostly for you who have been intimately involved with him; for whom nothing had been too much trouble in an effort to save him; to whom he had already shown so many indications of having improved. How is it possible, what has become of his good side? Is it possible that he has lost it entirely and that every expression of it has been merely a pretense? Oh, it grieves me so, it makes me so very, very sad when I think of it, and not the least because this also must affect you. In that respect all I can do is love you more, my dearest friends. You have always been such a support for us, and now will we not need you even more? I do hope that some final solution can be found to Kartono's strange behavior—to really bring him back to his senses. Is there perhaps something that is more sacred to him now than the memory of his father and his noble sister? Is there something that cannot be brought into harmony with that? Poor boy, as long as he continues to follow that which he has chosen over all else, that he believes is the most important thing.

How wonderful, on the other hand, is the news that the letters of Kartini will very soon see the light of day. I received the last news about this from the sisters, and let me tell you that it is an indescribable joy for us all—all those who loved her and respected her so highly. We are looking forward impatiently to the day that your noble work will achieve its outcome. Also we received—our thanks for this—the beautiful edition of the journal *Kunst Oud en Nieuw*, which includes the photographs of the exhibits at the Indies arts exhibition in Brussels.[239] What wonderful samples of the output of our compatriots are on display there. And how impressed I am by the visit of the Jaksa and his exhibit during that time. He must surely have really enjoyed it, and he would have been able to assess the true value of the work of the Natives who were sent for this purpose to the exhibition.[240] But the craftsmen are also an element that is recognized as belonging to an exhibition, something that expresses all that beauty. When I see them like this, so simple and yet the source of so much beauty, then I would also have had to say that they too must also have felt the intensity of it. So now, even in a foreign country, Indies arts are well known. What a fine task Mr. Jasper has now also been given.[241]

Do you remember that I still have the silk material from Pekalongan of yours which was intended as furniture fabric? Do you still want me to send it to you?

We are all well. Soematri is now married and the young couple lives in Semarang. The health situation here leaves much to be desired, you will have read that in the newspapers. We are very anxious about the terrible epidemic that is raging at the moment. The plague. Our menfolk are very busy carrying out preventative measures to try to contain the illness. My husband asks you to excuse him that he does not write himself.

With lots of love from us all,
I remain your loving,
Roekmini

Roekmini to Rosita and Mr. Abendanon

Mayong, 13 May 1911

Dearest Friends,

Another quick note,

I have just returned from Jepara and learned that Kartono's situation has improved again. I read his letter to Mama which said he could not possibly go wrong again. I hope to have confirmation of this from you again, dear Friends.

Lots of love from us all,
I remain your loving daughter,
Roekmini

Roekmini to Rosita and Mr. Abendanon

[Letterhead] *Raden Ajoe R. Santoso*

Mayong, 1 November 1911

Dearest Friends,

I will probably be the last to inform you of the safe arrival of your greatly appreciated gift, the book about our precious Kartini, and to thank you most sincerely for it.[242] And yet by an extraordinary coincidence, mine happened to arrive exactly on my birthday, so that it moved me even more, and in my heart I could not thank you enough. But at the time we were both experiencing very difficult days and Ori was quite ill, several times we feared the worst and for months afterwards we were still worried about her. Only quite recently has she returned to good health, but the poor child has certainly lost weight and is quite weak.

So only now can I send you my belated, yet not less heartfelt, thanks for that which we now have of our dearest one. But now, and I don't know what you will say about this, I have to say that as yet I have not been able to properly look at the contents of the book. Once I begin, I can't really go on. I am immediately overcome with sadness when I begin to read the words through which she presented herself to the world in a way that nothing else could do better. It conjures her up in my mind again as clearly as though she had never left us. You can understand, can't you, that I have to snap the book closed each time. Nevertheless, one day I will force myself to read the whole book.

Of course, because we sisters had always lived together so intimately, the contents of the book are not entirely foreign to me.[243] But we are so grateful to you for your fine work in collecting together all her noble ideas and feelings in that form—and also because the cause for which it is intended will also realize her principal idea: to provide education to Native girls.

We have no doubt at all that you will succeed in your beautiful work. Will you tell me later how that is proceeding? I am longing to find out. I myself can still do so very little for the cause that we both shared, but I do constantly spend much time with the wives of Native officials, trying to introduce Her ideas into their lives, and I constantly encounter a lot of interest. But thus far I have not yet been able to succeed in having girls—those who are already regarded as being of marriageable age—to come to me to learn, at least to read and write. Everything that the parents have heard about and that interests them and that would be valuable for the girls, they only regard as relevant for boys. Just as when "adults," although they know nothing of this yet, they will have to be satisfied with their lot. Even when I once invited the ladies to see a sugar factory in operation,[244] and I had great hopes that the younger girls would also form part of the group, I was disappointed. I was not even allowed to fetch them. But then we are living here in a desa; in the towns, especially the big towns, things are different. There the Native girl is much freer.

I have now dedicated the book to my two little ones, our youngest daughters. I will teach them to love it and respect Her, just as their mother does. As happy as I was before in having two daughters, now the book has appeared, my dear little ones can after all become totally the children of Kartini's spirit. We will raise them completely according to her ideas.[245] That which their mother herself was not able to realize, oh, they will be able to enjoy and make their own. With our oldest daughter, who is now 19, we have other plans.[246] I think I don't have to wait very long now before I become a mother-in-law. Also with her I have done everything within my means to let her experience what was previously unknown.

What wonderful memories the letters also contain of you, Moedertje. I am so moved by that. They fill me with sadness but still I love them so much.

You will no doubt have read that a girls' school will be established on the initiative of a friend of the Regent. Although this will not be in the spirit of the planned Kartini School, it has been influenced by these ideas.[247] We also received from Mr. van Deventer a copy of his article in *De Gids* that discusses *Door Duisternis tot Licht* and your aim in publishing it.[248] Let's hope that everything will lead to the success of your goal to realize the most beautiful idea of our dearest sister.

How is everything with you? As I am writing this I am informed that the doctor has advised that our youngest urgently needs to go to spend some time in the cool mountains. She has an enlarged spleen and an enlarged liver. Poor little thing. She also has to undergo a quinine cure.

How are things with Kartono? Can you not encourage him to write to us occasionally? We don't get any reply to our letters. We would so love to hear something from him personally. It was already such a joy to us to see that the address on the parcel containing the book was written by him. For a moment then he must have been thinking of us. May I enclose here a brief word to him to send him our love?

    With all our love and gratitude,
    You loving daughter,
    Roekmini

Roekmini to Rosita and Mr. Abendanon
[Letterhead] *Raden Ajoe R. Santoso*

Ungaran, 1 February 1912

Dearest friends,

As you will see by the address above, we are now in Ungaran, near Semarang. My husband has in the meantime been transferred to this district. A year ago he asked for a transfer to a place which had a school for the school-age child because eventually it would have become such an expense for us to have her go to school in Kudus. So now they have transferred him and we really deserve to be congratulated for this because, apart from the fact there is a [European elementary] school here, we also enjoy a wonderful dry climate. We are 1,000 feet above sea level here. For our little one it is also a real boon because she had begun to suffer from malaria. We had only just settled here when the signs of improvement already became evident. We arrived here in mid-December 1911, and till now we have been very busy getting the house in order. Your letter and the presents for the little ones arrived safely, for which we send you our sincere thanks. The dress is lovely and both items of clothing just fit. She happens to be of quite fair complexion so all that fine light material suits her very well.

When I received your letter it must have been exactly when you received mine in which I wrote that we had received the book you had sent. I reproach myself for having caused you so much anxiety because I had not written to you immediately after receiving it. Oh, I can assure you that it caused me twice as much grief to have to constantly make you wait on a letter, especially when you had sent me such wonderful news, which was really bad of me. There was no question of waiting for your felicitations with our youngest child though, dear friends, we know that very well.

I would love to meet John. It would be a great pleasure to meet someone related to you. Yes I could really long for that very much. Which company does he work for? Where will he be stationed? In East Java? Of course I will try to help him, as you have urged me to. We well understand that you both hated to see him leave and we also wish the best for you and him.[249] Is it really possible that we might finally actually meet him? I long so to meet someone who can speak about you, who was so recently in your presence.

Can you imagine, last week, to my surprise, I received a letter from Kartono. He must have written it when he was with you. He says he had read you some sentences out of this letter to me to you. He writes with such sadness, it was so full of self-recriminations, that it saddened me greatly to read his letter. I never know exactly how I should think about him. His unaltered love for us shines through clearly, and I believe that, but I think now, and this may be true, that he is too weak to connect to this great love for us the self-control necessary for him to be truly regarded as being of much worth in the eyes of others. No doubt an outsider would think what a complete egotist he is, but, oh, that's not it, he is just weak, terribly weak in character. In fact, one should feel sorry for him because I know that he must be the one who suffers most of all of us in those moments when he can be himself. Such self-reproach, such contrition in his writing: even I found them almost unnatural from someone whom we know as being of quite a different nature, someone whom we respected so much. Is there perhaps also some misplaced pride involved, which explains why he can get worse and worse? In fact, he also wrote of his gratitude to you. That made me feel a lot better. Yet it saddens me so much now to think how he can disappoint you, how your noble interventions can be rewarded with such ingratitude sometimes. That boy, oh that boy, surely it is almost unforgivable, one would think. God only knows how it will end up. We earnestly hope it will all turn out all right.

No doubt you already know the news that Dr. Hazeu has been appointed Director of O[nderwijs], E[eredienst] and N[ijverheid].[250] What a fortunate choice on the part of the government. Now we can expect good times, much better than previously, now that he is at the head of these branches of government. After you left our country, the loss of such a leader who devoted himself wholly to his task, has barely been compensated for and now we have your equal. Wish us well.

25 February

Another few days have passed without being able to continue writing this letter to you. In the meantime I have received a copy of the talk by R. M. Noto Soeroto.[251] It has again moved me greatly, just like every other heartfelt expression of admiration for Kartini and her idealistic work and the light that your noble work has shed upon it.

Because you have been waiting so long, I will send this piece off to you now.

    Remaining your loving,
    Roekmini

Roekmini to Rosita Abendanon-Mandri

Ungaran, 17 March 1913

Dearest Moedertje,

Your long letter and following that, your postal order (25 guilders) arrived safely. And I must tell you that I immediately did what you asked by giving Kartinah, who is still in Jepara, the request. I also clearly explained to her to use the design on the cover of *Door Duisternis tot Licht* as the design for the decorative carving work. Kartinah has already sent me news that the *tukangs* [craftsmen] have already started and, as long as you are not in too much of a hurry, the frame will be ready in time. The photo you sent is still with K. and I will send that back to you.

Mrs. [Hilda] de Booy[-Boissevan] also wrote to me several times recently seeking my assistance for her work in relation to our Kartini at the exhibition. I think it is very nice of her that she also wants to make the effort to contribute to the revival of Kartini's ideas.[252] It is such a touching gesture of hers. It's a great pity that such a great distance separates us and that we can't get these things done as quickly as we would like. And here is another example: we need to provide her with a description of Kartini's life as a child and as a woman. I only hope that I won't be too late. I will gladly give her an account of everything I know. It will be such an interesting exhibition and I am sure that the idea Mrs. de Booy has will be a great success.[253]

In the meantime Mr. and Mrs. van Deventer have returned to this country. How quickly he got to work in setting up the K[artini] V[ereniging].[254] And the latest news we have is that already 113 students have enrolled for the K[artini] School.[255] It was such a pity that we were unable to come to visit them as often as we would have wished in the time they were in Sem[arang]. For us it is still so difficult to get down there. But we could not appreciate enough their kindness when they came to make us so happy with a visit to us. They immediately made such a nice impression on us. It was like the way we felt when we were together with you, as if we had known them personally. It was such a pity that they did not find Mama and Kardinah at home and continued to miss them after that. Mama regretted it greatly. Quite naturally the conversation also turned to Kartono, but when I saw that they could not reveal everything to me—this topic was quietly passed over. It saddened me, but didn't they fall silent on this subject in my best interests? We continue to follow with great interest what he has to say about what he has seen and experienced in the Indies.

In the past two weeks we have also received letters from Kartono in which he wrote that he would be finished in June, yet he wrote in such a dejected tone. Oh, it continues to sadden me hearing from him without actually being able to sort it out, to get a clear idea what the true situation is. May God this time truly have pity on him and allow him to finish this time.

No doubt you know Mr. M. C. Brandes, Director of Cultures in the Principalities, the brother of late Dr. J. Brandes.[256] He will quite probably already be in Holland now. In the months shortly before his departure for Holl. he stayed in Ungaran and so we got to know him quite well. We found in him a great friend and came to know him as a fine person. Naturally you will also get to know him. He had also done so much for the Kartini Association and the K. School but because that can't be made public yet, I am not allowed to tell you yet. He is such a great friend of the Javanese. So many Javanese who needed it have benefited from his help. I am so glad that you will be able to get the latest news about us from him. Unfortunately he does not know Kartinah.

To get back to the question of the frame, I sincerely hope that the craftsmanship will be to your satisfaction. I let Kartinah read your letter so that she can see for herself what your intentions are. We like the design for the decorative work very much, but it will have to be explained very clearly to the tukang and I trust that Kartinah will do that, since all of us are equally devoted to the work of our woodcarvers.[257]

You have been to Spain, your fatherland? How you must have felt after all those years of separation. I can imagine how moved you must have been in seeing your beloved country again. And what a beautiful country Spain must be.[258]

At the moment here in the Indies much is being discussed and undertaken for the Javanese, as you will have read in the papers. There is much work being done in the public interest which will please you and all the friends of the Javanese. You will also have read that a female candidate has applied for the Native doctors' school but because a free course of studies for female pupils does not yet exist (which means she cannot be an intern), a fund is being established by several women so that such girls can be assisted in their studies to become a doctor.[259] The wheels are already in motion and the inspiration for everything is our own unforgettable Kartini. There is so much being done in all those organizations that hold her up as a model, to work for the good of all in the name of Kartini. Her ideas are taking hold and they provide encouragement.

If only you two could come and have another look at the Indies and especially in Java. Could that ever happen, dear Moedertje?

How are your children and grandchildren? Is John still in the Indies?

And now I hope that your last wish might come true that Kartono will continue as he is now. He has had his letters addressed to you. I am therefore hopeful that he will now arrange his life differently from before. I hope so. I hope you will have success from all that you have done for him. How could we ever make up to you for what you have done for him?

With us everything is fine and in May we are even expecting yet another citizen of the world.

Much love to you from all of us,
Your loving,
Roekmini

Roekmini to Rosita Abendanon-Mandri

Ungaran, 12 September 1913

Dearest Moedertje,

I don't know how I should come to you to explain this unfortunate situation, about a matter which had your fullest confidence and great expectations but which will now reach you as a complete disaster. Oh, I am so upset about it, I hardly dare to write.

The frame that you had ordered to hold the photograph of our dear Kartini has been incorrectly made.

Kartinah said that I had sent the incorrect measurements but she must be wrong because I had given her your letter as well as the photo that you sent with it and the former contained the measurements for the frame.[260]

What a shock I had myself when I received the frame, and it still saddens me. As well as that, as you can tell, the tukangs have certainly taken their time with it.

I could not write to you earlier, dear Moedertje. In May I had my third child. On the 10th day I became really ill, and since then, for the past month I have been suffering from trouble with my legs. Things are gradually improving. But my little boy is doing very well.

I am eagerly following the news about the exhibition, but I am constantly struck by how I have disappointed you. I can't forgive myself. I thought I had been doing the right thing by sending your letter to Kartinah so that she would have a clear understanding of everything. And I had regularly asked her if she had understood everything clearly. At that time she had to go out of town quite often to see my sisters, so no doubt because of that the tukangs worked at their leisure.

But for all that, I feel most responsible. Oh, I can't forgive myself that I have disappointed you in this. Kartinah has also written that the frame cost 20 guilders but forgot to also mention if she had also spent 5 guilders on postage.

Next time I will explain further.

Please be assured of my deep regrets about this sad affair, dear Moedertje. I hope that you will still be able to use the frame for some other purpose in relation to our dear Tini. I am also including the photo with this. I hope it arrives safely.

With my deepest apologies I take my leave from you,
Warmest regards from my husband,
Your loving,
Roekmini

R. M. Santoso to Mr. Abendanon

Ungaran, 4 May 1915

Highly Esteemed Sir,

I hereby take the liberty, also on behalf of my wife Roekmini, of writing to you on the following serious subject for which we have need of your greatly respected advice and assistance.[261]

As you will already have heard, our uncle, the Regent of Demak, Pangeran Ario Hadiningrat, died on 2nd of April this year, leaving behind two sons, the Jaksa of Salatiga, Poernomo Hadiningrat, and the clerk of the Controleur of Ambarrawa, Nooradiningrat. According to some opinions, neither of them will be eligible for the position that has now become vacant because neither of them has the necessary qualifications, as announced in the circular of the General Secretariat of 29 November 1913, no. 2744, and will consequently be passed over for the vacant position. A better-qualified candidate, even though not a relative of the deceased, will be appointed in his stead.[262]

In the abovementioned circular, among other things, it was expressly stated that to clearly ascertain the suitability of a candidate, he not only has had to serve in the lower positions but also to have successfully served at least two years as District Chief or as Patih and as well be able to understand and speak Dutch.

I believe that I have fulfilled all these abovementioned qualifications for the position of Regent, namely, I have already served 26 years, 18 of them as

Wedono. By decision of the Director of Internal Affairs of 3 July 1914, no. 1074, I have been awarded a salary increase from Jan. 1913, and I am in possession of the junior civil servants' diploma while my wife, Roekmini, is a niece of the deceased Regent.

We therefore wish to turn to you to respectfully request you to lend your kind support and assistance by agreeing to intercede for us with the government, to request that I be taken into consideration for this position.

We respectfully thank you in advance and extend our respectful regards to you and Mevrouw.

>Yours faithfully,
>Your servant,
>Santoso

R. M. Santoso to Mr. Abendanon

Ungaran, 8 November 1915

Highly Esteemed Sir,

In the first place we thank you for your communication with regard to what you have been able to do for us in relation to the Demak position.

We have had to wait a very long time for the government's decision, which has only been announced recently. However, contrary to all our expectations it was the Patih of Ngawi who was the fortunate person.

What kind of person he is we don't know. In the paper only his appointment was mentioned, no details were given about his career. It is said he must be the son of the Regent of Magelang and married to the daughter of the recently retired Regent of Panarago. In making the appointment it appears that the government has been very circumspect in filling this position and will have paid careful attention to the newly established criteria. Also in the appointment to lower positions, as of 15 June according to Govt. Resolution of 14 Jan., new criteria will have to be observed.

As of now, the only Natives eligible for appointment to the Native Civil Service will be those who possess specific documentation that confirms that they have completed a 2nd class Native school course or higher educational institution for Natives, while on first appointment, those with higher-level qualifications or who have received a higher vocational training will be appointed ahead of those with a lower qualifications or lesser training.

We believe that such prerequisites are the correct ones. However, there are too many alternative qualifications and vocational training courses allowed for Native civil servants. For instance, those eligible for the aforementioned position include, apart from those who have completed a 5-year HBS and the civil service training school, also those who possess a certificate from the trade school, the Catholic Orphanage School, and other educational institutions which have nothing in common with the necessary qualifications and knowledge that might be considered relevant to the functions of the civil service.

As a result, we will later have a corps of Native civil servants with different perspectives in terms of academic qualifications and proficiencies, which will be of less practical use to their position and as a result of which no or little improvement will be achieved among the majority of Native officials. Consequently, they will continue to be far below their European colleagues, of whom constantly higher academic and skill qualifications are required. The Native officials then, just as it is the case now, will be able to do little more than be the ones to carry out orders. They will then continue to be regarded by European officials generally as inferior in all respects since in fact they will not be able to work with the Native officials because of their partial knowledge and qualifications.

Any European official of whatever branch of the service, on the other hand, is especially qualified for his job because he has the requisite training for the job that is entrusted to him.[263] So, for instance, a forestry official would never be able to fulfill the position of a controleur, or a president of the Land Council would not be appointed as assistant resident, whereas, according to the new regulations, the appointment of Native officials is structured in a completely different way, namely, that persons trained in the law school or in the trade school can become assistant wedono or wedono if they happen to be in possession of a diploma of the civil service training school or an HBS. It would be better if it had been determined that only those who were in possession of a final diploma from the Training School for Native Officials could be appointed as a Native official (ass. wed., wedono, patih, and regent), while those who had certificates confirming their completion at European first-class schools would only be appointed up to and to the level of Mandur.

Persons trained at other institutions, such as the R.S. or Doctors School, must only be appointed to those specific positions for which they are qualified. It also seems to us as more appropriate if the Civil Service School is directly linked to the Training School for Native Officials just as the Higher Teacher Training School now is linked to the Teacher Training School for Native teachers, so that the former would act as a kind of higher institution for Natives intended for the civil service.

At the Training School and Civil Service School the candidate Native official, however, should receive a better and longer period of training so that these men can become not only better officials but also men of knowledge, of culture, and with practical expertise. A govt. official should be more up to date on the latest developments in every area and be able to discuss everything.

We will end this letter now in order to send it with the mail of this week. We will send a follow-up letter very soon because we still have so much we would like to say on this subject, and to whom else could we entrust it but you? There is no one but you both who has constantly evinced a strong affection for us.

How have you both been in the meantime?

We cannot tell you how the news about Kartono saddens us. On another occasion we will write about things at home.

With this please accept our warmest regards and sincere gratitude.

Your,
Santoso and Roekmini

Roekmini to Rosita and Mr. Abendanon

Ungaran, 6 June 1916

Dear Friends,

You both will no doubt have been surprised that we did not keep our word about writing to you again as soon as possible after our last letter. The reason for this is a very sad one. We lost a child on 17 November 1915. My firstborn, our dear little Ori, who was 6½. Now you can imagine why. It was so terrible, especially because it happened so quickly. Since childhood she had suffered from malaria, which did improve greatly with our move to Ungaran. This time it was also a malaria attack that affected her, but it seemed so insignificant that we hardly noticed it until, on the fifth day, it suddenly took a fatal direction and the child was lost to us. I can't remember what the doctor called it, that which brought our dear thing to her end, but it must have been something special because he had only seen three such cases in his 12 years' experience.

Oh, dear friends, you can imagine what a heavy blow this was for me. I myself became ill thereafter, so ill that people also feared for my life. After that there was a very long period of convalescence, I just could not regain my strength and I felt so tired—all I was allowed to do was to lie down and rest, rest. I was ill for more than 4 months, and it has only been in the last 2 months that I have felt better.

So for us it has been suffering upon suffering. Fortunately, we had Mama with us, whose wonderful presence helped me to recover as nothing else could.

And it is only now that I can write about our irreplaceable loss.

My husband has been so busy he has not had time to write. He does not have a single day off in the week in his job, not even a Sunday, no time to relax—the work of a "government official" is after all so all-encompassing.

Our little one was such a dear happy little thing. She had just been going to school for 6 months and was so keen about going, and she would always say, "I so love Aunty Kartini." It was really strange but when I talked to her about our unforgettable dear departed she would always say: "I want to go to Tante Kartini," and now she is actually there with her.

Oh, I can hardly write because my wounds weep so. God grant that I may one day be able to think back calmly on my dear one in peace—now I find it too difficult to think of her.

Can I ask a little something from you, dear friends? Could you pass this letter on to Kartono and Annie Bruyn for them to read? I thank you for that in advance.

> Please receive our regards,
> I remain your loving,
> Roekmini

Roekmini to Rosita and Mr. Abendanon

Jepara, 16 December 1916

Dear Friends,

Your letters in which you gave expression to how deeply you shared in our great loss we received here in Jepara—and for this our sincerest thanks. As it happened, my husband was been transferred to Jepara in September as *Ondercollector*. It is quite ironic that we have come back here to the district that has so much significance for us. Mama is of course very pleased about it.

The dark side, however, that hangs over this relocation is that my husband is coming here as Ondercollector, which for him means that it was not a promotion, and it also means that getting a little higher up the ladder is now more or less impossible for him.[264] It all happened rather suddenly. It was never something my husband had expected, nor at all the kind of promotion that it had been suggested he might one day be offered.

We had thought for a long time that my husband had an opponent whose influence was quite significant. For instance, all the work that my husband has had to do, all the difficult and almost impossible tasks for which, each time, he had been promised excellent recompense upon completion, had all been aimed to catch him out. All these things he was able to complete, so that we had always been optimistic. But no, each time some other task was dreamed up for him which was designed to bring the victim down.

That opponent was a highly placed Native official of the region who could not bear that my husband had sufficient courage to stand up to him, was not sufficiently servile and who in so many ways showed that he dared to be his own man. This of course is "not done" on the part of a subordinate. And for that reason my husband was constantly a thorn in the side of that official, who wanted him out of the way. European officials with whom my husband had worked were surprised at his transfer to deputy collector and asked whether this is what he himself had wanted. Yes, making use of the blind trust that the Resident placed in him, especially where it concerned a subordinate Native official, the opinion of this highly placed Native official has usually been accepted without question, resulting more than once in galling the lives of his subordinate officers.[265] At the moment we plan to patiently put up with everything; what good would protesting do given that the Resident is convinced of the correctness of everything that the Regent advises him on? We cannot live our lives only for ourselves; we must also, and more importantly, live for our children, mustn't we? You may perhaps receive another account of my husband's transfer, but as God is our witness he has only ever tried to do his best in the service. But that is enough on that subject.

We have had a photo taken of us by an amateur Chinese photographer. It did not come out particularly well, but you will still be able to gain a good impression of our children. I will send it to you with the next post. The eldest boy is not included. Yes, I also wanted to write to you about this one.

The boy has constantly performed well in his studies. Each year he was promoted with very good results, and now he is already in his fourth year of the HBS in Batavia. We therefore have every hope that next year he will go into the fifth class. And now, dear friends, because he has been continually doing his best, Mr. Hellwig, who is also a member of the Committee of Supervision for young Native students, has proposed that after completing his HBS he be sent to Holland for vocational training at a technical school. We have our reservations because we would not be able to afford this, but Mr. Hellwig reassured us that he would arrange for this and that we would only have to make a small contribution toward the expenses of his stay in Holland. Once the boy is in Holland, we would then love to see him in your care, that would be a great reassurance for us. He is a boy about whom the Committee has constantly expressed its satisfaction, also in terms of his behavior outside his studies. I hope that you will be pleased with him. Initially our plan was just to enter him in the local law school, but now that he is at HBS he will be studying law in Holland.[266]

In your last letter, Moedertje, I read with great satisfaction how much pleasure you had from your circle of Indonesian friends. What energy that Siti Soendari has. We have always admired her when she worked in the Indies as editor of the magazine *Wanita Soewaro*.[267] And now she is in Holland studying for her elementary school teachers' certificate?[268] Oh, dear friends, when I read how you are surrounded by Natives, what a deep melancholy comes over me, yet of course I don't begrudge any who have had the good fortune of experiencing all that they now enjoy.

With just as much interest we have been reading in the papers about the organizations in connection with which your names have been mentioned. Only it grieves us so when we think of Kartono, who has brought you so much disappointment. Till now we still don't rightly know what he is doing. You, who have for so long shared our lives with us, we can only thank and thank again for everything you have done for him, and if he has not conformed to your expectations we can only ask your forgiveness. Yes, if only we could meet you once more, and bring our children to you! What an unforgettable moment that would be.

I now have only two little ones, Kayati (Yati), who is 6 years, and a boy, Srigati, who is 3½. And if all goes well, next February God will compensate us richly in the form of another little one. We suffered so much with the death of our little girl. It was as if God did not want our trial to be too lengthy or too severe that we were so quickly recompensed. Wish the best for us, dear Friends. I am feeling very well, I try to face life with optimism.

Then there is another boy in the photo aged 13 who is still in the elementary school but is not very bright. We hope that he will improve as he gets older.

At the moment we are still living in with Ma because we still have not been able to get our own house.

My husband finds his work quite enjoyable. It is steady work and it will allow him to recover from the physical and spiritual damage caused by the disappointments and struggles he has had to live through in his previous position.

I am currently engaged in a regular correspondence with Kardinah about her sewing. We have agreed to try to establish in Jepara, the land of origin of all the beautiful new ideas concerning Native girls that are now springing up everywhere, a school just like hers.[269] The land of Kartini! Jepara has over the years become quieter and quieter, but we will do everything we can to realize our plans.[270] We will of course call on your much-valued assistance, dear Friends. Jepara especially must not be left behind! It must have some indication that it is the source of all that which is significant for the Native woman. You will soon also be able to read in the *Loc[omotief]* about the Van Deventer Fonds, which will establish a school for more extended education for girls.[271]

And now, dear friends, I must hurry to catch the mail. Next time more! We just read that peace negotiations have begun! We hope it's true that the great misery that affects the largest part of the earth will finally come to an end.

Please receive our warmest regards from Mama and us both and many kisses from the little ones,
Your loving,
Roekmini

Roekmini to Rosita Abendanon-Mandri

Jepara, 15 December 1919

Dear Moedertje,

In the first place let me thank you very much for your generous gift and your letter. It is a great relief for me since, to date, I have still not yet received my pension.[272] My health is improving after my having been feverish for the past month, but I have not yet completely recovered. People still think I am looking poorly. I have been resting and my appetite has returned. Gradually I will return to my old self again. My children are doing well and they are helping me to get back to being my old self; they are bringing me back to life.

In the meantime, however, Mama and I have experienced more miseries. Mama is living here in a rented house where she has been for the last year. Now suddenly the owner has been bankrupted, has had to sell all his houses including the one where Mama lives, and now the new owner wants to live there himself. There are no other houses for rent. You know how small Jepara is, and now we are obliged to leave. And to top it all off, we have been robbed. It was quite an impudent robbery. They stole items of silver of mine and Mama's tortoiseshell *sirih* bowl, which Ma always had beside her bed when she slept. This beautiful heirloom that Ma had had for half a century and which she greatly treasured was rudely taken from her. It was very fortunate, however, that at the time Ma noticed nothing of what was happening; what may have happened otherwise, had she been awake? Yes, those people must have noted well that in our house there would not be any danger of being confronted in their work by any members of the stronger sex. And now we are faced with the choice of going to live in either Tegal[273] or Semarang[274] or Kudus.[275] My brothers and sisters are offering us these choices and we still don't know what we will do, but at the end of this month we will hold an auction. For Mama, leaving Jepara is not something she wants to consider, but there is no other solution.

From your letter I gained the impression that you did not go to the Canary Islands. So, will you be spending the winter in Holland? How that will please Sardjono. I have just received a very lively letter from him. Yes, he certainly is a boy who is full of life and energy, especially when he is telling a story. Oh, I really had to laugh when you wrote that Mr. Abendanon almost wanted to take up horse riding when he was talking about that so enthusiastically. He had also written to me about the occasion when he had been given the wildest horse to ride, I literally feared the worst. I even wrote to him not to be so *brani,* but he will have thought me silly to have worried so. Hopefully all will continue to be well with him.[276]

His younger brother is just like him, full of life and energy, and an enthusiastic admirer of horses. And he also seems to take after him in his interest in studying. If he has to go to the Grandpa and Grandma in Holland,[277] then he thinks I should also go with him, otherwise it would not be so nice.

I should also tell you I have finally received some information about Singgih from the wife of the Resident of Rembang; I am sending part of her letter to you along with this. I hope you will be able to do something for him, whatever you think will be best. The Regent refuses to answer any letter that comes from any member of the S[osroningrat] family, and no one knows with whom he is boarding in Sem[arang]. We so long to see him, this child of our beloved Kartini, but none of us have succeeded in doing so. It is a very strange attitude on the part of the Regent.[278] What on earth can he be thinking of? During her life with him Kartini was always just as loving toward the other children as she was to him.

Now I should also tell you that I have also received a letter from my son Soedjono[279] in which he asked me permission to leave the Technical School. He finds the course there too difficult and wants to find a position. Judging

Letters from Roekmini 169

by his report it does look as though he is not cut out for study, although initially I thought that he would do well. But now he is complaining so much. He will be coming home during the Christmas holidays, and then we will discuss with him at length what he will do if the course is really beyond him. I am considering whether to suggest to him to take the training course for Post and Telegraphic Service. He is really quite a different character than Sarjono. Whether or not he follows a course or gets a position, for which, however, I think he is still too young, we will definitely be making a decision this month and I will let you know the outcome.

And now, dear Moedertje, to you both the thanks from our children and me and kind regards from Mama,
    Your loving,
    Roekmini

Roekmini to Rosita Abendanon-Mandri

Jepara, 24 December 1919

Dearest Moedertje,

Many thanks for your letter of 5 Nov. in which was enclosed a second postal order, which I put aside because, as you know, the first one also safely arrived and I have already received the money from the Ned. Handels Bank in Semarang.

For the moment I have enough for the children, Moedertje, but then it depends on Soedjono, the boy who is studying at the Technical School in Jogya, whether the amount you have offered will be sufficient. The situation is like this: the boy has been complaining, and this is the second time that he finds the course too difficult; he is not complaining about his boardinghouse. There he is staying with sons of wedonos and *mandur goeroes* who are attending the same school. His first report was not too good, the second he does not have yet. If that should also prove to be unsatisfactory I am considering transferring him to the Tech. School in Semarang, where the course is only three years. As well, he would be closer to home so that I would definitely be paying less for his board. I am going to try to find out if the Tech. School in Semarang is in fact easier. I will recommend to Soedjono to at least do one year of technical study and not to give up too soon. If it really appears that he does not have any talent for this, then I will enter him in the course for the Post and Telegraph Service. Then he would be earning a salary while undergoing training beginning at 45 guilders because he would be classified as someone who had passed the entrance exam for the K[oning] W[illem] S[chool]. So everything depends on Soedjono because the two little ones are still costing me so little. As soon as I am a little more certain about this I will write to you.

How pleased I am that Sardjono has passed once again. Let's hope he continues this way so that he will quickly move up the rungs of the social ladder.

I have read the reports of the K[oninklijk] O[nderwijs] C[ongress] with great interest, especially the last one on girls' education.[280] I really enjoyed this. Much wonderful progress has already occurred in this field, the attitude amongst young women and girls is already so positive, so that if everything that has been established and still has to be done is completed, what won't we see then?

I didn't yet know about the plans of the daughters of the principalities, and I would love to know more. I do know that in the principalities there is now more freedom for girls of the higher classes.

I received a letter from Dr. Adriani when he arrived in the Indies, which I thought was very nice of him. He was planning to come to Sem[arang] if he could. Who knows if he will not be able to stretch it a little further to Jepara? How it would please me to see one of our old dear friends again.

I only know a few poems by Noto Soeroto, which I think are very beautiful.[281]

Please receive our best wishes for 1920, my dear friends, accompanied by lots of love from us all,

Your loving,
Roekmini

Roekmini to Rosita Abendanon-Mandri

Kudus, 4 March 1920

Dear Moedertje,

I still have not answered either of your two letters. Please forgive me, Moedertje. I have had so many things to worry about and still do. But let me before anything else thank you for sending me your postal order for 250 guilders. I have already used up the second one.

I think I wrote to you last when we were preparing to move. Now we have already been here in Kudus for about 2 months. We live in a solid although rather small house but in a much better climate than in Jepara. We are fine and the children all look healthy and well fed.

How are you? Do you still have that pain in your face? And did you accompany your husband again on his travels? Yes, now that the road is free again such a lot of people are traveling to and fro. I hope that Mr. Pleijte will be coming to the Indies again.[282] I received a letter from Sardjono with very good news, including that he spent the Christmas holiday with you. I just hope that he remains healthy and well for the time he is in Holland.

What you wrote to me about Soesalip[283] did not surprise me, although I cannot understand what the Regent might have in mind in acting so strangely, also toward us the family, who he does not wish to have any contact with the poor boy. We do not know much about him. I sent you that letter from Mrs. Frolich,[284] which you must have received already. That letter was in answer to one of mine asking for information about Soesalip. It says exactly the same as what the boys wrote to you, although I find those letters, and especially that from Soesalip himself, rather unlikely. I hope that you two may succeed in rescuing the boy from that mysterious situation. The fact that S[oesalip] is still only in the first class of the HBS must be because that is what they have made of him. He must be a clever boy, and he could have got just as far as his half brother. It's so strange, and Kartini had always been so loving toward them, the children of her husband; so strange how they then should have treated that innocent boy, and the family of hers in such an unfriendly way after having experienced nothing but love from her. The only one who cares for him and shows him some love apparently is a loyal servant, a former garden boy of his mother. Isn't it enough to make you weep? Poor, poor boy. Let's hope that one day his lot will improve. They have not deserved this, his mother and he, poor Soesalip.

But now I must write to you about Soedjono. After the Christmas holidays he came home for good. Without informing me first he wrote to the Director of the Technical School where he was that he was leaving. He gave as his reason the fact that he found the course too difficult. Both his 3 monthly reports had been very poor, and although the Director advised him not to give up and to give it one more try, Soedjono chose to leave the school. He has never been intellectually very strong, and each time he is confronted by some difficulty in his work, he loses confidence and he gives up. That's what has happened this time too! Now he thinks he might enroll in the MULO[285] (or otherwise he would look for work), but just to be sure I have consulted with a head teacher who advised against it since a student with below-average abilities would not do very well there. Knowing the boy as I do, I think it would end up there just as at the Technical School and would be a waste of both time and money. So I told him what the head teacher advised and he became more insistent on looking for a job. I had the idea of finding him a job here in the immediate vicinity so that he could then live with us. I found one: he was able to get a position in the Afd[eeling] [branch] Bank. With a K[lein] A[mbtenaars] Ex[amen] [junior civil service examination] certificate he has the possibility of rising to adj[unct] ad[viseur] [assistant supervisor] at a salary of from 300–500 guilders and he would be able to remain stationed here. He liked the idea himself. Until on the day that he had to arrive at the office to begin work. He left home but after that he could not be found anywhere, not at the bank, nowhere. He had simply run away. You can imagine what emotions overcame me. However, in the evening he returned home but refused to answer any of my questions. Did he want to do something else? Would he please honestly tell me what he wanted?

The following day he came to me to tell me that he wanted to join the service, as a sailor. In normal circumstances I would have burst out laughing, but now—it seemed impossible to convince him of what that would entail so I am giving him some time to think of some alternatives. With the Post and Telegraph service perhaps. There he would have to undertake a course of about 7 months but would already receive an allowance of 35 guilders per month. I have heard nothing more from him.

Moeder, it is really not an easy thing to raise boys such as this, and as a woman I have felt myself powerless. Oh, if only Sardjono were here, if only his studies were finished, he would be able to help me make something of his brother, to make him see things more clearly. Well, my idea now, Moeder, is that if Soedjono is no longer going to school, I want to suggest to you not to send me any more money. Although my pension has not yet been organized I would prefer to arrange for the maintenance of my children by myself. Otherwise you will make it far too easy for me. I hope one day to be able to repay you the 500 guilders you have sent me, Moeder.

And now about my pension allowance. I naturally put in a request myself. But, as well, the Ass. Res. and the Regent's family and other European residents here have also asked on my behalf for more or a higher amount, as I wrote to you earlier. I knew nothing of this until Mrs. Kroesen, the wife of the Ass. Res., wrote to me about it. Well, I was of course very grateful to receive so much friendly interest in my situation but never thought that it would lead to any difficulties for me. From various things it has now become apparent that these friends have asked for a higher pension for me because they thought that I had to support the two older boys during their studies. I had never told anyone, Moedertje, what a noble gesture you both had shown me by paying for the education of the two boys. It has always been difficult for me to do this, but now, when it becomes clear to the Resident that I am receiving support from family and friends, there will be no grounds for the government to provide me with a pension. (The Resident is currently investigating this.) Against my better judgment I have therefore kept silent about this, Moeder; only my brothers and sisters know about it. My conscience about remaining silent about your noble deed has come to the end of its tether. And now, several days ago, I had to answer several questions that had been sent to the Ass. Res. telegraphically by the Director of B[innenlandsch] B[estuur].

1. How much did I pay per month for my son in Holland.
2. How much did I pay for the boy going to school in Jogya.

From this I first realized that these were the grounds, my having to pay for the education of the two oldest boys, upon which friends had requested a higher allowance for me. In the first few moments I didn't know what to answer. If I told the truth, that I did not have to pay anything on their behalf, what an unfortunate impression the Resident would get of the well-meaning friends! So then I took my second questionable step, this time, Moeder dear, to protect the honor of my friends here. Look, I answered as follows: For Sardjono I paid out 20 guilders pocket money; for Soedjono nothing since he was no longer attending school and is looking for a job.

Moeder, do you think this was cowardly? Oh, I did not realize that these matters would lead to such dark consequences. I felt deeply ashamed of my actions, but Moeder, in relation to Sardjono hadn't I always intended one day, one day to repay you the financial assistance you gave us? We can never thank you enough for your noble gesture, but were we able, we would do our best to return to you everything you had given us. Oh, your selfless act has so greatly embarrassed us, has moved us deeply, and we will not just simply accept it, Sardjono and I, once he has finished his studies.[286]

Well, when my pension will finally be paid I do not know. It has now become such an affair for me. And it is still not finished. To make matters worse I received a letter from the head of the 1st Office of the Dept. of War in Bandung. I will send it to you, you will appreciate its implications. It says that I should be "careful sending money to Sardjono."[287] Oh, I am so ashamed of myself about my big lie. Can you forgive me? I have now told you everything, I have hidden nothing from you. You who have been so good to us.

You had better let Sardjono read this letter also, it is better for him to know what I have done, then my real self will be revealed to him as well.

I am so grateful to God that Sardjono continues to do his best and that he remains such a good pupil of yours. God grant that he can resist all temptations that come his way that may lead him from the good path. There are so many terrible examples of this.

Now dear Moedertje, I grasp the hand of each of you and she who loves you embraces you,
    Roekmini

p.s. Adriani will visit us on 29 March.[288]

Roekmini to Rosita and Mr. Abendanon

Kudus, 16 September 1920

Dear Friends,

In the first place let me thank you for the two postal orders you have sent. I have wanted to write to you for a long time but till now was not able to, and again because of Soedjono. No doubt you have heard from Dr. Adriani that I had to go to Batavia to find a boardinghouse for S[oedjono]. Yes, when Dr. Adriani was in Batavia I asked him to put me in touch with the official charged with the supervision of Native youth. S. was going to take up the training course for beginning personnel with the Post and Telegraph Service in Batavia. Since I have no relatives in Batavia who could help me look for comfortable and moderately priced accommodation for S., I turned to the abovementioned official, Mr. Verschuur.

Mr. Verschuur was able to assist me with everything, and with his help S. was soon placed in a comfortable and moderately priced boardinghouse. That was in June. For one month all went well. Then in August I suddenly received a letter from S. telling me that he had resigned. You can imagine how shocked I was. Later I also received a detailed letter from Mr. Verschuur explaining about the resignation. S. had done nothing wrong—he had had to wear glasses and ordered a pair. But when they did not arrive and the Director constantly made it known that S. would be sacked if he did not wear glasses, S. decided he would resign first in order not to be fired. It was Mr. V. who managed to bring all this out into the open, that is to say, he managed to get the Director to readmit S. But S. was stubborn and left for Semarang. He remained there and didn't even come to me, doesn't even write to me any more. One fine day the Ass. Res. here received a letter from S. from Semarang in which he asked him to provide S. with a letter of good conduct because he wanted to enter the cadet school in Magelang.

He was given one, but I don't know whether he really did go to Magelang. I enquired as to whom he was living with in Semarang. Nobody knew. At least he is not staying with family. When your postal order of June arrived it was the time when I was able to buy him a bed and cupboard for his room in Batavia and arrange his board and lodgings. That furniture is therefore now superfluous. My intentions were good in putting S. into the care of real Europeans. But the boy refused to recognize this because of his inability to concentrate. In desperation I am now just willing to let him go to the cadet school, where I will no longer have any contact with him, because now he doesn't even come to visit me nor write and I don't even know anymore whether I would be able to discuss everything with him.

I regret it so much for Sardjono's sake that I have to tell you about this, especially since I think that it could only be him who could direct Soedjono. I wrote to him, therefore, that now more then ever I will welcome with great joy the news that he has passed because then he would be able to return home soon. His brother needs him, needs him desperately.

My fear is that his future will be bleak if he continues to be so willful, continually ignoring the advice of his elders and betters and thinking he can just jump from one position to the next without considering the consequences. I expect that Sardjono's forceful character would have a good influence on him if he were to take him under his wing. I am so sad that I have constantly to send such bad news about S.[289]

How are you both? I am so sorry to hear that you have cause to complain about your health. Didn't the stay abroad help any? Here we are all well, especially the children are in good health.

The little 7-year-old was promoted to the 2nd grade and continues to get good monthly reports. He has Sardjono's character and also physically looks a lot like him. His little sister of 3½ is also a clever little thing, she has such delicious fat cheeks. She is always demanding books, just like her brother.

In a few months time we hope to be able to move into our own house. You should know that Ma and I have come to the decision to have a house built. The shock of what we had experienced in Jepara, of having to move so suddenly, is still fresh in our memory, so we decided to slowly have our own house built. So I sold all my bits and pieces, and mother did the same. Many small things go to make one large thing. When we had collected an amount of around 5,000 guilders, a beginning was made with the construction of the house. That was on 20 May. It was fortunate that we had a good friend here who offered to arrange everything in relation to the building. So we have turned *pusakas* [heirlooms] into material value that will be of much greater use to us; we were driven to it but we will never regret it. For country people and older folk the safest thing to do is to be able to live in one's own home, and so that which is most important must be given priority. And given that brazen robbery, isn't the best thing to own nothing of value? And then again, there seems never an end to the increases landlords demand in rent. Also Kudus is a very lively place; there is a possibility that they will establish a higher elementary school here. It would mean a lot to our children if they were deprived of access to further education. We are so pleased to see that gradually higher education is being made available in Java.

Moedertje, I do so hope that you will soon recover from the pains in your face.

My recent bad experiences have turned me into an old woman, and I too have been unwell. No doubt Dr. Adriani also found me much changed physically.

It is true then that Sardjono has been granted a conditional pass? That's true, isn't it? When does he have to do his supplementary exams?

And now, Moedertje, until next time. Lots of love to you both from all of us,

Yours truly,
Roekmini

Roekmini to Rosita and Mr. Abendanon

Kudus, 21 December 1920

Dear Friends,

I received a letter from Sardjono in answer to mine in which I had explained to him my long silence. Together with that letter I had also sent one to you. Then I received a letter from you in which you asked me about what you had sent in the first half of the year.

But I had written in my letter to you that I had received everything and I expressed my gratitude to you for this. Now once again I have received from the H.U. (Netherlands) 250 guilders. Dear friends, once more my thanks for everything.

I can now tell you that in the meantime I have received my pension, and with a cost-of-living increase it is 52.50 guilders. Then, since October, by decision of the Director of Education, I have been appointed to teach needlework at the H.I.S.[290] here for 4 hours a week, for which I receive 50 guilders per month. In 1921, that will become 75 guilders if a new class is created. It is possible that something else will become available for me in the future. When recently the inspector spoke to me, he asked me whether I would be interested in entering government service as a Fröbel teacher when a Fröbel class is added at the same school.[291] If I was interested, he would recommend me to the Director of Education. I told him I would gladly make myself available if I had the complete support of the inspector—because I would never dare to apply on my own initiative since I did not have the qualifications. The inspector reassured me that if I put in an application then he would strongly support me. I think it's so kind of him. I only met him briefly, and now look what he is prepared to do for me!

I only hope that it will be sufficient because I do not have the diploma. On the other hand, it is true that I have read some Fröbel books, but it wasn't actually a study. And now that I am already earning 102.50 guilders per month I wanted to ask you, dear friends, not to send me any more money. Would you do that? Could I ever repay you what you people have done for me? We were at the edge of a precipice and you saved us from the fall. What would have happened to Sardjono without your very generous support?

He has already written to me that he has completed his supplementary exams, about which I am so pleased. The dear boy, how he does his best both for himself and for us. And now he only has one more exam to do. I hope he will complete that with flying colors. And now I want to tell you a little secret. You won't let on will you, dear Friends? Our dear Sardjono has a girl in mind with whom he would one day like to be united. She is apparently a sweet, intelligent girl, a Sundanese girl, the sister of the Patih of Batavia, and is currently working as a teacher at a HBS in Meester Cornelius. She has been a constant factor in his stay in Holland in keeping him firm and focused, and now, Moeder, S. has given me the task of going soon to ask for her hand. I will do so with pleasure, he certainly deserves it. But don't let on that you know about this. At the moment, while there is no certainty as yet, he is very shy about it.

As far as Soedjono is concerned I have nothing new to write to you. You know everything there is to know.

Mama is very well and the little ones also. And, apart from the fact that I am teaching at school, I am also giving lessons at home to grown-up girls in all kinds of domestic subjects.

How surprised I was when you wrote me that John's oldest boy was already 15. How time flies. How nice that the family has increased. May Didi's family also become so large.

And now dear friends, may the New Year bring you new good times. May you stay well.

    Love from us all,
    Your loving,
    Roekmini

Roekmini to Rosita Abendanon-Mandri

Kudus, 24 February 1921

Dear Moedertje,

I have received your letter containing a postal order. Once again I thank you very much for this. But have you not received my earlier letter, Moedertje, in which I informed you that I was now receiving 130 guilders a month altogether, so that, in my opinion I have enough for myself and the children? And also, that in January we moved to our new, our own, house, so that house rent is another expense that has been removed. I want to please ask you not to send us any more for our upkeep. Truly, dearest Moedertje, we now have exactly enough to allow us to live contentedly.

You are still so concerned about us. In recent days God has given me back my good health. Since I have been teaching I have regained my health and my dear little ones are also well. Even Mama is still *keras* [strong].

And now I can also write to tell you that after the *puasa* holiday, that is to say from the beginning of the new school year, I will get an appointment as Fröbel teacher at the same HIS where I now give needlework classes in the afternoon. As Fröbel teacher I will be a government employee. I had the good fortune of being recommended for the position by the Deputy Inspector. He was determined to help me get a government position once I had applied. Because I was capable of doing this work, I did it, submitted an application, as the Deputy Insp. had suggested. And now I have been accepted. I will be receiving as initial salary 75 guilders and I will only have to work till 11 o'clock.

What a life I will have then, Moedertje? I am so happy now that God has enabled me to work by granting me good health. My prayers have been answered, that one day I would be able to stand on my own two feet and not be a burden to my family and my children.

And the children have a right to an unfettered future so that when they finally have their own families, then their children alone will depend on them and I, their old mother, will not have to be a burden.

All is still not well with Soedjono. He lived for a time in Semarang without doing anything, and he never came home. Then an uncle of his, the head *Jaksa* of Semarang, forced him to come and live with him. Even then he persisted in not wanting to do anything until finally his uncle got him a job at the State Railways in Madiun.[292] For a month all went well, but now he has left once more to find something else. It is tragic. That uncle blames everything on to me. He blames me that I never paid any attention to the boy. Anyway, that uncle accuses me of being the wicked stepmother.

He doesn't dare say anything to me; evidence is that he didn't even write back to me when I wrote to him about Sardjono. I have heard everything from others. Maybe he thinks I am not worth anything, that might be the reason.

For this reason I would prefer that Sardjono not stay away for too long once he has completed his final exams, for Soedjono's sake. That boy is heading straight to his downfall. If only he had listened to me. I am prepared to make one more attempt to try to draw him (Soedjono) to me as long as he contacts me!

But it is so wonderful that Sardjono takes such care, it's such a comfort for me now, after all my grief. Everyone here is also so impressed by his steadfast character and his aptitude for his studies. In the beginning I had been so afraid that things would turn out as they did for Kartono. It was such a comfort to me in those days that he consistently showed that he was better than Kartono, and was able to appreciate your precious friendship far more than he could.

To you all the warmest regards from us all and with a warm kiss,
Your loving,
Roekmini

Roekmini to Rosita and Mr. Abendanon

Kudus, 25 May 1921

Dear Friends

Let me reassure you both of our sincerest sympathy in your time of deepest sorrow. I read in the Loc[omotief] the sad tidings of the passing of Mev. Cohen Stuart. May you both find comfort from life's sorrow and struggle. Is she Mr. Abendanon's only sister?

I earnestly hope that you will both be quite well when you receive this.

Are your grandchildren well? I have had very good news from Sardjono. I hope that he will be able to complete his state exams with great success. What a great satisfaction that will be for you, and for me it will be my greatest pride and joy if he can deliver you that happiness. He has such praise for the hostel for Native young people.

With us here everything is fine, although I am not able to tell you definitely whether or not Srigati will be promoted to the next class. I hope very much that he will, all his previous reports have been good.

Soedjono also appears to be doing well, as he himself wrote to me only a few days ago. Perhaps I will be meeting him in a few days' time. He is planning to ask for some leave. How fortunate it is that he has come to recognize that he had been going down the wrong path. He is progressing well and he is currently receiving a salary of 180 guilders per month and is still stationed in Madiun.

And friends, in a few weeks' time I will take up the position as Fröbel teacher. I am very anxious about it because I have never done any studies for it. But I have a good reference book and I hope that I will gradually work my way into it. Anyway, I will learn on the job.

I have heard from people who know that Soesalip was promoted to his next grade; have you heard anything more from him?

Please receive warm regards from Mama and lots of love from the little ones,

>   Your loving,
>   Roekmini

Today, 25 May, Srigati turned 8.

Roekmini to Rosita and Mr. Abendanon

No address, no date (c. 1921)

Dear Friends,

I received the wonderful news about Sardjono's success in his final exams. I thank you so much for letting me know so quickly. I was moved. And my deepest thoughts went out to his late father, and to you both who safeguarded the boy's welfare as if he were your own son. But I am also grateful to Sardjono that he delivered us that satisfaction by constantly doing his best for all this time. And he also has made up for what my own brother has done to you. How pleased he also must have felt at that moment, but also he must have felt sadness when he thought of his dear father. Who would have ever thought that we could have suffered so many setbacks in such a short period of time. And when can we expect him back?

I immediately told the members of my family and also our friends here of the good news.

We would now like to see him return as soon as possible, but for him to say farewell to you and the country that he has got to know so well will be difficult. But he is not intending to stay on to do further studies, is he? And how a certain young lady here must also be hoping to see him back soon. I think I have once written to you about her. I do so hope that the two will tie the knot soon. For the last month I have been working, dear friends, but because of my inexperience I have been suffering from a sore throat from time to time. I have 40 children in my class and it's no easy task to maintain order sometimes. Fortunately I only have to work till 11.[293]

Now that I am in government employment they have taken away my pension. I now get 167.50 guilders per month.

And now I must also tell you that Srigati has been promoted to the third grade. The boy is good at his studies and in good health, just as his 4-year-old sister and his mother are. He too was overjoyed by the news of the success of his brother. I haven't heard from Soedjono for some time, but he is still working with the railways in the Oosthoek. And how are you both? S. wrote that you were on a trip to Paris.

We send you our warmest regards,
Your grateful,
Roekmini[294]

Report by Roekmini for Maandblad van de Vereeniging voor Vrouwenkiesrecht in Nederlandsch-Indië

THE INDONESIAN WOMEN'S CONGRESS IN JOGYA[295]

On the 22nd of December 1928 a great event took place in the world of Indonesian women, the First Indonesia Women's Congress, whose aim is to form a Union of all Indonesian womens' organizations for the benefit of Indonesian women in general.

This event that symbolized the new spirit of the times for Ind. Women was a great success.

Hundreds of interested participants of the female sex attended the public forums, where lectures were presented on important matters relating to the woman, the child, marriage, education, etc.

These presentations were attended to with full attention. Lectures rapidly followed upon another especially because they were not debated. Further information, though, was gladly provided afterwards.

The Union, called Perikatan Perempunan Indonesia, has its headquarters in Jogya, where most of the executives of most of the women's organizations are also to be found. The executive is formed from their representatives:

President: R. Ng. Soekonto (Wanita Oetomo)
Vice President: Roro Moegaroemiah (Poetri Indonesia)
Nj. Ajar Dewantoro (Taman Siswo)
Secretary: Roro Soekaptinah (Jong Islamitische Bond)
Members: R.A. Hardjo Diningrat (Wanito Katholiek)
Roro Moendijah (Aisiah)

All organizations outside Jogya were admitted as ordinary members of the Union, whose representatives or members could be appointed to committees. Of the 24 organizations represented, 18 have so far become affiliated.

The PPI is completely neutral so that nothing of a religious or political nature was discussed at the Congress.

The PPI decided to publish its own journal which would be funded by the contributions from members of member organizations of at least ƒ1 per month.

It was also decided to establish a study fund for less well off girls who showed good ability for study and to work for the suppression of child marriage, for which support from the colonial officials will be sought as well as of members to explain the to people why it was wrong.

Apart from that, there was support for the promotion of the scouting movement and encouraging interest in it amongst girls, with free choice of uniform.

Subsequently, a motion will be forwarded to the government urging the provision of financial support for the widows and orphans of all Native civil servants and to establish more schools for girls.

It was also decided to direct a motion to the Islamic Court asking that a marriage certificate also be provided to the woman so that the respect accruing to her as woman and as wife will be increased. It was hoped that a congress would be held each year at different places to be determined.

As far as possible the Union will attempt to be self-supporting so that in the first instance it is proposed to refuse all outside assistance however much the offer of such support is appreciated.

Given the achievements of the Indonesian woman today, of which the Congress is a good example, we can look forward to a good future.

Kudus, January 1929   R. A. Santoso

Chapter 2

LETTERS FROM KARDINAH

Introduction

The initial letters in Kardinah's correspondence document not only the beginning of her adult life but also the initial crisis in the history of the "cloverleaf," the trio of sisters who, since at least 1897, had been reading, discussing, and planning their futures as reformers. For reasons that remain unclear, it was the youngest of the three who was selected to be married off to a distant cousin. The emotions generated by this crisis would emerge again upon Kartini's marriage two years later. Kardinah's apology to Rosita for allowing this to happen is echoed later by Kartini. Both women perceive that their "castles in the sky," which had for so long sustained the correspondence with their mentor, had crumbled. The correspondence suggests that the shame they felt in the presence of Rosita was of more significance to them than the experience itself. In a sense, they inhabited two worlds, and it was in the "modern" world that this shame produced the most pain.

Despite the earlier strength of feeling toward her, Kardinah resumes her correspondence with Rosita only after a gap of nine years. One wonders why she had not previously breached what seemed to have become a psychological impasse since, as Roekmini reveals, Kardinah had continued to correspond with her sisters. This sibling contact appears to have increased after each had received a copy of the 1911 publication. Each evidently felt reinspired by being reminded of the idealism of their youth. Kardinah then quickly recalls and rebuilds the historical bond with Rosita, thus couching it in terms of a recommitment to the ideals that they shared. The subsequent letters underline Kardinah's intention, as now the most socially senior (or successful) of the sisters, to take on the Kartini legacy for the benefit and advancement of Indonesian women. This renewal of commitment, as is evident with each of the sisters following the publication of Kartini's letters in 1911, leads in each case to quite distinct outcomes, expressive of their particular views, personal circumstances, and social contexts.

Central to Kardinah's story is her account of setting up a school for girls in Tegal, despite lengthy periods of serious illness. This, rather than the Kartini Schools, can be said to represent Kartini's immediate legacy. It was, first, a significant advance over earlier examples of *kabupaten* schools, such as the initial Jepara school, which had since become increasingly common. Like most nongovernment, nonmission Western-style schools at the time, it was centered and dependent on aristocratic patronage and local sympathetic European colonial administrators for support. In contrast to the Dutch-funded Kartini Schools, however, the driving force, curriculum design, funding, and control of Kardinah's Tegal school largely came from the Javanese community.

Apart from detailing the aims and progress of her school, the letters on this subject by both Kardinah and her husband Rekso Negoro guardedly but persistently express their criticism of colonial education policy. They reveal the distance that separated even the most "associationist" Javanese from the most "progressive" colonials in the definition and implementation of a reformist project, a distance that expressed itself in the detail and vision as well as in the implicit sense of national consciousness their letters suggest. This sentiment also permeates, as we have seen, Roekmini's correspondence and that of the younger Kartinah and Soematri.

Herein, as much as in the information the letters provide, ultimately lies the primary significance of the correspondence. As letters, as vehicles for the personal expression of feelings consciously intended to be conveyed to recipients on the other side of a racial—though not political—divide at a particular moment in time, they document a growing self-consciousness and self-confidence in a national conscience. By the second decade of the twentieth century, Kardinah reflects beyond her sense of a Javanese national trajectory, replete as it still was with a sense of noblesse oblige particular to the *bupati* class, an awareness of the land beyond. The rest of the archipelago remains, however, clearly "the land beyond," presenting no threat to her Javacentric view.

Kardinah's belief that her social position obligates her to do something for her people—a responsibility that, like her sister Roekmini, she thought should not be assumed by foreigners, although they clearly also had a responsibility—also reflects the political play within the wider Javanese political community. While one cannot doubt that the initiative for the Tegal school, Wisma Pranowo, was Kardinah's (as her husband's official correspondence in relation to the subsidy application attests), it can also be seen as reflecting the growing tensions within the political groupings in Java, between the *kaum muda* on the one hand and the Javanese traditional hierarchy on the other, and between the liberal-minded Javanese associationists and emerging Javanese radicals. In isolated Tegal or Kudus, these tensions were not yet (in the middle of the second decade of the twentieth century) so apparent. Yet, as a declared progressive, Rekso Negoro was linked to the politically aware bupati dynasties that ruled Central and East Java, who balanced their hold on the traditional sources of power with the need to conform to the ultimately telling requirements and arbitrary power of the colonial regime.

On the one hand, then, we see the Tegal bupati, like that of Ngawi and the Jepara, displaying his reformist credentials to demonstrate his right to rule. On the other hand, we hear of the *Wedono* Santoso and the sons of Roekmini's uncle failing to gain their expected promotions as a result of new demands—or corrupt intrigues. We see Sosrohadikoesoemo and Santoso—and indeed Kardinah and Roekmini—attempt to pull strings by appealing to well-placed colonial friends to assist in achieving expected outcomes in their pursuit of the gains to be made within the colonial system for both personal and altruistic benefit.[1]

Kardinah was ill for long periods of her life. Letters by her sisters reveal lengthy periods of medical treatment in Semarang and Batavia. From Soematri's later correspondence we learn, however, that by the thirties, after a life as raden ayu, much of it spent in the service of her people, she eventually retired to Salatiga, where she was joined by her mother, Ibu Ngasirah. In the end Kardinah outlived them all, passing away in 1971 at ninety years of age.

While all four sisters lived to see the birth of the new nation, the only surviving record we have of their response is the glimpse we get from the very last letter in this collection. The seventy-five-year-old Kardinah, writing in response to Hilda de Booy-Boissevain following the death of Roekmini, expresses the same, one might say, patrician, concern about "the people" that Soematri expressed in the thirties. The letter celebrates what was probably the last existing link between the olden times and the new: half a century earlier Hilda had met Kardinah and her two sisters for the first time in Batavia. In 1913, Roekmini had prepared a biography of Kartini for Hilda, which Hilda used in a series of speeches throughout the Netherlands to raise awareness of (and funds for) the Kartini School project in memory of their sister. The letter also serves to close the circle: Kartini, Kardinah reveals, had become officially recognized as one of the pioneers of the new nation.

Kardinah to Rosita Abendanon-Mandri

Jepara, 1 December 1901[2]

My dear, dear Mevrouw,

How can I express my deep gratitude and emotions for these lovely gifts to Moedertje, who is so sensitive and attentive, and gifts which *you* and only *you* could have thought of, and which your daughters so greatly appreciate. Thank you, our most heartfelt thanks, my own, dear Mevrouw, you have made Moeder so happy, as well as her daughters. I fondly take both your hands in mine and in my thoughts kiss them both repeatedly.

Moeder is so happy with her cloth and will keep it as a treasure with her other valued possessions. And what have you done: you have once again spoiled us. Had you not sufficiently spoiled us already when we were with you?[3] My dear, kind Mevrouw, thank you, thank you, and once again thank you for everything. Could I now but fly to you to warmly embrace you and tell you how happy we are with all these fine and beautiful things that you had given us and continue to give us! Have we really deserved this? Or I at least, your *kleintje,* has she deserved it that you continue to keep her in your thoughts? Is she worth every thought that is expended on her? No, no and once more, no, I have not deserved it, if you knew everything then you would never, never be able to think of me again. You will not be able to understand what troubles me at this moment, you must think I am mad, don't you, being so secretive. But be patient, I will explain everything to you soon, now I am much too overwrought and could not possibly think rationally and calmly.[4]

I am not able to write any more, forgive me. Should I have made you anxious, do not write back to me before I have written to you again and also do not say anything about this to my sisters—may I ask you this?

Now, good-bye dear, dear Mevrouw, many, many regards to you from everyone from,
Your kleintje

Kardinah to Rosita Abendanon-Mandri

Jepara, 2 December 1901

My own dear Mevrouw!

Forgive me, forgive me, you and Mijnheer also, that I have made you sad and that I have brought you this disappointment. Forgive me, I have accepted the proposal and the marriage will take place in January or February.[5] Do not despise me, do not push me away entirely, continue to love me a little, still feel some fondness for me, my very, very good friends.

I have not done wrong, I have simply done that which I regarded as my duty to my Parents. Oh, I plead and pray to you: judge me not. I suffer, I suffer because I know that I have disappointed you and have torn a wound into your heart. Continue to love me, continue to love me, that will give me the courage and the strength to make me happy, both now and in my remaining years. Pray for some happiness for your kleintje, pray for her future my dear Friend, my Good Angel, knowing this will allow me to meet my future courageously and make me happy. Do not grieve over me, do not think of me with sorrow, my dearest. I have made my Parents happy and I am grateful that it has been granted to me that I could bring these dear ones some happiness.[6]

I am writing you this with eyes worn out with crying and a prayer in my heart for forgiveness and for a little love.[7]

Comfort my sisters, my darlings; they suffer, they suffer, help them, oh, help them.

And also do not think too badly of my Parents, continue to love them, continue to give them your friendship and support. May I ask this of you, do I still have a right to do so? Oh God! Just reply with one word if you can and tell me that I am not wicked and that you are still fond of me. Do not write anything to my Parents about this before the engagement has been made public will you please.

And now adieu, my friends, forgive me, forgive your kleintje.[8] I will follow this letter with my heart.

Your kleintje

Kardinah to Rosita Abendanon-Mandri

Jepara, 13 December 1901

My dearest, dearest Mevrouw!

I must write you once more, I cannot rest for a moment before I have your assurance that, despite what has happened and what must still occur, you still love me a little. If I could only tell you how terrible it is for me, to cause you grief—yes, I know and I can feel that you grieve, that you suffer, and it is all my fault. Oh, forgive me, please forgive me, my dearest, please always love me and be kind to me, your kleintje, who so utterly, utterly loves you and who will continue to do so even should you deny me the right to love you. I know I deserve nothing else but your contempt and that I no longer have the right, or am able to make my claim to a place in your heart, oh, I know this only too well and I suffer terribly because of this. Know that my days are spent in a terrible state of anxiety eagerly awaiting the mail which may bring a letter from you in which you will tell me that you are still fond of me. But each day brings me nothing but disappointment and yet, despite the great disappointment and the sorrow I feel, I will not give up the hope, no, I will grasp it firmly with both hands, that I may yet receive a letter from you which will contain marvellous tidings for me. Dearest, you do want to make your kleintje happy in this way, don't you?

I understand that you were not able to write to me immediately upon receiving my previous letter, you would have waited with this until you had become a little calmer; after all, it is my fault, I should not have written to you so soon. But nevertheless it has happened and there is no possibility of my recalling it. I have become oh, so calm and have been made happy by the happiness of my Parents; I never tire of looking at my Parents' eyes sparkling with happiness.

Let us forget what there once was, please, dearest, try to do that, I already do so as do my sisters, but oh God, how hard it is to walk over the ruins of what were once my beautiful ideals with my head held calmly and proudly erect and at the same time not to lose my senses. But I want to and shall do so and will apply myself with all my strength to do what I intend. I laugh loudly every day and am always merry, and why not, no one, apart from you, need know what I think and feel, what it is really like in my heart, no, no one has anything to do with it. But I can still always write to you, can't I, I can still always pour my heart out to you, for you I want to open my heart always, and shall make you a partner of all I think and feel and will experience. I may do this, may I not? Now I pretend to everyone that he was my choice, do you approve of what kleintje is doing? You yourself don't even yet know who he is. He is in fact a child of my father's sister from a previous marriage, the Raden Ayu Regent of Tegal, and is the Patih of Pemalang.[9] Please write to me soon, I yearn so for a letter from you.

With this I am sending you my album with a request to you, Mijnheer and brother Edi, to write some wise maxims in it. You would make me so happy if you did, dearest.

And will I also get another photograph of you and of Mijnheer and if brother Edi has no objections, also one of him? We will now have to make our acquaintance in this manner, since if he comes later, I will no longer be here to be able to thank him in person for his support.

What impudent questions I have put to you. And now, good-bye, good-bye, my dearest, I always think of you.[10]

Your Kleintje

Kardinah to Rosita Abendanon-Mandri

Jepara, 29 January 1902

Dearest Mevrouw,

My sincerest thanks for your beautiful gift, I had better not say how pleased I am with it. You know how very precious the water jug that you have given me is to me and that I will keep it safely as a memory of that which now belongs to the past.

It is unnecessary to tell you how moved I was when I unpacked it. Even though I don't say much, you will know and feel what emotions traversed through me, won't you.

On Friday I am leaving Jepara and will be staying here and there briefly with members of the family.[11]

How are you and Mijnheer? I hope there is now no more illness in your house. I am not able to write much, dear Mevrouw, you will soon receive a letter from the sisters and will learn what has been happening.[12]

With this our very warmest regards and with all my love for you from
Your Kleintje

Kardinah to Rosita and Mr. Abendanon

[Letterhead] *Raden Mas Toemenggoeng Ario Rekso Negoro,*

Regent of Tegal

Tegal, 15 July 1911[13]

Dear Mevrouw and Mijnheer Abendanon,

How can I possibly find enough words to tell you both how exceedingly happy you both have made me by sending me the gift of a copy of the book *Door Duisternis tot Licht* by my late sister Kartini. I only know how deeply moved I was when I saw the book and opened it, and her picture looked out at me. It was as though the words printed there flowed from her very lips. I could hear her voice as though she were talking to me, telling me of our dreams, our youth, about all those wonderful things we imagined we would be able to do for others.

Thank you, thank you for your gift, you could not have made me happier. It was as though you gave me back a piece of my youth that had lain deeply buried in the past. Also, can I thank you, noble people, for everything that you had done for my late sister before and for everything; that you have never avoided anything and have done everything in your power to bring about that which our Kartini had always envisaged, and which become her life's work. I thank you in the name of my deceased sister. I know and I feel it, that if the dead could speak, she would in the very first place embrace you, with joy in her eyes, with happiness in her heart. And also Father: how happy he would have been.

Did I deserve it, that you still thought of me, the one who had dropped out of your lives so suddenly? Who gave you no sign or token of her existence, as if I were no longer of this world? Forgive me, oh please forgive me. So much has happened in the interim that I would need volumes to tell you about everything: what I have experienced, how I have been affected, and the trials I have faced since I bade my childhood good-bye to take my place beside my husband, who loves me dearly and with whom I am so happy.

But there can be certain moments in our lives that remind us that for us, young Javanese,[14] there is so much struggle and suffering awaiting us, especially for those who see themselves as having the task of being pioneers for the sake of the welfare of their fellow man. And that time has indeed come, with all its hard, cold reality, and has left its deep imprint. And I, weakling that I am, almost gave in to this feeling and would have completely surrendered had I not had the deep love of my husband, who gave me the strength and has always been and will continue to be my life's support.

But why am I telling you all this? Forgive me for boring you, but as I said before, your gift of this book for me was as though you gave me back my youth; it has made me come alive, and given me the strength to throw myself back into the struggle that has to be fought for the good of us all, especially for us women. So accept my gratitude, noble people, and forgive me that, unasked, I have written you this, telling you of my life. It is only that I feel that your gift and the words of my Sister have returned to me that fire of old, to take part again in everything that was once our dream and whose realization, because of your energetic support, is now so much closer. May I, and also my husband, even though you don't know him, offer you our services? I beg you, do not refuse us.

I am also very conscious of how life, as it were, has separated us three and how fate has not dealt with the three members of our union equally. She who was our greatest fighter, who we thought would never be defeated, fate rudely dragged from this stage, leaving us behind in deep sorrow.

Now I am writing to you with a prayer and a request: let us help you, even if we were only able to contribute but a grain at a time to the great work and its mighty goals that your publication of the legacy of our Sister has set for it. I feel it as my duty, my holy duty toward our Sister, with whom we once dreamed that dream, with whom we created those ideals, to offer myself now completely to the goal that we had always aimed for, for the good of us all. And, as I have said, forgive me for the fact that, till now, I have stayed away from the struggle, due to a lack of energy caused by my many experiences. Is it not my duty now, now that I have achieved such a privileged status in the highest rungs of Native society, as regent and wife of a regent? How could we not make use of the great privileges and advantages of this position? Is it not now part of God's purpose that you have now sent us this book, as a reminder of this holy duty? Now I have been, as it were, shaken awake, and I thank God for the moment that you set aside to think of me by sending me as a gift this work by my sister.[15]

You are no doubt aware that a new circular from the Department of O[nderwijs], E[eredienst], N[ijverheid] has just appeared regarding the admission of Native children to European schools which states that only those Native children may be admitted whose purpose is to go on to HBS, the School for Native Doctors, or the Native Law School. These children will have to be admitted even if they are unable to speak or understand a word of Dutch, and will be allowed to spend 2 years in the beginner classes, as long as their intention is to go on to the aforementioned schools. I and many others think this is fine, although it is another clear example of how it is becoming more and more difficult for us to send our children to European schools. How many of our nation, I ask myself, could afford to study at such schools? And if they cannot afford to study at such schools, they are refused entry to the elementary schools, and they would then have to pick up their Dutch language among other things at the first-class Native schools, where Dutch is also taught. And I don't need to tell you that the teaching of the Dutch language, among other things (except of course their Javanese language), is very limited at the Native school, with the consequence that what is learnt there is very basic so that one would rather not learn, speak, or understand any Dutch at all if it is so bad.[16]

Apart from that issue, where can Native girls go? Where are they supposed to get their little bit of education? What Native girl is able to set her sights on the more extended education of the HBS, the medical school, the law school? Isn't the implication loud and clear that the education of the Native school is sufficient for our girls? Is that fair? Or is that supposed to be an example of helping Native society to advance? Oh, ordinary people may well see it all as well and good since there are already more than enough *desa* schools, so what more would one want? I can hardly get my poor head around it; what can the government be actually intending with this regulation? Could it be that the intention is to force all Native children to go to the higher schools even though they would have to place themselves over their heads in debt to be able to pay for such studies? Surely it is obvious enough that only the higher Native officials, such as the regent, patih, and perhaps a few wedono, could afford such an education? So what can the lower officials and the masses do? And what about the girls? We now feel so clearly how they are trying to keep the Javanese out, how the brown race, the despised Javanese, is being as far as possible kept out of the elementary schools, [because they are] afraid that their white children will come into contact with the brown race.[17]

Oh, I could write a lot more about this, but then I would be afraid that I would bore you because so many other members of my race have already written about this theme so often. But is it not dreadful and irritating that we indigenous people are so put down while the Chinese, by contrast, the foreigner, is raised above everyone? Yes, the Chinese here get everything, and for them even the Chinese schools aren't good enough for those foreigners, they are even going to get Dutch Chinese schools.[18] Bravo!

You know that I now live in Tegal and that Tegal is now a large and important administrative district and will become more so with the prospect of the construction of the Semarang-Batavia [railway] line which will have Tegal as its center and head office of the S[emarang] C[heribon] S[poor].[19] As a consequence, therefore, more and more people will settle here, and Tegal itself is already so heavily populated. Now my husband and I are already planning to use the contributions collected from the Native officials here to establish a school for all children of Native officials, who, as a result of the latest circular of the Dept. of O.E.N., would have to go to the Native school—that would be about three-quarters of them—which would otherwise be their only opportunity to get to mumble and comprehend a ridiculously little Dutch.

From the book you sent me I was led to understand that it is your intention to establish a Kartini School in a healthy location in central Java. May I, and with my husband, now come to you with our request? But first, forgive us that we are so brazen in coming to you with this request.

Could we, on behalf of all Native officials of the administrative district of Tegal and their daughters, ask to have the Kartini School located here in our town, even if it were only a small school initially? Both my husband and I would devote all our efforts and abilities to help realize my sister's dream, to be able to work together on our dream, to make this dream come true, in honor of our Beloved Departed and for the welfare of our fellow human beings.[20] I feel it is my duty, my serious, holy duty, to direct this request to you, and to devote myself heart and soul to the proposed Kartini School. If we had not been raised up to this high position in Native society,

I would never have dared to ask you. We would already regard it as a great good joy to be allowed to work for the institution, and I pray you make us happy and give us what we ask.

Tegal itself may not be such a healthy place, but we have many healthy districts, and we would suggest to you the district of Slawie some 10 paal[21] from Tegal and about 200 feet[22] above sea level. It is easy to reach by tram and there is already a European high school established there with two teachers. There is of course also a Native elementary school and a clinic, as well as a European doctor and associated facilities and staff for all the workers of the 8 sugar mills in Tegal and Brebes. This is clearly an indication of how good the climate there is and how easily it can be reached from all directions. Ten paal higher up, at 1,000 feet above sea level, there is the *pasangrahan* Kalibakong, which is easily reached by car or carriage. Five paal further there is Bumijawa at 2,700 feet and Simpar at 3,000 feet, which can be reached by *tandu* or horseback. We, as well as all Native officials, hope that you will grant our request, and I am at all times ready to provide all necessary information that you may need about the area.[23]

Please don't regard this as some pedantry of ours in coming to you with this proposal. This does not spring from some hubris or exaggerated pretension. Oh no, it is purely to be able to contribute, were it only a grain, to the great work that you are planning in memory of my Sister. It would be my dearest dream to one day see that institution here, and we promise you with heart and soul to continue to work toward this to the best of our abilities.

May I now ask how you both are? Are you well, Mevrouw and your boys? Oh, I hope to receive good news about your well-being soon. Would you tell my brother Kartono that his sister, although she has not maintained a correspondence with him, still always thinks of him with all the sisterly love that she possesses? Give him my regards and tell him he is always in my prayers.

    With our very best wishes and my love to Mevrouw,
    I remain, respectfully,
    Your Kardinah

Should you wish to write to me then my address is
    Raden Ayu Toemenggoeng Ario Rekso Negoro
    Kabupaten
    Tegal

Kardinah to Rosita and Mr. Abendanon

Tegal, 25 May 1912

Highly Esteemed Mevrouw and Mijnheer Abendanon,

Just a few lines to inform you both about the telegraphic news that we received yesterday, that is, the 23rd of May, about the death of my brother-in-law, the Regent of Rembang, the father of Singgih.[24] I don't know whether they have telegraphed the news to you already, but I felt driven to inform you myself even though I myself am ill and the doctor forbids me to exert myself. So please excuse this untidy writing of mine, I am writing this in the long chair. I had not been able to reply to your letter any earlier since I have been rather unwell for the last 3 months with continual high temperature following an appendicitis attack, for which I had to go to Semarang to be treated by a specialist.

Oh, dear, dear people, whatever else it may be, this tragedy is a misfortune for my poor nephew. That child who, although still so young, has been constantly on his own, suffering the full weal and woe of this world by himself. And now he is utterly alone. I can't tell you how grief-stricken I felt. I telegraphed to the Regent's family to enquire about what was going to happen now with the little boy. Oh, it is my deepest wish, my dearest longing, to have the child with me. Will you hope with me that the family will give him over to me so that I can be a mother to him? Where else would he get it from, where else could he find one? I would so dearly like to care for him and spoil him. At the moment I am impatiently waiting for a reply.

As soon as I have somewhat recovered, I will be going to Semarang and then on to see the child. I had wanted to write to you at length, but I am still unable to. Perhaps my writing will appear a little strange to you, but later, when I have recovered, I hope I will explain it all to you. Again, please don't hold it against me that I write to you so briefly and so untidily but I can't refrain from writing and must turn to you in my state of grief.

Hope and pray for us that my dearest wish to be a mother for my little nephew is realized.

With respectful regards to you both,
I remain,
Your Kardinah

Kardinah to Rosita and Mr. Abendanon

Tegal, 25 December 1912

Dear Mevrouw and Mijnheer Abendanon,

You will think it very strange not to have heard from me for such a while after your last letter, which I received while in Semarang. So first, I ask you a thousand apologies and hope you will not blame me for it. But let me begin by wishing you both all the best with the new year of 1913. May this year bring you both the very best that can be imagined, and may good health be granted you.

I have not been able to write to you earlier as much as I wanted to. My last letter to you was at the time of the death of the Regent of Rembang when I wrote to you about Singgih. To my great regret we were not allowed to do anything for our nephew since the family, the Regent of Tuban and also the brother of Singgih himself, who has now become the Regent of Rembang, did not want us to have Singgih.[25] I cannot tell you how sad that made me, and I can do nothing but pray for Singgih's safety and happiness, that he may grow up to become a man worthy of his mother. Poor, poor little one. Since then I have heard nothing more about him, also because I have been so very ill and had even been taken to Semarang to a clinic to undergo a heavy operation. I was there from June to September, and the fact that I can now write you this letter is still a wonder to me since many friends had thought that I would not live through it. But thanks be to God, my suffering has ended and I am once again back to good health.

And now, how are you both? I hope that everything is well with you. Are you back in Holland? I was able to meet the van Deventer family.[26] They visited me in the clinic, and I am very grateful to have met them. And I am also so pleased that in Sem. work is already beginning on a Kartini School, and not only because thereby the dream of our sister *will be realized there*.[27] I only regret that no committee has been established for such institutions in other places but only an administration for Semarang itself. *There is so much support* for this movement, and we would love to contribute to the realization of that noble endeavor. I am so happy that I can hardly tell you, that I am able to witness this period of advancement of my compatriots!

People in Batavia have asked me for assistance for the SOVIA.[28] No doubt you will already have heard of this. I can't tell you how I applaud the fact that Native women are now admitted to the Native Medical School. The ladies who constitute the board of the SOVIA have asked me to work with them to encourage more girls to apply. Of course I accepted wholeheartedly and am so enjoying my work as correspondent of that organization. Our only regret is that the government does not pay the study costs of these girls as they do for the boys of the medical school. But now that the study fund has been set up, it will be free for girls as well. However, when they have completed their studies the government will still not be employing the girls as government employees, only because they are not considered suitable to examine coolies.[29] But I am so excited about this noble work and will devote all my time and effort towards that goal.

Will you also be coming for the opening of the Kartini School? The van Deventer family mentioned that you want to visit the Indies again. How happy I would be to see you and speak with you both again.

How is Kartono these days? Oh, my God, if only he would come back for the sake of our old mother, even if just for her. Is there no hope for this?

I will write you again soon. At the moment I have a lot to do for the SOVIA.

Our warm regards and with much love to Mevrouw,
Yours respectfully,
Kardinah

Kardinah to Rosita and Mr. Abendanon

Tegal, 30 March 1916

Dear Mevrouw and Mijnheer Abendanon,

Finally, I have been able to achieve that which has been my goal and has occupied my time for so many years, and what I thought might never be realized for girls of the people, the village girls: a school for the girls of the common people has finally been opened on 1 March 1916.[30]

I am now going to sit down and write to tell you and bring you up to date with all the news and activities concerning the school.

Dear Mevrouw and Mijnheer Abendanon, I should certainly have already told you about this but I hope you will excuse me because all my time has been spent in working towards the school. And then, before I go any further, I must thank you very much for sending me the report you wrote on the K[artini] F[onds] in the Netherlands. I thank you sincerely and with all my heart for the concern for us[31] that this demonstrates. I read it with the greatest interest and gratitude. And it is this that I want to discuss with you later.

How are you both? I wish good health always and as well as prosperity for you and yours.

Together with this I am sending you all kinds of documents related to our school and hope that I may get your comments on them.[32]

I had always had as my goal one day to be of use to our society and, in particular, to Native girls. I have always felt and had been convinced that my energies and activities should be devoted to provide practical help to the simple village child and girl. Given the growing number of government desa schools[33] my thoughts had been increasingly directed to focusing all my efforts in that direction. I thought about it long and hard until I came to the certainty that I could best realize my goal by establishing a form of domestic economy school for Native girls where the same level of education would be given as at government 2nd class schools but with an extended and complete course in instruction in domestic arts. Where the desa or ordinary child of the people now has to attend the desa or 2nd class school anyway, it seemed to me that such an institution would be the best kind of school for the child of the common people and would be of much more use to her in her future life as prospective housewife and mother than would the two institutions mentioned above.

It is now my aim to see that the education provided will be developed in this direction, and through it, that Native girls will be able to take the exams for the pupil teacher-training certificate as well as having the opportunity to obtain the necessary diplomas and certificates for teaching in the field of domestic education cooking, washing and ironing, batikking, women's handiwork, and theoretical and practical qualification for fancy and plain sewing. From the program you can see how we have tried to provide the domestic education in a thorough and systematic way.

At the moment I am writing booklets in the Javanese language, that is, schoolbooks, for all kinds of domestic activities that will also provide the method and direction for the domestic economy education at the school.[34] And, when I have finished the theory and text books, I have to send them to the Director of the O.E.N. and after they have been approved I plan to have them published and, if possible, to devote the money earned to the domestic economy school.[35]

Help me to realize my hopes and give me both your blessing for all this work of mine, that everything may be of use to the children of the people, that the school may produce useful and practical women who can join the work of developing our Native society, to develop the woman in all her simplicity, as useful and qualified to serve her immediate environment and family. Anyway for those who want to receive higher education there are now many opportunities, such as the K[artini] Schools and the HIS. I have already had the approval of Mr. Moresco[36] and I have already put in a request to the G.G. for several changes to the school regulations such as, that we now have a male head teacher for the school since there is no female Native *mantri guru* available. And I have also put in an application for a subsidy.³⁷

Would you please oblige me by looking at the documents I am sending with this and give me your opinion on them? I would be very grateful.

The school was opened on 1 March 1916 and because it still does not have its own building, the school is held in one of the former office buildings of the kabupaten which is situated on our property. Later we plan to build the school itself also on our large property.

One hundred sixty-two children have applied, including pupils from the HIS and all the girls from the 2nd class Native school but because of the lack of room we could only accept 15.³⁸ We had one male head mantri guru, 3 male pupil teachers and 1 female pupil teacher for cooking and batiking and one female guru and 1 female pupil teacher for needlework and associated subjects. There is also a teacher who gives religious education at the general request of parents and one apprentice guru, a helper. So altogether there are 7 teachers and a helper. School fees are 50 cents per pupil; their schoolbooks and all their school needs are free.

In contributions we have received (only from the *Native side*) the sum of 3,000 guilders; from the Eur[opean] side we have received much less interest and support except from some businesses that have made donations. The amount raised from the Native family fair that we held on 11 March produced 2,200 guilders net, from monthly contributions, 85 guilders. So you see we don't get that much money. If we were to build a new domestic economy school we would face very great costs. We would need, as classrooms, at least 5 or 6 large rooms, one room specially for needlework, sewing and cutting, 1 large kitchen, a large hall or shed next to the kitchen for batik classes, a *gudang*, a shed for preparing the *soga* and *wedel* coloring for the batik work, and a shed for washing and ironing the material. Based on the building and associated costs for establishing the K[artini] Schools—for instance that in Madiun where there are only classrooms which, without facilities for household economy, already cost a total of 18,000 guilders—a school with so many extra rooms would be cost a good 20–24,000 guilders. It is true that if we followed the new school regulations and were to receive a government subsidy then we would receive three quarters of the cost, but then we still would not have enough for everything since the school still does not have its own funds.

I had first thought to develop the school with only a three-year course and so would only take in girls older than 10 who had already completed the 2nd or 3rd class of the 2nd class Native school and who wanted to continue their education in this school of domestic economy that would commence at the 3rd and continue with the 4th and 5th levels, including the course in domestic economy. But if we did that we would not get so many pupils, only 50 or so applied. So, in response to the general request from the Native community itself, we have now made the school of domestic economy a six year course which would include the first 2 years of the ordinary school. This is, as the majority voice of the Native community has argued, "because if we have to send our daughters to school, then we would prefer to send them to a school where they can get all their education in the one institution."[39]

We regret that we have not been able to set aside time in our curriculum for a course in Dutch language in our domestic economy school, which would only be possible if we resorted to conducting an afternoon language course. However, were we forced to teach Dutch language in this institution, this would not really be possible as I am afraid that we would thereby lose sight of our goal as I outlined to you above.[40]

To my great joy and interest I read about your plans to establish a teacher training school for female mantri guru in Semarang. That is now something that will truly be of much importance for the Native girl today and in the future. That *has to happen!* Were the costs related to this and the associated problems not too great, then I would ask you to have the K[artini] F[onds] if possible, establish a training school for Native female mantri guru here in Tegal. I think such an institution must be worthwhile wherever it was opened but I am afraid that most gurus graduating from such a training school would not be readily placed in this region if they did not have the dialect that was spoken here and only the "pure Javanese" of such a school as proposed.[41]

I had wanted to write to you much, much earlier concerning the plans of this school but I thought it was better to be able to write you: "our School of Domestic Economy for Native girls, called 'Wisma Pranowo,' has been established and was opened on the first of March 1916."[42]

It is now my deepest wish that this school may continue to blossom and have the blessing and support of you both. That would be my reward.

The information I have received from the Director of O.E.N. that I enclose with this is in response to my letter to him requesting permission and advice. Given the large number of pupils (50) that we have accepted so far and the growing number of requests for a place—in March there were 18 requests for placement after *puasa* and then in the new school year we will once again take in new students, all girls, from 6 to 7 years of age—we will be obliged to take on more teaching staff which will naturally lead to more expenses. This year, that is to say the 4 months before puasa, we will enrol all pupils—girls of all ages who are older than 6 years but not older that 16. As a result we now have an unfortunate situation of having to conduct a parallel class of older girls who are older that 16 and who have not yet undertaken any education, in the morning in practical domestic science education first and then only after 11, when the little ones have left, can we actually provide their basic school education. I hope I have described all this clearly for you.

Once again I pray for your blessing.

With our best regards to you both, also from my husband,
I remain,
Your Kardinah

Kardinah to Rosita and Mr. Abendanon

Tegal, 16 July 1916

Dear Mevrouw and Mijnheer Abendanon,

To my deep regret and concern I learnt from Miss Ament who visited you and who spoke to you about me and our school, that you never received my letter of 30 March 1916 which included the entire documentation concerning the school, all the incoming correspondence about the initial plans for the establishment of the school up to the time of the opening of the school and all the associated correspondence.[43]

Herewith I am sending you the positive reply that I have already received to the request document of which I had sent you a copy.[44] But I regret very much and have been very upset because I really set my heart on knowing how you would react when you received that letter and to hear of your interest and support for my endeavors. That this did not happen was a great disappointment to me. But now you do know that I had not forgotten you in all this; on the contrary, in all the preparations and activity with regards to the school I was thinking constantly of you and only waited in writing to you about it so that I could announce to you with a loud, joyful cry: my school was opened on the first of March 1916. Give it your blessing and support so that I can achieve that which I set myself as a goal.

Please, write to me in just a few words that my letter did finally reach you and then write precisely what you both think of it. But let me first beg you both to excuse this untidily written letter. If I was not forced to do so by the shock and disappointment of the loss of my letter to you, and to thank you for your sympathetic interest in our school and your immediate assistance for us in the form of a gift of 250 guilders, this letter would not have been written. This is because at the moment I have a typhoid patient at home for the last two weeks and am therefore not in the mood to write. Hope for a speedy recovery for our 4-year-old patient. I love that child, who is one of my adopted children.[45] I am writing you this in the middle of the night in the sick room and have to constantly put down my pen to help the child. Consequently this clumsy writing of mine.

How are you both? I hope with all my heart that you are well.

When things return to normal here and I can think again I will quickly write you a letter telling you about everything. However much I would like to, I really cannot now send you all the documentation for the second time because the copies have not yet been completed and I want to send this quickly. I had sent everything to you because I wanted to get from you your suggestions and advice. For instance the application for subsidy has been returned to me by the Dept. of O.E.N. with the request to make certain changes. In relation to a few questions we had not given sufficient information. For example, in answer to question 25, asking if the children from well-to-do Natives get precedence in admission to the school, instead of saying "no" I should have said "yes" in accordance with a decision by the Dutch parliament. I had *so dearly* wanted my school to be open to all children without distinction of race or social status, unlike the village or 2nd class schools. But now that is not allowed. Because I have already commenced with the school, now it is not so difficult for me, in view of the subsidy question, and in the interests of all Native girls, to answer the question with a "yes." Now I may not let my own personal views take precedence.[46]

And then also, we "absolutely" have to appoint a female head of school even though in relation to that issue I had submitted a request to the G.G. mentioning that there was not a single female head teacher available. It was pointed out to me that the government would now accept, on the basis of the new school regulations, for appointment as a female head teacher, someone who was in possession of a declaration from a school committee of being "suitable to teach." As a consequence, now instead of having a retired mantri guru as head of this girls' school who provides both us and the department with the certainty that, given his experience, that there would be someone able to provide our girls with valuable education and leadership, we have to have a female teacher appointed on the basis of a declaration from a school committee.

No, for me the interests of the school bear more heavily on my heart than that I would allow the future of the school to be in the hands of a woman when at the moment there is no female mantri guru available. There are two in Java, but both are already married and both were unable to accept my offer to them to become head of the school. It would be a different matter if the school had already been running for a few years, then I would already have certainty about the way the school was running but now I do not dare take on the responsibilities of the school, and so, because now all the subsidies for the school will be refused, I am hoping there will be enough funds in the treasury to ensure the future of the school. At the same time that I sent those documents to you, Mrs. de Stuers, the wife of our Ass. Res., was corresponding with Baron van Hogendorp about our school and she sent a bundle of documents about the school to him.[47] Would you be able to ask about this?

I have turned directly to you for support and blessing but alas, none of this appears to have reached you and now there is no time to collect everything together for you because of my little patient. But I promise to write you a letter about all this as soon as all the illness has disappeared from our family.

In the meantime I thank you from the bottom of my heart for your interest and your financial help that means so much to us. Would you send the Kartini Association our thanks?

From us both our best regards,
Remaining yours,
Kardinah

Kardinah to Rosita and Mr. Abendanon

Tegal, 24 September 1916

Dear Mevrouw and Mijnheer Abendanon,

I have received both of your letters in good order and for them our deepest thanks and also for the interest you have shown and demonstrated in our school. How can we sufficiently express our gratitude, and also on behalf of the Native public whose interests are involved here? I have not dared to dream of such sympathy and support. Be assured of the fact that the school committee and the Native public of Tegal gratefully acknowledge your support and interest and we will not be able to cease encouraging your continued support!

Also thank you for the copy of the weekly paper, *Oost en West,* which included that piece you wrote about our school and immediately opened a collection for it. And we are grateful to have received the document from the van Deventer Fund entitled "The establishment of a teacher training school for Native female teachers."[48]

Before going further on that topic may I enquire how you both are? We hope you will both continue to enjoy good health so that you will be able to fulfill your dream of seeing the Indies again one day and hope of course to have the honor on that occasion to have you both as our guests! How fortunate I would then count myself. Please do not forget this!

The days of illness have fortunately passed for us and we cannot be grateful enough for the complete recovery of our little patient and the good health of us all, which in the terrible heat we are currently experiencing, is worth so much.

With the last mail I sent you a bundle of documents concerning our school intended for the board of the Kartini Fund together with a letter in response to its expression of support. I hope that that letter has already reached you. I also included with it a copy of the new curriculum because after this puasa month a fourth class has been added and the school has now grown to 160 pupils. Unfortunately, we could only take a small number of the 40 new pupils who applied because of the lack of space. Now I am giving serious consideration, if we have enough money, to begin next year with a fifth class, with a course on hygiene. While initially I had a plan to limit this to lessons in nursing and first aid for accidents, after talking it over with the doctors in Tegal, it now appears to me more advisable to begin with a course on midwifery and child care. Once again I express the hope that hereby I will be able to contribute even more to the welfare of the Native girl in general. And, as far as Dutch-language teaching is concerned, I very much hope that the time will come for our school one day, that the need for this will be widely felt by the mass of the people and then I will not hesitate to arrange it. I hope that time will come soon and that I will be able to write you the first letter about this.[49]

According to reports, a girls' school has been opened in Pringalek in imitation of the establishment of the Domestic Science School for Girls in Tegal, with 122 pupils. It is called Wijoto Kenjo Deso. Also on 1 June 1916 in Tulungagung, a girls' school, named Kenjo Pinardi, opened with 125 pupils while on 6 Aug. 1916 in Medan, a girls' school named Sekola Derma was opened with 85 pupils by the board of the Vrouwenkiesrecht Vereeniging under the direction of Mev. Gazan de la Meuse, which is completely in the spirit of our school and has been in correspondence with the board of the Wismo Pranowo. The two schools in Tulungagung and

Pringalek I know are also organized exactly like ours, that is, as 2nd class schools with domestic science education except that the Tulunagung school also offers some Dutch language, which is taught by a Native girl with a lower civil service diploma.

The Ass. Inspector of Native education has already visited our school and received a favorable impression. He was full of praise for our work, that is, for the books we are preparing in the Javanese language on needlework, cooking and batikking, which of course was very encouraging for us. My dearest wish remains, by the grace of God, to further the interests of the ordinary Native people for which I once again ask your support and blessing!![50]

We read with great interest the article about the proposed teacher training school for Native female teachers and continue to hope that that school will be established one day. As regards the curriculum, we are in complete agreement with you; especially as we have come to realize, that what is most essential in the first place is to gain the trust of the Natives. We also have come to recognize how the old tradition is still deeply respected and maintained and how the young girls are still carefully protected, as is evident by the appointment of a Native woman as supervisor of these Native girls because, regardless of anything else, the large majority of the people do not wish to see the Europeanization of the Native girl. And in that they are correct because the strength of our people can only be found in remaining steadfast! I also hope, both for you and for the sake of your school, that you will be able to find such a Native woman, preferably from the higher circles, who will be able to spread a beneficial influence. This has also been my experience with my female staff at my school: that through contact with the European environment and lifestyle they got to appropriate European culture and knowledge but by the presence and supervision of a cultured Native woman, they were able to maintain their own nationality and therefore keep it high.[51]

As far as the educational content goes, can I just say that the curriculum could not be more perfect. But that still leaves the biggest question: whether a sufficient number of Native girls would present themselves, whether in the Native world such an amount of money would be made available for the education of Native girls because, if I am not mistaken, one boarding student would have to pay between 25 to 50 guilders and the only students who would be eligible would therefore be the daughters of wedonos, patihs, and regents (that does not of course exclude the possibility that there are a small number of wealthy private individuals). I fear, therefore, that in the foreseeable future there would not be a great rush of female pupils.

We understand of course that the costs of boarding and establishing the boarding department could not be any lower than that proposed because of the extensive and heavy costs associated with it, and because of the size of the project, but this means it will not match the financial capabilities of the ordinary Native, especially when it concerns a daughter. And we would greatly regret, where we have become aware of the great lack of female teachers, if a sufficiently large number were not able to register.

I have already been promoting the project here in as far as it lay within my means through the local committee of the B[udi] Utomo but they also share my fear that the associated costs for the Native girl would be the major obstacle. Yes, we have not yet got so far that we can appreciate all this. At this stage the Javanese still would like to have everything for nothing. This too I have experienced myself in establishing the W.P. with the many costs associated with the domestic science school where all the study materials were provided free for which we at first planned to charge 1 guilder in school fees. There was such a general outcry that this was still beyond the Native financial capacity that we had to reduce it to 50 cents.

Expressing to you once more our gratitude for the greatly appreciated support and interest that you have shown, also on behalf of the Native school committee of our school,

> We remain, with a warm hand and love to you both,
> Yours truly,
> Kardinah

Kardinah to Rosita and Mr. Abendanon

Tegal, 26 January 1917

Esteemed Mevrouw and Mijnheer Abendanon,

In the first place, let me wish you all the best for the New Year. We wish for you from the very depth of our hearts all the possible happiness and especially good health. I had not been able to write you sooner because in December we took 3 weeks vacation and spent our time looking around the Oosthoek. It was mainly because I felt the need to get out after the recent period of hard work, and the journey did us a world of good. At any rate we have returned with renewed courage to take up our work again. And arriving home there was a great surprise waiting for us because what did I find waiting for me on my table but a resolution from the government in Batavia freeing us from the regulation regarding the mantri guru etc., a copy of the advice from Mr. Moresco and then, the biggest surprise of all, a decision to grant us a subsidy for the 1916 year.[52]

Dear Mevrouw and Mijnheer Abendanon, can you imagine how intensely happy I now feel? I am so grateful and gladdened by this that I feel like embracing the entire world. It means that finally now I have been granted what I wanted for Native society, that I am able to work for their advancement even though it is only just a little, and that is what made me so happy! With this I am sending you a copy of all the decisions. I hope it reaches you safely.[53]

But see how I have neglected to enquire first about your health. I do hope that you are both well. We also are very well, and it must not be otherwise, must it? Especially now, I have to remain well to help guard the interests of everyone!

I have received both journals that you sent me and thank you both for your kind thoughts with regard to the school that you expressed in your article, which are much appreciated.[54] Our school is going well and the results of the domestic science school are more than pleasing. I wish I could send you copies of all the handbooks and textbooks I have written. Oh, I so wish that you both were able to come and see everything that is being done at this school and that I could get your advice and comments on everything. I had our teachers take private lessons and later I wrote to the inspector of Native education, Mr. van Eupen, asking him to allow them to take their pupil teacher exams and he was quite ready to oblige me in this and immediately sent Kamil to arrange an exam for us here in Tegal. Two of our gurus passed and two did not gain the pupil teacher diploma, but I have not given up hope. In June they will repeat the exam.[55]

I have already submitted the budget for the building of the school—it amounted to 28,000 guilders, but since they will no doubt subtract some of that in Batavia I have every hope that the project will be approved and that we will soon be able to begin constructing a building of our own.

We hope next May or June to run a large *pasar malam*.[56] It has to be very good and we hope in this way to raise a bigger amount than last year because now we have to start thinking about that expensive building. The items already produced by our school such as crocheted articles as well as sewing and batik work we want to put on display and sell. Oh, I have really been surprised how in 10 months time our girls who had never before managed a *gunting* can now batik cleverly and artistically, following the batik method that I wrote for the school. If you could come and see all this for yourself how happy that would make me!

And now, finally, our best wishes for the success of the prospective Van Deventer School. It is a great achievement that so many, over 200, female pupils registered for the school. Now there is no doubt that it will be established. I learned from my sister and her husband in Semarang that in May a pasar malam was also held there, the proceeds going to the Van Deventer School. My sister is completely ecstatic about it but in Sem. those kinds of festivities have to succeed.[57]

From the government we are now going to get a qualified Native female teacher for our school but when speaking to Mr. van Eupen about the mantri guru, he said we could retain him for the first year until a woman with the necessary capacities has demonstrated her ability take the position as head of school.

As soon as the documents that I would like you to look at are ready, I will write to you again. At the moment I am busy making preparations for and organizing the forthcoming festivities.

Warmest regards to you both,
Lots of love from,
Your Kardinah

Kardinah to Rosita and Mr. Abendanon

Tegal, 7 August 1917

Dear Mevrouw and Mijnheer Abendanon,

Now that all the activity of the pasar malam is behind me, I can finally get down to talk to you. How are you both at the moment? I sincerely hope that you are enjoying good health.

I don't know if you have received my last letter, the one I wrote after I received your postal order together with the letter from Mevrouw. It has really become a hopeless task to try to keep up with the correspondence from the Netherlands properly, now that communications have become so difficult. To think that our letters full of intimacies and thoughts may have been written to no avail always makes me so sad. I just hope that my letters have not been written in vain and have all arrived safely into your possession.[58]

On 1 August our school was reopened for the New Year with an enrolment of 165 pupils. Our former head teacher has now stepped down and in his place we now have a female assistant teacher, Moerdiah, who has been seconded to us from the government as a teacher, while I have received another assistant female teacher to replace her.

In this new year therefore we are working exclusively with female teachers and I am happy to be able to inform you that that all now have their diploma. As teaching staff we now have 5 assistant teachers, 4 female staff for the academic subjects and one teacher for religious education. This year we have a fifth class and when we begin a sixth class next year I will be interested to see whether our girls will be able to pass their pupil teacher exams. When it gets to that time, end '18 or mid '19, I will be so gratified when our girls successfully pass and that in this way we can deliver up the products of our school into the service of other girls' schools who are still waiting on female teachers. How intensely grateful I will feel then, to have been able to make a contribution to this end.

Our pasar malam this time raised over 7,000 guilders gross. For Tegal that is to be called fantastic, but then we have still been bettered by Sem[arang] whose pasar malam raised over 12,000 guilders. We now have a treasury of 10,000 guilders and once the plans for our school building are approved we will be ready to provide one third of the cost of the construction ourselves. It is a wonderful idea to know that, in as far as we can work it out, our school will not experience any financial difficulty and once again I beg you both to bless this simple project that it may continue to flourish.

Until now Siti Soendari has not yet come to visit me even though she does live here locally. I very much doubt if she will ever come here, even though you had asked her to pass on your regards to us, simply because such people would never come to us. I mean, those from the higher circles of Native society. Although I would have loved to have had her here, I cannot ask her. She herself is a very ordinary woman but has become the object of the single-minded ideas of her father, poor child! Should she still want to come to see me one of these days I would always welcome her with open arms because as a woman I have a lot sympathy for her.[59]

How wonderful that the government now realizes how important teacher training schools are for Native female teachers. They could hardly think otherwise when girls' schools are now starting to spring up like toadstools. You will no doubt have already read that three such schools will be established in Java and one in the Outer Islands, and it will take another 3 or 4 years before one of these schools can produce. Nevertheless it is another step in the right direction.

How it must please you to see all this taking place having yourself done so much, and are still doing, for the advancement of our country and its people. Only it makes me so sad that our dear late sister was not able to experience it. But on the other hand, her memory lives on in a wonderful way. I would have liked to have sent you photos of our school but my fear that at the moment there would be little chance that these would reach you prevented me. As soon as the situation improves I will chance it.

Wishing you both our very best wishes, and also with warm regards from my husband to you both, I remain,

Yours truly,
Kardinah

Kardinah to Rosita and Mr. Abendanon

Tegal, 14 November 1923

Highly Esteemed Mevrouw and Mijnheer Abendanon,

The first thing I wish to do is to ask you to forgive me that I have remained silent for so long and that you had no sign from me, even after receipt of your kind and most welcome gift, *Door Duisternis tot Licht*.[60] Oh, tell me that you forgive me. I cannot write, I cannot, and the main reason has been that I have been suffering physically so much that I was regularly at death's door, and have barely been able to recover my health.

To write to you what I then felt, all the emotions and thoughts that preoccupied me at that time is not possible. I only know this: that it was my soul, the core of my being that enabled me to survive all the physical suffering, my spiritual side having saved me from my physical demise. And yet I would have liked nothing better had the final end come to this life that has been one continuous life of suffering. But no that rest was denied me; I had to go on, always further.

But let me not make you somber: a good time is awaiting me again. All of us, my husband and children, are well and thank you both for the book of my sister that will continue to be treasured by us.

How are you both, and where are you now? Is Mijnheer well and is his condition now satisfactory?

You know that my sister Soematri and her husband Achmad and two children are now stationed in Tegal which means for us both a wonderful period of being together and we are gratefully profiting from this.[61] How are things with all your children and grandchildren? How old we are becoming and have become don't you think. We also now have two grandchildren who are both developing well. And yet, despite this grandmothership, I still feel like I felt in former days. I think all people must feel like this whose internal life is stronger than their outer life. The times—life—passes by rapidly, with each day's changes and emotions, and while changes are not always for the better, we would not wish to miss all this even if it brings us pain when it gives us moments when we can think, feel, and comprehend the inner value of suffering. Too late I have come to the realization that only through suffering can we rise to that higher level, to the "Light," to the infinite.

And now my dear friends, I greet you both from far away. Be assured that you are never out of our hearts and thoughts even when there is no physical evidence that this is so.

Our warmest regards from my husband and I embrace you warmly in my thoughts,
> I remain,
> Your own,
> Kardinah

Kardinah to Rosita and Mr. Abendanon

[Letterhead] *Raden Ayu Ario Rekso Negoro*

Tegal, 24 October 1924

Highly Esteemed Mevrouw and Mijnheer Abendanon,

With a warm handshake we thank you profusely a thousand times for your letter and best wishes for the Royal distinction that has been bestowed upon us. Dear friends, I cannot express in words how surprised and deeply moved I was by this circumstance, all the more so because I know that the person who deserved it most is our sister Kartini. She was not able to live to see it but Her Name to this day is mentioned more often, bestowing an honor greater than any earthly distinction could bestow. For me, when I was first told and when I was called forward at the public occasion in Pekalongan, it was a moment I could barely contain myself.

Friends, please continue to give me your blessing as always so that I may be vouchsafed for a long time yet for the cause to which we have dedicated our lives. Once again both of us want to thank you for your letter and good wishes. We are so happy to learn from your letter that you are both in good health. Some time ago we learnt that you had been unwell so that we are now all the happier knowing that you have recovered.

I don't know if our letter in which I wrote you all the details ever reached you. I fear that it did not because I heard nothing about it any more.[62] I wrote to you about the takeover of Wismo Pranawo by the government and that it has now become a finishing school with preparatory grades, all for the sake of having to be coeducational. Alas however, all the success we had established is now lost.

I handed the school over with 135 pupils. Within a few months the average number of girls attending the school dropped to 42, which is more than tragic. We discussed this with the relevant education officers, but Batavia refused to recognize that it would have been better to initially keep the school going as it was. However, it's the government's decision so there is nothing that can be done about it. I have some hope to believe that it might become a girls' school again even if this should take some time. I wrote about it and argued it with the inspectors and the lady inspector of Native education.[63]

From the funds of the school that I am responsible for, a sum of 19,140 guilders together with a government and regional subsidy, we will establish a hospital for indigent Native people in Tegal. Building of this hospital is likely to begin this year and it will be opened next year.[64] Oh dear friends it is wonderful that I have been able to contribute to this and it is my dearest wish later myself to work there, even if it were only doing the simplest work because I have absolutely no qualifications.

For some time I have been responsible for a private study fund for Javanese girls. This fund was a gift by a European who does not wish to be named. As a result at the moment a Javanese girl has had the opportunity to study at the HBS to later continue at the STOVIA in Weltevreden. Since this study will take many years, with the agreement of the donator, I have nominated Soematri to take over this role when I have passed away.

I tell you all this in greatest confidence because the donator of this fund wishes to remain unknown.

At the moment I have several silversmiths working under my supervision with the aim to encourage the revival and development of the Native craft of silversmithing. Oh dears, I have so much wonderful work to do to which I can give my heart and soul.[65] We have already had devoted several exhibitions to it, in Aug. 1923 we had the first annual market and exhibition in Pekalongan, and in December '23 one was held by the N.T. Arts Society in Tegal. In Aug. '24 the second annual fair exhibition was held in Pekalongan and then in Nov. '24 we will have an exhibition by N.T. arts society of Cheribon. When I have the time I will send you several photos of the silverwork, then you can see what beautiful work it is.[66]

And now dear friends, for the time being I take my leave from you both. Receive my best regards from my husband and with lots and lots of love to you both.[67]

    I remain,
    Your Kardinah

Kardinah to Hilda de Booy-Boissevain and H. G. de Booy

Salatiga, 25 May 1951

Dear, dear people—can I address you in this way?

How very surprised I was to receive your letter, which expressed such sincere empathy and understanding concerning the passing of our sister Roekmini. A warm hand for you both and my thanks for your writing. The passing away was not a blow for those of us who understand and who have always been "one" with us. It was as if a dried up leaf fell to the ground and found itself a place amongst the grain. In my 70th year I also know that our separation will only be brief and that we old people will soon follow her.

I am pleased and grateful to have received your letter containing those words of understanding. It did someone like me a lot of good, especially in this time when the younger generation suddenly finds itself in a new world, so full of bright light and sparkle that it blinds them and now they can only see the correct and true path with great difficulty. God grant that our country, our people, one day will come to follow the one and only way to the glorious future. We are only at the beginning, we will no doubt continue to stumble and fall, but with God's blessing and that of my sister Kartini, who continues to lead the way for us, we shall finally reach the perfect goal.

Yes, our sister Kartini is now a national hero. Twenty-one April is now a national day for the whole of Indonesia. Thousands and thousands of women and people generally go on pilgrimage on 21 April to her grave in Bulu, Rembang. God grant that our people will always keep that fine, pure spirit in their minds, even though they are still traveling through darkness.

But I am charging ahead. Let me first ask you how things are with you both. The children have no doubt already become adults. I have already become a great-grandmother of four great-grandchildren.

Do please write again if you should have a spare moment. I will be very grateful. Once again my thanks for your letter. My warm regards to you and to your husband.

I remain still your,
K. Rekso Negaro

Chapter 3

LETTERS FROM KARTINAH

Introduction

Although Kartinah was not the youngest, and although her early history and correspondence replicate those of Soematri, hers is the smallest archive of letters. Her correspondence ends abruptly after her announcement of marriage (she was the last of the sisters to marry), suggesting that her husband may have intervened. Although there is no further information about his political leanings, he was of the same rank as many of the other brothers and spouses and thus, like the majority of figures in this correspondence, located within the emerging Western-educated class of lower *priyayi* members of the colonial bureaucracy. Within this burgeoning social class, however, a great variety of attitudes and perspectives were to be found during this volatile transitional period. Wedono Dirdjoprawiro may have been ideologically separated from his new relatives by having a less favorable opinion of the colonial regime or a more radical commitment to nationalism and/or Islam, or by being a member of the more radically nationalist organizations that Sosrohadikoesoemo criticized. Equally, he may have been one of those who remained wedded to the older traditions and values.

In any event, Kartinah's choice of marriage partner was constrained—as indeed, ultimately, was Roekmini's[1]—by institutionally defined circuits of physical and social mobility within the colonially defined society. Her prospective husband was *wedono* in an administrative subdistrict (Somoroto, of the district of Ponorogo) within the residency, Madiun, in which his brother-in-law, Boesono, was regent (of Ngawi). The small number of official appointees were all known to each other and could be thoroughly vetted, if not specifically introduced. At the same time, if one takes at face value her earlier accounts of youthful flirtation, it may be that Kartinah, who appears to have dedicated her young adult years to caring for her mothers, came to see herself as approaching spinsterhood and was happy to have a match arranged. It is clear that Raden Dirdjoprawiro, like many of the immediate family, remained in the lower ranks of the civil service, eventually rising, after fourteen years' service as wedono, to end his career as patih of his *afdeeling,* Ponogoro (1927–31). On his retirement, as Soematri confirms, Kartinah and her husband settled in the town of Madiun and the close bonds connecting the siblings were reconfirmed. Again it is the informative Soematri who provides the following impression:

> When the airmail letter from our child arrived, we were just sitting together, close and cosily, Roekmini, Kardinah, Kartinah, and I, just like the old days, looking for the comfort of our own family and home, together also with our two mothers. You can imagine how, with the reading of Arto's letter, all those memories were being recalled. An air of melancholy spread over us all, but yet we were filled with a warm feeling of happiness. We felt rich in the wealth of memories; there was not the slightest discordant note.[2]

Although nothing in Kartinah's correspondence distinguishes her history from that of her siblings, one senses that the personality differences between Roekmini and Kartini—differences that made Kartini the one who attracted the attention of outsiders and that led her to produce her prodigious output of writing—were similar to those between Kartinah and her younger sister Soematri. Being five years older, Kartinah must have had more involvement in the Jepara school experiment with Roekmini and experienced more extensively the social life to which both she and Soematri refer in their letters to Lien, and she would have been able to recall more clearly the days with her older sister Kartini. But Kartinah appeared to share Roekmini's more sober personality, perhaps inherited from the royal Madurese bloodline through their mother, the raden ayu, whereas Soematri and Kartini, the children of a village woman, inherited the more open personality of the common people.

Kartinah was already thirty-two when she married, seemingly a very advanced age, and her prospects may well have been affected by the death of her father and the family's social demotion. She was older than Roekmini at the time of her marriage and possibly, like Roekmini and Kartini, married an older man. After the last of her sisters left home, Kartinah had taken on the role of maiden daughter looking after the raden ayu. She writes, less as a complaint than as a justification for her life to Lien: "I am now everything at home, *dame de la maison,* secretary and whatever for my old mother, so I am constantly busy."[3] Nevertheless, the accounts she provides Lien of Jepara suggest that she is bored and lonely.

We do not have, as we do for her sisters, a record of how in later life she translated the ideals that were cultivated in the Jepara *kabupaten*, or indeed the precise date of her death. Given her stated views, articulated with the same enthusiasm as her sisters', it seems unlikely she could have married anyone who held traditional views about women's social position. Before her marriage, Kartinah had taken on what had once been Kartini's role, that of establishing a network of correspondents, with whom one imagines she conducted a steady correspondence about the ideas she had grown up with. She was one of the signatories to "A Call to Young Java," and indicated in her letters to Rosita her interest in and awareness of contemporary events in the Netherlands relating to the Indonesian student movement there. Her summation of the contemporary situation echoes the intellectual and emotional sentiments expressed by Kartini years earlier:

> The situation in the Netherlands Indies regarding the education of our girls remains miserable; there has been no response yet to the numerous earnest pleas to provide to women too the opportunity for spiritual development. Everywhere the cry for more education is being silently expressed. Who would dare to suggest that Javanese women do not feel the need for more knowledge and new skills? This would surely be a cowardly assertion. Yet among our most highly educated male countrymen there are still some who continue to dare to hold to this view. Is that not scandalous? When will the time finally arrive for us Javanese women to open up a broader pathway in our society? As long as conservatives retain their hold over most minds we will just have to observe passively the developments that surround us. Oh, may the times soon bring great changes to this situation.[4]

These words, while less severe in their criticism of Javanese men than those uttered by Kartini in 1899, may well indicate the tenor of the correspondence she was planning to commence with her network of socially well-placed young women.[5]

It is perhaps significant that this paragraph, which begins with an implicit criticism of the colonial regime, ends with "feminist" criticism of her own countrymen. In this it is reminiscent of the criticisms expressed by Sosrohadikoesoemo, whose vehemence is also reserved for his own countrymen rather than the colonial government. It effectively marks the conservative position of this circle of Javanese, whose nationalism was defined in terms of a commitment to the progress and modernization of Java that was apparently at the expense of solidarity with their fellow colonized subjects. Their vision of a modern Java—and indeed their social and political position—depended on encouraging the colonial regime to provide the necessary leadership, guidance, and support, together with, if necessary, the suppression of outmoded values and the physical constraint of those—such as "the exiles," as Sosrohadikoesoemo had derogatively called the leaders of the Indische Partij—who threatened the orderly achievement of the goals this circle had in mind. Their perspective trapped them into a dependence on the colonial regime.

Unfortunately, lack of later correspondence prevents us from tracking Kartinah's subsequent activities as a married woman within a particular social class in the rapidly shifting sands of Javanese nationalism. It can be supposed, however, that like her sisters, Kartinah continued to give voice to the feminist ideals with which she had been raised. Unlike the political jockeying that preoccupied their menfolk, this would have continued to have evinced a strong commitment, as it had for her sisters, to the welfare of women of all classes. Therein lay the real progress of Java.

Kartinah to Rosita Abendanon-Mandri

Jepara, 3 December 1901

Dear Mevrouw!

Many thanks for the fan which you have sent me as a present.[6] It is a delightful one, and I am so very pleased with it. I think it is very nice of you, Mevrouw, that you also did not forget us two; I will be very careful with this fan and always use it and each time think of the dear person who gave it to me.

But tell me, how are you and Mijnheer? Have you now both completely recovered? I heard from my sisters recently that you were both unwell? How awful!

But now all that unpleasantness has passed, has it not? Well, I certainly do hope so! Also with us everything has returned to normal. We are all as healthy as fish; wonderful, isn't it?

Well, Mevrouw, I shall end, because my sister also wants to write something on this letter. My warmest regards to you and Mijnheer and once again thank you for your present,

by your Kartinah

The young writer of this is the best one of us all: a model of goodness and gentleness and so honest and conscientious. That she loves neatness you can see from her beautifully written letter. We older ones can in many ways learn from her example.

Forgive us our sisterly pride. We are truly privileged creatures: to have such sisters—and such friends—as you two are. Good-bye!

[Kartini][7]

Kartinah to Rosita Abendanon-Mandri

Jepara, 14 June 1902

Dearest Mevrouw!

May I offer you this small present as a souvenir of your visit to Jepara? I hope very much that as often as you will wear these slippers, you will give a thought to our little Jepara and the giver of this present! I think it is wonderful, dear Mevrouw, to be able to give you something, and so, as soon as I learned of Juffrouw Glaser's trip to Batavia[8] and that she was certain to pay you a visit, I set to work on a pair of slippers which she was only too happy to bring to you. Nice of her don't you think that she was prepared to do this for me?

Do you know from what I made the [decorative] flowers on these slippers? Mevrouw, can you guess? I don't think you could and so I will quickly tell you. They are nothing else but the caterpillar dolls which my sisters brought back from their visit to Batavia. They had been given them by the daughters of the Regent of Kutaarjo and later they were given to me to make all sorts of things, handicraft things, out of; because you see, Mevrouw, I am very fond of needlework and do an awful lot of it whenever I get the time. I so enjoy doing this and would *very, very* much like to gain training in it. Yet I do not dare to discuss this with my Parents for fear that I may receive a refusal to my request to take further lessons in my favorite pastime, and that would disappoint me terribly, I know.

So mum's the word about this desperately desired permission from my parents, although I regret terribly not daring to express this one wish; but to comfort myself, I *shall* and *will* ensure that I maintain what I do already know. Perhaps then later, says Roekmini who gave me this advice, something good may eventuate from it to my advantage. So now I am often making something or other for my sisters or girlfriends. There is no harm in that, is there, Mevrouw?[9]

But how are you and Mijnheer in the meantime? Both in good health, I hope?

I am able to report about us that we are all in perfect health, despite the bitter winds which daily beset us. Wonderful that Juffrouw Glaser will soon be seeing the beautiful Prianger and the great Batavia. Oh goodness, I would so love to take a look at both these residencies, especially the Preanger. It is meant to be absolutely *marvelous,* isn't it? My sisters never stop talking about it and are never too tired to tell me stories of that beautiful place, or I to listen to them. Wondrously beautiful Preanger, I wish I were sitting in your heart. It would be heavenly, wouldn't it?[10]

Well, Mevrouw dear, I will end, because I still have to wrap up the slippers. Hoping I will bring you some pleasure with this little gift, I remain, with my warmest regards to you both, always

Your Kartinah

Kartinah to Rosita Abendanon-Mandri

Jepara, 17 December 1902

Dear Sinterklaasje![11]

Oh, how you surprised the young ones of the Jepara Kabupaten with your parcel in which so many wonderful things lay buried which you, dear Sint, had intended for us. Thank you, thank you, many thanks for everything.

We are so happy with them, those sweet fans, how they beckon to us in such a friendly manner when we open the parcels, we cannot stop ourselves from briefly waving them. Oh, how nice, a gentle coolness blows towards us. Oh, dear Saint, how happy you have made us with these delightful presents which so totally suit a girl's room or a young girl's treasure chest![12] We therefore quickly deposited them in our chests among our many beloved souvenirs, those dear little fans. Oh, how I long to use one of mine as an ornament; as soon as there is an opportunity for it I will take out the most beautiful and I will be constantly thinking of the dear giver while I wave myself a heavenly coolness with the fan. And then the edibles, those sweets for which every young girl's mouth waters when she sees them, they look so delicious. The children[13] are enjoying them and for that matter so are we.

Dear, kind Saint, you will ruin us if you go on this way. Last year you also did not forget us; in fact we received so much then, too much in fact.— And from others we also received such nice, sweet surprises this year, so many: books, silk handkerchiefs with lovely white embroidered edges, gorgeous calendars for 1903, little statues and wall plates like the one which Roekmini received from you, and a heap of sweets. Isn't that a lot? And on top of that, a parcel from you. Oh, we were so pleased with it. So nice of you to still think of us this year and to send us so many nice things. Once more many thanks, dear, kind Mevrouwtje for these kind thoughts. I hope that we will be able to repay you!

There was no doubt a big celebration there with you to honor the Saint's arrival. Here in the town there was no celebration; nothing was happening on that night; the days passed uneventfully. How sad for the poor schoolchildren, they had so counted on there being at least some toys and some biscuits handed out. Poor dears! I really felt sorry for them. Then like a ray of sunshine Mijnheer Both came to the schoolroom with a tin in his arms from which he distributed cakes to his pupils, who accepted them eagerly and with gratitude. Poor things, how their sad and disappointed faces lit up when the generous hand offered them those delicious things. Nice of Mr. Both (he is the new teacher, the replacement for Juffrouw Glaser) that he, despite the large number of children, still wanted to remember them all, don't you think?

Speaking of this kind man, did you know that for the last couple of months Soematri and I have been receiving lessons from him in the beautiful French language? We think it is wonderful, marvelous!!! Those dear, kind Parents of ours, how very kind of them to allow us to have these lessons in this elegant language which we had so much wanted.[14]

Oh, we think it is heavenly and we are so grateful to our Parents for their permission that we both promised with all our hearts that we would do our best as long as we were able to have these lessons so that Pa and Ma would be utterly pleased with their children. What a blessing that Mijnheer Both, that clever man, has been posted here. Now we are able to take advantage, with several others, of his talents, his ability. We are already relatively well advanced in the language, and between us we can already undertake several short conversations. Nice, don't you think? The Boths are a very dear family, the children are real treasures.

Finally our house has been finished: four whole months, yes four long months they have been at it; we have had to listen for four months to the maddening tapping, the hammering, and the banging. It was dreadful! But now all that deafening noise has finished and we are going to get a beautiful wide back veranda in the place of the previous untidy corner. It looks very attractive, and we have also got an additional two rooms of which one will be especially set up as our workroom, nice isn't it?[15]

Well, that is all, dear Saint. I will end here because it is late. Warm regards to you and Mijnheer and once more many thanks for all the kindnesses you have shown us, by your grateful

    Kartina [sic]

Kardinah, Kartini, and Roekmini, probably taken in Semarang, c. 1900. *Collection of the KITLV, Leiden, the Netherlands, photo number 15465. Reproduced by permission of the KITLV.*

Kartini, Kardinah, and Roekmini, probably taken in Semarang, 20 January 1901.
Collection of the KITLV, Leiden, the Netherlands, photo number 15467. Reproduced by permission of the KITLV.

Kartinah and Soematri, probably taken in Semarang, c. 1902.
Collection of the KITLV, Leiden, the Netherlands, photo number 15480. Reproduced by permission of the KITLV.

Ibu Ngasirah, probably taken in Semarang, date unknown. *Collection of the KITLV, Leiden, the Netherlands, photo number 9585. Reproduced by permission of the KITLV.*

Raden Ayu Moeryam, probably taken in Semarang, c. 1900. *Collection of the KITLV, Leiden, the Netherlands, photo number 44000. Reproduced by permission of the KITLV.*

Raden Mas Adipati Ario Sosroningrat, regent of Jepara, probably taken in Semarang, c. 1900. *Collection of the KITLV, Leiden, the Netherlands, photo number 43099. Reproduced by permission of the KITLV.*

Jacques Henri Abendanon, director of the Department of Education, Religion, and Industry, 1900–1905, Batavia, 1903. *Collection of the KITLV, Leiden, the Netherlands, photo number 34600. Reproduced by permission of the KITLV.*

Rosita Manuela Abendanon-Mandri, c. 1912. *Courtesy Mr. G. A. Abendanon.*

Home of Jacques and Rosita Abendanon, Kebon Sirih, Batavia, 1896. *Courtesy Mr. G. A. Abendanon*

Interior of Kebon Sirih home: piano room and Rosita's boudoir, 1896. *Courtesy Mr. G. A. Abendanon.*

The three sons of Jacques Abendanon, c. 1895: *(left to right)* Eduard (Edi), Dolph (Dop), and John. *Courtesy Mr. G. A. Abendanon.*

Kartini and her husband, Raden Adipati Djojoadiningrat, regent of Rembang, 1903. *Collection of the KITLV, Leiden, the Netherlands, photo number 15469. Reproduced by permission of the KITLV.*

Kartini, Raden Adipati Djojoadiningrat, Soematri, Roekmini, and Kartinah in Rembang, 21 November 1903. *Collection of the KITLV, Leiden, the Netherlands, photo number 15472. Reproduced by permission of the KITLV.*

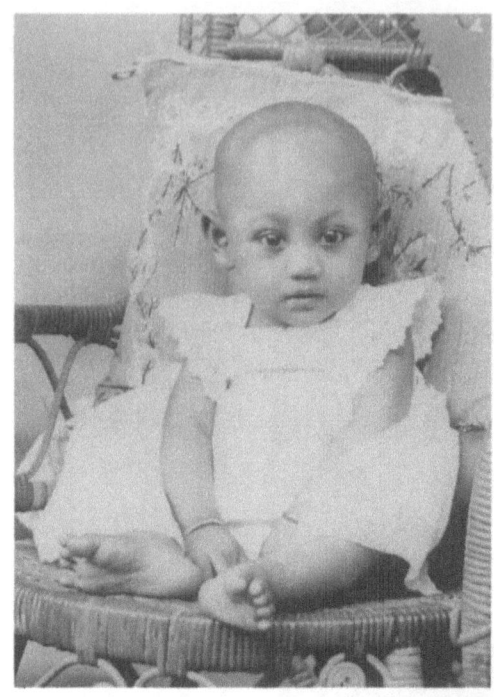

Raden Mas Singgih, Rembang, 13 September 1904. *Collection of the KITLV, Leiden, the Netherlands, photo number 15475. Reproduced by permission of the KITLV.*

Roekmini and her husband, Santoso, probably taken in Semarang. *Collection of the KITLV, Leiden, the Netherlands, photo number 15479. Reproduced by permission of the KITLV.*

Kartinah, probably taken in Semarang, 2 November 1909. *Collection of the KITLV, Leiden, the Netherlands, photo number 15481. Reproduced by permission of the KITLV.*

Soematri, probably taken in Semarang, c. 1910. *Collection of the KITLV, Leiden, the Netherlands, photo number 15483. Reproduced by permission of the KITLV.*

Soematri and her husband, Achmad Sostrohadikoesoemo, probably taken in Semarang, 1911. *Collection of the KITLV, Leiden, the Netherlands, photo number 15484. Reproduced by permission of the KITLV.*

Soematri and her son Soearto at three and a half months, probably taken in Semarang, 7 April 1912. *Collection of the KITLV, Leiden, the Netherlands, photo number 15485. Reproduced by permission of the KITLV.*

Jacques Henri Abendanon in The Hague, c. 1925. *Collection of the KITLV, Leiden, the Netherlands, photo number 15501. Reproduced by permission of the KITLV.*

Rosita Manuela Abendanon-Mandri, c. 1925. *Collection of the KITLV, Leiden, the Netherlands, photo number 15504. Reproduced by permission of the KITLV.*

Kartinah in 1930. *Collection of the KITLV, Leiden, the Netherlands, photo number 4437. Reproduced by permission of the KITLV.*

Three sisters with friend, 1935: *(left to right)* Kardinah, friend, Soematri, Roekmini. *Collection of the KITLV, Leiden, the Netherlands, photo number 15486. Reproduced by permission of the KITLV.*

Kartinah to Rosita Abendanon-Mandri

Jepara, 22 July 1904

Dear Mevrouw,

How surprised you will be when you receive this letter. No doubt you will have asked yourself who it could have come from before you opened it—or do you recognize our handwriting already, Mevrouw? I think so because even though it does not happen often, we had written to you several times already, hadn't we?

And here we are once again and with a big request to you both. Can you guess what it is? I think not, so I will quickly whisper in your ear what has driven me to write to you, otherwise I might forget, and that would be a pity! Do you know what we both, Soematri and I, have always wanted and what is one of our dearest wishes? Nothing other than a photograph of you and Mijnheer! Truly I envy my sisters that they have such a precious souvenir, do you know that? After all, aren't we also your children who, just like the sisters, are so fond of their parents? And that is why we also claim to ourselves the right to carry a souvenir of you both in our hearts. What do you think of this, dearest, dear Mevrouw? Oh, how happy I would be if I could have my dearest wish fulfilled. Really, with a dear photograph of you both I would feel myself to be as rich as I would if I had hundreds and hundreds of bags of gold. And we would care for the photograph as if it were gold. So I fervently hope that these so much desired souvenirs will not be refused. You would make us extremely happy, you know that, don't you? My deepest thanks in anticipation and a couple of big kisses on your cheeks for that wonderful, and for us so desired, souvenir.

And now, how are things with you and with Mijnheer? I sincerely hope that he will be feeling much better now after his stay in the cooler and healthier climate and that he will now be able to get back to his work with renewed enthusiasm and energy. Mijnheer needs lots of rest, doesn't he, dear Mevrouw, after all those tiring days and all that hard work? A couple of months were much too short a period to get the complete rest that he must have needed, to have had its full effect. But Mijnheer cannot stand doing nothing, can he? My sisters have often told me that. I suppose he could not endure staying any longer in that cool climate. Oh, sometimes how I admire him his enthusiasm, his energy and his ability to work, and I sincerely hope for you both that God will grant you his constant support.

Is it true you will soon be going to Europe with Mijnheer? Oh, I am very happy for you both about this, dearest Friends. Enjoy to the fullest that healthy Dutch climate and don't return until you are certain that all your strength and health have returned. We will then wish you a hearty welcome back here to beautiful Insulinde. But first rest in Europe and only then come back, isn't that the idea, dear Mevrouw?[16]

We have received good news from our married sisters. It's wonderful. We were so worried recently about our Kardinah. She had been so ill, poor thing. But, thank God, she is in the care of a clever specialist now, Dr. Schmidt, and is now recovering well under his treatment, and we can breathe again. And then Kartini had also been ill but that was because of her being pregnant and now she is again her sweet, happy, fat self again. Isn't it wonderful, Mevrouw, that she is expecting a baby in September? Who would have thought this last year at this time! She, a mother! Oh what an excellent and loved mother she will be. She left us a wonderful reminder of herself that we have inscribed deep in our hearts. We will never, never forget the time we had together. She was for us little ones such a dear little mother and she is that still, even though she is now so far away from us. But we will never stop loving her, really, never.

Well, this is it, Mevrouw. Would you give Mijnheer our warmest regards and to you too, after once more begging you for a photograph,

Lots of love,
From yours truly,
Your Kartinah

Kartinah to Rosita Abendanon-Mandri

Jepara, 24 November 1904

Dear Mevrouw,

How surprised I was when cousin Hassim brought us that parcel from you and especially when, after opening it, it turned out there was something in it for us as well, which was a photograph of you. You could hardly have made us happier. Oh think, it is so lovely of you to have thought of us and have sent it to us. Dearest *mevrouwtje*, may I give you a big kiss for it and warmly clasp your hand for this wonderful souvenir that I now have of you. And I will look after it so well, you have no idea. Oh, I have longed for a photograph of you for a long time and now that this wish has been realized, I would now love to be able to fly to you to show you how grateful I am. Oh, it has made me so happy.

At the moment that I am writing this I have you next to me, dearest Mevrouw, and am fondly gazing into your eyes that seem to be telling me something, how fate has dealt us such sorrow, it is terrible. And when I think back to the time we had spent together last April, and how we had enjoyed your being with us. Then it is as though my heart is torn open, it hurts so much. Did it in fact happen, or was it not just a frightening dream, I often ask myself. And then a voice inside tells me, it is true. Her child, the sweet treasure of us all which is now so utterly alone, brings everything back to me in stark reality. Oh God, oh God, why? Why did it have to happen this way? Didn't we all love her deeply and was she not always our dearest one, our pearl, our jewel. Why then was she taken from us? Oh, it is so hard, so hard, and I don't know if I shall be able to carry this heavy trial calmly. Oh, I would sacrifice everything, everything, yes even myself if I could, just to recall her back to earth, to let her nurture her child with all her love, and to once more stand beside her husband.

Oh, that poor, poor brother-in-law of ours, how that loss must press down on him. He is suffering terribly, and then to have no one who can comfort him, to give him strength. Isn't that terrible? Oh, Mevrouw, if I could go against my *adat* then I would immediately go to him, take his hands in mine and tell him how we suffer with him and, as well as I were able, to whisper words of comfort to him. That would be wonderful for us all. But now, things being as they are, all we can do is glance at each other fleetingly, and even that may only occur occasionally, which I regret so much. Oh, it is so very different with us than with Europeans. It makes me so sad sometimes, especially in situations like this. Do you then just have to watch someone suffer without being allowed to stretch out a hand of sympathy? You can understand, Mevrouw, that I think such an attitude is very strange.[17] Oh, how I would love to extend a hand to this fine brother-in-law as warmly, as warmly as possible. But this too will probably never happen, and that is why I seek my own comfort in the child that can lie so sweetly and quietly on its mattress, it is so peaceful to look at. Carefully I pick him up and press him tightly to me while my trembling lips cover his little cheeks and lips with countless kisses. Poor, poor thing, I think then. Can you yet comprehend what a huge and irreplaceable loss has befallen you?

Oh, Mevrouw, if only you could see him, the dear little poppet. So healthy and so well formed, and so bright and sweet. It's really a gorgeous child. Oh goodness, that it should experience such a loss at so young an age. Our little thing, if only we could hold on to you, how wonderful that would be. But I do not think this good fortune will be our lot because our brother-in-law is so opposed to giving us the child because he himself can't bear to be parted from it, the poor man.

Well, adieu, dearest Mevrouw. Once again thank you for the wonderful souvenir and a big kiss from,
Yours always,
Kartinah

Kartinah to Mr. Abendanon

Jepara, 10 May 1909

Dear Mijnheer Abendanon,

Would you be so good as to withdraw your thoughts from your work for one infinitely small moment to listen to someone who, on behalf of her entire family, comes to you to offer her sincere thanks for the great support you have shown to Kartono in his difficult time?

Oh, dear Friend, how we thank you for what you have done and are still doing for Kartono. How very joyful we were when Kartono wrote and told us all about this himself. Were it possible, we would all fly to you to personally express our gratitude to you. God be praised that in life, however somber and sad it may be, there is usually a solution by which those whom Fate has touched can take up their lives again with renewed strength and confidence.

Oh, what a life full of care and difficulty Kartono has experienced. Although we don't know all the details, I feel that his suffering in recent years must have been great, and what worries he has had to cope with! His life has been marked by misery, a series of obstacles, and all kinds of problems just when he had to complete his studies. Most certainly his life has been far from rose-colored in recent years. In his letters he has revealed clearly how tragic his situation has been, and time and time again it caused us great sadness and concern. And learning about and hearing of so much suffering without being able to provide the necessary help and rescue—isn't that terrible too?

It is therefore impossible to describe our joy when Kartono told us of your generous assistance that, like a warm clear ray of light, fell and kept shining on his tragic and hopeless life. As a result, like magic, his tragic situation changed into something more hopeful. His exhausted spirit was able to taste once more some of the joy of which he has been deprived for so long. New courage and strength surged through his body and spirit and this enabled him to finally complete his studies. How overjoyed we were with the news that he has finally passed. Father and our dear sister Kartini should have been alive to witness this—how overjoyed they too would have been.

Dear Friends, for the thousandth time, please accept from afar our expressions of deep gratitude. God grant that from now on a happier life may await my brother who lives there, utterly alone, in a strange land.[18]

Also our thanks for sending us your sensitive article about the "Education of Native Girls in the Netherlands Indies," which we have read with great interest.[19] I was touched in finding there several passages from the letters of our beloved sister Kartini that you included. We were so moved to read them, and to read between the lines her passion and utter happiness at receiving Father's permission to continue her studies. Oh, if only she had been allowed to live longer, she would have been able to achieve *much, much* more for her fellow countrymen, specifically for her fellow women. May her spirit rest in peace!

The situation in the Netherlands Indies regarding the education of our girls remains miserable; there has been no response yet to the numerous earnest pleas to provide to women too the opportunity for spiritual development. Everywhere the cry for more education is being silently expressed. Who would dare to suggest that Javanese women do not feel the need for more knowledge and new skills? This would surely be a cowardly assertion. Yet among our most highly educated male countrymen there are still some who continue to dare to hold to this view. Is that not scandalous? When will the time finally arrive for us Javanese women to open up a broader pathway in our society? As long as conservatives retain their hold over most minds, we will just have to observe passively the developments that surround us. Oh, may the times soon bring great changes to this situation.

We warmly applauded the establishment of Budi Utomo and have attached ourselves to it. May it be a support for us in many ways! May its efforts be rewarded![20]

Kartono keeps us well informed about the [Indies] Association in Holland.[21] He also told us the boys of the Association occasionally gather at your house and that you have very pleasant and friendly discussions there. Knowing how you and Mevrouw continue to interest yourselves in the Native, I can easily understand that.

In the meantime, how are you both? I can report only good tidings about the three of us, Soematrie, Ma, and myself. Time has taught us to accept and understand. Even the great suffering of recent years has been educative and has allowed us to see life from all sides. We have come to accept it.

Dear Friend, would you be so kind as to give Mevrouw our warmest regards.

We take our leave of you, once more with a warm handshake,
Remaining yours,
Ever grateful,
Kartinah

Kartinah to Lien (Johanna Wilhelmina Caroline) van den Berge-Kelder, Padang[22]

Jepara, 20 September 1909

Dear Lien,

Together with this comes my thanks for your dear letter of 1 Sept. and for the book you sent us as souvenir. Lien, you simply cannot imagine how *overjoyed* we were when we saw those wonderful books for us. You know how we always longed to have them. They contain such a lot of fine things about women so that it really will be a great pleasure each time when I pick mine up to read. Oh, dear Lien. Let me give you another big kiss in my thoughts for your wonderful souvenir. As soon as I have time I will read it and then I will tell you what parts of it most grip me. Now I am still up to my ears in other work and, moreover, I am still busy with another book which I had already begun when your letter arrived. So I will finish this one first and save your book because to do everything at once is an impossibility, isn't it?

Up till now there is no sign of any improvement in the life of this deserted town. Phie Castens remains the only one with whom we spend any time. From time to time we go for a stroll, and then the destination of our walk is always the sea. And when we are on the beach, that huge expanse of the sea before us with the ever-changing color spectacle of the setting sun, as it were, spread out across the gently swaying water, across which hundreds of birds are flying like little souls, we enjoy it so much we would never want to leave such beauty. You know amongst the fishponds, many little pathways have now been made with here and there little bamboo bridges and these pathways all lead out to the sea. Apart from these, they have also made a larger road intended for vehicles, and we have also walked along there. And on both sides of these paths are the well-tended fishponds. All this creates a wonderful impression and really, it is very enjoyable strolling along there. And then to know that this is all the work of Terburgh.[23] Phie says that he really has earned a medal picturing a two-faced image on it. Oh, such ungrateful creatures we are!!

On Friday the 17th this month it was Mev. Casten's birthday and the next evening, that is, on the Saturday, they gave a dinner where we two were the only invited guests. It was more like a private occasion, you know. That same evening Mr. C[asten] came back by car with Lucie and Chris and Mr. Monod with whom Phie is secretly engaged.[24] It was an enjoyable evening. Mr. C. is looking well and has even put on weight. He was really very nice to us.[25] Mrs. C. is always very friendly to us and has an inexhaustible supply of jokes.

Lien, I just said before that Phie is sort of engaged, but Lien, you must not tell tales out of school, okay? Please wait till it has become publicly announced, and then you can congratulate her. We both think he is the type of "Handsome Man" (Donkers[26]), but of course in Phie's eyes he is a charming fellow. Oh, she is so happy and is always talking about him. And we are always teasing her. He lives in Semarang and comes over every Saturday by car. He's an extremely rich young man, Lien. I have no doubt that they will be marrying in February.

Oh, by the way, this month we will be going to Ngawi and will probably be staying there quite a while. Please don't ignore us while we are there and send us a note from time to time. The best thing to do will be to just address your letters to Jepara. Mr. Blom[27] will arrange to send them on. I am taking my Hilda[28] with me. Thank goodness, we will be seeing something new.

We received from the firm Grese and Conrads some samples of fine material but not the kind of material that we really wanted to buy. It seems they have not got what we want. What are we going to do now? Perhaps we will order some anyway.

What unpleasant types the Van Bengens[29] are.

[incomplete]

Kartinah to Lien van den Berge-Kelder

Jepara, 20 December 1909

Dear Lien,

From the postcard we sent you, you could read that we were still staying with Marietje and Guus when we received your letter of 23/10. That's the reason why we were not able to place your order and why, because of all that traveling and visiting, we were not able to reply to you any earlier. Lien, I hope however that our silence did not make you think that that you are out of favor with us. You must not have such mean thoughts about those fine ladies (à la Marietje), absolutely not. Well, you know us well enough to be able to work that out for yourself surely.

Well, I am going to tell you about all the things that have been happening recently and especially about our fantastic vacation we had not so long ago. Oh Lien, that was such a great time. Us, away from J[epara] for about 2 months! What do you think of that? Everywhere we had such a crazy time, as you can imagine. First we stayed a long time with my brother and sister in Ngawi, who, as you know, have a child of about a year old. It's a real treasure and very big and very clever for its age. He looks just like our father, which really struck us. I won't have to tell you that we spent a lot of time with that little boy. His older brother, a boy of about 11, was also overjoyed that his aunties had finally come to visit again. We could not get rid of him. Yes we had so much fun with those little fellows.

Then Marietje also came to Ngawi for about 5 days with the intention of then taking us by train to Boja, which is what happened. What a steep climb it is from Jerakak to Boja. Marietje and Soematrie were sitting in a *bendy* while Guus and I arrived sitting very proudly and sophisticatedly in a rattling post carriage.[30] It was a case of constantly climbing, up and down mountains. The terrain is terribly steep, and then the carriage swayed so much that I was dead tired when we finally arrived. But I could immediately feel the cool air, directly after the first part of the climb. Lien, the air is so wonderful, healthy and cold. I loved it and I gulped down the fresh air in large drafts. To the right and left of the road were the dark teak forests, coffee plantations, palm and coconut palm plantations, and every now and again in a valley you got a wonderful view of the Sumbang, Sindono, and other mountains. Wasn't that marvelous? I so enjoyed all of that and Guus just kept explaining everything to me.

We finally arrived at our destination at 8 o'clock at night. They have a lovely house that they have furnished and arranged in a very cozy way. We had inspected the entire house in a flash. Marietje flew from one corner to the other along with us, truly. Altogether we stayed there for 4 weeks and every day we four just had a great time. We made some wonderful excursions to tea and indigo plantations situated 1,100 to 3,000 meters above sea level where it was deliciously cold. And there one is surrounded by the beauty of nature, which is simply overwhelming. We also entered real primeval jungle, riding through its dense wilderness, which was full of monkeys, wild pigs, and that sort of thing. M. and I sat in a bendy while the others drove through the forest in a car, and because of the carelessness of M., who was in charge of the horse, we almost ended up in one of the spectacular ravines. Frightening, really.

M. was excited and full of life while we were there, and G. also showed the cheerful side of his personality, so that in the beginning I thought everything was fine again between them. But this was far from being so, Lien. The relationship between them is all right, and for people who have only just met them, that is also what it seems. But I noticed that things were not as they should be between two people who love each other, and this knowledge can make me very sad. They lead completely separate lives, don't you think that's sad? Although we had a really fine time staying with them, I should tell you that I am also happy now to be at some distance from them. To witness their separate existence is far from pleasant. And yet, whatever the situation, we still feel great affection for them, and this is mutual. Will they never return to the right path? In March they will be going to Buitenzorg. Guus has received an offer to work at B., and given that the people there have already accepted all the conditions that Guus had laid down, they will soon have to pack their bags and to go to that smart city. M. is absolutely cut out for that kind of life, but G. is not.[31]

Lien, it's a very sad state of affairs here now. The few souls who still live around here don't get on with each other—they have their own separate clubs—this is the outcome of what that famous *kaum* generation has achieved.[32] Kroes and family have withdrawn from public life and now only remain friends with the Blommetjes. No one notices the little Jews anymore, these people are fully occupied making money, and have disagreements with everybody. St. Nicolas was celebrated, we heard, but relations between the people here were such that only the Regent's family, van Bengen, and then the two van Pengkols came. Van P. came loyally with his wife and child and, altogether there were only ... 2 ladies. Great, isn't it?? Kroes and his family decided to stay home and celebrated *Sint* themselves with the Blommetjes.[33] Isn't the social life all going well here! We want to keep ourselves entirely out of it, and remain friends with everyone. One evening we had van Kroes, Kees, and the Blommetjes visiting us. They were very pleasant and talked about everything. Kühr is leaving and we are going to get Wiggers in his place. About this, a little later. We tend to see the Castens family fairly regularly. Mien and Phie are busy preparing an outfit for the bride who will be leaving the family home on 7 Feb. The Castens themselves are seriously thinking of retiring in March or April. The man is finished and must have rest. Who will we then get to head the government here?[34]

Lien, *Hilda* is now so dear to me, you don't know the half of it.[35] Time and again I open it and never tire of rereading the words. Or rather those beautiful sayings, which relate so much to our situation in this life, full of struggle to achieve what is noble and good. For instance: "Everything is born in tears and in these periods of transition, most of us will only be able to enter life fully after a period of struggle." Isn't that beautifully expressed? I find the characters of Corontje and Frank very sympathetic. I always reread the book with great pleasure. Once again a big kiss for giving it to me.

How did you celebrate Sint? We two poor wretches were also given a surprise.

Okay, good-bye, Lien. Don't forget to give your husband our regards. For you a big kiss and embrace from,

Kartinah (the little one)

By the way, Phie's handkerchief was not so heavy that extra tariff had to be paid, don't worry about it.

Kartinah to Rosita Abendanon-Mandri

Jepara, 12 December 1910

Dear Mevrouw,

We have read both your last two letters to Roekmini. God, what wonderful news is contained in them for us alone, and for all of that we have you to thank, to thank from the bottom of our hearts, you who have never ceased to offer us so much help in our troubles. Dear Friends, how will I ever be able to thank you enough for everything that you have done. I am and will remain *deeply* grateful. Yes, let us hope that from now on K[artono] will be able to persevere with his work and that everything may still come to a good conclusion.[36]

We are certainly pleased to hear that everything is well with you. We can say the same about our old mother and us two. We are sending you, together with this letter, our most recent photographs as a small token of our friendship for you. Well, can you still recognize the Kardinah and Soematri who were still little things when you were both here in Jepara and stayed with us?

At Roekmini's house recently we saw a nice group photograph of you both with your children and grandchildren. You are both looking very well in the photograph, and goodness, how big your grandchildren are already. One can see from the photo that you are both not half proud. And do they often come to stay with Opa and Oma?

You will no doubt have already heard that in Nov. last Roekmini had her second daughter. Wonderful, don't you think? It is a darling of a child. And her oldest has already become quite big. R. is very fond of her little treasures and is now already full of plans for them. May all her wishes for them become realized and may her daughters grow up to be women who will one day succeed in achieving that goal that we always had in view. We should therefore constantly pray for the health and well-being of these children!

We have not once had Kartini's little boy here with us, even though we would have been so very delighted had he come. However we continue to send our little darling our best wishes. I hope he will always be well. Recently his *babu,* who had to be in Jepara, brought us a message from Singgih that he had received from his Oma a slate, some fine slate pencils, an automobile (a real one), and a beautiful carriage. What do you think of that little dear? We have sent him several small gifts that he was so pleased with. Oh, how sad that his mother is not able to see this.

Dear Moeder, can I ask you a big favor? It concerns the letters of our Kartini that will be published in book form. As soon as the first ones appear, will you tell the publisher to send a copy to us? My sincere thanks for this, Mevrouw.

No doubt you had already met Mr. Jasper here in the Indies, the man who had made such a name for himself by devoting himself to the Native arts and the training of Native girls. We also had the pleasure of meeting him and his family when they were still living in Surabaya. A likable man, isn't he, who will never run out of energy or the like. He has just received a fine position in Holland. Won't he enjoy that![37]

We also know the monthly paper, *Oedayana Para Prayitna,*[38] in which Mr. Noto Soeroto[39] often writes. He seems to us such a fine person, doesn't he? For the last year or so we have been corresponding with the Raden Ajengs of the Pakualaman House.[40] If I am not mistaken, one of them is the sister of Mr. Noto Soeroto while another is an aunt of his. No doubt you have also met over there R. M. Amby-a, an uncle of the Regent of Kastoardjo?[41] Do you know that his brother, R. M. Soemoto, passed away not so long ago? The pity of it is that he was apparently a very clever boy! So you see here once again how strangely things can turn out in the world at large. People of whom the world has high expectations bid farewell to life while the great gross of mankind who account for nothing live on, yes, forever. Objectively seen, life is really a sea of misery, don't you think?

Mevrouw, I have to end here because the mail will close soon. On another occasion I hope to be able write you more about everything.

Please accept, with Mijnheer, once again our deepest thanks for everything, and imagine that we warmly take your hand,
Your,
Kartinah

Kartinah to Rosita Abendanon-Mandri

Jepara, 27 February 1911

Dear Mevrouw,

May I call on your help, Mevrouw? We would love to send Kartono a letter but do not know where he is actually living. And since Mijnheer last wrote that K. was now again living with you, we took the liberty to enclose our letter to him with this. We can, can't we for this time? Would you therefore please give K. our letter? Many thanks for your help Mevrouw.

Last December we sent you a letter with our latest photos—did they arrive? In that letter, Soematri told you about her engagement, didn't she? Well, since then the date for the wedding has been decided. It will take place on the 7th of April forthcoming, in other words in a month's time. It seems as if time has wings these days, it's flying past and before I know it, the 7th April will have come around. God grant that everything will go off smoothly.

And how are you and Mijnheer faring? Here with us all is well. The two daughters of Roekmini are little treasures and Oma of course dotes on them, the aunties no less.

What wonderful news about K[artono], Mevrouw. I so hope that he will keep going this way. And when he submits his dissertation will he then graduate immediately? My God, let us not wait again helplessly. Our thanks to you and to Mijnheer for everything that you have done do date.

Mevrouw, you won't mind if I stop now, will you? All kind of busy activities prevent me from sitting too long at my writing table. We hope to hear from you soon.

Please accept with Mijnheer our warmest regards and our deepest thanks for everything.
Your,
Kartinah

Kartinah to Rosita and Mr. Abendanon

Jepara, 14 July 1911

Dear Friends,

On the 4th of this month the mail brought us your thousand times marvelous gift. Oh, how utterly, utterly grateful my Ma and I both are for your priceless gift, in the form of a book in which are published the wonderful, beautiful ideas of our unforgettable Kartini.[42] Oh, Mevrouw and Mijnheer, what a swarm of ideas filled my head when I took the book in my hands. It is indescribable; no words could sufficiently give account of it, dear Friends! I held it tightly and a powerful, indescribable feeling took hold of me when I saw her picture in the book. I looked into her dear eyes, and looking at her, felt the tears coming to my eyes. It was just as if she was standing before me. Oh my God, I could never forget her, or my beloved Father.

Oh, Dearest Friends (I can call you that, can't I?), how wonderfully dear and good you constantly have been to us. What have you not always done for us and how you continue to do so! Mevrouw, Mijnheer, in my thoughts I warmly and heartily clasp your hand! We pray fervently to God that one day we may still be given the opportunity to see you both again in person, here in Java to give you in person that token of our deep acknowledgment and appreciation. Oh, may this prayer be realized one day.

Dearest Friends, I am still too overwhelmed by my great joy in being in possession of your wonderful souvenir that writing is still too difficult. Hence my brief note—you won't mind, will you? But I promise that I will send you with another mail a more detailed letter. My thoughts are still confused and I am oh, so happy with my book. Once again, many thanks for this.

I hope this note finds you both in good health. In your thoughts accept my warm handshake,

Your grateful and happy,
Kartinah

Kartinah to Lien van den Berge-Kelder

Jepara, 20 October 1911

Lien, dearest Lien,

Finally you are getting a letter from me. Well, aren't you pleased? You can see from this that your poor little Javanese mate is still alive and is still doing very well. Also my dear old mother is still enjoying good health, that's wonderful, isn't it? And I am right in thinking the same about you two, am I not? On the photo, for which I thank you very much, by the way, you are all looking very well. The little prince I think is simply gorgeous, I could just bite into those little arms. He looks most like you, Lien—am I right? Oh, what will your husband say when he reads this. He obviously will also want his fair share? I mean of all the little attributes such as a baby has. Am I right? Yes, yes, the gentlemen can also have their pride, I know that lot.

Oh yes, thanks also on behalf of our mother for your good wishes on the occasion of the *hari raya*.[43] We had a fabulous time on that day. Matri and Mad visited us so that the set was complete again.[44] Oh, it was so nice for me to have her again, Lien. I enjoyed every moment of the time we were home together. Matri stayed with us for one long wonderful week and throughout that whole time we chatted nonstop about everything! Such a pity that that has now all come to an end. Once again I am sitting here all on my own. Can you imagine? I hope furiously that she (Matri) will come to visit often and that she will remain in Semarang for a long time!

Lien, my dear Jepara is looking worse and worse; it's terrible the way society here is now. On the square they established a tennis court some time ago but I believe that barely one quarter of the people play there, nice, isn't it! The ass[istant] res[ident] has left his wife and children in Holl., the contr[oleur] is not yet married. The post officer the same. The Wiggers family has already disappeared with the Nordessens and the administrator of the regional bank is also still without . . . a wife![45] Only the teachers (Bergma and de Boer) make up a jolly group because at least they came here with their women. What do you think of all this? A bit frightening, yes? So I don't really have anything to do with anyone here and so I am not seen anywhere.

But on the other hand, at home I am leading a hectic life. I am now everything at home, *dame de la maison,* secretary and whatever for my old mother, so I am constantly busy. For reading matter there is always the newspaper that I now get every day like an old friend, and every now and then Mr. Ginsil brings us some good reading material. From him I get books from the W.B. and the N.B., which are really good and educational. Do you know them, Lien? And when Mr. G. is here again for some time then I can once again have hours of enjoyment. That poor man knows so much about the arts. It is really a pleasure to hold a conversation with him. It is as a result of this also that I have gained *a reputation!* Because I constantly choose his company over that of the young people. What fools you can encounter in this world, can't you? But all that talk leaves me completely cold.

We have had several attacks of cholera here, Lien. And oh, what a terrible lot of young lives were taken here, it's terrible.[46] The heat in the last few months has also been unbearable. Everything was completely dried out. But thank God, it has been raining again here since the last few days and I hope that then very soon the west monsoon will take hold. What a blessing that will be for the people!

Well then, dear Lien, you have once again caught up with my news. Once again, many thanks for your nice letter. Send me some news again quickly, won't you. Give your husband my warmest regards and a kiss from me for you and your little treasure.

    Your,
    Kartinah

Kartinah to Lien van den Berge-Kelder

Jepara, 6 December 1912

Dear Lien,

What a delicious little fellow you two have! It's such a lovely photo of you three. I love having it, really. Many thanks for that and also for your letter and the efforts you made for me in getting those addresses that I requested. Thanks, thanks for everything, Lieneke dear! Everything is all right between us now, isn't it? I am so very happy about that, you know!

Forgive me for not having written back to you earlier, Lien. When your letter arrived I was out of town for an entire week. Firstly I went to stay with Roekmini and after that with Soematrie. They were such wonderfully enjoyable days. I only returned home on the 3rd of November and we had only just got back when Moeder became ill, very, very ill. I was desperate and was so afraid you cannot imagine. Fortunately the Dokter Djawa (you will still remember Dr. Moertar) came immediately and helped Moeder to get better. "Thank God!" was the cry that came from the bottom of my heart! And now Moeder has completely recovered.

And I had barely rested from the efforts and anxiety that that had occasioned when my married sister arrived with her family. They came to see Moeder and stayed a week. That again gave me lots to do, but it was a pleasant busy-ness, I could love more of that, you understand!

So there you are, dear Lien, the reason for me not having written. I was constantly so busy! Because here at home I am master and mistress of the house. Moeder has earned her rest that she needs. I, on the other hand, have the energy of youth and can cope with all that work. What do you think, hey!

It was also nice of Mr. Lekkerkerker[47] to help me with getting those addresses. Would you also thank him for me at some opportune moment? Lien, I have already written to the Nawani ladies and have already received a reply. Their reply was very brief, so I cannot yet tell you what impression I have of them. I hope that later they will be a little freer in their communication with me. As to the other ladies, I had better not carry on a correspondence with them because I don't know the Malay language, as you probably know. That's a pity, isn't it! I already have quite a number of Native girlfriends with whom I am writing in Dutch. Some write particularly well—and have good ideas. At the moment we are planning something, you know, Lien. We would very much like to do something together to help our sisters in general. But what? Actually, I already have an idea but I first need to consult with all my Native girlfriends for advice. Oh, this exchanging of ideas with all these girls is such fun! I haven't ever seen any of my correspondents.[48] What do you think of that?

Nice, isn't it, Lien, that Mr. Ooievaar will be visiting you again next year! How that will amuse your Jeremiah![49] I hope everything ends up well.

Lien, Lien, I also still like Marietje Versteegh[50] a lot and would give anything to know where she is at the moment. She left a year or so ago for Holland, no doubt you know that too, but what her address is now I really cannot tell you. She was such a sweet thing, with a heart that always thirsted for lots of sincere, warm love. My God! That it had to end so tragically. Poor, poor woman! My love for her has not changed despite everything, really! May fate one day bring us together again.

If nothing intervenes next year in April I will once again leave this dreary town for a few months, Lien. That's a nice prospect isn't it? I will then be going to Kendal, where my oldest sister is currently living and from there I will go on to Tegal, where my no. 4 sister has been living for many years in her position as wife of the Regent. And whom I haven't seen for some 8 years. Remarkable, isn't it! Very likely I will then be staying there for a month or so. At any rate I don't think my sis will be throwing me out too quickly. Well, for my part, I'm very happy to be wandering around in the world.

Adieu, dear Friends. Wishing you three all the best. My warmest regards to you all.

Your old *sobat,*
Tinah

Kartinah to Rosita Abendanon-Mandri

Jepara, 11 April 1915[51]

Dear Mevrouw,

On behalf of my mother, I am able to inform you and Mijnheer that I have become engaged to Raden Dirdjoprawiro, Wedono of Samosita (Pomorogo), and that, if nothing intervenes, our wedding will take place on 20 June next. As you have both shown great interest in everything that concerns our family, we hope that now also this news of ours will also please you.

Also, now that last bird will fly out of the parental nest to build and live in her own nest in S., the old Mother of ours will consequently then be alone, although with the comforting thought that her children will be well situated and happy. It seems to me that for a mother this is the most important thing.

But now, how is everything with you? You will probably never see Java again, I think. In the meantime an incredible lot has been achieved in the interests of our people. It's such a pleasing sign for Java.

You probably already know that my uncle from Demak has passed away. The last representative of Tjondronegoro dynasty has thus finally made his appointment with the eternal judge. It was a terrible blow for the whole family. Who will follow in his footsteps? The eldest son is the Jaksa of Salatiga and the youngest has only just been named scribe of the Controleur of Ambarrawa. Will the government in this case make an exception and allow one of the sons to replace the father? That is a question that absorbs the attention of many at the moment.[52]

Dear Mevrouw, I have to be brief, unfortunately. But I hope that you will not hold this against me.

Mother sends her warm regards. And I warmly squeeze your hand.

    From,
    Your Kartinah

My address will be:
    Raden Ayu Wedono Dirdjoprawiro
    District Samosita
    Panorogo
    Java

Chapter 4

LETTERS FROM SOEMATRI

Introduction

Soematri, the youngest of the five siblings, appears to be the most "modern." Her letters are descriptive and practical, and she is an astute observer of the changing life around her. Her character also seems the closest to Kartini's, at least in the outgoing liveliness that Nicolaus Adriani had noted, if not in the intellectual depth revealed in Kartini's writing.

Soematri lived the most public and modern life of all the sisters. Her engagement and marriage were less traditional even than Roekmini's, but her reaction to tradition seems to have been less emotionally charged than that of her three previously married sisters. For her, the break with tradition seems to have been something already achieved, with which she no longer needed to struggle. Soematri was also the most mobile, and her correspondence, together with that of her husband, reflects and is informative about the new Indonesian middle class that evolved in the first decades of the twentieth century. As in her sisters' correspondence, Soematri's sentiments, reflecting her class and its perception of the ideological enemies that threaten its view of a modern world, suggest firm personal convictions. There is no sense that they simply echo her husband's sentiments. Her jolly letters to Lien, the young teacher's wife, indicate the easy relationship she was able to form across what, for many, remained clear racial boundaries. Her husband, although these boundaries were especially clear for men, also appears to operate easily in the European half of the colonial world.

This modern urban couple found themselves in the midst of the internal political battle of an emerging nationalist movement. They may not have been central players, but they were clearly located on the edges of the key political debates of the second decade of the century, as the earlier and apparently straightforward demands for progress and greater autonomy became muddied. They participated in the emerging definition of the competing objectives and strategies of various political movements in Java at the time: of European and Javanese progressives; of Indo, Chinese, and Indonesian nationalists; and of the competing streams of Javanese nationalism, ranging from associationist-liberal to Marxist-radical nationalists.

Soematri's husband, Raden Ngabehi (Achmad) Sosrohadikoesoemo, is the most confident and representative member of the new Javanese political elite to appear in this correspondence. Kardinah's and Kartini's husbands, although younger, represented *bupati* of the old school like Soematri's father and uncle and Kartini's old husband, appointed on dynastic principles. Even so, these bupati were already representative of a new generation of appointees, selected for their Western education and Dutch language ability and their support for colonial reform.[1] Sosrohadikoesoemo's influence, however, was exercised not through the traditional Javanese hierarchical structures but through the new channels provided by the structures of modern colonial administration and urban society. His accumulated cultural capital enabled him to gain a position on the newly established municipal council and to become a member of the organization for Javanese colonial officials and the Kartini School committee.

Like Roekmini's husband, Mas Santoso, Sosrohadikoesoemo was a "self-made man," although apparently from a more privileged background. More importantly, he represented the new generation, selected from an early age to undertake a Western education, which apparently involved boarding in urban Semarang from the age of six until he completed both European elementary and secondary schooling (HBS) and education in the Netherlands, followed by sitting for the civil service examination. He became one of the first Javanese employed in what came to be known as a "class C" civil service position, traditionally reserved for Europeans. Unlike Soematri's brother, the slightly older Sosrokartono, whose preparation his paralleled, Sosrohadikoesoemo succeeded in making the transition to the modern world of colonized Java, and did so more successfully than Soematri's other brother, another secondary school graduate, the slightly younger Sosro Moeljono.

Moreover, he avoided the fate of Santoso, who found himself trapped within the traditional Javanese hierarchy, embedded in a colonial service that still took account of family background. Sosrohadikoesoemo's problems stemmed from the political conflict he had to confront, standing as he did between the more radical and, he would argue, extremist nationalists on the one side and, on the other, the demands to conform to a colonial regime to which he was so closely tied but of which he was also immensely critical. Soematri only refers to this indirectly when she writes in 1932:

"The years that lie behind us have not been easy ones for us, but we won't linger on that—they have been difficult but now, fortunately, lie behind us, and after all, those difficult years also had their golden edges."[2]

Of all the correspondence, Soematri's has particular interest because it continues long enough to give a sense of how this first generation of Javanese nationalists reflected on the tumultuous years of the twenties, as her words above suggest. As indicated in the introduction, across the years of the correspondence Soematri provides regular impressions of a changing Java and its domestic life. In the 1930s, as a mature woman, she reflects nostalgically on a life now lost:

> Times have changed, Moedertje, they bring with them sadness and suffering. You see I am gradually becoming part of that older generation who sees with regret how everything has changed, at least according to my old-fashioned opinion. . . .[3]
>
> . . . We are of course the oldies, whom the young ones no longer feel comfortable with. Our parents left us with very pleasant memories of home that we have carried with us as a precious possession throughout our lives, but now that we ourselves are confronted with the fact, many parents don't know what to do. The chaos that has resulted from this has led in many cases to the need to reestablish a sense of family life.[4]

However, she also remains aware of what her generation had achieved: "It is unbelievable how much has been achieved in such a short time. We now already have our female doctors, our lawyers. People no longer question whether they should send their daughters to school. We have come a long way, but whether people are happier as a result?"[5]

A sense of generational change is emphasized when she refers to her teenage daughter and her student friends beginning their adult lives. They are so much more "advanced" than she had been at her age, Soematri sighs. The early struggles of her and her sisters, especially Kartini, are now so far in the past that their achievements are in danger of being taken for granted by a new generation.

In retirement in the cool mountain climate of Salatiga, Soematri's generation—or circle—may have felt that enough was enough. The real battle, however, was still to take place, though unfortunately the correspondence does not extend long enough to cover it. Soematri and Roekmini and their cohorts were not likely to have welcomed the radical upheaval of

Sukarno's revolution, no matter how much they accepted the ultimate goal of independence and becoming, as Roekmini had stated years earlier, able finally to undertake the responsibility that was theirs.

Soematri remained a cheerful and active correspondent, continuing to write to Rosita until it became apparent, five years before the elderly Rosita's death, that she was no longer able to reply. Significantly, Soematri also continued the correspondence for a decade after Abendanon's death, unlike her sisters, whose correspondence—at least their extant correspondence—ended at the beginning of the 1920s,[6] on the eve of the beginning of the political phase of the Indonesian nationalist movement. For them, it may be that the personal relationships that had generated two decades of correspondence had run out of emotional steam by 1920; the fragility of correspondence as a historical source, after all, lies in its dependence on the live bonds established between people. It may also be that the historical archive has been shaped by coincidence or happenstance. However, another possible conclusion is that, close as the personal contact had once been, relations between colonial and colonized had ineluctably drawn them apart. By 1920, for a growing circle of similarly positioned Javanese, the possibility of emotional or cultural association, let alone political association, had increasingly come to be seen as unlikely.

Soematri to Rosita Abendanon-Mandri

Jepara, 3 December 1901[7]

Dear Mevrouw!

Many thanks for the dear gifts which you have sent us. How pleased I was when my sister gave me the pretty fan, I really cannot tell you how happy I am with it. That very afternoon when we received your parcel, Kartinah and I were just talking about fans, that we would buy a nice fan from the hawker who often came by our house, but now that is of course not necessary, because we already have a beautiful fan from you.

How are you and Mijnheer? I heard from my sister that you and Mijnheer had been ill, but now all that is behind you, isn't it, Mevrouw? It must be terribly busy in Batavia at the moment, isn't it, because of the forthcoming *Sinterklaas* celebrations? Last year I received from the good Saint a beautiful postcard album and now I have already collected fifty postcards.

It's marvelous that the holidays are almost here and that I can rest for 10 days. My brother who is at the H.B.S. at Semarang[8] had his long vacation in September, four long weeks, and each day I saw him pass by the school, sometimes on a horse, other times on a bicycle. Oh, I was so envious of him that he could go each day to the beach, while I had to sit on my narrow school bench and work out difficult sums. But in the Christmas holidays, the roles will be reversed.[9]

Well, I will end my little letter now because I have nothing more to write.[10] You must not be angry that my writing is so untidy and so full of mistakes. Once again thank you for the fan and my warmest greetings,

By your,
Soematri

Soematri to Rosita Abendanon-Mandri

Jepara, December 1902

Dear Mevrouw

Many thanks for the presents you sent for Sint Nicholas, which were a great surprise. I am over the moon. I think the fans are beautiful and I will be using them at the first suitable occasion. What a good idea of yours to send us fans because we really need them in this unbearable heat. The biscuits were also very welcome; we feasted on them without thinking of the consequences! Fortunately toothache and stomachache did not eventuate so that we can still think back on that feast with pleasure. Our happiness, our joy, everything we did out of pure happiness on receiving that box was caused by you and your kindness that we can never repay because with what could we repay you?

Mevrouw, how are you and your husband? Here we are all well and I hope to be able to hear the same about you. Here in Jepara it has already rained heavily several times. Has it also done so in Batavia? We hope that the west monsoon will commence its journey across Java very soon because otherwise it will be very bad for my countrymen, especially in relation to planting the paddy. My poor countrymen, how they have had to cope with misfortune this year, but we hope that the new year will make up for that.

Our back veranda has been enlarged and we are now getting two nice if quite small new rooms added.[11] It is now so nice and roomy in the back. The sisters wanted to have chairs and benches made out of rough timber, such as from branches of the banyan tree and other types of trees too many to mention, and decorate the veranda with these. Up to now they have only one chair completed. We had such fun preparing that chair. When it was finished we all had to take turns sitting on it, yes even Pa and Ma, to see if it was strong enough and also if it was comfortable to sit on. The chair was perfect and we decided to quickly make some more. You will have to come and see us again and then I can show you our wonderful chair.

I am still going regularly to school and I am now in the highest grade. Our new teacher is very educated because he has all the qualifications, for French, German, and English.[12] Now, each Tuesday and Friday afternoon from 4:30 to 6 he gives private classes to some of the children, which includes us (Kartinah and me). We are very excited because it has always been our wish to be able to speak foreign languages. We never thought that our wishes would be fulfilled and see, along comes someone from the far north who comes to fulfil our wish. We also had once lessons from the *juffrouw*.[13] but that didn't last very long, just a month, and so we now hope that these lessons will last a little longer. The new teacher is a quiet man and when I see him then I always think of Mijnheer because he also has a beard which he wears in the same style as Mijnheer. Also his quiet manner and calmness remind me of Mijnheer.

Now I had better end my letter. No doubt it is full of mistakes, but you will overlook these won't you, Mevrouw. Regards to all in your house and my warm greetings to you from
    Soematri

Soematri to Rosita Abendanon-Mandri

Jepara, 22 July 1904

Dear Mevrouw,

Before I begin to tell you about this and that, I first have to know how Mijnheer is because I heard from Roekmini that he has been often unwell recently. I sincerely hope that he has now completely recovered. And how are you? I hope well.

It is a very bad time at the moment, one hears about illness from all sides. We are well and our sister Kardinah who was sick is getting better. However, we are not getting good news from Kartini. She has been often ill recently. After that time with you we have not been back to Rembang, although we have been to Pemalang. Kardinah regretted so much at that time that she had been unable to meet you at the station when you were passing through Pemalang. She had so wanted to see you again. In the first place she didn't know that you would be passing through Pemalang on that day, and secondly it was just at that time that her husband was very ill.[14] It's a pity, isn't it, Mevrouw, that a meeting never eventuated! Let's hope that we will meet again one day. Who knows whether one day we might not still come to Batavia to say farewell to you both. Oh, wouldn't it be wonderful to be able to see you both once more before the wide ocean separates us forever. Holland is so far away from Java.[15] We will not be going to Batavia to visit you though, but just to know that you are still residing in the same country that we are living in is already a great comfort to us.

Oh, if only we could come with you to Spain, that sunny land full of flowers and natural beauty. How we should enjoy that! You would of course show us everything, wouldn't you, Mevrouw! I can already see you, as lively and jolly as ever, running out in front of us to explain something to us or point something out to us. But I am just building castles in the air. I had better change the subject because I do this so often dreaming up things that never eventuate.

Let me tell you about our little school because I know very well that this interests you.[16] The little children are progressing well, not only in writing and reading but also in needlework. One of the married ladies has embroidered a runner and some chair covers which are quite good for a beginner. The little ones are still enjoying the toys that Mijnheer had sent us. They are only allowed to play with these if they are well behaved. What fun these little tots have. Their little eyes shine with pleasure when they have to color in a picture or have to build a house. It's really a great pleasure to watch these children working. They pull such serious faces and they are very diligent. That is already reward enough for their teachers.

As you know there are 2 married women with us at school. And, just imagine, they are both expecting a baby. Funny, isn't it? Later they will both be coming to school with their baby strapped to their back.

Before ending this letter I must ask you something. Can I have a photo of you both? Roekmini has put the photo of you two in her album and now we don't have a photo anymore of you two on our cupboard. May I have one, Mevrouw, just for myself? Please don't refuse my request, you would make me so happy if you do because it has always been my wish to own a photo of you both.

And now, good-bye, dear Mevrouw. My thanks for the photo in advance. Please point out to me any mistakes in my writing. Good-bye, good-bye.

With Mijnheer please receive my friendly greetings from us all and also from your,

    Soematri

May I also call you Moedertje? Because after all I am also one of your daughters. Good-bye!!! Lots of love from your,

    Soematri

Soematri to Rosita Abendanon-Mandri

Jepara, 12 November 1904

Dear Mevrouw,

Thank you, a thousand times thank you for the portrait photos which we received via our cousin Hassim. Oh, Mevrouw, what a surprise! Since we had heard from our sister Roekmini that you are presently very busy, and, as well, often suffered from headaches, we no longer dared to think of the possibility of ever being able to own your portrait. But, like people in need who are helped when their need is greatest, we also received help when hope was almost given up. Because just when we had given up any hope of getting your portrait, our cousin arrived with a parcel which, apart from the photographs, also contained two very sweet cloths for Roekmini.[17]

Oh, Mevrouw, I can't tell you enough how glad and happy I am with the portraits. It is such a shame that you live so far from us otherwise I would immediately embrace you to thank you for the wonderful surprise. But now I must make do with expressing my deep felt thanks by letter. But however I express my gratitude, it is and remains genuine. Kartinah has your photo in regular size and I have the one which you son made himself. As soon as possible I want t go to Semarang and have a copy made of it and have an enlarged and a normal size made because the one I have now will perhaps be too large for the pocket album that I plan to buy. I do so want to keep my loved ones by me at all times wherever I am. When I have such an album I will put in all the photos I have of the people I love so dearly and can therefore have them with me everywhere. Hey, that will be wonderful. It's a pity I now don't have a photo of Mijnheer, but as soon as you have one I will get one from you, won't I, Mevrouw? Since I don't yet have a photograph of him, I have cut one out of *Bintang Hindia*.[18] That will be the temporary replacement for a real photo that I have still to get.

Mevrouw, how are you both? Well, I hope. We are all in good health. Recently Roekmini had some teeth extracted, fortunately without further complications.

We continue to get good news from Rembang! The little fellow[19] is in good health and in the last four weeks has been able to turn himself to his right and left. He cries very little but sleeps and drinks a lot. I hope sincerely that it will continue like this because he is now such a source of comfort for his poor father. May the good angel give him the noble character and the brilliant spirit of his much loved mother so that later he may realize the goals which his mother had been striving for. Also give him the courage, oh dear angels, so that later he may be able to stand up to all the difficulties that life may present. Oh merciful God, hear our prayers.

Mevrouw, I would give anything, everything for his happiness, I would even give up my life without a moment's hesitation if I knew that thereby he would gain happiness. He looks very much like his mother, especially his mouth and his sparkling eyes. It's a pity there is not yet a photo of him otherwise you would be able to see him yourself.

But now I have to say good-bye because the paper has now been filled up and anyway, it is already so late. And otherwise the post would leave without my letter.[20]

Once again thank you for the photos. My warm regards to your husband and a warm kiss for you from your,
Soematri

Soematri to Lien (Johanna Wilhelmina Caroline) van den Berge-Kelder in Padang[21]

Jepara, 20 September 1909

Dear Lien,

We received your letter of 1 September in good order. Thanks a lot. Well done, old fellow! Write us a note every now and again, won't you, you'll be doing a noble deed if you do! Do you know that at the moment the mail makes up our entire conversation, and I don't mean the postman, but that which the post brings us, and thank God that our friends aren't too lazy these days.

Yes, that is really mean of your husband to read your letters first. It's a pity that at the moment I don't have much time to write. But then, I am not allowed to sit writing for too long on orders of Herr Doctor because otherwise I would have written you a whole big sermon about the lack of trust men have in their wives etc. etc.[22] Why don't you just pull his ears yourself, this could have a good result. Men! They are such impossible things, and yet . . .

Many thanks for the little memento that came together with your letter. Lien, you can imagine I am giving you a big kiss for that. I still have the book here on my desk. Some parts of it are really heart-stopping. As soon as I am allowed to write at greater length we will exchange thoughts about it, okay? Don't you find that Reverend Moisette the type of person you would like to throw in the river? And don't you think those comments about women's emancipation on page 130 are just right? Will the day ever arrive that this book becomes well known in Javanese circles?[23] That would be wonderful.

We, my boyfriend and I, have such wonderful plans for the future.[24] God grant that we will see them come to be. Oh yes, do you know already that we are now officially engaged? As I had told you earlier, the matter had been only recently finalized between ourselves. We had to, or rather he had to, discuss it first with his family. These matters always need to be done formally among us Javanese. Well, all this has now been done and I pretended the whole time that I didn't have the slightest idea about what was happening, but in the meantime, you know . . . !! They spent so much time to-ing and fro-ing—which by the way, is also traditional with us—but in the meantime we were nevertheless waiting anxiously, 4 whole months in suspense. I reckon that was quite enough. Well, now all that is behind us. The family has given its approval. You can imagine how absolutely excited we are. Let's hope there will also be no more obstacles in the future for us.

You ask how I am at the moment. I am not back to my old self by any means, but hope to be fully recovered soon. In a day or so we will be going to Ngawi. It certainly is high time that we got out of here for a while. Here in Jepara we are becoming estranged from the world and boring. By the way, if you might be writing to us (just address as normal and they will arrange to send it on), would you be a dear and not say a word about my secret? What we are doing on the sly is still a closely held secret. We are however looking for a way to get the family's agreement to be allowed write to each other etc. openly. Hopefully we will succeed.

Thanks for the warning about v. B[engen]'s tricks.[25] We don't run much chance of becoming affected by that because the family has remained so antipathetical to us. Recently they asked to stay with us but we simply invented some reason to say it was inconvenient. It is no joy to have that tribe staying with you.

And now I have to take my leave of you, Lien, my eyes are still hurting me from staring at these letters. For the time being just be satisfied with this scribble of mine. Once again thanks so much for that beautiful memento which has so many lovely thoughts attached to it.

    Good-bye,
    Say hello to your husband from me,
    Yours affectionately,
    Soem

Soematri to Lien van den Berge-Kelder

Jepara, 20 December 1909

My dear Lien,

We have now been back in this wonderful district of Jepara for the last three weeks, where, like little animals, we can exist for who knows how long on the memories of all the nice things which, alas, now belong to the past already. Oh, what an ungrateful creature I am to immediately begin on such a pessimistic note, and this after having just had such a good time. But it is just a little bit difficult to lock yourself up in such a little place, especially when you know that there, outside, there is so much life, so much action. We're not really socialites, actually more like sparrows than butterflies, but still that kind of life in the city really attracts us. There is so much more to enjoy there in all sorts of ways; people live more, in a little place such as this you often find such narrow-mindedness.[26]

Lien, we had such a wonderful vacation.[27] First we spent about 3 weeks in Ngawi where we had lots of fun with our nephews, one boy of 10 and one of 1 year, the latter especially is so sweet you could eat him, he is such a cutie.[28] We could also talk there to our hearts' content about our favorite topic, that is, the emancipation of the woman (here we also have to miss out on that because there is nobody here any more with whom we can discuss frankly all those things that we hold dear).

After those 3 weeks we went to stay with Marietje [Mühlenfeld].[29] She came to collect us herself in N[gawi]. You don't need me to tell you what a fantastic time we had with her. Boja is an ideal area, wonderfully cool, and one is not so isolated there. Boja is only a few hours' drive from Semarang. So if life in Boja becomes a bit boring then one can refresh oneself in city life in just a few hours. And, as far as the house is concerned, they are living there in a palace with a garden in which you could literally get lost. In front of their house they have a large stretch of grass with a pond and a music rotunda, where, however, there has never been any music played. The district around Boja is beautiful. Behind it lie the beautifully rounded shapes of the mountains Sumbing and the Sindoro, and the Praku with its saddle, the Ungaran, and on the opposite side a beautiful view on to the Java Sea from the coast of Pekalongan to the Bay of Jepara. The road through to Boja goes through an almost unending teak forest.

In fact life here is not so bad. There are three ladies at the moment. The forest industry is well represented and there are several enterprises in the vicinity. No, in my opinion Bojo is a kind of place where one could last for quite some time. Although you are out in the country, you are not totally cut off from the world.

You asked how things are currently with M[arie]? It is not what it should be, but then this could be our problem. We, after all, know what happened and maybe this knowledge means that in our eyes their relationship is not what it should be. We did not raise the issue in any way during the 4 weeks. You can imagine what a relief that was for us. It is such a d——— nuisance to operate under such conditions. I sincerely hope that their relationship will get back on track again. Both are now in good spirits, she is singing and laughing again as of old and Guus ditto, ditto. In May or March they will be going to Buitenzorg, where Guus will join the staff of the [colonial] secretariat.[30] Yes, they will become a sophisticated couple; what insignificant folks we will be by comparison, hey, Lien?

Thanks very much for your good wishes for us. Are we up in the clouds?? How can you ask! We are crazy with happiness. I wish everyone could experience such joy. The world would then be a paradise. Isn't it so, if you are so absolutely happy you cannot be bad. Happiness makes a person good, doesn't it, Lien? Oh, then the world would be one and everything all goodness and uprightness!! We hope that our little sister will also soon experience this happiness also. You have experienced it so I don't have to describe it to you and then I wouldn't be able to anyway. Lien, if someone asked me what love was, all I could do would be to quote them a poem by Caspidot Swart that goes more or less like this:

> How people look at me
> They suspect my secret!
> It's as though they know
> That it is no longer me but us

But that's enough on that subject. I have obviously already bored you. But more importantly I have to tell you that my *boy* is doing very well and has been promoted again. The best thing is he now has a humane and clear-thinking boss. It would be great if later we could get posted to Padang, but would you still be there in about 3 years' time? We are in no hurry to marry; we first need to get a better understanding of the world.

How are you two at the moment? You can count yourself lucky that you are now no longer in J[epara]. Amongst the European community, relations are in a terrible state at the moment. The van B[engen]s and the de B[oer]s are still always quarreling. The latter is well supported by his intimate friend, the mail. De B. no longer wants to have anything to do with anything related to the Soos[31] any more. You remember, don't you, that the whole affair was started by a piece of ham, a leftover from the party in Aug. which van B secretly devoured together with the committee, entirely excluding the members. De B. then became terribly angry, wrote a letter to the committee full of accusatory language such as "greediness," "avarice," "vulgarity," etc., etc., and declared he no longer wanted to be member of the Soos. What do you think of this as a good example of *Magnanimity of the Soul?* Well this quarrel has settled down a bit, but they remain terribly reserved towards each other. The educational inspiration that now flows from the school is now obviously marvelous! All the children are aware of the whole situation. What a situation!

Have you received the back money from van B. yet? If I were you I would set the bailiff on him. He can quite easily afford the money now. He is giving so many private classes that it will surely make him a rich man, the Jew![32]

Kuhr, that prissymouth, is leaving and he will be replaced by Wiggers. Hopefully he is married or is at least not so on the prowl as his predecessor was.[33]

We will soon be left to our own resources. In February Phie will get married. It will really become a dull place here in J[epara]. We won't have anybody with whom we will really be able to have a *really* good laugh anymore. We never see Keetje. They are really narrow-minded, you know! Imagine, recently for 5 December a party was held for the children at the Soos. And neither Mr. nor Mrs. van B., not even their child, turned up for the occasion. Why are they so stupid? What must the children have thought of them? They are certainly giving a great impression of *Unity is Strength!*[34] Really, you could thank the Lord on your bare knees that you have moved a long, long way from such an atmosphere as exists here at the moment.[35]

Well there's nothing much else to write about J[epara]. Oh, yes, there is something. Our neighbor, the 12-year-old Raden Ayu, had a little girl and the R.A. Regent is expecting her 4th.[36] Well, now I have told you all the news.

I take your "Hilda" [van Suylenburg] with me everywhere. It's such a marvelous book, some chapters are really moving, especially for us who are just beginning to live almost the same time situation. That chapter, for instance, where you have that discussion between Corona and Frank in which Frank tries to convince her to share the future with him but she, thinking of the many women who, through her efforts, had gained a belief

in themselves again, she refuses steadfastly even though inside her heart was breaking. Don't you think also?
[incomplete]

Soematri to Rosita Abendanon-Mandri

Jepara, 11 November 1910

Dear Mevrouw,

What wonderful news your two letters to Roekmini contain. I can't tell you how extremely happy we all are with the happy tidings. Kartono has left us without news for more than a year; our letters to him have remained unanswered, in the end we were becoming quite desperate.[37] Thank God, thank God that we can hope for better times again. Oh, and for this we have you two to thank! Mevrouw, our very sincerest thanks for everything that you both have done for Kartono, for us all. I hope that the efforts you both have made will soon be rewarded! How wonderful to know that once again we can be hopeful. Kartono was always our dearest brother, and has continued to be; despite everything we were never able to give him up. Does he now come to your home regularly? Kartono must now stand firm, he must not allow himself to be led astray again by one or other so-called good friend. God grant that this will have been his last straying!

Kardinah happened to have just written to Kartono a few days ago to ask how things were with him. Nice that we will also be able to tell her the good news. How happy she also will be. No doubt you never heard anything more from our sister Kardinah.[38] She is well, as are her husband and children. She has just written that Mr. Henny, the Assistant Resident of Tegal, and Dr. van Bussen have asked her to provide them with some information about the midwifery support available to Native women, which she gladly provided.[39] She did not write where her account will be published. She has certainly struck it lucky with that Assistant Resident and his family. Mr. Henny seems also to be an advocate of the advancement of the Native woman.

Mevrouw, when will the letters of our Kartini be published? What a wonderful idea of your husband to publish them in the aid of a goal that is entirely in line with her thinking.[40] For us, who still feel her loss so intensely, it is such a beautiful idea to know that our dearest did not live in vain. Oh, may her ideas overcome the prejudice that is still expressed against the educated native woman. Isn't it strange that people can still think that education can make a woman unsuitable for her task as wife and mother? Even Javanese men, who make out that they are very enlightened and cultivated, still think like this. But we aren't giving up. The pioneers—we can call them that, can't we?—who have had the privilege of being allowed and able to read, must thoroughly appreciate what their task is!

The details of the speech, or rather the information provided, by Mr. Jasper on Native education and Native handicraft have just appeared in *De Locomotief*. It was so good to read there the great interest being expressed in these issues.[41] The protection of native handicraft is surely very necessary, we know this from what we know about the woodcarving industry here in Jepara that has deteriorated badly. A big mistake made by the *tukangs* is their inability to make ends meet. We have done everything we could to deal with the problem of lack of money, but they have to try to compete with the Chinese, who are always after making a profit, it's really shameful. It would be a great help if a museum was established, along the lines suggested by Mr. Jasper. The low prices and the system of providing advances are slowly but surely doing the tukangs in.[42] Thank goodness we have a number of orders again for these poor people, but, then, what good is this? With it we can only help a few people, and there are so many who need help.

Knowing your interests in our family, I can't neglect to let you know that quite likely very soon a change will occur in my young girl's life. I have become engaged. How coolly I am writing this down; perhaps you might be thinking that I am in revolt against this change?[43] No, that is far from the case. Indeed, I am looking forward to the future with great joy. I know Achmad, my future husband, very well, and I could not be in safer hands than with him. We have the same ideals, and so, with God's help, we hope to contribute our small portion to the realization of the ideals of the Indies and her inhabitants.[44] Achmad works in the Criminal Investigation Department, where he plans to remain for some years, during which time he wants to learn more about the work of a head *jaksa*. His plan is to apply for that job later on when there is a vacancy. Will something like that be possible? Mevrouw, would you be so kind as to ask your husband on behalf of these two foolish children whether such a thing is possible? It would be so wonderful for him if he could do it. He has already had to give up so much for that dreadful matter of money, going to Europe for further study, etc.[45] Anyway, we don't want to be dissatisfied. Will you give us both your blessing?

Mevrouw, once again, from us all our sincere thanks for what you both have done and will continue to do for our Kartono. Warmest regards, also from Ma, to your husband.

And now, dearest Moedertje (may I say this also?), a warm embrace from your,
    Soematri

Wedding Invitation

7 March 1911

Raden Ayu Adipati Ario Sosroningrat has the honor to inform you of the forthcoming marriage of her daughter Raden Ajeng Soematri with Raden Ngabehi Sosrohadikoesoemo, civil servant. The marriage will take place on the 7 April at the home of the bride.

Soematri to Rosita Abendanon-Mandri

Semarang, 6 June 1911

Highly esteemed Mevrouw and Mijnheer Abendanon,

You will, I hope, not hold it against us that it is only now that we send you some sign of life but I have been so taken up in getting acquainted with domestic arrangements that there has literally been no time left for anything else. She is becoming a real little housewife, I can hear you saying. A housewife in the meaning of that word that people usually give it, I am not and will never be. But my domestic affairs must be neat, even very neat, don't you think? After all, in the eyes of the opponents of girl's education I belong to that unfortunate group of women who, by learning to write and read the a. b. c. will become completely unsuited for a married life.[46] Is it now not the duty of any woman who has had the good fortune of being allowed to learn, to work against this prejudice, not only in relation to domestic affairs but also in terms of her duty as a young Javanese? Oh, my dear friends, both of us carry such big plans in our heads: we will dedicate our lives to contribute, however minutely, to the welfare of our people. Give us your blessing, so that we may be able to achieve our goal.

Perhaps you can still recall that some time ago I wrote you asking whether or not it was possible for Achmad to transfer directly to the Native B[innenlands] B[estuur] as head jaksa.[47] For the time being Mad has decided to remain in the service of the Criminal Investigation Department, where the chief inspector has promised him a fine promotion. In any event, with the recent reorganization in the service, young people with the diploma from the five-year HBS now have good financial prospects. And to have a position that is completely independent of Native BB and of the "printah aloes," or pressure from above, as we call it and what will not be unknown to you, is also of great value to us. How many Native officials have not had to give up their own fine ideas because their liberal ideas did not agree with the opinions of their superiors? It is a sad but undeniable fact.[48]

Together with this letter we present you as an initial introduction to my boy[49] a snapshot of ourselves taken a month after our wedding. May Achmad also, just as his wife, find a small place in your circle of friends? Would you be so kind as to give the other photograph to Kartono with the letters that I have also enclosed for him. Our sincere thanks for your efforts in doing so.

Dear friends, what wonderful news that was for us, the news that Kartono has returned to you. Oh God, may it be the last time that he stays away. Thank you, thank you so much, dear friends, for your perseverance, for all your efforts that you have devoted to our brother. I cannot express in words what I feel the moment. If I were standing before you at the moment I would kiss your hands in gratitude.[50]

But now I must stop writing. I have already taken up too much of your time. Once again our sincere thanks for all the good wishes that you sent us for our marriage.

With the warmest regards from us both,
Soematri, Achmad

Soematri to Rosita Abendanon-Mandri

Semarang, 14 July 1911

My esteemed Friends,

We received "Door Duisternis tot Licht" in good order. Thank you, thank you so much, dear Friends, for sending us this wonderful book, and once again especially for what you have done for our dear one, our Kartini. Will we ever be able to thank you enough for that? Our dear sister did not live in vain, what a wonderful realization, what a great comfort that is for us, for everyone who loved her! Oh, may your efforts not have been for nothing, may the people for whom you have so much love, show themselves worthy of it!

We have just come home from visiting the Stokvis family,[51] with whom we had an enjoyable cup of tea. We found the family sitting in the garden with our dear sister's book, and so immediately started talking about her. There also we found a great interest in our Kartini. We have spoken to a number of people about the book, its purpose, etc., and everywhere we found the same interest, isn't that wonderful? Mr. Stokvis will soon write a review of it for *De Locomotief*. He has high hopes that the book will attract many, many readers. Wonderful—who knows how soon the dreams of our dear sister will be realized. Dearest sister, you have not been allowed to see your dreams come true, but others are now carrying your noble work forward, you have not suffered in vain.

Here in Semarang I have not yet been able to do anything about our beautiful plans. Soon after all the activity of setting up our little nest I became ill, that is now more than a month ago but I have still not completely recovered. I do hope to be my old self again soon. I have to be able to take advantage of living in a place like Semarang, where so much can be learned about all kinds of things that can be of use to us when later we end up somewhere in the interior.[52]

And how are things with you both? And Kartono, is all well with him? In the letter from him that we received some time ago he sounded so depressed. Give him our fond regards and also tell him that we will never cease to love him, and to pray for him. This month two young Javanese men left for Holland to complete their studies, both are former students of the grammar school in Semarang. Have they come to visit you yet? They are both nice, straightforward boys, Soorjopoetro and Soegiarto.[53] May the sense of duty which they, as privileged sons of the nation, owe to their compatriots to fulfill continue to inspire them with energy and dedication to their studies, and keep them from all temptation.

And how are the other Javanese students doing? We were speaking recently with a young person recently returned from Europe, who told us that the Javanese had presented a very sad image of themselves this year. Is that true? We can hardly believe it, that our boys could forget that they are actually our pioneers, that upon their shoulders rests the task of sweeping aside a powerful prejudice, including the too often expressed hateful opinion that we Javanese are not susceptible to higher education. And they also have to convince parents, who are still hesitant about sending their children to Holland. Oh, our boys must not forget their duty, their duty toward the country and their compatriots. What a comfort it is therefore to us that a number of friends of the Javanese continue to increase—under their guidance the studies of these boys will succeed, won't they.

Recently we had the pleasure of speaking briefly with Mr. van Kol.[54] While in transit on his way to Bali and Lombok, he stopped over for a few days in Semarang. Mr. van Kol told us that the aim of the current Governor General is to appoint more Javanese to European positions [in the civil service].[55] Wonderful news, don't you think? We therefore fervently hope that this attempt will be maintained and that our compatriots will demonstrate that they are worthy of it. That would really be an important solution for our young people, who, because of their financial situation, cannot continue their studies in Europe but don't see they have a future with the native civil service, or in the private sector, where there are also still many unacceptable conditions. What a lot of bad feeling the Javanese must have created before that, as a result, until today we are still denied the right to look forward to the same opportunities as their European colleagues even though they undertake the same work, and possess the same qualifications! Poor nation, when will you be treated as human beings! Mr. van Kol promised us personally that he would ask the GG if we, that is, my husband, will have the right then, just as his European colleagues, to an overseas furlough. The chief inspector of that service did once assure Mad that he could expect the same privileges without his having to obtain [Dutch] nationality. But then, what does an oral assurance amount to; when the chief inspector leaves and a new one takes his place who wants to have nothing to do with what happened before, what are we to do then?[56] So we are looking forward with some impatience for news from Mr. van Kol.

And now, dear friends, I must not hold you up much longer with my chatter. When my condition allows me to go out again, I plan to go out with my husband and make a proper study of Semarang. May I then later describe this and that to you? The people, at least those whom I have met to date, don't impress me greatly, they are noisy when they speak, and the women especially are so coquettish, they saunter more than they walk. No, then I would prefer to see my simple *desa* women, with their *kain loerik* up to their knees, revealing their muscled calves, with which, by energetic strides, they have managed to traverse many long roads.[57]

Have our photos and letter that we sent some time ago arrived safely? Good-bye. Once again thank you for the book, for your love of our dear unforgettable sister. Imagine that you are receiving a warm handshake from,
    Your Soematri and Mad

Soematri to Nellie van Kol[58]

Semarang, 8 August 1911

Dear Mevrouw [van Kol],

I can begin my letter this way, can't I? Before this I have never written to you, so I am completely unknown to you, but I know you; I have already been told so much about you.[59] But you don't yet know who this rude person is who dares come to take up your time and for which interruption she offers many, many excuses.

I am Soematri, Kartini's youngest sister. Since April of this year I am married to a dear, fine husband and am now living here in Semarang as a very happy and fortunate wife. How is it that I am now writing to you? There are many reasons for this, but the main one is the desire, which I feel very strongly, to make the acquaintance myself of someone who brought so much happiness to our beloved Kartini.[60] Mevrouw, will you therefore forgive me for the liberty I have taken?

We have just had the pleasure of renewing our acquaintance with your husband. In the beginning of last month he was in Semarang for a few days, during which time your husband was kind enough to spare us a few hours of his precious time. It was a very nice time that we had. And now the mail has just brought us a postcard from your husband from Solo. Oh, Mevrouw, what a kind man your husband is, despite all the work he has, he still had time to think of us. You see, when he was in Semarang and we were talking about my husband's work here, an occupation that till now has only been open to Europeans, the conversation turned to this question: whether a Javanese, without being officially integrated into a European branch of the civil service, would have the same rights as his Western colleagues. Your husband promised us then to enquire from His Excellency the Governor General. And today he wrote that Buitenzorg has formulated a set of clear answers that will please us and which will be sent to us soon. I do not have to tell you how grateful we are. Our thanks to you, also on behalf of our compatriots since the clarifications that the GG has provided will also be of benefit to them.[61]

Oh, it is so wonderful to know that there are more and more individuals among our conquerors who are prepared to give their attention to a consideration of the possibility of the closer relations between white and brown, who are sympathetic to the evolutionary spirit which is now beginning to stir the spirit of many a Javanese. What a noble task Mr. Abendanon has performed in publishing the letters of Kartini! We pray to you earnestly that the goal he intended may be achieved. Kartini suffered so very much that the struggle must not be allowed to have been for nothing. May our dear sister not have lived for nothing.

Mevrouw, the good God has heard our dearest wish. We just read some wonderful news in the newspaper. In Purbolinggo, Banjumas Residency, a school will be opened for the daughters of Native leaders which will be under the direction of a lady from Middelburg. Thank you, a thousand times thank you, our rulers! You won't regret this. Our menfolk also are slowly beginning to realize that there cannot possibly be any development of the people where men prevent the progress of women. An acquaintance of ours, a Doctor Jawa, allowed his wife, during the period of their engagement, to undertake education to prepare herself for her role. Isn't that a wonderful sign? This, and so many other things indicate that the spirit of the times is beginning to force its way in.

Mevrouw, unfortunately I have to end my writing here because that which cannot be set aside awaits me. May I come to chat with you once again?

I wish you all the best! Please greet Lily for me, I have read her article.[62] How she is revelling in her work, that fine girl.

Please receive with this our warmest regards,
Yours truly,
Soematri

Soematri to Lien van den Berge-Kelder

[Letterhead] *Raden Ngabehi Sosrohadikoesoemo*

Semarang, September 1911

My dearest Lien,

I had better not fill my letter with a thousand excuses, had I? We both know only too well how, through no fault of our own, we are required to set our correspondence aside. Knowing this, it would be silly for us should we let our declared friendship lapse because of a period of silence. Hey, dear girl, you totally agree with me, don't you?

Dear Friends, my deepest thanks, also on behalf of my husband, for your good wishes for the goal that has been finally achieved. Our wedding days were not so very enjoyable, that is, for those who had plans to celebrate the occasion with a lot of fanfare.[63] You know that with us Javanese, a wedding has to be celebrated with a lot of fuss, otherwise the occasion is not complete. However, both of us became ill just before the wedding, the approaching realization of our goal appears to have been too much for our nerves, which had already been constantly on edge. Anyway, our illness caused our doctor to provide a medical certificate that enabled us, after the main ceremony, to depart for the mountains. So it turned out that our illness could be regarded as the silver lining in our misfortune. That which would have been completely denied to us had we been well, was offered to us: we were allowed to take our honeymoon and were released from the round of visits we would otherwise have been obliged to make. You can imagine what a joy that was, and we took full advantage of it.[64]

What did I look like as a bride? I can't tell you because I was not allowed to look at myself. Our *adat* forbids a bride to look into a mirror. But didn't you do so secretly, I can hear you say? I couldn't do that either because I was not left alone for a second. I just accepted it all and remained satisfied with the description of my appearance that my sisters and friends gave me. It's a pity that you two were not able to see me, you would not have recognized me at that moment. For the whole time I had to sit completely still and look straight ahead with a serious expression. Later Mad, who was not used to seeing me so serious, said that for a moment he thought he was looking at a stone statue. Anyway, thank heavens that that is all behind us now. That is the first and last time.

And now we are here already in Semarang for 5 months. What is it like here? Well, if Mad could find a position in Jepara I wouldn't hesitate for a minute, I would have no regrets or concerns to immediately bid this entire city of Semarang good-bye. We are living here in a house with a 10 square meter garden, which, believe it or not, is completely tiled, which is totally unpleasant in this dreadfully hot city. I so miss our gorgeous garden, our beautiful flowers and most of all my Moedertje and my little sis, Tinah [Kartinah]. In every letter I receive from home I notice how those two are missing their tomboy. Moedertje has become much grayer and thinner in those five months someone has recently told me. Loving someone also brings with it suffering, doesn't it, but yet for all the money in the world I would not do without the love that joins us three so closely together.

If nothing intervenes then we will be going home for a few days in September, to celebrate the end of *puasa* month with the old folks. I am already looking forward to it. How we will enjoy seeing each other again. My dear Mad is also looking forward to it. He himself is not so specially attached to his family like his silly Soem. This is no wonder because since he was 6½ he has been living with strangers and only came home during the holidays.[65]

Lien, perhaps we may meet each other again. Will you be staying a while in Padang? How terrific it would be if we could see each other again. Of all the places in the Outer Islands, Bali and Padang attract me most. The first one strikes me as so mournful. But I very much hope that we will never have to go to the Outer Islands. To be on the same island as Moedertje and the sisters would be the best. I hope that life will be kind to us in this respect.

But now I won't say another word about myself. Goodness gracious me, it's terrible, I have been talking about myself all this time. Tell me, quickly, how are you three? Is the little Jan still shooting up? What is he already able to do? I can easily imagine, people, how happy you two must be with this little fellow. Let's hope that he that he will always be a source of happiness for Father Gerard and Mother Lientje. Well, you can imagine how surprised we were when the mail brought us a postcard from Father Gerard informing us of the arrival of the little prince. My first exclamation was: how happy they must be! And we were not wrong were we?

Well, people, you are going to get Luci Castens in your area, well at any rate on the same island. She has become engaged with Ir. [engineer] Cloux, Controleur in Medan, if I am not mistaken. I have already met Dotje here in Semarang, still the same, full of laughter. She has also had a child, but it only lived a few hours. And do you know already that Mühlenfeld has remarried? He once again stepped into the state of married bliss on 3 August with Corie Becker. I hope sincerely that they will be happy. And Marietje [Mühlenfeld] has returned to Holland with the same boat which 5 years ago brought her, full of life and dreams, to the Indies. I wrote to her before her departure saying that I had happened to hear about it. Lien, I can't not continue liking her because of her failings and her mistakes. Poor Marietje, how cruelly life has treated her. She wrote back to me, so sadly. Poor thing, that she had first to have such an experience before coming to her senses. She is going to live in The Hague with strangers—she has broken with her whole family. Really, Marietje has been punished enough for her mistakes. Imagine, arriving in Holland and there is not a single person to welcome her, even though she has her grandmother there whom she idolizes, her father, uncles and aunties. Don't you think she is being terribly punished, Lien? With all my heart I pray to God that one day the sun will shine in her heart again.

Lien, have you read the book by our sister Kartini, *Door Duisternis tot Licht?* A friend of ours has taken the trouble to collect her letters and to publish them in the form of a book. As you know, she lived with heart and soul for the uplifting of the Javanese woman. She was not able to see her efforts come to fruition but now our friends want to try to make them come true. With the profits from the sale of the book a school will be established for Native girls that will have the name of our sister. Will you also buy a copy, dear people, and help to realize the dream of so many Javanese women who are feeling the awakening of the spirit of the times?

And now, dear girl, this brand-new housewife has to get back to work, so I will leave it at this. I had better not ask you for a quick reply because I wouldn't get it anyway, would I?

Well, good-bye, Mother Lien. All the best to you three,
From your Mad and Soem

Should you write then address this letter as follows:
De Heer R. Ng. Sosrohadikoesoemo[66]
Toll Collector
Semarang
Good-bye!!

Sosrohadikoesoemo to Rosita and Mr. Abendanon

Semarang, 18 December 1911

My Esteemed Friends,

In the sincere hope that you will accept this letter as it is intended, I am taking the liberty of writing this letter in order to introduce myself to you. My name is Sosrohadikoesoemo, the husband of Soematri, Kartini's youngest sister. I have wanted to correspond with you for a long time, but a good opportunity to do so has never presented itself.[67]

Before continuing I would like to wish you and your family, also on behalf of Soematri, all the best for the New Year although the letter will not arrive on time, that is before or on 1 January. Nevertheless we both hope that you will regard it as having arrived on time. For all kinds of reasons I was unable to write this letter any earlier.[68]

On behalf of Soematri I need to bring the following to your attention. In June last, my wife had sent to your address a letter and a photo taken after our wedding. Enclosed in that letter there was also a letter for Kartono. Till now we have not received any reply. It is to be hoped that the letter and photo arrived at the right address. You would do us a great pleasure if, in a few sentences, you would let us know whether both have arrived safely, the letter for you and also the letter intended for Kartono. Also could I ask, on behalf of Soematri, whether you could ask Kartono to reply to that letter. His mother, my mother-in-law, who is currently living with us in Semarang, and who intends to so for some time, would dearly love to receive some news from him. Would you, sir, be so kind as to inform Kartono of this?[69]

In anticipation of your willingness, may I express my gratitude to you for undertaking this task.[70]

I have read Kartini's book, of which Soematri has received a copy from you. I read it with great pleasure and enthusiasm. May Kartini's noble efforts find a receptive ear among many people, European as well as Native. Excellent reviews of this work give me the impression that many Europeans agree with Kartini's ideas. We *Jong Javanen*[71] have been expecting this. We have you to thank that the authorities are concerning themselves about the condition of the Javanese, especially that of Javanese women.[72]

On behalf of the Javanese people I offer you many thanks for everything you have had done to bring the bundle of Kartini's letters into book form. I hope that you may succeed in achieving the aim you intend in producing the book, the achievement of an idea which is in accord with the times.

Well, I will leave it at this. On another occasion I hope to write you a more detailed letter.

With my respectful regards to you both,
Sincerely,
Sosrohadikoesoemo
Postcard

Sosrohadikoesoemo to Mr. Abendanon

Jepara, 8 April 1912

Most esteemed Mr. Abendanon

Just a few words to respectfully inform you that my wife Soematri was delivered of a healthy son on the 7th of this month. The birth went well, and the condition of both mother and child up to now leaves nothing to be desired. As you see we are at the moment also in Jepara. I can say that it was my privilege that I was able to be present the whole time. It happened during the Easter holiday when I had intended to visit Soematri, who has been here in Jepara since 28 March with her mother to await the event. It seems that the Almighty had wanted it to be so. The dearest wish of us both has now been fulfilled.

Now, my highly esteemed friend, I had better leave it at this. I hope sincerely that you, sir, will accept these few lines, I still have many letters to write.

With respectful greetings, also from Soematri,
Sincerely,
Sosrohadikoesoemo

Soematri to Rosita Abendanon-Mandri

Semarang, 16 July 1912

My esteemed Friends,

Finally, I can get around to starting a letter that I have so often begun in my imagination. Dear friends, please excuse us that we have allowed so much time to pass before replying to your letters containing a photo of Mijnheer, for which we thank you sincerely. We received this just at the busiest moment, just before I left for Jepara, where, as you perhaps already know, I awaited the birth of my child. And when the little one finally arrived, others things occupied all my time so that there was hardly any time to think about writing. But we did not forget you; indeed, many things occurred which we know would have interested you very much, and that ensured that our thoughts often flew towards you, Friends of the brown people!

Dear Moedertje, before I go on, may I on behalf of my little treasure, thank you so much for the gorgeous little dress that the mail has just delivered together with your husband's letter. Thank you, thank you dear Friends, for all your kind wishes. May we succeed in raising our little one to become a useful member of society. Also may this time of struggle into which he is born influence him; may he always hold women in high regard for their struggle against injustice. Oh, Moedertje, we have such wonderful plans for our child, our life now revolves entirely round him. I am now doing everything to ensure he remains healthy, and till now my efforts have not been in vain. He is getting all his sustenance from me, and he is doing so well on this, that everyone is amazed. Even Nellie,[73] who has seen so many babies, thinks that he, my little Soearto, is a wonder child. He is now only 3 months old and already weighs about 18 pounds, a wonderful piece of meat, in other words. If I could only bring him to you, I can't possibly put everything down on paper, I would have to fill pages and pages and even then I would not have told you everything. But can a mother ever finish talking about her child?

As soon as possible we will bring him to a photographer and then you can convince yourself that I haven't been exaggerating. Moedertje, don't you think the sudden death of the Regent of Rembang is terrible?[74] Our poor little Singgih, so young and so surely tried. Let us hope this is the last thing he has to suffer in his life. He is now in Tuban with his uncle. Kardinah tried to have the little one with her but her efforts were in vain. The Regent of Tuban will not allow it.[75]

21 July 1912

Moedertje, I was not able to finish the letter. As a result of the inoculation my little one developed a temperature and I have been so anxious that I forgot the whole letter. Today, in tidying up my writing table, I saw the unfinished letter and I now I am hurriedly finishing it.

We have met the van Deventer family.[76] You have certainly not exaggerated, Moedertje, they are such a nice couple who do have a great interest in welfare of the brown people. They are very hopeful that the Kartini School will be established, but not entirely as envisaged by Kartini, but that's not important, is it, as long as we get a school, then at least we have taken another step forward.[77] Of course there will, as always, be some opposition, and in this case there will be opposition not just from the conservative side but also from those who can't see the sun shining in the water.[78] Perhaps you cannot or will not believe it but it is a fact that there are many among the menfolk who cannot forgive Kartini that she, as a woman, has been able to impress the world, was able to inspire with her beautiful and fine words. We especially made some enquiries amongst some Native top officials to see what they thought of the Kartini book, and a typical all-encompassing reply that we got was: "Oh yes, we read the book. It is well written." That was all we got to hear. Don't you think that was petty-minded? And it is doubly sad that I have to say this, but it is a fact that we in our struggle to advance received the greatest opposition from our own compatriots.[79] And if only it were people who did not speak their mind publicly. Oh, Moedertje, let it suffice to say that sometimes I have an overpowering urge to reveal who are the little minds among them who through their position and cunning believe they are safe.

You know how Kardinah, the princess, is. She is not well, Moedertje, at the moment she is in a clinic here in Semarang where she has to take six months rest. She still speaks a lot about you, and when I spoke to her last about you, that I was writing to you, she asked me to pass on to you both her warm regards.

Moedertje dear, I regret I can't chat with you any longer. Little Soearto has missed his mum long enough and is now already crying impatiently for her.

Thank you once again, dear friends for everything. Our warmest regards to Mijnheer and for you a warm embrace from
 Soematri and son

Soematri to Lien van den Berge-Kelder

Semarang, 4 November 1912

Dear Lien,

Perhaps you were thinking that you would never get a reply from me, I made you wait so long. Lien, is it necessary for me to give you a complete explanation of my silence? Surely not, we both know only too well that we can't always do what we want to do, especially when there is a little tot that is taking up all our attention.

I am happily now back in my own home. As you may already know, I went to Jepara to have my baby and stayed there for about 3 months. Back at home there was of course a pile of work waiting for me, but that appeared not to have been enough because on top of all that I also had a lodger for 2 months. You can imagine how busy I was then. Fortunately all that activity has not had a bad effect on my little one. Despite all the activity he has just calmly continued growing and blossoming and has now already become such a sturdy little man. He is now 6 months old and is now already beginning to become so attached to his mother in such a lovely way. It's such a delicious, cuddly little thing, a first-class fidget.

Oh, Lien, he's such a little treasure, our Soearto. I can't really say who he looks like, I only know he is beautiful, with large black eyes with which he regards the world with such a wise look. Lien, Lien, what a joy he brings with him, it fills your entire life and every day there is something new about him to note. Well you can imagine then that we are not half crazy about him. Recently he is allowed to join us in bed in the mornings, which he seems to like very much. And the pleasure he gets from that, it's wonderful! But that's enough about my little child, who knows how long I have already bored you with this. Oh, Lien, if I get started on my baby I cannot stop myself, the material for this is endless.

You ask how the housekeeping is going. Well, according to me and to Mad it is going wonderfully well, but according to my sister, who has already been married for 10 years,[80] who came to visit us recently, she turned up her nose at it. Completely perfect housekeeping it will never be, we lean too much in the direction of the free-and-easy village for that.

And how are things with you, Lien? How are things with your little Janneman?[81] He has so much of you in him, your little treasure. Will you give him a kiss from his brown aunty who from a distance wishes him all the best? No, really, Lien, in all seriousness, you have not exaggerated about your little fellow. With this letter the hope from us both that he will continue to grow and keep well.

Thanks for your interest in the Kartini book. Yes, it is a great comfort for us to know that our beloved sister did not suffer in vain, that not only in the immediate family but also far beyond she continues to live on. In 1913 in Semarang the first Kartini School will be opened. Hopefully this school will attract a lot of pupils so that it won't end with just this one school!

And what is the state of progress of the people? Are the schools here being attended by Native girls? In Java the desire for education is becoming more and more evident. Although very slowly, many parents are beginning to see at last that it is useful to also have their daughters educated. Just like everywhere else, with any new movement often silly things manifest themselves, so here too, often mistakes are being made, but we can overlook these, can't we, as long as a beginning is being made, everything will turn out all right in the end.

I have not been able to do anything in this regard here in Semarang. The people in S[emarang] really disappointed me, they are mostly lazy, rude characters whom I would rather not have anything to do with of course. It's very unchristian of me, isn't it? Yes, but in the face of such rudeness I really can't do anything, and I have too aggressive a character to have much patience and calmness to deal with all that rudeness.

I have not heard anything more from Marietje Mühlenfeld recently. As you will probably know, she went back to Holland. Before she left she wrote me a letter which was so very sad, she was no longer the jolly Marietje of old, poor, poor woman. And Guus remarried, you know that?[82] And now, almost a month ago he has become father of a little girl, called Génane.

How strangely things can work out sometimes in this life, don't you think, Lien? I often think back to those fun days, you remember, we could be so wild sometimes. Do you still remember that day when the four of us visited Keetje to see her beautiful hat and to relieve her of a bottle of lemonade and a pound of ice? She was so stingy that she wouldn't get ice for you, you remember? And she could never stop talking about Jan Donkers, who was n[ota] b[ene] my furious admirer.[83] He was rather the type for whom you could go through fire. Those days really were great fun, weren't they, Lien? And now Tinah is completely alone with all those nice memories. She was just recently staying with me, the first time since my wedding. We also had to get accustomed to this and conquer some of those ingrained *adat* traditions. You don't half know what kind of trap these idiotic habits are that we are still entangled in. Anyway, we were finally able to get Tina with us and we had so much fun, tremendous. We wandered through the streets, went window shopping, went for drives, went to the cinema, etc., etc., it was just crazy fun.

Lien, but now I have to stop writing. [Soe]Arto is calling for his food and the mail has to go out the door soon. I hope to write you again soon, in the meantime be satisfied with this will you. Bye, bye, best wishes to your husband and child.

    I remain as always your
    Sobat baik
    Soematri

Soematri to Rosita and Mr. Abendanon

Semarang, 9 November 1912

My highly esteemed Friends,

After what the post has brought us this afternoon, I cannot neglect to come and briefly interrupt you with a chat on paper, dear noble friends, to tell you how I can never thank you enough for what you have done and are still doing for our Kartono. We were so happy this afternoon when we saw that together with your letter there was also a letter from him, who we still all love very much. Also I have to tell you how very happy it has made his mother, who impressed upon me several times that I must not forget to pass on to you her deepest thanks to you. God grant that everything will now go according to plan.[84]

Together with this writing we are also sending to you a few photos and a letter. Would you be so kind as to give these to Kartono. Dear Friends, once again, God bless you for your noble work.

Mevrouw, I was also grateful to receive your letter safely, but because of all kinds of things I was unable to reply any earlier. I will write to Roekmini about the design you mentioned, she knows more about this sort of thing than I do, but won't the order arrive too late? Mrs. Boissevain also asked for our help (Roekmini, Kardinah, Kartinah, and Soematri and I). We want to try to get an exhibit ready in time, but there is not much time left.[85]

I have nothing but good news to tell you about the Kartini School. There is lots of interest. A European teacher has been found prepared to teach some girls to prepare them so that later they can assist the girls in the first grade of the Kartini School. How marvelous all this interest is. Approaching the work in this way will ensure that the women's interests will proceed well. And don't you think it is wonderful that it won't become a status school. It was such a great relief for us when this proposal was unanimously accepted.[86] And those who cannot yet accept this change will soon realize that it is just in this way that the school will be able to contribute best to the character formation of both sides. I am firmly convinced that much of the current situation will disappear when no sharp boundaries are drawn between those of aristocratic and nonaristocratic background. It is so rare that noble birth coincides with real nobility of character.[87]

May the coming year bring you fulfillment of your wishes, and my best wishes to you both. With our warmest regards,

Your Loving,
Soematri, husband and child

Soematri to Mevrouw Nellie van Kol

Semarang, 19 November 1912

Dear Mevrouw,

If there is any need to speak of neglect, then it is I who have beaten you at it, Mevrouw! What a long time I have let you wait for some word from us. I had to postpone replying to your warm letters many times because of the pressure of work that has overtaken me.

Mevrouw, how is your husband now? The papers reported that he was ill and in Japan. I hope very much that everything is now back to normal. It is so sad to know that our dear ones are ill when they are so far away from one. And how is Lily coping in her new domestic situation?

Here things are very well, our little boy is growing like anything, as you can see from the photo that I am enclosing with this letter. What do you think of my little treasure? Sweet, isn't he? We so hope that our little Soearto will later have the advantage of a good set of brains. Our dream is later to send him to Holland to study to become a doctor, that is, if he has the capacity for that and a calling for this demanding but noble work. I am getting a little ahead of things here, am I not, but doesn't any mother do that, Mevrouw? How I would like to be living somewhere in your neighborhood, for his sake, for the sake of our child who we later hope to send in to the world with a deep spiritual sense. Which direction we will go in his upbringing I cannot tell you yet, I only know that I will guard against the kind of superstition that we were brought up with and whose less pleasant consequences we still experience. Help us realize our hope that we may succeed in raising our child to become a worthy adult who will be of service to his community.

Mevrouw, I need to point out to you a misunderstanding. It is unfortunate that there was a misunderstanding because I would now feel much happier if that hadn't happened. My words in my previous letter, "God has heard our prayers...," seem to have given you the idea that I had a religion, had a belief. In the first place, my apologies for what I have done, that is, put you on the wrong track. These words flowed out of my pen like the cry "May God save us from that!" that so many who don't have a belief often use. To mislead you therefore was never my intention. Mevrouw, once again, forgive me for it.[88]

I do not have a belief, Mevrouw. Not that religion leaves me indifferent. I have been raised free from any pressure with regard to religious belief.[89] That is surely a very fine principle and we are very grateful to our parents for this. Nothing we abhor more than trying to squeeze the brains of a little child full of all kinds of prayers of which they would not understand in the slightest. Mevrouw, I have been indifferent to religion until the birth of my little treasure. This dear little thing has brought an entire reversal in me. From time to time I began to ponder these things but unfortunately could find nothing that spoke to me. What am I seeking? I am looking for a place of refuge, one of which De Genestet[90] spoke so truly: something that comes and stays, that can hang on our heart, around which everything turns.

Mevrouw, please help me as you have helped Kartini, tell me which direction I should take. Someone has given me the book by Thomas à Kempis, *Imitation of Christ*. Mevrouw, I was not able to finish that book, a lot of it was incomprehensible to me because of my ignorance. What in heaven's name should I do now? It seems to me I can't go on like this. I feel like a caged bird that is looking hopelessly for a way out so that it can once again enjoy the wonderful feeling of freedom. I hope life will be kind to me.

To your question, how things are now with Kartini's son, unfortunately I can only say this, that since the death of his father he has gone to live with his uncle (the Regent of Tuban), where, according to the Resident of Rembang, he is being well looked after. We very rarely get news from my brother-in-law's family. Let's hope things continue to go well for that boy, not only in his material life but also in his spiritual existence.

From the newspapers we gather that people are very busy establishing an organization from whose funds a Kartini school will be established.[91] It is hoped the first Kartini School will be built in Semarang in 1913. Let's hope that the Javanese parents know how to appreciate it.

Mevrouw, I have to leave it at this. Greetings to your husband from the two of us. With our very best wishes,
 Your,
 Soematri

Soematri to Rosita and Mr. Abendanon

Weltevreden, 1 December 1913

Esteemed Friends,

May I also come and interrupt you with a little chat? It is a long time since I last wrote to you and so much has taken place since then, at least in our lives, in that relatively short time. After much *soesah* and traveling to and fro we are finally settled here in Batavia—but for how long? I think we will also be leaving again soon, which on one hand I think is a pity; we would have loved to have integrated into the life here that is so different from that of the *orang jawa,* the name that the Batavians give to us people from Central Java.[92] However, living in Batavia much longer would severely affect our current financial position. Well, what aspect of life doesn't have its drawbacks.

We find Batavia a beautiful city, and especially the quietness on the street struck us. Here there is not that hustle and bustle on the street that we have in Semarang and Surabaya, which we could never get used to. And the people? They are definitely more civilized than those in Central and East Java. Once we went into a few kampong houses that we came across, and these were in very good condition. If only our central Javanese could learn from that. The condition one often finds in Javanese houses is really terrible. And the rudeness about which many people complain there we have also not found here, although the occasional rudeness will be experienced anywhere, in all parts of the world, of course.

What we really don't like here is the style of life. People here live beyond their means, also those of the *priyayi* class, that is, the educated class.[93] A typical example of how people here, without any concern, can live in this manner is the advice we received when we arrived in Batavia. People said to us, "Raden, moesti idoep begitoe, halau tida begitoe, orang Batawi tida kassi hormat,"[94] more or less in those words. Don't you think that's terrible? You should also have had a look inside the homes of these people. Everything we saw there was beautiful and modern, but, goodness me, don't look behind the wings. That was just shocking. The children hardly got anything to eat, but the world outside did not see that and didn't know about it. We saw this kind of thing a lot. I have seen this so often, yet it still cuts me to the quick. I think such circumstances are so terrible: how can intelligent people so degrade themselves.[95]

But, thank God, we don't only see such sad things as this, we also have made good friends here whose company is really wonderful. And we were also fortunate when we had just arrived here that Mr. and Mrs. Adriani happened also to be in Batavia.[96] You can imagine how we enjoyed their company. They have now returned to Poso.

3 December

It is only now that I can resume my letter. Sister Gildemeester sends her regards to you both—you remember her, don't you? We got to meet her through the Adriani family and now she often comes to visit me, which of course I like very much, she is such a fine upstanding person.

And dear friends, how are things with Kartono? We have not heard from him for a long time, we are concerned, very concerned about possible new difficulties. In the past these have also been preceded by periods of inexplicable silence. We comfort ourselves in the hope that this would be impossible, but past experience does not provide us with much confidence. How thankful then we would be if you could give us some news. In February I will be going to visit my mother, and I fervently hope that before that time I might have some news about Kartono for our poor dear mother. Should he still be visiting, could you then ask him on my behalf if he could write a brief note to mother? At the moment she is living with Rawito, who is working with the S[emarang] C[heribon] S[toomtram].[97] From February I will also be staying with her for several months, so I will read the letters to her. Oh, as long as Kartono is willing to write letters to her, he doesn't need to do anything more than that. I will enclose a postcard to him in this letter, would you give it to him? Thanks for everything, dear friends.

And now I won't hold you up any more. May all go well and my very best wishes to you both for the coming 1914. Should you wish to write us then please address the letters to my husband. You have his work address at the Pasar Senen, Weltevreden.

With warm regards from us both,
Your Soematri

Just one other thing. We recently visited Mr. and Mrs. Hazeu, and on this occasion Mr. Hazeu told us that the government would establish a school for Native midwives and nurses.[98] It was especially His Excellency the Governor General, who insisted that efforts be made in this regard. People are now getting advice from qualified Javanese authorities.[99] I sincerely hope that this will prove to be supportive so that this plan does not just remain a dream. Please consider this as confidential I am not sure if I am allowed to reveal it but you have expressed so much interest in the people that I will forget about that.

Soematri to the Mindere Welvaart Onderzoek

Weltevreden, 26 January 1914[100]

I sincerely regret that I cannot fulfill your request, at least not as you would have liked, because I do not consider myself qualified to do so. I have, however, carefully considered the current situation in our society, which is far from rosy, and I also realize the necessity for making changes therein. But I too am still examining and searching for the right direction to bring us to the desired goal and thus do not have the right to write something for your report, which is of such significance for our society.

How I think about some of these issues personally, I am setting out herewith. What you may want to do with this writing I will leave entirely to you.

Vocational Training for Various Occupations for Javanese Girls and Women[101]

Given that we are at the beginning of an evolution, which is to say therefore that we still have many things to overcome, it is in my modest opinion to be recommended—at least for the time being—that as many girls' schools as possible are established along the lines of the existing Kartini Schools, where, apart from the ordinary school subjects, outside the normal school hours girls must be given the opportunity to prepare themselves for one or other occupation. With this they can later become financially independent or apply themselves completely to everything that a *good* housewife must know, one who, both as a life partner of the educated and cultured man and as an educator of children, knows the meaning of the beautiful significance of her task.[102] In this so-called domestic course she would also be instructed in the essentials of first aid and the principles of good health. Experience shows—and doctors can confirm—how the best of medicines can fail when the nearest nurses—the family members—have not the faintest idea of the necessity of strictly following the doctor's advice, or are totally unacquainted with the requirement of good hygiene.

Where trust in the doctor is slowly but surely sinking in among the people, I definitively believe it would not be too presumptuous to think that a school for training midwives would be attractive. Of less interest would be one for general nursing: as a nurse one should be ready to assist any patient who was brought in for treatment, regardless, and this, I think, would present a major problem for parents. Before going on to discuss the question of marriage, I would also want to urge strongly that, in admitting candidate pupils to a school for midwives, careful consideration be given to the background from which such students have come. It should not be forgotten that here one is dealing with an occupation that demands much tact and experience.

With the increasing spiritual development of the woman, undoubtedly a real reorganization will need to be brought about and maintained in marriage and of married life itself.

A pleasing sign is already apparent within the priyayi class, where child marriages are hardly in evidence anymore, and undoubtedly that will also have its influences on the other levels of Native society. And, with vocational training, further change will be brought about in this serious and delicate question. After all, once in possession of some training by which a woman can make herself financially independent of her family, she would no longer be subject to the family's pressure for her to enter a marriage that she was opposed to. The woman who has learned to recognize that she is not an object, but a person just like a man, with the right to live, will also be imbued with a sense of the seriousness of marriage. She will learn to appreciate that marriage is not an escape for the woman but a step in her life which needs to be carefully and seriously considered because, alongside the good fortune of being able to dedicate herself to the man whom she has chosen above all others, it will also involve the difficult but beautiful task of being a good mother for the children.

Many will agree with me that the state of *selir* is a cancer in Native society and must be got rid of. Men also are coming to recognize this, as is evident in the following response of a Native official when replying to his superior, who, as a stranger in the region, had asked him about work and lifestyle traditions there. This official said emphatically, among other things: "Sir, . . . what's also of significance, and what we need to aim for, is the abolition of the practice of having more than one wife because this is definitely the cause of our downfall, economically and spiritually." All praise to this man who believes this and lives accordingly—because he is not just saving himself and his wife much suffering but also his children will bless him. Anybody who is not blind can see the depressing effect in families where polygamy exists and tragic relations between the children among themselves. It is ridiculous and superficial to claim that the Javanese woman does not suffer in these circumstances. She is silent because from a very early age it is drilled into her to be silent, to accept everything that life may bring her. And what difference would complaining make to her? Even her parents would not accept her back should she run away from her husband if it was only because he had taken another wife.

So what alternative does she have? Often totally unfamiliar which the world at large and as well having no skills by which she could earn a living and lacking the moral fortitude, despite everything, to go out into the world with which she is unfamiliar just so long as she could escape her husband.

Oh, don't allow yourself to be lulled to sleep by that superficial assertion that the Javanese woman does not suffer under those circumstances. It is very definitely felt and suffered, and intensely so. I have had the opportunity to speak about this with women from several classes who are themselves in this situation, and none of these women has given me any cause to change the view I have expressed above. And then, think of how excruciatingly unjustly the children of the selir are treated—although of course there are exceptions to this, thank goodness.[103] But how significant are these exceptions: so many innocent children are suffering as a result of polygamy. No, I will say it again: polygamy must not be allowed to exist any longer. It damages the family and thus the entire society. And that is enough on that subject.

Hoping that that my reply will not cause you to think that I do not appreciate your attempt to improve the condition of women—in fact, the opposite is true and with this I also add the thanks of my sisters— I am, respectfully,

Your humble servant,
S. Sosro Hadikoesoemo

Achmad Sosrohadikoesoemo to Mr. and Mrs. Abendanon

Weltevreden, 18 February 1914

My Highly Esteemed Friends,

It is now some months since I received your letter from 8 November, and it is still awaiting an answer. I must beg your forgiveness for the late reply and can only say that the delay was due to my circumstances. I will now try to make up for this and I hope I will not suffer any consequences from my forgetfulness.[104]

Yes, I believe that in the Pawnshop Division I will have a better future ahead of me than in the customs service. The work environment here is also much more congenial and till now I have no regrets about the decision I have taken. My immediate superior is Dr. Nittel, the son-in-law of the late Mr. Dr. de Wolff van W., who when he was alive was an assistant resident. Dr. Nittel is the head of the service.[105] Initially I am *mayong* of the technical instructor, who is training me.[106] If I understand it correctly, my boss is quite pleased with me, and in the copy of the confidential report which I have enclosed herewith you can see that it gives evidence of his satisfaction with me. As an indication of his good will towards me he agreed to sign the copy of that report. As soon as I am officially appointed as technical instructor, which I hope will occur in the course of this year, and then not the technical instructor, Ostmeier,[107] but only this Mr. Nittel will supervise me. I would come to work directly under him, which will be very pleasant.

Although eventually the final salary of the technical instructor would be the same as that of a *controleur,* which I believe is 600 guilders, as technical instructor I have to start on a lesser salary of about 200 guilders, while the controleur begins at 350 guilders. The difference is therefore not insignificant, as you see. I am unable to say at the moment if I will ever succeed in becoming a controleur. I have dreamed, as you know, of becoming a controleur, not an instructor. But people here still don't dare, I believe, to appoint Natives to that position. People fear that a Native controleur will not have the ability to deal with the European administration, a concern that I think is groundless. I also believe that I will be the only Native appointed to the Pawnshop Corps. How much effort it has cost me to achieve this position, Messieurs v. Deventer and v. Kol will be able to tell you. Without their help I would still be working in Customs. Anyway, I sincerely hope that my aim—that is, to become a controleur—will eventually be realized.[108] In the meantime I hope that my superiors will be pleased with my work.

I am very pleased to hear that you have taken an interest in the fate of the Native exiles.[109] I fear, however, that as long as both Natives remain in contact with DD they will not want to recognize their mistake. The action by these young Javanese I reject completely. What in fact do they want? Do they entirely forget the fact that people here in Java are not yet ready for autonomous government? This will still be the situation for the next 50 years in all aspects of society, so that self-government is still a long way off. To tell you the truth, I would not like to serve under our own compatriots, and on no account under the Indos, that is, the so-called "census Europeans." That would present insuperable problems. It would be impossible for me. Even now, now with the native rulers under the strict control of European colonial officials, they continue to be guilty of abuse of power, let alone what the situation would be like if they were free to do what they like, as we so often see from their behavior in the *desa* and in the Native households. Oh God, no, I much prefer the situation that now pertains to an administration directed by our own rulers or by Sinjos. Yes, and it would definitely be better—there could be no doubt about it.[110]

Mr. van Kol is doing the right thing in not providing the IP any support. And why the SDAP[111] does not condemn the childish pranks of these exiles is a mystery. The ridiculous aspect of the action by the SDAP becomes clear in the fact that their key spokesman, Mr. van Kol, the only soc[ial] dem[ocrat] in the Indies and who knows the conditions in the Indies, has declared himself against the approach of the former IP.[112] That is enough about this. I hope that you will be able to succeed in bringing those native young men to see things differently.

I wrote Kartono from Batavia, but till now I have not received a reply. In relation to his aim to be appointed as a teacher of Malay at the trade school in Rotterdam, I conclude he still has no plans to return. Our old mother will be very upset. Anyway, you cannot make a silk purse from a sow's ear.[113]

Recently Kartinah sent me a letter from Mr. Brandes,[114] who is in Holland at the moment, in which he mentioned that Kartono faithfully promised him that he would complete his studies in June this year. I sincerely hope that this time Mas To[115] will keep his word, which he promised on oath to keep. Should you meet him would you then be so kind as to pass on to him our regards and also to ask him why he has not written to us for a long time? In anticipation I thank you for your efforts.

At the moment I am here alone in Weltevreden. My wife and child are staying with Kardinah in Tegal, where I had taken them on 30 January. I did so because of the fact that in December there had been mention of the possibility that in that month I would undertake a study tour of Central Java. Due to a series of circumstances these plans fell through. Everything happened suddenly and unexpectedly. My instructor, Mr. Ostmeier, may not travel for medical reasons. Yes, the doctors who are treating him have declared him unfit to continue undertaking the technical instruction. As a result, Mr. Ostmeier yesterday lodged a request to be transferred to the position of administrator 1st class in the Pawnshop Division, accompanied by a medical report signed by two doctors. He was the official who had been appointed to show me around, and now that he was ill, it was obvious that the trip would not proceed. And so I am sitting here without my wife and child. I don't need to tell you that this situation depresses me. Nevertheless, my plan is to leave them in Tegal until my appointment, when I will have more certainty about where I will be stationed.[116] It is still an open question whether Mr. Ostmeier will get his wish, and whether he will be staying in Batavia. Anyway, now he would not be able to instruct me further. The best solution now, I think, is to calmly await the outcome and practice patience.

Soematri and the little Soearto are very well. Our little *boy* has progressed well. We speak Dutch with him and he replies in Javanese. Doesn't that surprise you? He understands us very well. Oh, we so hope that our *boy* will later become a person of good character. He is already able to win the hearts of people. He is never bad tempered, never a nuisance. And so everybody loves our little boy. Oh, may the Almighty grant that our wishes for him will be realized.

Now, my esteemed friend, I will leave it at this. I think I have already detained you too long. Please receive the warmest regards from Soematri and me and also for your wife,
   Your friend,
   Achmad

Achmad Sosrohadikoesoemo to Mr. and Mrs. Abendanon

Semarang, 26 February 1916

My highly esteemed Friends,

Your letter of 8 Nov. last reached us safely. It pleases us both greatly to learn from it that you have not forgotten us, and it is clear to us that only the fact that you have both been so busy has prevented you from writing to us. We had not at all supposed because of the long absence of your letters that we had been completely forgotten or that you no longer had a kind heart for us. It would indeed give us both the greatest pleasure to meet you again to exchange ideas over a wide range of subjects. I am sure you would not be able to recognize Java again, such a lot has happened in recent years. The Java of the present is no longer the Java of 10 years ago. Java has indeed undergone a metamorphosis.

What a pity that in the last year one of the cornerstones of Java's progress was taken from us; I mean the passing away of Mr. van Deventer. What a great deal we have to thank him for. The memory of Mr. van Deventer will therefore always stay with us with gratitude. In particular I will always remember him with respect and gratitude because I have Mr. van Deventer to thank for the fact that I was appointed to the government Pawnshop Office. With the death of His Excellency, the Kartini Vereeniging especially has lost a great supporter. Unfortunately, human beings desire but God decides! May he rest in peace. May the Almighty also safeguard those companions left behind—companions understood in the highest and truest sense of that word—to live through this dark hour, to allow her to undergo this trial imposed by the On High with courage.

Mr. Mühlenfeld will already have told you that during the festive season, at the request of the Freemason's Lodge, I gave a paper on "The Education of the Javanese Woman."[117] I asked Mr. Mühlenfeld to pass on to you my paper to read. Theoretically, and logically, the passing of a funding law to support the education of women would be a *conditio sine qua non* for the uplifting of Javanese women. However, the practical problems related to this question are so numerous, in my opinion, that it would not be wise to promulgate such a law.[118] At the moment there are not enough schools and a lack of teachers and so it is likely that the current situation in the colonies would not allow the great expenses that would result from it. Whatever the case, the huge task that awaits will not be able to be realized for another 50 years.

Nevertheless, we can comfort ourselves with the thought that the Dutch government is willing this year to increase the number of Holl. Indisch schools and to extend the number of Native 2nd class schools. And it pleases me greatly to know that in the former, school instruction in Dutch will be greatly increased. This issue is just now an issue being raised by the Ind[ische] Soc[iaal] Dem[ocratische] Partij,[119] which is arguing just now to begin to use the Javanese language as language medium in those schools, which, in my view, is humiliating. I am prepared to accept that the gentlemen Soc. Dem. have good intentions; I will *readily* admit that for the Javanese people it would be an *ideal* situation if the people could gain a knowledge of technical areas via their own language. But, given the way things are now, giving in to the ISDV would take us out of the frying pan into the fire. The gentlemen seem to have forgotten that Russia, by means of the German language, and Japan, by means of the English language, were able to develop themselves and that both countries, while they developed technically, also managed to maintain their own language. Moreover, it would be stupid to declare that the Dutch language would entirely suppress the Javanese language. The Javanese people must possess the key whereby it can open the door that opens out on to the Temple of Western Knowledge. At the moment, it is the Dutch language that can be regarded as being that key. Only when we also are in possession of Western knowledge will we be able to begin to shape the Javanese language in the desired way. Where we are now just beginning to make use of that key, then it would be inappropriate to now already begin to develop a modern Javanese language. That would produce a defective outcome and would cause language experts great difficulty later to try to fix the defective product.[120]

Fortunately, the ISDV is still in a minority and the Javanese are not letting themselves be misled by the pied piper. Because should they do so, we would be wandering even further away from our purpose, with the result that in the wider arena of life in the struggle against the Indos we would lose outright.[121] These latter—99% of the Indos are supporters of the ideas of Mr. Westerveld[122]—would love to see that it was the Javanese and not the Dutch language that became the language medium of the H.I. Schools. Looking at the issue from their perspective, I could agree with them entirely, since as a result their struggle for existence would become so much easier. Now, there is a possibility that they will become extremely hard pressed. The efforts being made by Mr. Westerveld mean for the Indo world a reigniting of their aspirations for glory.[123] Should the Netherlands government be inclined to accept the request of the Javanese to receive a good education in the Dutch language, then that would mean the death knell for the Demi-rulers. They would then be obliged to either merge in with us completely or lead the life of a trapped tiger. For these rulers it would indeed be important to bridge the gap that stands between them and our people as quickly as possible, not to widen and deepen it.

And now, highly esteemed friends, I need to bring you some good tidings. Our family has been increased by one. On the 22 Jan. last Soematri gave birth to a daughter. The birth went extremely well, although Soematri suffered quite a bit. This was no doubt because for a Javanese baby it was quite large. At birth the little one weighed 10 pounds. The little [Soe]Arto is of course in love with his sister, the little Annie (short for Soenniani) and especially when the new little citizen of the world is being bathed, he is very keen to help bringing this or that. Soematri and the little Annie are progressing well. Highly esteemed friends would you both pray for our little princess that she may grow up to become a woman worthy of her aunty Kartini.

Highly esteemed friends, I had better end my letter. Very soon I must leave to attend a meeting, and I want to post the letter myself. Please be assured that we both look forward to hearing from you.

    Yours truly,
    Achmad and family

p.s. Should you meet Nic (Mr. Adriani), would you be so kind as to pass on our regards and inform him that I will write soon. Thanking you in advance for your kindness.

Achmad Sosrohadikoesoemo to Mr. Abendanon

Semarang, 26 April 1916

Highly Esteemed Friend,

No doubt you have already received the report of the meeting of 2 April last from Mr. Raden Kamil, responding to your writing about the possibility of establishing a teacher training school for Native female teachers.[124]

From this rather short report you will have been able to see that, in principle, the meeting enthusiastically welcomed the plan. Unfortunately, although all those present were unanimous in their belief that this plan, the costs of which would be completely covered by the Kartini Fund, would hasten the development of our people, they concluded that, given the existing educational circumstances, there would be insufficient numbers of female pupils capable of benefitting from that training, so that such an educational institution would not be able to be established for another 5 or 6 years.

Although this report referred only to this single objection, there were also—and this is my personal opinion—other equally weighty factors considered that certainly need to be kept in mind if one is later to avoid the impression that one jumped to conclusions too hastily.

In the first place, I draw your attention to the fact that the government, as far as I know, still lacks the funds even to accept *in principle* the idea that for the *speedy* as well as for the *harmonious development* of the entire Javanese population the establishment of Native schools for girls would be desirable. Where private initiative has already done its part, where private initiative has already incontrovertibly demonstrated that the demand for girls' schools definitely exists, then it completely escapes me why the government cannot decide to establish a girls' school itself, even if only as a trial.[125] Where the government is not yet inclined to do this, it means that in the near future there would not be sufficient girls' schools in existence to guarantee the appointment of female school teachers or, for the time being, the demand from the Native community for their daughters to be trained as teachers will be near enough to zero.[126]

Then it should not be forgotten that Native parents would prefer girls' schools as an area of employment for their daughters rather than coeducational schools. Westerners may regard such a view as conservative, but that does not take away from the fact that account has to be taken of this. Moreover, I question whether the average Native female teacher, teaching the higher grades of a school, would be able to maintain the necessary order amongst the boys or gain the necessary respect from her male pupils. Social relations between our men and women are still at that level—and this shouldn't be surprising because we are still at the dawn of evolution—that one is justified in anticipating that it will be tens of years even before our female teachers will be ready to teach even our girls.

Should the executive of the Kartini Fund want to implement its plan as quickly as possible but also successfully, then, in my view, it would be essential that it convince the government as soon as possible to establish Native schools for girls—and for the time being only in the provincial and large residency capitals, where no private girls' schools have been established—and at the same time, provide a guarantee that Native female teachers, from whatever training institution, who have completed their training but have not yet gained a position in private Native girls' schools would be appointed to government girls' schools. This guarantee would be necessary to convince Native parents, who, for the duration of their daughters' education, have had to shoulder what is for them a fairly heavy financial burden, that all those burdens were not for nothing.[127]

I personally believe that the Kartini Fund could succeed in convincing the government of this. It could, without any scruples, claim that the great majority of Native parents prefer to send their daughters to girls' schools rather than to coeducational schools. Apart from the fact that the *large majority* still, as it were, maintain this orthodox position, at the same time we need to make sure that we *don't* turn our girls into learned academics; rather, we want to form intelligent women (mothers) so that this education will indeed be productive. And the education at coeducational schools cannot be productive since the period of puberty in the case of both sexes does not coincide, so that at this time there needs to be a separation in their education.[128]

If the government is indeed serious in wanting to improve the condition of the subject people it rules materially, spiritually and morally, then it is ethically obliged to respect the reasonable request to establish government Native girls' schools in those centers, as I mentioned earlier.

Only when there is a sufficient number of Native girls' schools in existence, whether private or government, can the rapid placement of certificated girls be guaranteed—the problem should be considered not only from the idealistic side but also from the materialistic side—only then will the supply of pupils be great enough to justify the establishment of a training school, and not before.

And once the time has come to put the plan into action, then, it will be advisable to establish a residential facility in relation to it and make residence a compulsory element. The dangers of the typical environment to which students are exposed after school cannot be sufficiently emphasized. Any educational influence in this kind of environment is usually lacking. And where the duty of the Native female teacher will be mainly to prepare the Native girl, as it were, for a society in transition, a task, therefore, which is noble but also serious and very difficult, then the environment of the trainee educator of the people must be such as to be nothing but capable of having a good influence on the student And this influence can only be created in the restricted environment of a school and residential facility at the head of which one has to appoint a highly respected European (Dutch) lady. Given the fact that in the first years it is unlikely that a suitable Native woman would be found for this position (since, apart from having the necessary qualifications for teaching, she must also possess those character traits and personal qualities essential for an educator in the purest meaning of that term), it will be desirable that a Dutch lady be appointed to the directorship.

However, it seems to me that it could also be useful to also appoint a Native lady to the residence who is acquainted with the etiquette that still operates in cultured Native society, who would see to it that the pupils were not transformed into half-baked beings. I mean by that, that one must be seriously on guard against the girls metamorphosing into pseudo-European women. Even after the completion of their studies, Native female teachers, even if they are real *modern* Javanese women, must still be able to feel at home not only in the European but also in Native society. Given this, it would be advisable to simply forbid these pupils to wear European clothing. Wearing such clothes, after all, brings with it a freedom of movement which later, when she returns to the completely Native world, would *definitely* be inappropriate. But not only that, it would *make her less admired by the parents of the girls* who would be put into her protection.

Above all the aim surely needs to be that the Native parents can place their trust in the compatriot female teacher. And this trust can certainly not be created when Native female teachers *take on the allures* of European ladies. Such Native women would have to be regarded as being *lost* to our cause. They will no longer be able to feel at home in our circles, will completely alienate themselves from their own people, and . . . the conclusion of this drama will be: marriage to a European, which, note well, would be regrettable. But I am also critical of the opposite situation. I would not like to see that our educated young men were to marry European ladies. The Native young man who does so is also lost to our cause. The educated Native young man must, in the interests of the great task that awaits him—to raise up his own people—must, in the arena of life, remain at the side of his educated compatriots.[129]

From the above it should be apparent that *in principle* I am against mixed marriages. That however does not mean that there are not cases that might disprove my objections. And such cases are for instance when a (European) party indeed has a warm respect for Native interests.[130]

Highly esteemed friend, I believe that I have herewith set out everything that I feel on this matter. I grant you complete freedom to regard this writing as a memo attached to the report of the recent meeting in case you are free to put my ideas forward to the directors of the Kartini Fund.

With the greatest respect for Mevrouw,
I remain,
Yours truly,
Achmad

Achmad Sosrohadikoesoemo to Mr. Abendanon

Semarang, 5 September 1916

Highly Esteemed Friend,

I received your friendly letter and the accompanying memorandum dated 14 July in good order yesterday and I am now hurrying, given the last sentence in your letter, to reply.

It pleases me greatly to be able to conclude from reading your memorandum that, in relation to the school that you are planning to erect, you have a sufficient number of pupils. Now it will only depend on the parents themselves whether or not they will send their girls to the school. As a kind of test of our evolutionary development I hope with all my heart that the Native parents will allow their daughters to attend the "Van Deventer School."

The organization Mangoenhardjo[131] has already turned its attention to assisting the school. At the meeting held on 13th August, at the request of the committee, I introduced the topic. I did so to the best of my ability. Knowing that you have been one of the first to take the initiative, I now take the liberty of offering you herewith a copy of my speech. I was successful in my presentation in as far as the general meeting agreed unanimously to support the project. The executive, of which I am a member, was ordered to make arrangements to raise the necessary funds from the side of the Native community. All Native officials will get a copy of my speech together with the Malay translation. Apart from that, we will immediately organize wayang performances, etc. Mr. Atmodirono,[132] whom I gave your latest letter to read—Mr. Kamil is no longer living in Semarang and has moved to Yogya after his appointment—has since approached Mr. Dr. Joekes, secretary of the Kartini Vereeninging here, who has agreed to receive any funds that may be donated. Whatever happens, like you, I am hoping that the project will be successful.

We are all well at the moment, although mother and children were recently quite ill—they all had influenza—but that has now fortunately passed.

On the 31 August we had an emotional day. In all the main cities in Java meetings were held on behalf of "Indië Weerbaar."[133] In Semarang, Dr. H. H. Berkenhouwer—president of the committee—Atmodirono—member of the committee—and the undersigned gave speeches. I was rather nervous when I took the stand, but fortunately I became calm and I was able to complete my speech without hesitation. I was certainly glad when it was over. At another time I would be happy to send you a copy of the speech, and I sincerely hope that you will also agree with the sentiments I expressed therein.

Now, my highly esteemed friend, I will leave it at this. Please present our respects to Mevrouw

I remain,
Yours truly,
Achmad

Soematri to Rosita and Mr. Abendanon

Semarang, 25 April 1918

Highly Esteemed Friends,

How is it that I have the audacity to take up the pen once more to commence a letter to you? It is out of a deep, deep feeling of guilt, dear friends.

So many times we planned to write to you. Yes, and not infrequently we did make a beginning, but, as so often happens, children arrived and the letter writing was postponed. Unfortunately, this has happened more often than that we resisted and continued writing. And yet recently you have been more often in our thoughts than ever because of events that have taken place and are continuing to take place here in the Indies, the land that has so attracted your attention.

The Indies are waking up! Those who have been saying that the Indies have been woken up are correct. That this "being woken up" is not always accompanied by clearheadedness should not be held against the Native. Great changes await the Indies! Could such changes take place without excesses? It is now up to the ruler to get to work with care because the power of the awakened creature should not be taken for granted! Because of the bad connections with the Motherland I don't know whether you have yet heard about the new actions of several S[arekat] I[slam] branches, the agitation for a strike here in Semarang, the disturbance of the good order, etc. It is here in Semarang that all this is manifesting itself most strongly. Given the nature of some of the actions of several S.I. members, it is thought that those well-known gentlemen, Baars and Sneevliet,[134] are behind this new movement and the president apparently is allowing himself to be influenced [by them].[135] Poor, poor people, who, because of their bitterly scarce education, are allowing themselves to be used as obedient cattle. Should this letter reach you, things will have progressed several more months in this direction, and what the situation here will be like then, God alone knows! My most earnest prayer is that these poor people will not have to pay too dearly for their ignorance, for the great trust they have placed in their leaders who are abusing it.[136]

Dear Friends, the education of girls is going ahead in leaps and bounds. You really cannot imagine how the recognition of the need for schooling has now reached down to the lowest levels of society as a demand of the times. Everywhere one becomes aware of the good effects that education is having. What our dear sister once said, that progress develops from the lap of mothers, is beginning to come true. What I wouldn't give if you could just see these young native households, headed up by young women, unselfconsciously contributing to the advancement of their people by the new atmosphere that they have brought into being in the native world. Among my friends there are lots of young housewives from all parts of Java, East, Central, and West Java, where, oh, it is such a pleasure to see this personification of Kartini's wise words; as young mothers I can admire them because they are so doing their best to be good mothers. If in the past, it was usual to have a baby tended by 2 or 3 *babus,* this practice has now been almost completely abandoned. The baby now finds itself in a baby carriage or box with the little mother sitting beside it doing her sewing; didn't that use to sound like a fairytale? And this is now the case in almost every household. I even saw a wife of a regent with her child in a *slendang*[137] getting into a train. Friends, when I saw that I was moved to my very soul and I felt like kneeling down in front of her, not because she was the wife of a regent but because she had felt and come to understand the message of what it was to be a mother, even as wife of a regent.

People are still studying the issue of which schools would be best for Native girls. Kartini Schools like those which we are fortunate enough to have in our city or kabupaten schools like those which Kardinah has established in Tegal. It seems to be a difficult problem, at least a solution to it has not yet been found. In my modest opinion both kinds of schools should exist; there should be as many girls' schools, based on the same principles as

European elementary schools, as there are 2nd class Native schools, don't you agree? It is no doubt that, at the moment, the majority of people are getting most advantage from the latter type of school rather than from those that are purely directed at academic education, although this is the direction in which, later, they will also have to go, won't they. Our girls must later be able to provide themselves with an independent existence. We have not yet got that far, but it is our duty to think about it and to start to make a beginning in that direction, don't you think?[138]

27 April 1918

This letter has been lying around for a few days unfinished. The post has just brought us the calendar that you sent us. Thank you so much for your kind thought, dear friends. I feel myself even more guilty now. God knows how often you are in our thoughts despite the fact that we have been so unfriendly as to not give you any news of us for so long. What a nice effect that batik theme of the border around the calendar creates, and what fine sentiments are contained in the quotations printed on the different pages. We are doubly grateful that you have sent us this.

The steamship "Nieuw Rotterdam" has also brought ISO[139] to Java. He brought us your regards and also told us a lot about you. He is one of the few young Javanese who are pleased to be back home in the land of their birth. It is so good to see that intense happiness shining in his eyes and expressed in his words. It promises much for the future, namely, that he will devote himself heart and soul to his country. God bless this young man. He has been stationed in Demak. Friends, such a sharp pain went through my heart when he was sitting here with us. My thoughts rushed to him, who is so dear to us, and for whom we continue to long. Whatever happens, we can't forget him . . .

1 May 1918

Once again this letter has had to be put aside. Forgive me. On Tuesday it was not possible for me to continue writing. It's so strange, there are moments in life where our feelings play games with us, leave us as it were paralyzed in our thoughts. Friends, no doubt you also would like to hear how we are faring. At the moment that I am writing this letter, all reports we have received from my sisters and brothers are good. And of course both our mothers are fine. They have become a lot older, but generally remain in good health, and it is then our dearest wish that these dear people will be with us for many more years, to be able to enjoy the fruits of their labors. We ourselves have a son who this coming January will already be starting elementary school, and our little girl is also growing up fast.

About Kartini's child we never get any news, we only know that he is still in Rembang attending an elementary school. What will become of him we don't know. The Regent is keeping all of us at a distance. Oh, friends, if you were here we would have asked you to take the child with you. You know that with us Javanese it is only the family on the father's side who has the ownership of the child in the situation like that of our little nephew. Oh, it is such a terrible thought to think that the only child of our dear sister is being neglected. The Regent, whom I have only spoken to once about Singgih, complained about his reluctance to read, but, going on the stories that he told me about the boy, Singgih is terribly spoiled. Are you still getting reports about him? Kardinah and Boesono took a lot of trouble to try to get the child to stay with them. The Regent, however, refuses to let him go. I hope that we will soon be able to bring you better news.

Dear friends, with this our warmest regards and our gratitude for your friendship,
    Yours truly,
    Soematri

In reading the letter again I realized that I completely forgot to tell you about the huge success that Nellie has had with her association for Native nurses.[140] It was incredible how much the demand for medical support has grown in native society. Nellie has certainly succeeded wonderfully in her attempts through tact and patience to achieve what, after years and years, male doctors have attempted unsuccessfully to bring about. Nellie's tactful approach is quite unique, and people have such trust in her. It is therefore no exaggeration if I write that Javanese women are extremely grateful to Nellie for the inspiration that brought her here, and many hope with me that we will have her here for a long, long time.

    Once again, a warm embrace,
    From your,
    Soematri

If you see the Adriani family please give them our warm regards. We will be sending a letter to them by the same mail, but whether these letters will reach you? Well, I hope so.

Soematri to Rosita and Mr. Abendanon

Semarang, 26 November 1918

Highly Esteemed Friends,

On behalf of Kardinah I am sending you herewith several copies of schoolbooks that she has compiled as a way of contributing to the development of the Native woman. There are some other works in print, copies of which she will be sending you. Dear Friends, Kardinah asked me to pass on her apologies that she could not write to you herself. Since July she has had to undergo a very strict regime of rest, which unfortunately will still have to conclude with an operation that will take place here in Semarang in December. I don't know whether this letter will reach you before that operation takes place. Kardinah has asked me to ask for your blessing for the success of the operation so that she may yet be of some use to Native society.

I have just received in the mail your letter to Ngawi for me to read. Dear Friends, I hope you will succeed in your attempt to provide for a future for the little Singgih as his dear mother had imagined it. From all of us, our most heartfelt thanks, my dear friends. I regret it more than I can tell you that I have no better news to write to you about our orphaned nephew than the following. By accident we learned in August this year that Singgih was in Semarang, had been so since June, and moreover was boarding with a family who lives no more than 5 minutes' walk from our house. The fact that we were not informed about this at all did not make a very good impression on us because what wouldn't we do for the child of our dear sister? We went to visit him where he was staying with the family with three other stepbrothers. Singgih gave me the impression as if he had been constantly kept under the thumb, he looks so frightened when he looks at you. When I saw the boy, my first thought was to take him away out of the environment. The impression I had of him, from his whole manner, was so pitiable. Oh God, isn't it ironic, that incredible contrast between mother and child? Alas, we are completely helpless in this case. It seems as if the child has been forbidden to come to visit us. It is now 3 months ago that we visited him and asked him and his brothers repeatedly to come to visit us, but up to now, this moment when I am writing this letter, none of the boys has come. Why? They do visit other families, but it seems that they have to avoid us, although, as far as we are concerned, we have done nothing wrong in relation to the boys. The head of the boardinghouse, however, did tell us that one of Singgih's brothers told Singgih not to come to visit us until he had the permission of his brother, the regent of Rembang. The fact that we had been left completely in the dark that S. was in Semarang while the regent knew we were living here brings us closer to the truth. S. is still in elementary school. Dear Friends, you should not think that the reason I am telling you all this is to blacken someone's name in your estimation. What I wouldn't give if I could be writing you the complete opposite. The R of R[embang] has for a very long time kept his distance from the family of Kartini. The reason for this we have endeavored to discover, but alas, to no avail. Dear Friends, could I be expected to keep all this from you? Wouldn't that be akin to being a crime against Kartini, against her child? Forgive me if I have made a mistake here, it is so cruel, that Kartini's only child will, probably forever, be neglected. Nellie Stokvis, whom I discussed this with, advised me to seek the counsel of Mr. Hazeu.[141] But we have to go about this very carefully because the R will resist any attempts if he should learn that Kartini's family is behind it. You know that he refused to allow either Kardinah or Boesono, who had immediately attempted to do something on the death of Kartini's husband, to have the child. Dear friends, it's all quite desperate that I have to write you all this. Oh, let's hope you may succeed in helping Kartini's child.

With our warmest regards to you all,
Yours always,
Your Soematri

Soematri to Rosita and Mr. Abendanon

Semarang, 1 December 1919

Highly Esteemed Friends,

Finally we can sit down to write letters in the certainty that they will not be months underway in getting to Holland. Dear Friends, let me first begin by wishing you a happy New Year. For the first time after all these years a New Year will be ushered in without the anxiety-inducing bulletins bringing us news about war zones. The cannons have stopped their murderous action, thank goodness! Please God that, with the end of this year, a period that is shameful for all civilized people will be forever closed! Even though everywhere misery still reigns, at least they have stopped murdering on a large scale, isn't that already a great improvement?

But it has been a very long time since we have written to you. I read your letter to Roekmini, dear Mevrouw, which she, at your request, sent to me to read, and for that I thank you sincerely, not only for the great interest you have shown, that you have always shown, in our family's affairs but also, in particular, for the practical support that you have always shown us. I cannot tell you how very grateful we are to you for your belief in us. What you have offered to do for our poor dear sister Roekmini could never be calculated. Dear Friends, it is not possible for me to set down on paper everything I feel. If I could at this moment stand before you, all I could do would be to kiss your hand. Be assured that we are striving, dear Friends, to be worthy of your faith in us and your friendship.

Regarding our nephew Singgih, unfortunately I have nothing to write to you. You ask if it would not be advisable for me to write to the Regent. Forgive me, Friends, that I have not yet been able to do this. His arrogant attitude toward us has till now prevented me to do as you suggest. Small-minded and cowardly of me, isn't it? I will do my best to overcome this.

From the newspapers you will already have a good idea of how things are here in the Indies. The days of peace and quiet have passed. Everywhere there is tension and dissatisfaction. People are finally trying to get to understand each other, but where for hundreds of years people have lived and worked side by side but as two completely separate nations, it is difficult for them now immediately to get to understand each other's way of thinking. This won't happen without some problems, unfortunately. Many have wanted it differently, but what can an individual do against the majority which is still too stupid to comprehend that many of these leaders only get up as leaders out of self-interest. How often, without realizing, do the masses not place the yoke on their necks themselves, such as in the case of those strikes and other protests where they are completely vulnerable? The history of Western peoples tells us however that in Europe too, as a result of new ideas, clashes are unavoidable in the advancement of the Indies and her inhabitants; that here too more extensive experience of the meaning of life will result in outcomes that will be of lasting benefit for those now feeling their way.[142]

One good sign is that there are now more young Native people who have completed their education; even though they may not be participating in all those political goings on, their own education and broader view of life will definitely have an educative influence, in the first place on their own families and later on, on wider and wider circles. If you were able to take a look at the family life of young people in our society now, you would be surprised at what great changes for the good have occurred! One can feel that spring is in the air; everywhere one can already see the buds forming which will later transform everything into a beautiful blossoming field. But, at the same time, one still feels the cold and the chilling winds of winter. Dear Friends, do not turn away from us when you see excesses increasingly occurring. We Javanese also are seeking the right direction, but the way there is still very unclear.

How wonderful that it is now so easy to get a scholarship to study in Holland. Had the government done this earlier, then the huge amounts of money that the government now has to spend on the ever-increasing salaries of imported workers could have been saved. Well, let's not now start complaining. The government has made a beginning in providing young people with ability with the opportunity to continue their studies in Europe. Let's hope those who are selected are able to profit from this.

In September 3 boys from Semarang's HBS left for Holland.[143] One of them, Raden Mas Darsito, lived with us for 3 years. At that time he was a quiet, shy boy. If he comes to pay you a visit with his friends, would you be able to keep an eye on him? He comes from Solo and has always been in a Javanese environment. I hope that the great change will not have any negative consequences for him. His younger brother is still with us. He hopes to complete his final exam next year and also to go to Holland. I know this boy better than Darsito, who came to us when he was already in the 3rd class and therefore someone whose character was already largely formed. His younger brother, on the other hand, came to us directly after his elementary schooling. We have therefore had a better opportunity to study his character, and I don't think that I am mistaken in thinking that he shows great promise. We are expecting a lot from these boys who are now going to Holland with the realization that they have a duty to their country to come back qualified. Let's hope that these expectations will be realized.

All is well with my little family. The children are shooting up. Our oldest boy, who will be 8 in the spring, is now in the 2nd grade of the elementary school. And my little daughter is gradually becoming a real little lady. She is now 4 and a dear little thing. It is so wonderful to watch these little lives blossom, and the support that they need now and then is always so gratefully received. We feel ourselves so richly rewarded. I don't follow any particular method of child-raising, but I do agree in many things with the ideas of Ligthart,[144] the man who describes the character of children so beautifully. But I could not stop if I once started on my hobbyhorse, and I have held you up for too long already, haven't I? Forgive me that I so rudely robbed you of your time.

Once again we wish you all the best with the beginning of 1920. May the New Year bring us all closer together to the realization of our ideals!

With our warmest regards and respect,
As always,
Your Soematri

Soematri to Rosita Abendanon-Mandri

Semarang, 17 November 1920

Highly Esteemed Mevrouw,

Many thanks for your letter of 25-9-20, which I received several days ago in good condition. I could not, however, reply to you by return mail since just when I received your letter I was tending to my little daughter Soemiani, who was ill at the time with influenza.

I can now, however, report good news about Roekmini. She had been quite ill for a time but has now, thank God, completely recovered and since October has been teaching a course in practical sewing twice a week at the HIS, for which she receives 50 guilders from the government. She is very well now, as are her children. I will write to her and send her your letter to read.[145]

I understand from your letter that my letter, which I wrote to you in February or March, did not arrive. We had a lot of misfortune at the beginning of the year. My husband suffered from nerves so seriously that it required an emergency certificate ordering a month's rest. One month appeared not to have been enough, and so we stayed up in the mountains for 3 months. Hardly had we returned home than we had to bury our highly esteemed friend Atmodirono.[146] We have certainly received more than our fair share of what one calls life's trials. Hopefully this period has now closed for us.

How are our children going? Thank you for your interest, Mevrouw. They are well. Our eldest, a boy of 8 years, is now in the 3rd grade of the elementary school, where the head teacher calls him the most successful of all the Javanese children that he has ever had. That is certainly a flattering compliment and we hope of course that our boy will continue to earn it. In June he will go up to the 4th grade. Our youngest, a four-year-old girl, will be going to the Fröbel school till next year. It's so wonderful to have, these little children, but, oh, how desperate we become when they are ill. Then it seems to me that doctors are so stupid because they can't cure our children immediately. It's very silly of me, of course but, oh, the anxiety drives you mad. We hold the most wonderful dreams about our children's future, especially for our daughter, who must become worthy of her aunt who departed from us so early in her life.

From the newspapers you will already have gathered how things are now in the Indies. There have been many changes for the good, but along with that we have also gained elements in our society to counterbalance these, which are still the consequences of the terrible war. The revelations recently about the S[arekat] I[slam] are very, very bad, don't you think too?[147] They make us Javanese ashamed, but in one respect it is probably good that the crisis has occurred now. This is likely to have its good effects. We must go on, despite the disappointments, to uncover our faults and improve them. It is impossible that one day we will not reach that goal which other countries have already had for so long before us. Mevrouw, in August this year another boy has left for Holland whom we had with us for 5 years. His name is Surwedo Mangoenkoesoemo, the son of the *Patih* Regent of the kingdom of Mangkoenegoro.[148] We asked him to call on you. He is a very nice boy and we hope that he will also leave a good impression with you. What a lot of young Native youths are now going to Europe! Do they take their studies seriously? We get to know so little about them here.

About Kardinah I can only report to you that, thank God, she has now completely recovered after being under doctor's care for about 2 years. Her school is going very well and, looking at the number of European government school lady teachers who have been coming to her school for research, and the school in Aceh, and possibly the one in Lampung, which has been modeled on hers, it could be seriously considered that her school can be called a success.

In January she will get a daughter of a raja, a girl of 18, to train as a teacher for the school that will be opened in Lampung. How marvelous of that girl to leave behind home and family, to come, completely on her own, to a country where everything is totally foreign to her, both language and people, solely for the purpose to be of use to her people when she returns.

Then I also have some good news to tell you about us. Perhaps you still remember what a lot of trouble we had when my husband was appointed to the Pawnshop Division of the civil service—appointing a Javanese to a not completely subordinate position, well, that really troubled those gentlemen at the time. But now they have changed their mind. In June my husband will be appointed as controleur in the same office and the successor in my husband's old job will again be a Javanese. The trial succeeded. Hopefully Westerners will now have more faith in us, and from our side, hopefully this trust will not be shamed. We will be stationed in Tegal. There I hope to be able to help Kardinah with her social work. When this letter arrives in Holland the year 1920 will have come toward its end and a new year, full of promise, will be dawning.

A happy year, Highly Esteemed Friends,
From us both our warmest regards,
Your Soematri

Mevrouw, with this same post I am also sending a letter to Mevrouw Ovink-Soer.[149] However, I don't know her current address so I have addressed the letter to your house. Would you be so kind as to readdress it correctly? In advance many thanks for your efforts.

Yours Soematri

Soematri to Rosita and Mr. Abendanon

Tegal, 3 November 1923

Dear Esteemed Friends,

This afternoon we received your kind gift of *Door Duisternis tot Licht*,[150] which after a long journey of several months finally arrived at our present address. The parcel was sent in June, we saw by the postmark, and we only received it today, 3 November. So it really must have made a trip around the world.[151] Dear friends, this does not in the least diminish the fact that we really appreciate your kindness and express our sincere gratitude to you for your gift. What a large place the Javanese people occupy in your hearts. Neither the hard work nor disappointments have proved an obstacle to your noble work; undaunted you have devoted all your energies to the struggle to secure our welfare. You can feel assured, my esteemed friends, that your name will always live on in our hearts; we pray that those who have remained standing firm despite the world's storms will continue to be worthy of your devotion.[152] Java, alas, has also not remained uninfected. The seeds of the illness that is currently threatening to wreck the West have also gained an increased presence here, alas not without effect, where just now the air is filled with dissatisfaction.[153] One would so wish to be able to save one's people from being infected, but that is of course an impossible wish where the Javanese people also form an inseparable element of the great universe. The sober soul of the people will, however, not lose its way. May the Javanese people emerge purified from the struggle!

Dear friends, how are you both? It is already so long since we have heard from you? We sincerely hope that you are both well and will be assured many more years to remain a secure haven for our boys, who, in that strange land, may feel at home with you with their ideas and aspirations. Here in Tegal we are both well. My husband has the trust of his superior, and that of course makes work all the more enjoyable. You can imagine how much that means to us now, when, at first, we were immediately mistrusted in and about everything. In that unpleasant time, when we were often pushed to the extreme, and often were driven up the wall and felt like writing, "Dearest, I am going to chuck it all in!" it was only the thought of you, my Friends, that held us back from doing so, and also the thought of our dear ones who preceded us as models of righteousness and patience, they too we could think of at those times.

Our children are now both going to school. Our *boy* is now 11 and is in the sixth grade and our girl is 7 years old and is in the second grade. They both learn easily and we have many hopes for their future. Let's hope they come true. Do you ever hear anything about Kartini's son? The Regent of Rembang seems to want to continue to prevent any approach on our part. Now that we are here in Tegal we don't hear anything from him anymore.

Dear friends, once again many, many thanks for your kind thought. Believe us when we say you will also remain unforgettable for us.

With our best wishes for your good health and happiness,

Your Soematri

Soematri to Rosita Abendanon-Mandri

Semarang, 24 November 1932

Dear Mevrouw,

The airmail just arrived with a letter from our boy in which he wrote that through the intermediary of Miss Adriani he had received an invitation to come to The Hague to meet you. Arto[154] wrote that he could not afford time out because he is studying hard for his entry examinations, which he has to sit on 4 January, but that after his exams he will come to visit you. Then he would have all the time and as a reward for his hard work we will allow him to stay a little longer in The Hague to look up old friends of ours, and in the first place you, dear lady.

When I read Arto's letter and came to the section in which he wrote about you, it was as if I fell through the floor in remorse and shame. How could I have neglected to have informed you of Arto's presence there, so relatively close to you! We did not know your address, the last time we heard from you was that you were going abroad. Your son Dolf was in Batavia at that time and we would hear about you from him from time to time. But that correspondence ceased long ago. We don't even know whether Dolf is still in the Indies.

The years that lie behind us have not been easy ones for us, but we won't linger on that—they have been difficult but now, fortunately, lie behind us, and after all, those difficult years also had their golden edges. And now our eldest is in Holland. Sometimes I can't believe it, you know. Up to now Arto is doing his best. To support his studies we sought the help of the Oost en West Student Commission, and we can only sing the praises about the way it has gone to work. It will be wonderful when Arto will be able to visit you—I will write to him immediately to remind him that he must not forget to do so as soon as he has time.

Does Roekmini still write to you?[155] Her daughter is now living with me; she is already in the third grade of the MULO and after her final examination will continue her studies at the teacher training school. Her son will do his final exams next year at the AMS and then will continue in Bandung at the Technical Institute. Roekmini herself is still living in Kudus, where, since the closing of the Fröbel class at the HIS, she now teaches at the Fröbel school in the same locality. Kardinah and her husband now live in Salatiga. Perhaps you know that her husband retired 3 years ago. Their son is now the regent of Tegal, and now the old couple are living in Salatiga and are enjoying the delights of now finally being able to live for themselves. Kartinah and her husband are also already retired and live in Madiun. The brothers live far apart but are all doing well. Our mother has also become quite old but is in good health. My own mother[156] is living with Kardinah in Salatiga while *Hibu*[157] continues to live with Roekmini and Soelastri in Kudus. We too have been living in Semarang for the last 3 years with our daughter Soemiani, who is in the 4th year of the HBS and has plans to continue her studies at the medical school—the same aspirations as her aunts had but for whom these remained only dreams.

Much has changed in Java, the people, the surroundings, and everything which together actually we call the world. There is much good but also much that is bad—but both are needed to build upon, isn't that right? Here also the depression has brought many victims with it and the coming year is being anticipated with much trepidation. "What will it bring?" is on everyone's lips.

Dear Moedertje, may everything go well for you and yours in the coming year. If Arto visits you I am sure he will find much love. Moedertje, my sincerest thanks in advance for your kindness. Moedertje, if you are no longer able to write, leave it, you do not need to reply to my letter. I am so happy that I can write to you—I feel as though in this way I have been able to repay a small portion of my debt towards you.

Good-bye, dearest, dearest Moedertje. My best wishes. The warmest regards from us three,
    Your old,
    Soematri

Soematri to Rosita Abendanon-Mandri

Salatiga, 20 January 1935

Dear Moedertje,

How lovely it was for us to read the news in the last airmail that my son has finally been able to meet you. We had told him so much about you both and he knew he was doing his parents a great favor by making time to visit their friends. But he didn't do this just to make his parents happy: he wrote in his letter, "I am glad to have made the acquaintance of Mrs. Abendanon. Please write to her and also ask the other aunts to write, it would make Mrs. Abendanon so happy. Neither the future nor the present has much attraction for her since, with the passing of her husband,[158] who you all know and learned to love, she lost everything that was of value in her life." The impact you had on him must be contained in those last lines, we are so pleased with that. Respect and love for older people who have struggled on our behalf, who have opened up the way for us—these are feelings which one finds so rarely in young people these days so it does us good, us parents with old-fashioned principles, to detect these feelings in him.

Moedertje, was it really good to have had our child with you? Wasn't he too rowdy? It was more than three years ago that we brought our child on board the ship, and he has not neglected for a single week to write to us, which we have appreciated so much, and yet we look forward to the end of his period of study. We parents, in our love for our children, really are big egoists—only with great difficulty do we relinquish our children to the big turbulent world but forget so often that we ourselves also longed to fly from home.

Moedertje, how time has flown. How well I can still imagine your last journey to Rembang to say farewell to Kartini. Roekmini, Kartinah, and I then formed the cloverleaf, and we were allowed by Father to travel to Rembang too, to meet you both, not knowing that this would be our last happy time together, because not long thereafter, Kartini departed from this life, unexpectedly.[159] Moedertje, we were desperate, why was there never an answer?—We had just to accept it, but can feel that we have been granted some mercy because we have only happy and sunny memories of those who went before us. Kartini's son has now himself become a father. Unfortunately, there is no contact between him and his aunts, but this does not take away from the fact that for us he will always be the beloved child of our dear Kartini.

Times have changed, Moedertje, they bring with them sadness and suffering. You see I am gradually becoming part of that older generation who sees with regret how everything has changed, at least according to my old-fashioned opinion. The world is restless, internally and externally, one is always looking for variety, change, sensation. Why this is I don't know, I can't understand it. The youth will be able to accommodate to it.

When the airmail letter from our child arrived, we were just sitting together close and cosily, Roekmini, Kardinah, Kartinah, and I, just like the old days, looking for the comfort of our own family and home, together also with our two mothers. You can imagine how, with the reading of Arto's letter, all those memories were being recalled. An air of melancholy spread over us all, but yet we were filled with a warm feeling of happiness. We felt rich in the wealth of memories; there was not the slightest discordant note.

Arto no doubt also told you that Kardinah, after her husband retired, came to live in Salatiga, where we are now also living. Roekmini and Ibu had also come to visit for the company, and as well Kartinah, who lives with her husband in Madiun, came over for a few days. Moedertje, we spent that time together like four silly little girls—very old-fashioned but still, in the eyes of those who saw us, we could see their approval and recognition of the riches that flow from love. Roekmini and Kardinah will also write to you soon.[160] In June Roekmini lost her youngest daughter, our poor sister is sorely tried, she has lost both her daughters and now only a son remains, who is studying in Bandung to become an engineer. He is a good, well-mannered boy—may he be able to make up to his mother the love and warmth which she lost with the loss of her daughters. Tante Janie[161] will no doubt have told you a lot about us all. Our paths happened to cross quite accidentally—but then, could it have been otherwise? A deep friendship has developed from this chance meeting, not only between Soematri and Tante Janie, but also Soematri's children have found in Tante Janie a maternal friend. Our son always enjoys meeting Tante Janie, which we are very happy about. It gives us a feeling of peace, a sense of security knowing that in that foreign country he has friends who, through their own experiences and maturity, can help him through his difficulties. Last year we also had to bring away our daughter, fortunately not to Holland, but for a mother it is already a big step to send your daughter away. Fortunately, because of his role in the Volksraad, my husband is often in Batavia, which comforts me with the knowledge that she is not there alone. Mothers shouldn't really be so possessive, but unfortunately I am—I would prefer it that all the people I love would always remain by my side.

Moedertje, Arto wrote me that you are not able to write anymore—well, you don't need to. We will keep you informed, either through letters or via Arto, about the things that interest you. The Indies has changed very, very much, unfortunately not always in the best way. Education has brought a lot of good, but also many black spots, but is that not a natural phenomenon in life—don't we need the shadows to appreciate the light more? It is sad that because of the Depression so much that had been brought to fruition with great difficulty has had to be discontinued, but this too may have its good side which we can't at this point yet see.[162] But perhaps after a few years we can look back at all this with different eyes.

How well I can remember your first visit to Jepara, when your husband wanted to get the opinion of regents about the question of establishing schools for girls.[163] It is unbelievable how much has been achieved in such a short time. We now already have our female doctors, our lawyers. People no longer question whether they should send their daughters to school. We have come a long way, but whether people are happier as a result? What else can one expect where character remains far behind development? It is a situation that applies all over the world. Perhaps after this things will move in a different direction.

Dear Moedertje, am I not boring you with my chatter? I have to end this letter now if it is to make the post. With lots of love from us all, from Ibu, Soe[miani] and the sisters,

and your Soematri

Soematri to Rosita Abendanon-Mandri

Batavia, 18 January 1936

Dearest Moedertje,

I cannot thank you enough for your letter. I know how you are suffering from neuralgia, but despite that, you did set down to write. Do I need to tell you how doubly dear this letter of yours is to me? I immediately passed your regards and best wishes on to the sisters. Moedertje, the link between you and our family can never be washed away; on the contrary the children will carry it with them as a talisman throughout their lives. A friendship made up of such tight bonds can bear nothing but good fruit, even for the younger generation. I am very happy that you have been able to make the acquaintance of our son, and we are delighted that you have developed a good impression of our child.

Moedertje, the young lady on the photo with Roekmini, Kardinah, and me that Nellie gave you is not our Soemiani but Jo An van de Broek d'Obrenan, a colleague of Nell's who is now practicing as a doctor in Salatiga. Her parents knew Father very well, and now Fate has brought her to Salatiga, no doubt to draw the old bonds tighter. Our daughter herself is a student at the medical institute, a choice which she really made against our wishes but which we did eventually have to accept, as she has demonstrated a deep commitment to her vocation. For her sake we are now also living in Batavia, a more expensive and hotter place than Salatiga, where we had been living. Strange, isn't it, when parents are confronted by a choice between living quietly in a pleasant climate and their child, the decision is made quite quickly and the child can cry out, Victory! We hope that with all our experience that we can be of assistance to her.

Yesterday's mail brought with it the news that our son had passed his Dutch agriculture candidature, so now he has both qualifications and this year he will go abroad to do his practical training. After that he will return to the Indies in 1937. By that time I will find out where you are living because we would like it very much if Arto bade you farewell before he returned to the Indies. Unfortunately, I cannot tell you much about Kartini's child. We tried to approach him, but till now with no success. All we know is that he is now Assistant *Wedono,* is married and father of a child. Let's change this subject, it's too painful not to know anything about the child of her who is so dear to us. We will, however, not give up our attempts and hope one day to succeed. Soetino, Boesono's[164] oldest son, is now Wedono in the same regency where Soesalip is Assistant Wedono with the Criminal Investigation Division. Perhaps the two cousins will be able to come closer together and succeed where the aunties and uncles could not.

Roekmini's own son hopes to complete his studies as engineer next year. If together with our son he can then immediately get a position, then we will feel as rich as a king. The terrible unemployment our young people are experiencing is so bad; a job is just so important for them to occupy the tumultuous energy of youth. We don't want to be too pessimistic about the future. During our lifetime surely we have experienced enough to know how often human predictions are wrong. If the young people can begin at the bottom and take on everything they are given, then I think they will get there in the end.[165]

Kardinah is still in Salatiga with her husband and Kartinah in Madiun. Our two mothers are in good health, but don't travel much anymore, unless they can travel in a good automobile which allows them to stop every now and again when traveling becomes too much for them. We hope very much to have them with us for a long time yet and share with us the harvest years of a life to which they have devoted themselves with so much love. During *Lebaran,* our so-called New Year, we went to visit our mothers. We found them in good health and alert. They were so happy to see all their children, grandchildren, and their children who had taken the trouble to come to celebrate the special day in the company of their family.

Can you still remember which old acquaintances of yours here in Batavia might still be living here? I would love to take on the task of bringing them your regards. Are none of your children here? I thought Dolf had a son here, or am I mistaken? We are of course the oldies, whom the young ones no longer feel comfortable with. Our parents left us with very pleasant memories of home that we have carried with us as a precious possession throughout our lives, but now that we ourselves are confronted with the fact, many parents don't know what to do. The chaos that has resulted from this has led in many cases to the need to reestablish a sense of family life. There are exceptions, of course, but generally it won't be so easy to bind the young people, who have found more pleasure in the cinemas and dance halls than in the calm and peaceful atmosphere of the interior of the home. Moedertje, how happy I feel that I have kept to that which my father and mother passed on to me. How will our children look at these things? Their work, especially that of our daughter, is such that they won't have much time for this, but we hope their homes won't be poor in warmth and cosiness, because this life won't leave that unpunished.

Your Christmas greeting is hanging next to the photo of our Kartini in Ani's room. You understand that we have told our children everything about our dear Friends, and when your letter came together with your Christmas greeting Ani immediately asked if she could have it: "It must be hung next to Aunty's photo because it comes from she who loved her." It is bound to have a good impact on her surroundings.

Dear Moedertje, I should not hold you up any longer. You don't need to tire yourself by replying to this letter, although of course we would love to receive a letter from you. If I know your address I would like to keep you informed about all of us here in the Indies. Your husband has passed away but his work lives on. Ani often has girl students visiting her who have no idea with how much difficulty the freedom they enjoy was achieved. I then tell them about those who have gone before them, about the Dutch people who were here, inspired by warm love for the land and its people, how they moved heaven and earth to realize their ideals. It is wrong to keep the younger generation ignorant of the heavy struggle undertaken by their elders, to achieve. What they already regard as their right they should in fact be more grateful for toward those who made this possible after so much difficulty.

Good-bye, Moedertje, our very best wishes to you. May your new dentist save you from more suffering. I am sending this letter to Nell, as we don't know your address nor that of Marie and Dolf. Nell will no doubt be so kind as to take care of the matter of sending it on to you.

With many warm regards from all of us and much love,
From your Javanese girls,
Your Soematri[166]

Appendix

DOCUMENTS RELATING TO THE ESTABLISHMENT OF THE WISMO PRANOWO SCHOOL

R. M. Rekso Negoro to Mr. Abendanon

Tegal, 20 February/30 March 1916[1]

Highly esteemed Sir,
    Respectfully we take the liberty of offering you the patronage of the Tegal School of Domestic Economy, Wismo Pranowo.
    The Raden Ayu of Tegal has long held the idea of doing something for Native girls and believed she could realize this through the establishment of a school for domestic economy, a plan which she carried out as soon as she as she gained the support of Mevrouw de Steurs.
    We will not bore you with the reasons that delayed this project, but the fact is that the plans did take shape and that now we can respectfully approach you with the request that you would provide practical assistance for an institution for which Native society has an urgent need.
    In the month of December, discussions were held with Native leaders, teachers, and several individuals in Tegal with the aim of finding out if there was support for the idea, how one envisaged such an institution, and whether people were prepared to make voluntary financial contributions for the establishment of a school which would undoubtedly involve great expense.
    After receiving written replies from many interested parties, we developed a plan that we now would like to submit to your scrutiny with the hope of having your greatly appreciated comments.
    We plan to establish and furnish the school in the following way:
    The school will be named "Wismo Pranowo," which means "the house that expands the vision," and this will be opened on 1 March 1916. It will be

temporarily housed in an office of the kabupaten, the former army barracks until the time comes when it will have its own building. The initial furbishment and maintenance will be paid for out of voluntary contributions of interested parties, thereafter from school fees. At the moment fees are around 1,000 guilders initial payment and a monthly payment of 50 cents. As soon as possible a subsidy will be applied for to begin construction of a school building, to contribute to the salaries of the teaching staff and to the initial cost of furnishing the school, etc. School fees have been set at 50 cents per month, and it is expected that 100 students will be enrolled.

The curriculum will include:

- the course as provided in 2nd class Native schools
- the teaching of cooking
- teaching of batikking
- teaching of fancy and practical needlework
- if possible religious education (2 hours a week Koran reading)

The course will run over 6 years.
The teaching staff consists of:[2]

- a head teacher (male or female)
- 2 assistant female teachers (at the moment we have 4 assistants)
- 1 female teacher for cooking and batikking
- 1 female teacher for fancy and practical needlework
- 1 female teacher for religious education (who is also a teacher in training for needlework)
- 1 assistant trainee teacher
- 1 assistant in the kitchen
- 1 guard

The estimated budget at the moment is as follows:

Income for the first year:

– subsidy school fees	ƒ190
– subsidy for 2 pupil teachers	ƒ280
– subsidy for initial establishment costs	ƒ100
– subsidy for other personnel	ƒ180
– subsidy initial costs for the establishment of the domestic economy school	ƒ200
total subsidy	ƒ950
– initial payment	ƒ1,000

– initial payment paid monthly	ƒ500
– school fees	ƒ500
TOTAL	ƒ3,000

Expenses:

Current[3]		Original	
1 head teach.	60	head teacher 10 months @ 50 guilders p.m.	ƒ500
1 ass. teacher	30	2 pupil teachers @ 30 and 25 guilders p.m	ƒ550
3 pupil teach.	60	1 batik and cooking teacher @ 30 guilders p.m	ƒ300
1 guru batik & cook.	35	1 needlework teacher @ 30 guilders p.m.	ƒ300
1 guru needlew.	20	1 religious education teacher @ 8 guilders p.m	ƒ80
1 p.t. needlew. & rel. educ.	20	1 kitchen hand @ 7.50 guilders per month	ƒ75
1 kitchen hand	5	1 guard @ 10 guilders p.m.	ƒ100
1 guard	10		
TOTAL			ƒ1,905

150 pupils

– 3 sewing machines	ƒ105
– sewing equipment	ƒ150
– batik equipment	ƒ100
– kitchen equipment	ƒ100
– 1 kitchen (temporary construction)	ƒ50
– food purchases from the market	ƒ125
– books etc.	ƒ200
– initial purchase of furniture	ƒ250
	ƒ980
TOTAL	ƒ2,885
Miscellaneous expenses	ƒ115
Total expenses	ƒ3,000

Because we fear that the monthly fees may not always be paid on time, a reserve fund will be necessary, for which in time a permit for a lottery of about 10,000 guilders will be applied for, while on 26 February a Native "fancy fair" will be held to raise money to cover initial costs because it is unlikely that the subsidy will be received in time.

We have tried to provide you, sir, with a brief overview of our plans but we are more than willing to provide you with a more detailed oral account should you wish further information.

Yours respectfully,
R. Negoro

R. M. Rekso Negoro to
The Governor General
of the
Netherlands Indies

Herewith, with the greatest respect, you are informed that:

Raden Ayu Adipati Ario Rekso Negoro, wife of the Regent of Tegal and sister of the late Raden Ajeng Kartini;

Will open, on the 1st of March 1916, a School of Domestic Economy for girls in the district capital, Tegal;

That several interested persons, including Mevrouw H. H. de Stuers, wife of the Assistant Resident of Tegal, Mevrouw van den Bos, wife of the Controleur of Tegal, Raden Ayu Soemodirdjo, wife of the Patih of Tegal and others, have promised her their support for the proposal for a school whose goal is namely, to provide Native girls with the opportunity to learn different skills so that they can indeed become "mother and wife" of the family;

That despite everything she has been unable to fulfill all the requirements of the subsidy regulations as outlined in Government Decree 1914, No. 592;

That on the basis of article i, line 3 of the said Decree, she directs this request to you, requesting you grant her exemption from the following conditions and substitute different conditions as His Excellency may see fit;

That, in several classes, namely in the 3rd parallel class of the first year and the 2nd parallel class of the second year, only 1½ hours per day are taught in reading and writing "in the local or the Malay language with local or Latin characters" and "the four rules of arithmetic with whole numbers" because in these classes girls of 11 to 16 are enrolled who mainly attend school for the purpose of receiving practical instruction related to domestic economy (article I, clause 2, point 4);

That she requests to receive a subsidy forthwith on the basis of the total number of enrolled pupils since this money is required immediately (article I, clause 2, point 6);

That she requests to be permitted to appoint a male teacher as head of the school, a retired head teacher and graduate of the teacher training school in Magelang because no female teacher is available;

In conclusion, we respectfully request Your Excellency to authorize the Director of Education and Religion to issue the requested subsidy.

R. Negoro

Document[4]

ADVICE RECEIVED BY THE CONTROLEUR OF TEGAL (H. L. VAN DEN BOS) FROM THE DIRECTOR OF EDUCATION AND RELIGION [IN RESPONSE TO MY WRITTEN REQUEST FOR SUPPORT AND ADVICE]

A subsidy can be received on the basis of the regulations set out in Government Decree 1914 No. 592 even if not requested by an organization.

The Director is sympathetic to the proposal and supports the proposal. He hopes that such schools might be established in more places in Java so that eventually the Government can benefit from the experience gained in such schools. The administration of the Kartini Schools also feels the need for instruction in domestic economy but finds that to do so it would have to drop other subjects from the existing program in favor of such subjects or to resort to running an afternoon school which would be a problem for many.

The government has plans to establish continuation schools, connecting to the 2nd class Native schools where only domestic economy would be taught, although it does wish to maintain its preference for the principle of coeducation rather than providing separate education for boys and girls. Given this, the requested subsidy will not be refused by the government for the kind of school under consideration.

Undoubtedly the government will more readily approve a request to conduct a lottery where it is submitted by an organization but it is completely impossible to grant permission to a private individual unless it is made very clear what the purpose of the requested lottery would be and that this is approved by the government.

The Director suggests that a subsidy request be submitted as soon as possible and where such a request may somewhat differ from the requirements listed in the decree, that a request be sent to His Excellency the Governor General.

Asked if he would give his personal opinion as to the necessity for such a school, His Excellency replied that he would be strictly guided by the government decree in making a judgment with regard to the subsidy request and that he will not exercise any personal influence in the case.

The Director recognizes that it may be difficult to find a female head of school so that a request to the Governor General to be allowed to appoint a male head would receive his positive advice.

The Director emphasizes that female assistants be encouraged to sit for the pupil teacher exam as soon as possible.

Batavia, 29 November, 1916

No. 32175
Copy

The request by Raden Ayu Adipati Ario Rekso Negoro concerns an exemption from article 1, clause 2, points 4, 6, and 7 of the subsidy regulations of law 1914 No. 592 in relation the private Native girls' school that she plans to open in Tegal on 1 March of this year. This relates to her application for a subsidy for the coming year and which is within the competence of the head of this department to grant.

In relation to the first of the relevant conditions—that the instruction in the compulsory subjects must given for three hours each day—I advise that a request for exemption is only necessary for the lowest classes, Ic and IIb, where instruction is provided in domestic economy subjects alongside normal school subjects. A separate exemption issued by the government need not be necessary if, as the last clause of article 1, clause 2, point 4 of the subsidy regulations allows, the curriculum and timetable are approved by me. I would have an objection in principle to giving my approval of [the curriculum described in] those documents which were included as appendices to the application, since [this indicates that] instruction in the normal school subjects in those lower grades would be restricted to 8¼ hours per week. This to me would not be in accordance with the intention of the subsidy regulation, which, while it does allow for domestic economy as an addition to normal school instruction, does not allow for the situation, as applies here, where the latter was entirely pushed into the background.

However, as it can be seen that this is a worthy attempt to meet the urgent needs for education for Native girls, it seems to me that in the first school year it would be appropriate, and I believe there would be no sufficient reason to omit from a calculation of the subsidy, that which would relate to the abovementioned pupils. On this basis, I have no objection to approving the curriculum and timetable for the current year. I intend nevertheless, after payment of the subsidy has been made, to enter into correspondence with the applicant with regard to removing this conflict with the existing regulations for the following school year.

Further, given that the number of students to be enrolled in the first month would be increased by the enrolments in the following two months (as indicated in reply to my further enquiry with regard to the initial response to question no. 15 of the subsidy application), thus ensuring that the second of the two previously indicated conditions would also be met, there remains only the request for exemption from the condition outlined in point 7 of the regulations, namely that only female teachers will engaged by the school.

The request for exemption from this condition is based on the circumstances that a male teacher will need to be temporarily attached to the school because all attempts to engage an appropriate female head of school have thus far proven fruitless.[5] Given that schools such as the present one should receive all the support we can give them, I believe I should advise in support of the requested exemption, although only temporarily.

Respectfully, I consequently recommend that your Excellency give consideration to the attached request in accordance with the accompanying draft resolution.

Were a decision to be forthcoming in accordance with this draft, I would recommend that the Resident of Pekalongan and the applicant be provided with copies of this advice.

I would respectfully request to have returned to me the attached documents with the exception of the application and the abovementioned correspondence of the Resident of Pekalongan.

>The Acting Director of Education and Religion
>On behalf of the Acting Director
>The Secretary
>(Creutzberg)

Attachment

Extract from the Register of Resolutions of the Director of Education and Religion

Batavia, 20 December 1916

Having read the government resolution of 8 December 1916 No. 8 . . .

And with reference to . . .

It is resolved that:

Firstly:

For the duration of the school year 1916/1917, the curriculum and timetable of the below mentioned Native girls' school as presented with the application for a subsidy for the year 1916 is approved.

Secondly:

On the basis of the regulations laid down in the ordinance of 25 August 1914 (Decree No. 344 and 619), the private Native (Islamic) girls' school, Wismo Pranowo, opened on 1 March 1916 in Tegal, Subdistrict Tegal of the Residency of Pekalongan, will be granted for the year 1916 the following financial support:

a. ƒ300 (three hundred guilders) for payment of salaries of the teaching personnel;

b. ƒ125 (one hundred and twenty-five guilders) as contribution towards employment of teaching staff;

c. ƒ117.50 (one hundred and seventeen guilders and fifty cents) for the normal costs of upkeep of the school building and their furnishing, and for the provision of schoolbooks and writing and drawing equipment;

d. ƒ150 (one hundred and fifty guilders) for the wages of personnel employed to teaching female handicraft and other subjects of a domestic nature;

e. ƒ235 (one hundred and thirty-five guilders) for the purchase of items necessary for the teaching of female handicraft and other subjects of a domestic nature.

Notes

Introduction

1. A summary of the correspondence appears in J. Coté, "The Correspondence of Kartini's Sisters: Annotations on the Indonesian Nationalist Movement, 1905–1925," *Archipel* 55 (1998): 61–82. Since the preparation of this English translation, an Indonesian translation of the sisters' correspondence has been published: *Surat-Surat Adik R. A. Kartini*, trans. Frits G. P. Jaquet (Jakarta: Djambaant, 2005).

2. While a selection of abridged letters by Kartini to a variety of recipients has been available in a variety of editions and languages for almost a century, the unabridged corpus of letters to Rosita became publicly available only in 1987, first in Dutch and later in Indonesian (1989) and English (1992).

3. The history of this archive is described by Frits Jaquet in his introduction to *Brieven aan mevrouw R. M. Abendanon-Mandri en haar Echtgenoot* (Dordrecht: Foris, 1987).

4. H. Sutherland, "Notes on Java's Regent Families," part 1, *Indonesia* 16 (1973): 113–47.

5. Jepara was involved in two more naval attacks on the Portuguese in 1551 and 1574, when it was ruled by a queen, Ratu Kalinyamat. M. Ricklefs, *A History of Modern Indonesia since 1200*, 3rd ed. (London: Palgrave, 2001), 44-45.

6. H. Bouman, *Meer Licht over Kartini* (Amsterdam: H. J. Paris, 1954), 8–9. Van Kesteren was to have a major influence on colonial thinking via his influential and progressive newspaper, the Semarang-based *De Locomotief*, and the Netherlands-based journal the *Indische Gids*.

7. Kudus was one of the early centers of Islam in Java; its name is Arabic.

8. See Kartini to Stella Zeehandelaar, 6 November 1899. Kartini and her four younger sisters all attended a European (Dutch-language) elementary school.

9. Details of the genealogy are derived from A. S. Tjitrosomo, "Dr Sosro Kartono" (typescript, 1967).

10. For details of Kartini's "feminist credentials," see J. Coté, "Reading Kartini 1899–1999: Education and the Colonial Experience in Java," in Joyce Goodman and Jane Martin, eds., *Gender Politics and the Experience of Education: An International Perspective*, 199–224 (London: Woburn Press, 2002); J. Coté,

"Our Indies Colony": Reading First Wave Dutch Feminism from the Periphery," *European Journal of Women's Studies* 6 (1999): 463–84.

11. See J. Coté, "Exhibiting Women's Labour: R. A. Kartini and the Dutch Women Exhibition of 1898," in M. Waarbeek and F. Dieteren, eds., *Een Vaderland voor Vrouwen/A Fatherland for Women* (Amsterdam: IISG/IIVA, 2000), 119–35.

12. See J. Coté, *On Feminism and Nationalism: Kartini's Letters to Stella Zeehandelaar* (Clayton: Monash Asia Institute, 2005).

13. Kartini had argued their case at length in an earlier letter. This makes clear that Rosita had specifically advised against the plan in a personal message that she had asked Annie Glaser to deliver in person. Kartini to Rosita, 15 July 1902. Significantly, the sisters discussed their Europe plan with the visiting Henri van Kol, the Dutch socialist parliamentarian and acquaintance of Kartini's pen friend, Stella Zeehandelaar, before revealing it to Rosita and Jacques Abendanon.

14. Roekmini to Rosita, 29 July 1902.

15. Their brother, Sosrokartono, who arrived in 1897, was the first of a very small but regular trickle of male students. By 1921 there were 70 Indonesian students studying in the Netherlands, in 1922, 115; in 1924, 130; in 1929, 125; and in 1930, 150. The first woman to undertake a university course was Ida Lamongga Haroen Al Rasjid from Lampung (medicine) in 1923–31. The only others recorded were Oemijati (1927–29), Siti Soendari (law, from 1927), Maria Ullfah Achmad (law, from 1929), and Raden Ajeng Kamar Roekmi (medicine, from 1929). Several women also trained as nurses before 1930. H. A. Poeze, *In het Land van de Overheerser* vol. 1, *Indonesiërs in Nederland, 1600–1950* (Dordrecht: Foris, 1986), 222–23.

16. Kartini to Rosita, 12 October 1902.

17. Significantly perhaps, this letter was addressed to Jacques Abendanon, not Rosita, who had, however, previously indicated her opposition.

18. There is no indication that Roekmini was involved in writing the petition. The earlier document, "Give the Javanese Education," was definitely written by Kartini alone. The formal letter appended to the petition sent to the government was signed by both women.

19. Kartini to Jacques Abendanon, 4 March 1903.

20. He continued: "Given that it is generally accepted that popular education must also include the influence of women in order to really take root, and now that two cultured women of good birth are offering themselves to work for this, it would make sense that his offer be gladly accepted." Resident Sijthoff to Gov. Gen., 27 April 1903, KITLV Archive, H 897 (copy from Arsip Nasional Indonesia).

21. Kartini both was embarrassed by and made fun of Sijthoff's clumsy attempts at intimate conversation. He apparently had no interest himself in returning to Dutch "social circles," and on his retirement he came to live in Batavia, where, years later, Soematri visited him.

22. Kartini responded that she would hate to become part of his "salon furniture" as a married woman, as he had implied. She explained to Rosita: "We would be foreign furniture, as it were, exotic plants in his salon. . . . We simply told him that social life was certainly not where we saw ourselves since we would feel most uncomfortable, because we had learnt to appreciate content over form and that form without substance was of no interest to us." Kartini to Rosita, 9 March 1903.

23. Director of Education to Gov. Gen., 26 June 1903; Formal decision, 7 July 1903. KITLV Archive, H 897, copy from Arsip Nasional, Indonesia.

24. Kartini announces the arrival of the first pupil in a letter to Rosita of 4 July 1903. She writes: "Moeske, we have begun our wonderful work. Thank your husband for his suggestion to begin at once, even without qualifications. Just imagine Moeske dearest, our little school already numbers 7 pupils, and we keep getting new enquiries. Wonderful, heavenly! We had not dared to hope that it would be so successful. The children are enjoying it and the parents are very pleased. . . . The children come four times a week from 8 to 12:30. They learn writing, reading and needlework and cooking. We don't teach according to the proper method but in the way we think that these little Javanese prefer to be taught." Roekmini, who soon took charge of this school, describes it in greater detail.

25. Although Kartono was two years older, it appears that prior to his departure for the Netherlands he and Kartini were close and that he shared much of his learning—and books—with his sister, with whom he continued to correspond. His widely reported speech in 1899 and his involvement with other Indonesian students in the Netherlands in the establishment of the Indische Vereeniging, a precursor of the Indonesian nationalist movement, as well as several publications, demonstrate the parallel trajectories of Kartono and Kartini.

26. Kartini to Stella Zeehandelaar, 18 August 1899.

27. The account by Roekmini of the visit to Jepara of Kartini's husband-to-be describes how young women were excluded during a "traditional" visit. By contrast, we see in several earlier accounts by Kartini how the women were completely involved in visits by Europeans and were normally active participants in ensuing conversations.

28. A more detailed description of the domestic environment emerges from Kartini's letters and also from an account written by Kardinah in 1958.

29. A further 247 native pupils attended private European elementary schools. The number at government elementary schools peaked in 1920 at 5,387 but had dwindled to only 3,659 in 1935. S. L. van der Wal, ed., *Het Onderwijsbeleid in Nederlands-Indië, 1900–1940: een bronnenpublikatie* (Groningen: J. B. Wolters, 1963), Statistical Tables, 691–700.

30. A further 99,204 indigenous pupils were registered at private elementary schools for natives. In 1907, three-year village schools began to be established, initially in Java, and the number of pupils at such (subelementary) schools

quickly equaled and then overtook attendance at regular elementary schools: in 1910 these schools had achieved an enrollment of 310,867 compared to 320,974 in elementary schools. Van der Wal, ed., *Het Onderwijsbeleid in Nederlands-Indië,* 691–700.

31. Although Kartini herself provided an account of her early days, she does not make clear whether she completed her elementary school, nor is there a detailed account of Roekmini's or Kardinah's schooling. It can be assumed that these three attended school together and were withdrawn together. Kartini appears to have stopped going to school in about 1892, that is, at age thirteen, at the time of her sister Soelastri's marriage. Kartini then took on the domestic responsibilities of the eldest daughter.

32. Both Kardinah and Kartini, in announcing their impending marriage to Rosita Abendanon-Mandri, described a similar sense of humiliation and failure in view of the ideals they had earlier declared and that had been confirmed by her.

33. Kartini to Rosita, 14 July 1903.

34. Kardinah to Rosita, 13 December 1901. This and the previous letter by Kardinah are couched in terms of an apology to Rosita, who represented for them (and to a certain extent acted as) their external conscience in the context of the new morality they had defined.

35. T. Shiraishi, *An Age in Motion: Popular Radicalism in Java, 1912–1926* (Ithaca: Cornell University Press, 1990).

36. This ceremony, conducted by President Soekarno, took place in 1964. Kartini was being celebrated as a "national hero" by Indonesians—although not in Dutch-curriculum schools—at least as early as the 1930s in Sumatra and no doubt elsewhere. Personal information, Din Zainu'ddin, Melbourne, 2006. Dutch feminists regularly cited her as an example of modernizing trends in Indonesia.

37. Approximately half of the Chinese population resided in towns throughout this period. The Chinese population rose from approximately 180,000 to 350,000 between the 1905 and 1930 censuses.

38. These figures would not account for the large numbers of day and seasonal workers employed in urban areas or generally operating in the informal sector.

39. W. F. Wertheim, ed., *The Indonesian Town: Studies in Urban Sociology* (The Hague: W. van Hoeve, 1958), 8–9. Such census figures should be recognized as indicative only. They give little indication of the large informal sector—rural migrants and temporary workers—in urban areas. In rural areas, the influx of a range of professional and technically trained personnel, in line with colonial development policies and the expansion of commercial agriculture, was bringing with it an increasingly "modern" lifestyle.

40. The letters in *Door Duisternis tot Licht* and its various editions and translations are to only ten recipients, all part of a small linked group of colonials. However, they contain indications that Kartini also wrote to others, including

other Indonesians. No letters from the four sisters to anyone apart from Rosita and Jacques Abendanon and the three other recipients in this volume are known to exist.

41. Beyond the letters themselves, this occurred through the draft memoir Roekmini wrote in March 1913 specifically for Hilda de Booy-Boissevain for a lecture, initially presented 20 June 1913, at the De Vrouw exhibition in Amsterdam, and thereafter at least seventeen times across the Netherlands. The lecture was in support of fundraising activities for the Kartini Fund and generally to attract support for girls' schools in Java. KITLV Archive, H 897, no. 7. A further account was written by Kardinah in 1958.

42. See Coté, "Exhibiting Women's Labour."

43. The history of her brother Kartono, who was trapped in Europe, also shows the danger that Europe represented. Kartini as well as her sisters in numerous letters nevertheless emphasized the dangers of "Europeanization."

44. See Coté, introduction to *On Feminism and Nationalism*.

45. C. Penders, ed., *Indonesia: Selected Documents on Colonialism and Nationalism, 1830–1942* (St. Lucia: University of Queensland Press, 1977), 225–27.

46. As the correspondence reveals, however, the sisters did not proceed to join more radical organizations. Soematri's husband specifically rejected any sympathy for Soewardi when he was exiled to the Netherlands, and even more vehemently rejected the aim of the party. See Achmad Sosrohadikoesoemo to Jacques and Rosita Abendanon, 18 February 1914.

47. Traditionally, in the literature the reference has been to "Rosa." However, all family references both written and in oral interviews have been to "Rosita." It may well be that the less "foreign"-sounding name "Rosa" was considered more acceptable in Dutch colonial circles.

48. That is to say, all the letters written after 1904.

49. Only one further meeting transpired after the two meetings in 1900.

50. I am indebted to Mr. Dolf Abendanon and Mrs. An Stork for the generous access to the family history.

51. This appears not to have been conducive to Abendanon's health. Kartini's letters contain numerous references to his ill health and his need to leave the city to recuperate in the hill country of the Preanger.

52. C. Fasseur, "Abendanon, Jacques Henrij," *Biografisch Woordenboek van Nederland*, vol. 3 ('s-Gravenhage: Instituut voor Nederlandse Geschiedenis, 1989).

53. See S. Stuurman, *"Wacht op onze daden": Het Liberalisme en de Vernieuwing van de Nederlandse staat* (Amsterdam: Bert Bakker, 1992).

54. This and subsequent details on the lives of Rosita and Jacques Abendanon are drawn from H. van Miert, *Bevlogenheid en Onvermogen: Mr J. H. Abendanon en de Ethische Richting in het Nederlandse Kolonialisme* (Leiden: KITLV Press, 1991), and interviews with descendants in the Netherlands in November 2005. Abendanon had left the region before the sisters were born but may well have known his father and other members of the Tjondronegoro family.

55. Abendanon's attempt to introduce girls' schools was opposed by the colonial bureaucracy on the ground that it had also been opposed by the majority of the Javanese regents. See Coté, *On Feminism and Nationalism,* App. 5.

56. These men had arrived in Indonesia at about the same time, together with the other influential "ethical" figure Pieter Brooshooft, editor of the Semarang-based newspaper *De Locomotief,* who coined the term "ethical policy." Each had been critical of colonial policy and used his subsequent European career to promote colonial reform. Brooshooft, van Kol, and van Deventer, like most returnees, were able to finance their second careers with astute colonial investments. It is not clear to what extent Abendanon had colonial investments.

57. The more influential "colonial lobby" was that constituted by economic interests. As A. Taselaar shows, one-third of the "elite corps" of administrators of key colonial enterprises were also active in the Kolonial Instituut, the cultural institution founded in 1910, "which expressed the ideology of the colonial lobby." A. Taselaar, *De Nederlandse Koloniale Lobby: Ondernemers en de Indische Politiek, 1914–1940* (Leiden: Research School CNWS, 1998), 5. The "liberal progressive" lobby groups increasingly lost out against economic and conservative political and capitalist interests, epitomized by the former colonial official (of a slightly later generation) oil magnate and later Dutch prime minister Hendrikus Colijn. See H. Langeveld, *Dit Leven van Krachtig Handelen: Hendrikus Colijn, 1869–1944,* vol. 1, *1869–1933* (Amsterdam: Balans, 1998).

58. For the latter group see W. Otterspeer, ed., *Leiden Oriental Connections, 1850–1940* (Leiden: E. J. Brill, 1989).

59. See E. Locher-Scholten, *Ethiek in Fragmenten: Vijf studies over koloniaal denken en doen van Nederlanders in de Indonesische Archipel, 1877–1942* (Utrecht: HES, 1981). A key link here was common membership or orientation toward theosophy. See L. Sears, *Shadows of Empire: Colonial Discourse and Javanese Tales* (Durham, NC: Duke University Press, 1996).

60. Quoted in van Miert, *Bevlogenheid en Onvermogen,* 58.

61. Quoted in van Miert, *Bevlogenheid en Onvermogen,* 77.

62. Abendanon published *Rapport van den Directeur van Onderwijs, Eeredienst en Nijverheid betreffende de maatregelen in het belang van de inlandsche nijverheid op Java en Madoera,* 2 vols. (Batavia: Landsdrukkerij, 1904). This report ran to 536 pages. Although dismissed, after his retirement Abendanon continued to promote his recommendations for several years at various conferences and in the press. See Van Miert, *Bevlogenheid en Onvermogen,* bibliography.

63. Quoted in H. W. van den Doel, *De Stille Macht: Het Europese Binnenlands Bestuur op Java en Madoera, 1808–1942* (Amsterdam: Bert Bakker, 1994), 381. Van Miert argues that the departure of Hazeu and Governor General van Limburg Stirum marked the effective end of ethical politics. Locher-Scholten first elaborated the problem of defining the nature and timing of an ethical politics. See Locher-Scholten, *Ethiek in Fragmenten.*

64. The poet and writer Noto Soeroto's attempts to transform traditional Javanese culture and define a moderate nationalist vision are now largely forgotten. See M. Djajadiningrat-Nieuwenhuis, "Noto Soeroto: His Ideas and the Late Colonial Intellectual Climate," *Indonesia* 55 (April 1993): 41–72.

65. Van Miert notes that he was very active, not missing one meeting and contributing numerous reports, which, however, were not always taken note of. See van Miert, *Bevlogenheid en Onvermogen,* 117–18.

66. Van Miert, *Bevlogenheid en Onvermogen,* 138.

67. Stella Zeehandelaar considered at least half of the letters she received too personal to be published; Anne de Bruyn-née Glaser refused any permission. See Bouman, *Meer Licht over Kartini;* Coté, introduction to *On Feminism and Nationalism.* The more intimate letters were also held back from publication by Abendanon and not released till 1986.

68. Publication was limited, however. An initial printing of 1,000 in 1911 was followed by a further printing of 3,000 exclusively in the Netherlands in 1912. Not until 1923 would a further 4,000 be printed. See R. Mrazek, *Engineers in Happy Land: Technology and Nationalism in a Colony* (Princeton: Princeton University Press, 2002), 255n38. The first Indonesian-language edition was published in 1922, and the first Javanese-language edition in 1938.

69. See Poeze, *In Het Land van de Overheerser;* F. Jaquet, "Introduction: Archief Oost en West," n.d.

70. While Kartini and Roekmini are very critical of their uncle, in particular for his forthright rejection of their attempts at advancing the position of Javanese women, Hadiningrat was highly regarded in progressive colonial bureaucratic circles, as indicated by, among other things, his report on the need for education in 1896 and his involvement in the Semarang Colonial Exhibition in 1914.

71. H. Bachtiar, "Pahlawan nasional dan R. A. Kartini," *Kompas,* 8 December 1987.

72. By the end of the first decade of the twentieth century, a number of girls' schools had been established on the initiative of Javanese elites with or without colonial support. These included schools established by the wives of the bupati of Garut and Karanganjer and a school in Solo established by the wife of Prince Mangkunegara. A growing number of schools had also been established by private Dutch individuals. P. A. Toer, *Sang Pemula* (Jakarta: Hasta Mitra, 1985), chap. 3, H. G. de Booy-Boissevain, draft speech, 1913 KITLV Archive, H 897, no. 7.

73. See the discussion of the emergence of a *kemajuan* discourse in A. Adam, *The Vernacular Press and the Emergence of Modern Indonesian Consciousness* (Ithaca, NY: Southeast Asia Program, Cornell University, 1995).

74. By World War I, a belief in the good faith of the colonial side of the implicit political contract—Javanese support for maintaining the security of the colony in return for political participation—had come under increasing suspicion,

and after the war it lost its support among most Javanese intellectuals. This change in attitude can also be detected in this correspondence, even among the closest associates of the colonial progressives.

75. Noto Soeroto arrived in the Netherlands in 1907 after completing his secondary school at the HBS in Semarang. His father, who was administrator of the Paku Alam princedom and brother of its ruler, Paku Alam IV, sent four sons to study in the Netherlands. Alongside his law studies, Noto Soeroto contributed many articles to Dutch and Indonesian-related newspapers. See Poeze, *In het Land van de Overheerser,* 66–68. Noto Soeroto set out his (by then very much outdated) ideas in *Van Overheersching naar Zelfregeering* [From Colonization to Self-Rule] ('s-Gravenhage: N.V. Adi-Poestaka, 1931), published by the Nederlandsch Indische Verbond.

76. During his stay in Semarang to arrange the establishment of the Kartini School, Conrad van Deventer had met Soeriosoeparto, who had been working for Kartini's uncle in Demak, and arranged for his study in the Netherlands, which commenced the following year. Poeze, *In Het Land van de Overheerser,* 99–103. This intellectual climate is well described in Sears, *Shadows of Empire,* chap. 3.

77. See J. Coté, "Tirto Adhi Soerjo and the Narration of Indonesian Modernity, 1909–1912," *Review of Indonesian and Malaysian Affairs* 32 (1998): 1–41; Toer, *Sang Pemula*.

78. This interpretation is proposed by Ricklefs, who argues that Javanese cultural revival at this time was in response to the rise of modern (urban) Islam. See Ricklefs, *History of Modern Indonesia since 1200,* 221–22.

79. The decision in 1987 to publish only the correspondence up to the announcement of Kartini's death fitted the historically inscribed conventional view of the pioneering significance of Kartini.

80. Kartono's speech in 1899 and Hadiningrat's memorandum in 1896, both explicitly demanding greater access to Dutch-language education, were both made public at the time; a memorandum by Sosroningrat is described by Kartini in a letter to Stella.

81. See P. Chatterjee, "The Nation and Its Women," in P. Chatterjee, *The Nation and Its Fragments: Colonial and Postcolonial Histories* (Princeton: Princeton University Press, 1993), 135–57.

82. Soewardi Soerjaningrat's address, *Eerste Koloniaal Onderwijs Congres 's-Gravenhage, 28, 29 and 30 Augustus, 1916, Stenografisch Verslag,* 62–67. He stated firmly, "For the time being we should agree to regard Malay as a social language which makes it possible for the different groups of the one and indivisible Indies people to communicate with one another. Javanese for instance will never be supplanted by the Malay language in the sense that Malay would ever become the language medium in Javanese schools. Javanese is much too important to allow this to happen.... Moreover that language is still being spoken by more than 20 million people who have the clear determination to con-

tinue speaking it. As far as the other indigenous languages are concerned, events will have to show if they are able to maintain themselves, or whether, as a result of natural processes, they will become extinct" (63–64). Returning to Java, Soewardi, like Kardinah, dedicated himself to establishing modern Javanese-language schools.

83. The newspaper's then editor, J. E. Stokvis, with whom Soematri and Achmad Sosrohadikoeosmo were personally acquainted, promoted Abendanon's publication of Kartini's letters, *Door Duisternis tot Licht*. The most influential review was that written by van Deventer and published in the influential Dutch intellectual journal *De Gids* in August 1911.

84. Van Deventer admitted the influence of Pieter Brooshooft, long-time editor of the city's progressive newspaper, *De Locomotief*. He had long advocated the essence of what van Deventer declared in his pamphlet: that the Netherlands was honour-bound to return some of the wealth that had been taken from the colony. On his return to the Netherlands after twenty-five years as editor, Brooshooft coined the phrase "the ethical policy" to characterize the policy of increased native welfare provision. Details of van Deventer's life and writings from H. T. Colenbrander and J. E. Stokvis, eds., *Leven en Arbeid van Mr. C. Th. van Deventer*, 3 vols. (Amsterdam: P. N. van Kampen, 1916–17).

85. Roekmini to Rosita, 18 February 1904. By contrast, Kartini had been enthusiastic about Chinese culture and the assistance provided by the Chinese entrepreneur Oei Tjing Ham during a local crisis. In a letter of 12 December 1902, Kartini explicitly rejected the racist attitudes of her compatriots directed at Chinese and Arabs.

86. Soematri to Rosita, 11 November 1910.

87. Kardinah to Rosita, July 1911. Tegal, like all north coast cities, had a significant and long-established Chinese population. Sarekat Dagang Islamiyah, the predecessor of Sarekat Islam, was founded in 1911.

88. Adam shows how extensively this idea was articulated prior to 1913. See Adam, *Vernacular Press*.

89. Mangkunegara to Abendanon, 23 July 1923, KITLV Archive, H 1200, no. 248. In 1918. the Comité voor het Javaansch Nationalisme, established in 1917 with the support of Mangkunegara, commenced publishing *Wederopbouw* to articulate a Javanese nationalism.

90. Ricklefs, *History of Modern Indonesia since 1200*, 221–22.

91. Kartini, however, did express her criticism of traditional Islamic prescriptions as applied to women. See in particular her letters to Stella Zeehandelaar.

92. Ricklefs, *History of Modern Indonesia since 1200*, 225.

93. Kartinah to Lien, 6 December 1912.

94. *Cariyos Bab Lampah-lampahipun Raden Mas Arya Purwa Lelana* (Account of the travels of Raden Mas Arya Purwa Lelana). See Quinn, *The Novel in Javanese* (Leiden: KITLV Press, 1992). Quinn lists a long series of similar works (travelogues) in Javanese that followed.

95. Krisprantono, "Conservation of the Tuntang Railway Heritage" (typescript, n.d.); T. Stevens, "Semarang, Central Java and the World, 1870–1900," in P. Nas., ed., *The Indonesian City* (Dordrecht: Foris, 1986); Djoko Suryo, "Social and Economic Life in Rural Semarang under Colonial Rule in the Later Nineteenth Century," PhD diss., Monash University, 1982.

96. Official Tourist Bureau, *Illustrated Tourist Guide* (1913).

97. The *kraton* was established in Surakarta in 1746.

98. Soematri to Rosita, 14 July 1914.

99. Soematri to Rosita, 23 April 1918.

100. Roekmini also notes that the family, specifically the regent of Demak, had made it known that the sisters were not to marry men of position. One can only speculate as to his motivations.

101. Soematri to Rosita 1 December 1919.

102. In 1920, Roekmini compares the fate of her stepson with that of Kartini's son Soesalip, by then completely estranged from his aunts. Noting that Soesalip was then "only in the first class of the HBS," she ascribed this to the fact that this "must be because that is what they have made of him. He must be a clever boy, and he could have got just as far as his half brother. . . .The only one who cares for him and shows him some love apparently is a loyal servant, a former garden boy of his mother. Isn't it enough to make you weep? Poor, poor boy. Let's hope that one day his lot will improve. They have not deserved this, his mother and he, poor Soesalip." Roekmini to Rosita, Kudus, 4 March 1920.

103. Roekmini to Rosita, Jepara, 8 March 1908.

104. Sosrokartono became a protégé of leading orientalist scholars at Leiden University, Professors Kern and Snouck Hurgronje. His publicly acclaimed speech presented to the Nederlandsch Taale en Letterkundig Congres in 1899, demanding greater access by Javanese to Dutch-language education, established his notoriety soon after his arrival in the Netherlands in 1897. See Coté, *On Feminism and Nationalism*, App. 4.

105. Sosrokartono embarked on a brief career as correspondent for several American and European papers. After World War I he worked briefly for the League of Nations in Geneva. In Geneva he reputedly healed a young child suffering from high fever, which suggested to him that he might have special powers. He tried unsuccessfully to enroll in the University of Paris to study psychometry. In Bandung, unable to find other employment, he initially and briefly taught at a recently established branch of the Taman Siswa school, founded in 1922 by Soewardi Soerjaningrat (Ki Fajar Dewantoro), with whom he had became acquainted when the latter lived in the Netherlands from 1914 to 1922.

106. He claimed these letters would prove that he had been a significant influence in shaping Kartini's ideas.

107. The libraries, he said, would "be a symbol of a new understanding of a new ideal." Neither libraries nor employment eventuated.

108. Kartono to Rosita, Bandung, 19 July 1925. From 1924, serious unrest led by the Indonesian Communist Party, the PKI, swept Java, climaxing in major revolts in Java in 1926 and later in Sumatra, both of which were ruthlessly suppressed by colonial authorities.

109. After Kartono's death in 1951, Roekmini's son, Srigati, became chairman of the foundation established in his memory. Details of Kartono's life from Koentjoro Purbopranoto, "Ter Nagedachtenis van Drs RMP Sosro Kartono," 1973; Amin Singgih, "Djiwa Besar," 1967.

110. Soematri to Rosita, 1 December 1919.

111. Soematri to Rosita, 1 December 1919.

112. Soematri to Rosita, 18 January 1936.

113. P. Chatterjee, *The Nation and Its Fragments: Colonial and Postcolonial Histories* (Princeton: Princeton University Press, 1993).

114. M. Laffan, *Islamic Nationhood and Colonial Indonesia: The Umma below the Winds* (London: RoutledgeCurzon, 2003).

Chapter 1

1. Of the 106 extant letters written by Kartini to Rosita, three-quarters were written after the announcement of Kardinah's marriage. All letters written by Roekmini up to September 1904 were previously published in Jaquet, *Brieven,* the collection later translated into Indonesian and English.

2. Adriani to Abendanon, August 1900, KITLV Archive, H 1200, no. 237.

3. As critics of the Kartini "icon" have pointed out, of course, the efforts of other pioneers in women's education outshone this attempt by Kartini, and indeed what were effectively *kabupaten* schools had been established in a number of kabupaten throughout the island of Java in the first decade of the twentieth century.

4. Roekmini to Rosita, 6 November 1904.

5. I am grateful to Susan Blackburn for alerting me to this reference, which, perhaps remarkably, receives no mention in the correspondence. For the context of Roekmini's involvement in the women's movement, see S. Blackburn, "Political Relations among Women in a Multi-cultural City," in K. Grijns and P. Nas, eds., *Jakarta-Batavia: Socio-cultural Essays,* 175–98 (Leiden: KITLV Press, 2000). In particular, it is surprising (and a pity) that there is no extant correspondence from Roekmini for this period.

6. The *Maandblad* reported (incorrectly in terms of the details) in July 1927: "Raden Ayu Santossa, sister of Raden Ayu Reksonegoro [Kardinah] Kartini and Roekmini, has indicated her willingness to take her place on the Executive." The spelling of "Santosa" was eventually corrected.

7. Some indication can be gained from examining the names of new members listed in the *Maandblad* for November 1927, which included ninety-four European, sixteen Indonesian, and two Chinese women and six European men. One of the new members reported that month was Etti Wawo Runtu in Surabaya.

8. This is the conclusion drawn by Blackburn, "Political Relations among Women," 184.

9. Roekmini's report states it was in imitation of the Madiun branch, taking the same name. The latter, however, included European women in its founding structure.

10. The VVV executive applied to the Indonesian organizers of the Congress, Poetri Indonesia, to attend and was told only Indonesians would be permitted but that the VVV could send an Indonesian member. That member, however, could attend only in a private capacity, not as VVV representative. *Maandblad* 3, no. 2 (December 1928).

11. Roekmini's name no longer appears on the list of executive members in the second half of 1931. Blackburn notes that the organization sent her to the All Asian Women's Conference in Lahore in 1931. "Political Relations among Women," 184.

12. The letters by Roekmini to Rosita Abendanon-Mandri from 1901 to October 1904 have been published previously in English translation in J. Coté, *Letters from Kartini: An Indonesian Feminist, 1900–1904* (Clayton: Monash Asia Institute; Melbourne: Hyland House, 1992). Four letters by Roekmini written previous to this initial letter have not been reproduced here. This letter by the twenty-one-year-old Roekmini is her emotional response to this initial crisis in the plans that the three sisters had developed.

13. Unlike Kartini, who from the start addresses Rosita as "moedertje," or "little mother," Roekmini, who had only twice previously written to Rosita, uses a formal term of address until 1903.

14. There were in fact three younger siblings: Kartinah, then aged eighteen; Moeljono, then aged fifteen; and Soematri, then aged thirteen.

15. *Sinterklaas* or St. Nicholas Day, a Dutch celebration on 6 December, specifically focuses on children. Children traditionally expected to receive surprise gifts on the morning of this day. Rosita Abendanon was childless. As the correspondence reveals, Rosita marked Saint Nicholas Day each year by sending gifts to the sisters.

16. Kartini, in a long parallel letter about Kardinah's arranged marriage, written over three days and completed on the night of 2 December, recounts in similar terms the moment when Kardinah announced her decision to accept the arrangement. She was too emotionally overwrought to write to thank Rosita for the presents, so it was left to Roekmini to write on her behalf. Kartinah and Soematri also each wrote a letter, their first to Rosita, to thank her.

17. Annie Glaser was the young teacher especially assigned (and paid for by a special government fund) to the European elementary school in Jepara by Jacques Abendanon in his capacity as director of education, so that Kartini and Roekmini could get further private instruction in preparation for taking their teaching qualification examinations. Director of Education to Gov. Gen., 19 March 1901 KITLV Archive, H 897, no. 35. As Roekmini states later, Annie

initially lived with the family in the kabupaten. See further references to her in letters by Soematri and Kartinah. Annie's later refusal to allow her correspondence from Kartini to be published is perhaps indicative of the depth of her relationship with the sisters and her own moral character.

18. As she describes later, this is an allusion to the fact that the women's plans had become a matter of public knowledge after they were reported in the colonial newspaper *De Locomotief*.

19. This metaphor also alludes specifically to Kartini's description (in a letter to Stella Zeehandelaar) of the requirements of Javanese etiquette for young women to walk sedately, not raise their voices, and suppress any signs of strong emotion.

20. Henri van Kol was leader of the parliamentary Social Democrat Party and a prominent colonial reformer. Kartini had written to inform Rosita of their discussions with him on 10 June. This was the first time she had specifically set out their aim to study in the Netherlands. Prior to his departure, van Kol had been requested to meet Kartini by her supporters in the Netherlands. Van Kol ensured that Kartini and Roekmini's petition for financial support to study in the Netherlands was addressed and approved by the minister of colonies. On learning of these plans, the Abendanons attempted to dissuade the girls. On 15 July, Kartini wrote back justifying their plan and politely rejecting their opposition, since, in particular, they had at last succeeded in gaining their parents' approval.

21. Roekmini uses the term "Inlander" or "Inlandsch" when drawing attention to colonial concepts and contrasts. When speaking of herself, however, she refers to herself as "Javaansch" (Javanese).

22. In a separate letter, Kartini makes explicit that "this family" was her uncle, the regent of Demak, whom Kartini on numerous occasions had pilloried as her key enemy. Ultimately he appears to have been the cause of her "downfall"— that is, the arrangement for her marriage.

23. Javanese custom requires that younger daughters wait until their older siblings are married. Why the twenty-year-old Kardinah was selected for marriage over Roekmini, the daughter of the raden ayu, or Kartini, the eldest, can perhaps only be explained by the parents having selected the one least likely to offer resistance. In any case, this was clearly an arranged marriage, following a practice they had previously criticized.

24. If this conversation did take place, it is evident that Abendanon and van Kol disagreed about the best direction Kartini and Roekmini's future should take.

25. Kartini and Roekmini were very close to this *controleur* of Jepara and his wife.

26. Both Kartini and Roekmini were introduced to European-style painting and drawing by Marie Ovink-Soer, wife of the then Jepara controleur in the period before 1899. Rosita Abendanon was also an amateur sketcher, and her sketches decorated the first (and subsequent) editions of *Door Duisternis tot Licht*.

27. There is a suggestion of irony in Roekmini's remarks here: whereas "modern" Javanese families denied girls the opportunity to "fly"—that is, be educated—being modern in the domestic sphere was seen as very fashionable. Thus, Roekmini suggests, providing domestic education would be good advertising for their cause. Kartini and later Kardinah speak much more passionately about the importance of domestic science than Roekmini does here.

28. Annie Glaser was transferred soon after, and the younger girls were then taught for a number of years in school and privately by the new teacher, Mr. Both. Although remaining a correspondent, Annie Glaser refused Abendanon permission to include any of the letters she received from Kartini in *Door Duisternis tot Licht*.

29. The reference is to Eduard C. Abendanon (1878–1962)—also referred to as Edi—one of the three children of Abendanon's first marriage. He became a well-known Indies geologist and later university professor in the Netherlands.

30. It was Rosita's birthday.

31. A letter by Kartini on the same day carries the same sentiment. It suggests that Nellie wrote again in response to Kartini's insistence that they wanted to study in the Netherlands. The gratitude is for Rosita's concern for their welfare, not, however, because she agrees with them, as is apparent later in this letter.

32. This other couple is Henri and Nellie van Kol.

33. That is, permission from their parents to study in the Netherlands, which received the support of the van Kols. Kartini had written a long letter to Rosita on 15 July describing the support they had received from both Henri and Nellie van Kol.

34. Kartini had become known to the editor from the days in 1897–98 when Kartini, Roekmini, and Kardinah were involved in arranging an exhibit for the National Exhibition of Women's Work in the Hague.

35. The relationship with Oost en West, the organization established to promote Javanese craft and the welfare of Indonesian students studying in the Netherlands, dates from 1900, when the organization sought Kartini's assistance in arranging woodcarving orders with the Jepara woodcarvers, for whom initially Rosita was a conduit. However, prior to this, in 1898, Roekmini's brother Kartono had been involved in the establishment of Oost en West. In the first decade of the twentieth century its membership came to include all known Dutch "Java friends" in Holland. Before this time only male students had been assisted.

36. This represents a polite but very firm rejection of the position adopted by the Abendanons.

37. Despite the effusion of sentiment, Roekmini continues to make it quite clear here that she and Kartini intend to pursue the Netherlands study option over Rosita's objections. It is also implied that, unbeknownst to Rosita, they had already been making plans for their accommodation. Roekmini here is reiterating what Kartini had insisted upon in her letter of 15 July. Ominously, as

Roekmini also suggests, the final decision depended on the local colonial hierarchy, and indeed both the resident of Semarang and Abendanon effectively blocked the proposal.

38. This is the first time Roekmini addresses Rosita by this term, as Kartini had done since 1900. "Moedertje," a diminutive form of "moeder" (mother), was a term of endearment, but for Kartini it had also expressed the sense of Rosita's being a kind of mother for them in the way she provided support and guidance. Given that the sisters already had two Javanese mothers, the Dutch terms also allowed a different idea of mother to be expressed. The letter celebrates the fact that they had now reached agreement about their future plans while, at the same time, the sisters shared Rosita's concern over her son's accident.

39. As clarified in a letter by Roekmini of 26 December (not included here), since December, Rosita had been in Sumatra attending her stepson, Edi Abendanon, a mining engineer, who had been injured in a mining accident.

40. Having just completed a major memorandum at the behest of a Dutch official, "Give the Javanese Education!" Coté, *On Feminism and Nationalism,* App. 2. Kartini was busy studying in preparation for her preliminary teacher training examinations.

41. The postcard provides a brief summary of the behind-the-scenes events that were generated by Kartini and Roekmini's attempts to gain further education. Nellie's report would seem to relate to Dutch initiatives to lobby the colonial government to support the proposal to study in Batavia, not the earlier plan for study in the Netherlands, which the sisters had now set aside.

42. The reference is to Edi Abendanon, who, instead of coming to Jepara as had been planned, decided to proceed directly to the Netherlands. The effusive expression of disappointment seems extreme but does not imply any other intentions on their part.

43. As an engineer, Edi would presumably have enjoyed being taken to see the oil-boring operations, which would have been uninteresting to the women.

44. This confirms that all the plans are in place for the sisters to begin study in Batavia. On Abendanon's advice, Kartini had visited Resident Sijthoff in March (Kartini to Rosita, 9 March 1903) to secure his support, and a subsequent letter confirming his own arrangements (reported in the previous letter by Roekmini) had apparently assured their parents. Kartini was then required to write a petition, dated 19 April (Coté, *On Feminism and Nationalism,* App. 3), which was supported by an official memorandum of the resident of Semarang of 27 April 1903. KITLV Archive, H 897, no. 35, copy from Arsip Nasional Indonesia.

45. As Abendanon was soon to set out in his memorandum, Roekmini would undertake nursing training, for which she was now sent the requisite information. Medical training had not been part of Roekmini's plans, but its importance had been highlighted by Kartini in her memorandum on education of January 1903, and she had herself once considered it, though only if no other opportunities were available.

46. This is not indicated in Kartini's correspondence. Abendanon had suggested in his memorandum that the two sisters live together in residential accommodation provided by Kartini's proposed school and that Roekmini be an external student at the nursing institute. Rosita apparently disagreed with her husband, but thereby further reduced the possibility of Roekmini developing her painting interests.

47. That is, Roekmini supports Rosita's plan to find accommodation for the sisters equidistant from the two educational institutions.

48. Given the forms of Javanese politeness, this amounts to a very firm objection to Abendanon's proposal. The final solution to the question of what Roekmini would study and where she would live was never resolved, as the entire plan fell through after Kartini was confronted by the proposal of marriage.

49. It suggests there was some disparity in the views of Rosita and Jacques Abendanon that Roekmini was keen to exploit. It was Abendanon who had convinced Kartini against continuing their plan to study in the Netherlands at a time when Rosita was unavailable, and she may well not have held the same view as her husband (who, after all, was a colonial official) about this.

50. After his accident, Edie Abendanon returned briefly to the Netherlands. Both Kartini and Roekmini had expressed their keen disappointment at not having met him in Jepara as had been planned earlier.

51. The reference is to Sosrokartono, or Kartono, who, with the support of private benefactors, had left for the Netherlands in 1897 after graduating from the Semarang HBS (grammar) school in 1896. His unfortunate subsequent academic career and the Abendanons' care of him are documented in Roekmini's correspondence. In 1899, he had made an influential speech demanding Dutch-language education for Javanese. Coté, *On Feminism and Nationalism*, App. 4; Poeze, *In het Land van de Overheerser*, 30–36.

52. This is a reference to Abendanon's third son by his first marriage, Galdolph (1880–1956), who was the same age as Roekmini and was studying in the Netherlands.

53. The ruler of Solo's historic visit to the city of Semarang, including the visit to the resident, must surely count as a sign of the times, a reflection of the rapid modernization taking place in central Java.

54. The resident of Semarang, Piet Sijthoff, knew the family well, and Kartini recounts several very intimate conversations that took place between them. Sijthoff did not support her plan to study in the Netherlands but did support her petition for funding to study in Batavia.

55. Kartini later wrote an account of this occasion for a Dutch ladies' journal.

56. Although signed with both Roekmini's and Kartini's names, this and the following letter were clearly written by the former. Letters of 4 July, 7 July, and 14 July also carry the initials and/or names of both sisters but are listed in the inventory as being authored by Kartini and have not been included here.

57. This ominous allusion to interference with their plans—that is, to arrangements being made to marry off one or other of the women—was confirmed in a letter written three weeks later (9 July). Kartini immediately thereafter contracted measles and smallpox, and later Roekmini became seriously ill.

58. The reference is to the Training School for Native Administrators.

59. Five days previously, Kartini had written that, despite the marriage proposal, she was still "making efforts to come to Batavia." Kartini to Rosita, 10 July 1903. Roekmini here briefly refers to what Kartini had written the previous day. Kartini describes the tone of a letter they had received: "It was a proposal of marriage—what a tone. My God—that man already half regarded me as his property!" She also refers to the use of *guna-guna* (black magic) by her unknown suitor and the invasion of the kabupaten by "those strangers together with one of their servants rummaging through our house, as it were, to find us. Father locked us in our room. It still makes me shudder when I think of it." Kartini to Rosita, 14 July 1903. This convinced them that they would not be safe even in Batavia. As she goes on to make clear, however, this was a separate proposal from that received almost simultaneously from the regent of Rembang.

60. Raden Ario Djojo Adiningrat had been part of the official delegation to attend the coronation of the new Dutch queen in 1898 and was close to the colonial government. As Kartini writes after her marriage, he had been specifically appointed to Rembang to clean up the problems of opium consumption and corruption.

61. Gonggrijp was the assistant resident of Jepara in 1899 and resident of Rembang in 1907. He was acquainted with Abendanon.

62. Kartini wrote on 9 July that the telegram announcing the outcome of the government's deliberation was received one day too late—one day after her father had written to accept the proposal of marriage.

63. The first half of this very long letter by Roekmini has been omitted. It deals largely with Kartini's response to her impending marriage and a complicated woodcarving order. The second half of the letter, provided here, commences where Roekmini discusses the consequences of Kartini's marriage for her own situation.

64. This refers to her brother Boesono. He had previously been appointed to a post he was not happy with and had threatened to leave the colonial service. Kartini to Rosita, 27 October 1902.

65. It comes as a bit of a shock, given the modernness and outspokenness of the young women and their habit of being fully involved with European guests—not to mention the openness of their communications with Rosita—to read of the imposition of more formal traditional customs at what was, no doubt, a ceremonial occasion. Although Roekmini makes fun of these traditions, she is nevertheless obliged to adhere to them. We also see the gap between their ideals, partially realized in their private world, and the public world they sought to change.

66. Given foreknowledge of the way the regent, and more specifically his sons, later refused to allow Kartini's son to associate with Kartini's sister, these declarations might seem hollow. The following sentence could also be read as an equivocal conclusion.

67. This (unknown) person appears to have been linked to the plan for Roekmini to study nursing in Batavia, for which Rosita had previously sent her information. See above, Roekmini to Rosita, 15 June 1903.

68. The letter also carried Kartini's initials.

69. This was the day Kartini married.

70. For Roekmini these proved prophetic words. While her life had its rewards, Roekmini was to experience many bitter blows.

71. Significantly, the "note of approval" was from Abendanon, not Rosita. The suspicion remains that colonial interests orchestrated the marriage, which certainly resolved a number of difficult issues for both the Javanese and colonial elite of all persuasions in this matter.

72. It becomes clear from this letter that Roekmini's life was radically affected by the series of events that had taken place. Not only did she lose Kartini's companionship, but the plan to study in Batavia was also brought to an end. Now, as the eldest daughter at home, she had become responsible for both the demanding task of arranging woodcarving orders for Oost en West and for carrying on the classroom that Kartini had established but had spent little time in.

73. This comment referred not necessarily to Kardinah's health but more likely to the fact that, since she had become the wife of a prominent official, her lifestyle had changed considerably and she no longer spent time outside in the garden or walking to and on the beach, which, the correspondence indicates, was the girls' favorite pasttime.

74. Hassim, a distant relative from central Java, was a student at STOVIA, the school for training indigenous doctors. He initially struggled with his studies in Batavia but eventually went on to study in the Netherlands. His youngest sister was one of the pupils in Kartini and Roekmini's school. See also below, Roekmini to Rosita Abendanon, 18 May 1904.

75. *Lebaran* marks the end of *Puasa*, the fasting month. It is marked by family gatherings and celebration. Significantly, reference to this socially oriented annual celebration is the only reference to Islam in the correspondence.

76. This is a most revealing comment, raising questions about the precise nature of Kartini's accounts of her new life in her correspondence with Rosita. This was conjectured by Stella Zeehandelaar. Coté, preface to *On Feminism and Nationalism*.

77. P. A. de Genestet (1829–61) was a popular nineteenth-century Dutch poet who had become a favorite of the sisters and is regularly referred to in Kartini's correspondence.

78. This is a comment of some significance. Kartini's correspondence indicates that the women had accumulated the extensive, up-to-date, feminist oriented li-

brary in the second half of the 1890s, which had inspired their vision as well as their participation in the Dutch national exhibition of women's work and the subsequent contact with Dutch feminists. Since 1902 their attention had been largely occupied by the immediate events in their lives, while Abendanon's emphasis on teaching and teacher training had apparently dampened their earlier absorption in contemporary progressive literature. It is also clear from this that Kartini was the driving force in this intellectual pursuit.

79. Roekmini's experience with Fröbel methods allowed her to take an appointment as Fröbel teacher after her husband passed away.

80. This discussion of (practical) education philosophy relates to but in some ways goes beyond Kartini's statements about education. Roekmini's comments here can be compared to similar sentiments expressed later by her sister Kardinah.

81. Abendanon significantly expanded subsidies specifically to promote mission and private schools. There may have been a misunderstanding here. In fact, around this time the number of first-class Native elementary schools, in which Dutch was taught, was increased but access to European Dutch-language schools was restricted. It is odd that Abendanon had apparently not mentioned school subsidies for their school earlier. The reason may have been that normally subsidies depended upon teacher training and a minimum number of enrollments.

82. Roekmini implies they had only just arrived in the colony. This would have to mean they were children or relatives of Bervoets senior, who had already built a reputation in running the mission hospital at Mojowarno and had offered to train Kartini there in 1900. That plan had been arranged by their mutual links with the Ovink family, the former controleur and his wife mentioned here also. See also below, Roekmini to Rosita, 6 November 1904.

83. Evidently an official gift being prepared for the Dutch queen.

84. This seems to be Mr. Zeilinga, president of the Java Bank. It is apparent from the amount of interest from well-placed colonial and metropolitan people, including royalty, for Javanese carved wooden furniture and artifacts, that the fashion—and market—had grown dramatically since 1900, when Kartini was first asked to arrange some small orders. The manufacturing had now dramatically expanded in output and location, with craftsmen being transferred to Batavia. With her departure, this significant responsibility had been passed to Roekmini, who continued to be a major factor in its expansion, at least until the end of the decade, by which time the craftwork had certainly become an industry.

85. Given the persistence of strict traditional Javanese hierarchies within the Javanese civil service, the association of children of the second-highest official (*patih*) with the lowest official (*mantri*) was a significant factor, as was the fact that they were being entertained by the daughters of the *bupati* (regent) in the kabupaten. After the regent's death, when the remaining family was forced to leave the kabupaten, the school folded, primarily because it no longer had the advantage for the parents of providing contact with the regent.

86. It is unlikely that this is a reference to Kartini's memorandum, which had been written a year before. It would appear to refer to a memorandum Roekmini would need to write to accompany a subsidy application.

87. Roekmini notes in a postcard dated 9 December 1903 (not included) that she had read a report in the newspaper that Abendanon was planning to travel to Europe. Here also she appears to believe that the departure would be temporary, but now Rosita would accompany him. In fact, as it transpired, Abendanon was planning to retire back to the Netherlands but had apparently not yet informed Roekmini.

88. Plans had been made for Edi Abendanon to visit Jepara in March 1903. Both Roekmini and Kartini wrote with great emotion (29 and 30 March 1903; Roekmini's letter is not included) about their disappointment that he would not be able to visit Jepara. After recovering from the mining accident, he left immediately for the Netherlands.

89. In March 1903, Tjokrohadisosro was appointed *wedono* to a place Kartini described as "the worst district in the residency." She reported to Rosita that the resident had written to her that if her brother-in-law could improve the welfare of the district he would immediately be promoted to patih (one rung lower than regent). Kartini to Rosita, 19 April 1903. Tjokrohadisosro was eventually appointed patih of Kendal in October 1912. The sisters were evidently on good terms with their older sister Soelastri's husband. Earlier Kartini had been hopeful that Tjokrohadisosro's mother would act as her chaperone if her plan to establish a school in Magelang eventuated. She was confident that she would support her, but the plan did not eventuate.

90. This letter is from the KITLV Archive, H 897. It was donated from the private collection of Mrs. A. M. Wawo Runtu, of Manado, not part of the Abendanon archive. The mutual acquaintance linking Roekmini and Etty was probably Dr. Nicolaus Adriani, a missionary Bible translator, who had spent many years in Central Sulawesi. However, Kartini refers to Etty in a letter of 17 February 1903. "It was wonderful to hear that in the Minahassa there is also a native girl who has 'crazy ideas' like us! So you see we are not the only mad ones." Etty was a teacher in Manado. She was the only daughter in a family of five children of a prominent family of Sonder, Menado, North Sulawesi. Like Kartini and her sisters, she had attended a European elementary school. She "could play piano paint and gave lessons to young Chinese girls" at home, and was "very cultivated and read a lot." She married a graduate of the medical school for Indonesians (STOVIA). After independence she was active both in Menado and in the service of the Indonesian government. C. Vreede-de Stuers, "Augustine Magdalena Wawu Runtu," *Archipel* 38 (1988), 9–11.

91. This was a Dutch-language women's journal published in Yogyakarta.

92. In this declaration of their goal, Roekmini is clearly going beyond a specific gender objective and making a nationalist declaration. Although "our world" would seem to be limited to Java, she ascribes in the following sentence

a similar (if separate) goal to her correspondent. The idea of taking from the West only what was "beautiful"—i.e., certain ideals and modern technologies—to enrich Javanese life was only just being articulated by male contemporaries and affirms a nationalist consciousness that denies the hubris of Western colonial pretensions. Later she spells out the more specifically feminist goals.

93. This elliptical summary history refers to the early marriage of Kardinah and the opposition that Kartini and Roekmini experienced in gaining support and permission to continue their studies.

94. Such familial terms of address were typical in colonial circles. They suggest that this correspondent (also a friend of Abendanon) remained on close terms with Roekmini.

95. Here Roekmini makes quite clear what a dramatic impact the Fröbel equipment must have had and how different her classroom must have been from any formal government school, European or "native." In Europe, too, progressive methods were having an important impact on pedagogical approaches. Culturally, in the Javanese context, her classroom must also have been quite revolutionary.

96. Dislike of this Chinese appropriation of an indigenous cultural reference—if not of the Chinese generally—is apparent here, both as a personal expression by Roekmini and implicitly as a reflection of the Oost en West society's concern for "authenticity." See also the correspondence by Soematri reflecting her dislike of the Chinese. This can be contrasted with Kartini's interest in Chinese culture.

97. Kartini reports on this meeting in a letter of 17 April, written apparently very soon after the visit that took place in Rembang.

98. In a brief letter dated 31 May (not included here), Roekmini refers to the facts that Abendanon intervened to ensure speedy payment for the craftsmen and that one piece, a stand for a gong made by her Jepara craftsmen, "received the unanimous acclaim of the Exhibition" in Batavia.

99. It becomes clear that Roekmini was kept busy not only with the work associated with the classroom, but with arranging the order, supervision, and supply of items of woodwork for a number of different interests.

100. Nellie van Kol began her children's library in 1898, and by 1914 it consisted of eighty-eight volumes. *Biografisch Woordenboek,* http://www.inghist.nl/Onderzoek/Projecten/BWN/lemmata/bwn3/porreij, s.v. "Porreij, Jacoba Maria Petronella."

101. Kartini died on 17 September 1904. Roekmini had written several brief letters to Rosita Abendanon on 4 August, 13 August, and 31 August (not included), which dealt mainly with matters related to the production and delivery of further woodcarvings.

102. H. Bouman, in researching in 1959, reports an anonymous informant, interviewed as part of the research for a projected biography of Kartini, as recalling about this doctor: "I would not even have entrusted my horse to him." Bouman also refers to rumors of Kartini having been poisoned. None of this

has been, or can be, substantiated. Bouman to Nieuwenhuys, 9 September 1959, KITLV Archive, H 897, no. 2.

103. G. L. Gonggrijp was, like the Abendanons, a supporter of a more progressive colonial policy supporting Javanese education and development. He was also personally acquainted with Kartini's husband, R. M. Djojo Adiningrat, who had been regent of Rembang since 1889.

104. That is, in time for Kartini's funeral, which according to Muslim custom needed to take place as soon as possible.

105. This reference was in recognition of Rosita's Spanish origins.

106. This refers to Annie Glaser, the former Jepara teacher.

107. Dr. Bervoets was a highly regarded medical missionary stationed at the mission complex at Mojowarno, East Java. In 1900, he had suggested that Kartini could train at his clinic, and this was one of the options that Kartini had contemplated. See Kartini to Rosita Abendanon, 21 December 1900.

108. In this and the following paragraph, it is noticeable how forthrightly Roekmini was prepared to express her nationalist sentiments.

109. Van Emmerit was director of the Witte Kruis colony in Salatiga. Dr. Bervoets was missionary doctor at Mojowarno. It was not possible to identify the two women, but they were probably also associated with medical missionary work.

110. It is a customary token to offer a sarong belonging to the dear departed to a close friend.

111. Because Lebaran marked the beginning of the Islamic New Year, it was an appropriate time for new arrangements to be implemented, such as withdrawing children from the school and bringing the project to a close. As Roekmini notes, the previous year this time also marked what was to be the advent of a new life for the two women.

112. Firecrackers. This word and the tradition to mark the New Year derived from Chinese tradition.

113. Roekmini implies she has been suffering for more than six months.

114. If another meeting had been suggested by Rosita, it appears not to have taken place.

115. Rosita had earlier indicated that Abendanon would retire in 1905 and they would return to the Netherlands. The first intimation that Roekmini was aware that they might leave Java is reported in a letter of 28 January 1904.

116. The onerous task of supervising the execution of orders by the Jepara woodcarvers, which also dominated much of the earlier correspondence between Kartini and Rosita, became Roekmini's responsibility after July 1904. This effectively included acting as agent for the Netherlands-based arts-and-crafts association Oost en West.

117. J. E. Jasper (1874–1945) was associated with the establishment of annual native craft markets in Surabaya from 1904, following the successful annual markets in Batavia held since at least 1900. This is the first intimation of Roekmini's

longer involvement with Jasper's project (see further below). He later co-wrote a major five-volume report on traditional crafts: J. E. Jasper and M. Pirngadie, *De Kunstnijverheid in Nederlandsch Indië* ('s-Gravenhage: Mouton and Co., 1912–30).

118. This may have been A. L. Mensinga, a teacher in Meester Cornelis (Batavia).

119. Sosro Moeljono was twenty at this time. Sosro Rawito, "the youngest," was thirteen.

120. The reference is to Kartini's child, later renamed Soesalip.

121. There is a double tragedy here: physical incapacity and loss of position and income. Although Roekmini is not directly alluding to it, the implication is that the highest-ranking Javanese rulers were effectively only colonial employees and entirely dependent economically on their appointment in the colonial service. Heather Sutherland, *The Making of the Bureaucratic Elite: The Colonial Transformation of the Javanese Priyayi* (Singapore: Heinemann Educational Books, 1979).

122. Raden Mas Adipati Ario Sosroningrat died 16 January 1905.

123. This self-reference as "we natives"—"wij Inlanders"—is uncharacteristic; more typically, as in the next letter, Roekmini refers to matters pertaining to herself as "Javanese." Perhaps here, because the reference is to the feudal, male world, it is more distant from her.

124. The reference here is to the Raden Ayu Moerjam, the principal wife and Roekmini's biological mother.

125. Singgo or Singowirio from the village of Blakang Gunung was the head craftsman with whom Kartini and Roekmini arranged the supply of orders for furniture and other wooden craft objects. See Kartini to Rosita Abendanon, 25 August 1903.

126. This declaration of love and devotion by Roekmini is in strong contrast to the rebellious statements expressed by Kartini on their behalf against her (step)mother in 1901 and 1902.

127. Here Roekmini uses the more characteristic phrase "we Javanese" rather than "we natives," as in the letter before. The request for an item of personal clothing here can be compared to Roekmini's offer to Rosita the previous October of one of Kartini's sarongs.

128. Ships to Australia would have passed (or called into) Semarang, and thereafter Surabaya, Bali, Makassar, and Port Moresby.

129. This would be her sister-in-law, Abendanon's sister, Mrs. Cohen Stuart, wife of another prominent bureaucrat.

130. Henri Borel, *Wijsheid en Schoonheid uit China* (1895). Borel was a popular novelist; much of his writing at the turn of the century contributed to the popularization of interest in oriental philosophies. J. Bel, *Nederlandse Literatuuri in het Fin de Siècle* (Amsterdam: Amsterdam University Press, 1993), 160.

131. This is the first reference to the idea of publishing Kartini's letters. That project eventuated in 1911 with the publication of *Door Duisternis tot*

Licht: Gedachten over en voor het Javaansche Volk (From Darkness to Light: Ideas about and for the Javanese People). The impact of that book's reception on Kartini's sisters becomes a major theme in the subsequent letters. Rosita can be considered the main force in pursuing the project, and her sketches decorated the text. It was her husband, however, who exploited its political implications.

132. This was her older brother, Sosro Boesono (b. 15 June 1873). While it had been traditional for an oldest son to follow his father in the almost hereditary role of bupati, the new colonial policy was to interfere more radically in these appointments. The new qualifications demanded of senior Javanese appointees also had a dramatic impact, as later letters also reveal. It is not clear why this "difficulty" had been created, but the new appointee, R. M. A. A. Koesoemo Oetoyo, was very close to the colonial government.

133. This was her brother Sosrorawito (b. 16 September 1892).

134. The move from the kabupaten would have represented a mayor social demotion for the raden ayu.

135. A market town in the mountainous district south of Semarang.

136. The sisters did indeed retire in later life to Salatiga.

137. To "flâner" is to parade ostentatiously in a public place, and is here used in the sense of girls making a public spectacle of themselves. There is a strong touch of sarcasm in Roekmini's use of this word in referring to the excuse parents were giving for withdrawing their daughters. Roekmini clearly recognizes that the children have been withdrawn because the school no longer has important social links with the incumbents of the kabupaten, rather than for reasons of tradition or religion.

138. Kartinah and Soematri had been attending the European elementary school for some years. They commenced extra classes in French in around July 1902. See Kartinah to Rosita Abendanon, 17 December 1902.

139. The extended family had always been against the girls' education and, according to Kartini, had consistently pressured her father to restrict his liberal leanings. In particular, Kartini regularly railed against the attitudes of her uncle, the regent of Demak.

140. Carmen Sylva, pseudonym of Queen Elizabeth of Romania (1843–1916), was a well-known poet and writer who published extensively in the late nineteenth century.

141. The awkwardness arises from the possibility that the young regent would want to marry the daughter of the former bupati and so establish a sense of dynastic relationship with the region. Roekmini's father had similarly married the daughter of his predecessor bupati of Jepara and his raden ayu. Roekmini was thus a "full" priyayi with an excellent pedigree. There may have been an expectation, therefore, that she would marry the new incumbent, an expectation that she declares would have been countered by her family and that she evidently rejected herself, possibly out of principle. Later she declares her happiness in marrying a man of lower status.

142. Another abbreviation for Moeder, although Roekmini rarely applies the Dutch term to her mother, the raden ayu, who is usually referred to as "Ma," as later in the paragraph.

143. This seems to have been no exaggeration. Sosroningrat had provided his daughters an extraordinary degree of latitude, despite the very real restrictions that they felt had limited the possibility of achieving their goals.

144. Roekmini's willingness to compromise in these stressful circumstances, as suggested here, points to her more practical nature compared to that of her sister Kartini, but does not diminish her commitment to the ideals she held. It suggests the importance of the supporting role she played for Kartini, and perhaps her role in convincing Kartini to conditionally accept the marriage proposal in 1903. This character trait is also suggested by Adriani's initial characterization of her. Her letters reveal a strong character and a sharp intellect.

145. This was Abendanon's eldest son, John Ferdinand (1877–1946).

146. Mevrouw van Zuylen-Tromp initiated the establishment of Oost en West in 1898 after the National Exhibition of Women's Work in The Hague, which featured, among other exhibits, the work and contributions of Kartini and Roekmini. She advocated the maintenance of "pure" indigenous traditions in craftwork in the face of European consumer pressure and poor-quality indigenous production. M. Grever and B. Waaldijk, *Feministische Openbaarheid: De Nationale Tentoonstelling van Vrouwenarbeid in 1898* (Amsterdam: Stichting, 1998), 184–86. Roekmini's brother Kartono had worked closely with the organization.

147. The youngest boys were Sosro Moeljono (b. 1885) and Sosrorawito (b. 1892).

148. The reference is to the negative reaction Abendanon had received to his proposal to encourage traditional crafts as a means of developing the Javanese indigenous economy. Abendanon, *Rapport*. Broader investigations into native welfare—the concern of supporters of ethical policy—were subsequently initiated, most notably a major long-running (and long-winded) investigation, the *Mindere Welvaart Onderzoek*, which continued, with inconclusive results, from 1904 to 1914. Apart from the question of the role of native crafts in the economic development of Java, there was a continuing debate about cultural authenticity and the impact of Chinese entrepreneurs in expanding this industry.

149. The colonial bureaucratic system had also rejected his plans as Director of Native Education for developing education for Javanese girls and increasing access to Dutch-language education.

150. This suggests the continuation of an extensive correspondence with E. C. Abendanon. Extracts of some earlier letters to him by Kartini were included in *Door Duisternis tot Licht* and subsequent translations.

151. Poppy, or Dop, was the nickname of Geldolph Adriaan (1880–1956), Abendanon's third son. His wife was May (Mary).

152. It was politic for central and east Javanese bupati to be related via marriage to the royal houses of Solo. Multiple wives—as Kartini had noted in her

critical comment on the Javanese aristocracy—ensured a ready supply of princesses. Roekmini here is expressing her own criticism of the Javanese aristocracy and, of course, contrasting the Solo princess with the bupati's previous wife (Kartini).

153. In a 1958 memoir, Kardinah writes that the child was looked after "for some years" by Ibu Mangoenwikromo, "who was also very much loved by Kartini. When Soesalit was six years old his grandmother, the Ngasirah returned to the regency of Jepara accompanied by Ibu Mangoenwikromo. From then on Soesalit was cared for by the older succeeding heirs of the family of Rembang." Ibu Kartinah Reksonegoro, "The Three Sisters," trans. A. King (typescript, 1958).

154. Boeatan was the commercial and exhibition organization established by Oost en West to "promote an interest for indigenous arts (and crafts) by organising temporary and permanent expositions in Europe." M. Bloembergen, *De Koloniale Vertoningen: De verbeelding van Nederlands-Indië op de Wereldtentoonstellingen (1880–1931)* (Amsterdam: Wereldbibliotheek, 2002), 395n95.

155. Particularly after the successful major international exhibit at the Paris Exhibition of 1900, interest in native arts and crafts became increasingly popular, not only in the Netherlands but in the colony itself. Local exhibitions were held, initially in Batavia. Bloembergen, *De Koloniale Vertoningen,* chap. 4. Kartini and Roekmini had been key intermediaries in this development since their involvement in the National Exhibition of Women's Work in The Hague in 1898. Abendanon had hoped to involve Kartini in providing exhibits for an exhibition in Batavia in 1900, and Kartini herself had discussed establishing a native crafts shop in Semarang in August 1903. These plans included the construction of a factory to accommodate fifty workers as part of her plans for her new life in Rembang as wife of the regent. See Kartini to Rosita, 25 August 1903.

156. Since the late nineteenth century, it had become increasingly popular to display "natives at work" in re-creations of native villages. Bloembergen, *De Koloniale Vertoningen.* However, Kartini's earlier plans had also included relocating Jepara workers to Rembang, which suggests that skilled craftsmen in Java were becoming increasingly mobile.

157. Guido Gezelle (1830–99), a Flemish Catholic priest, is regarded as one of the most significant nineteenth-century Dutch-language poets.

158. This person is later referred to as Mientje but later still, correctly, as Nellie Cohen Stuart.

159. This was a significant recognition of the work that had been undertaken by Roekmini since Kartini's departure from Jepara. It is not clear whether the younger sisters were also included.

160. As well as increasing mobility and interaction between ethnic communities in urban areas, cultural exhibitions such as this contributed to the development of a broader sense of an Indonesian identity at the beginning of the twentieth century, although this one may only have reinforced Roekmini's sense of Javanese nationalism.

161. While this particular plan failed to materialize, Jasper's reports were instrumental in establishing technical schools in Semarang and Surabaya. Bloembergen, *De Koloniale Vertoningen*, 249. See below, Soematri to Rosita, 11 November 1910, where she refers to Jasper's report on native education and craft industry. The schools that were subsequently established, however, were primarily aimed at training prospective workers for colonial industry.

162. After retiring to the Netherlands in 1905, Abendanon was very active in numerous international congresses and activities related to colonial administration, in particular in relation to colonial education and welfare. He was involved in the organization of the Arts and Crafts Exhibition in Krefeld in 1906, which earned him an official recognition from the Prussian government. Van Miert, *Bevlogenheid en Onvermogen*, 24.

163. R. M. A. A. Koesoemo Oetoyo was something of a favorite among colonial progressives. He was well known as an advocate of native arts and crafts. In 1902, as regent of Ngawi, he had published an influential paper on the need for training schools to develop native crafts; it appeared in an important colonial journal, *Tijdschrift voor het Binnenlandsch Bestuur*. He later became a prominent conservative political leader and was a member of the Volksraad. Roekmini points out, as Kartini had earlier, how the new generation of Western-educated male Javanese progressives nevertheless maintained traditional notions of gender roles.

164. The energetic Abendanon had been regularly forced to leave Batavia to take periods of rest in the cooler climate of the West Java mountains. After his return to the Netherlands, he continued to lead a hectic public life but also continued to suffer from ill health, necessitating periods of recuperation in health resorts and spending the winter months in the warmer climate of southern France.

165. The new controleur was August (Guus) Mühlenfeld, appointed to Jepara as his first posting. Roekmini seems to have been mistaken in referring to a sister; she was in fact his wife (see below, correspondence of Soematri to Lien). After several other postings (see below), he joined the central administration, rising eventually to the position of director of the Department of Binnenlandsch Bestuur (colonial administration) (1929–33). In 1918, he became a founding member of the Comité voor Javaansche Cultuurontwikkeling, an influential group of Javanese and Dutch intellectuals concerned with promoting Javanese cultural revival.

166. Roekmini later indicates this was *Het Damesweekblad van Indië*. Published writing by Roekmini has not been located. Three published compositions by Kartini are extant and suggest a typical turn-of-the-century "women's journal" writing style.

167. Kartini had been involved in collecting Javanese fairytales at the request of Nellie van Kol, with whom she had corresponded after meeting with her husband, the Social Democrat parliamentarian Henri van Kol. See Kartini to Henri van Kol, 7 August 1902, discussed in J. Anten, "De ontbrekende brief van Kartini," *Indische Letteren* 20 (2005): 24–32. Nellie, once a leading figure in

the Dutch feminist movement, was the author of children's books. See above, Roekmini to Rosita, 4 January 1904.

168. There is no indication that this eventuated, or what its subject matter may have been.

169. A specific and much admired decorative style of batik from the Pekalongan region.

170. This can be read as a perceptive comment on modernity: on the one hand, communication was facilitated, but on the other, modernity imposed a greater self-consciousness and a set of social constraints that channeled and shaped communication.

171. Kartini's correspondence indicates that Lawick van Pabst, then chief inspector of (sugar and rice) cultures, had been a regular visitor to the Jepara kabupaten.

172. The scientific name is *Dalbergia latifolia*.

173. She had first met Adriani in August 1900 at the home of Rosita and Jacques Abendanon in Batavia.

174. The Dokter Djawa school, or STOVIA, was the highest-level educational institution in the colony. The majority of Western-educated Indonesian intellectuals at the beginning of the twentieth century had graduated from it. STOVIA graduates also formed the majority of students going on to further study in the Netherlands. A. Nagazumi, *The Dawn of Indonesian Nationalism: The Early Years of Budi Utomo* (Tokyo: Institute of Developing Economies, 1972), chap. 3; Poeze, *In het Land van de Overheerser*, 68–71. Hassim's future career is not known, but this is a rare reference in the correspondence to the Islamic religious awakening in this period.

175. *Eigen Haard* was a popular illustrated Dutch journal. It had already published articles by and about Kartini.

176. While generally Roekmini's older siblings had remained distant from the "modern ideas" being expressed and activated by their younger sisters, Kartini reported that Boesono had "silently" supported her and that "not all idealistic urges had been killed in him." Kartini to Rosita Abendanon, 14 January and 1 February 1903.

177. At this point Kartono had been away for ten years.

178. Kartono was initially supported by the generosity of several colonial benefactors, but his "bad behavior" appeared to have led to this financial support being withdrawn. Thereafter, he had to work to support himself, and economic difficulties, as well as problems with his academic supervisors, continued to make life difficult for him. Kartono was one of the first Javanese university students in the Netherlands. Oost en West initiated support schemes in the Netherlands and established a *Studiecommissie* in 1909 to "to advise and act *in loco parentis* to Indonesian students." Poeze, *In het Land van de Overheerser*, 142–44. The various private Dutch schemes to support Indonesian students were consolidated and reorganized in 1916. This also facilitated greater supervision and control.

179. The first craft exhibition and market of this kind was held in Semarang in 1908. The later published account makes no mention of Roekmini's involvement either in the organization or as contributor. The regent of Jepara was a member of one of the jury panels and provided items of silver. *Verslag van de Eerste Semarangsche Jaarmarkt-Tentonstelling, 1908* [1911]. The first such event in Surabaya was held in 1905, and it continued annually thereafter.

180. Concern about the Chinese domination of the indigenous economy motivated the establishment of agricultural credit banks, a key innovation of the ethical policy inaugurated in 1901. Earlier expressions of concern about the financial difficulties of Jepara craftsmen take on an anti-Chinese sentiment here, which becomes increasingly present in subsequent comments.

181. Roekmini's future husband, Santoso, was a member of the local bank's advisory board, as was the Jepara regent, Koesoemo Oetoyo, of whom she was to become highly critical. The latter was vice president of the Jepara branch of the bank and may have been influential in blocking the appointment, given Roekmini's later comments about his views on women.

182. Along with her direct involvement in the Surabaya exhibition for two years and her published writing, the application for the position at the credit bank and the possibility of teaching at Jasper's proposed vocational school represented real attempts to enter the public domain in fulfilment of her and Kartini's long-held goal to be publicly active. These activities extended and went beyond those initiated by Kartini. The short-lived Jepara kabupaten school, after all, had remained largely a private initiative.

183. Kartono commenced studies in the Netherlands in 1897 at a polytechnical school in Delft, probably with the intention of training as an engineer. Shortly afterwards he sat for the entrance exams to enroll at Leiden University, where he commenced reading Oriental languages. Even prior to 1907, but particularly after Kartini's death, concern regarding Kartono's progress and anxiety about his return increased, since it was hoped he would be able to protect the interests of the women against the conservative elements of the family. Kartono's behavior, however, caused the sisters, as well as the Abendanons, many years of anxiety. He did not return to Java until 1925, twenty-eight years after leaving the country.

184. The English word "boy" was used as a term of endearment. See particularly the use of the word by Soematri.

185. Gonggrijp had been stationed in Jepara in 1899 and became resident of Rembang in 1907. He became famous for his anonymous and satirical commentaries on colonial policy, *Brieven van Opheffer*.

186. This was controleur August Mühlenfeld. He became a major figure within the colonial progressive movement. Mühlenfeld's father had also worked in Java in the 1850s and personally knew the sister's grandfather and uncle from his period. Letter to A. Mühlenfeld from his father, 4 July 1911, Kartini Archive, H 1200, No. 259.

187. This was both insightful and prophetic. Kartono maintained a precarious existence as a journalist in Europe before finally returning to Java, where, after announcing grand plans to establish a school and embark on a career of writing, he became a well-known mystic and healer.

188. Kartini had also written at length and often to Rosita about the continued opposition of the regent of Demak, Raden Mas Adipati Ario Hadiningrat, the younger brother of their father.

189. This was in fact Piet Ducroo, an artist sent out by the administration of Boeatan to investigate and evaluate the artistic merit of native craft production, in particular of batik, "in order to investigate subsequently how the standard of this may be lifted by introducing these into items produced and in demand in the European market, yet maintaining their purely Indies style and designs" as well as promoting its production as a cottage industry. The project failed as such, but Ducroo experimented with developing modern designs that would be attractive to Europeans, a development opposed by Boeatan as being inauthentic. Bloembergen, *De Koloniale Vertoningen*, 262.

190. The problems apparently were largely financial, as Kartono had incurred serious debts. Poeze, *In het Land van de Overheerser*, 127.

191. This was Professor Kern, professor of Oriental languages at Leiden University. Professor Kern in particular had initially taken a supervisory interest in Kartono's academic career in Leiden. See Kartini to Rosita, 29 May 1903.

192. In other words, it was believed that Kartono was trying to keep up with his wealthy compatriots, apparently the root cause of his financial troubles.

193. This comment does appear to confirm that the preparation of the collection of Kartini's letters for publication as *Door Duisternis tot Licht* was being undertaken by Rosita.

194. This was the same position her father had held in the 1870s. It could therefore have been expected that her husband also would eventually have been appointed to the position of regent, although Roekmini stresses he was not of high birth. His expectation of career advancement, based on his education and possibly on his marrying Roekmini, underpins the tragedy of the subsequent history.

195. Roekmini emphasizes here that Santoso is representative of a new generation of Western-educated Javanese men—a new priyayi class—not a privileged member of the old aristocracy that dominated the native civil service in the nineteenth century. In normal (traditional) circumstances, a woman of Roekmini's position, as daughter of an old regent family, could have expected to marry a future regent.

196. This proposed school can be compared to the remarkably similar one established (quite independently) several years later by her sister Kardinah; both are quite different from the contemporary colonial- and Dutch-initiated Kartini Schools. Opting for teaching at the proposed school in Jepara saved the problems of having to relocate to Surabaya.

197. This "letter, calling on young Western-educated Javanese to unite," was appended to Roekmini's letter. It is almost identical to that circulated by

STOVIA students in establishing Budi Utomo, reproduced in the Budi Utomo tenth anniversary publication *"Soembangsih": Gedenkboek Boedi-Oetomo, 1908–1918* (Amsterdam: Nederlandsch Indië Oud en Nieuw, 1918), 15. In a letter published in newspapers on 23 July 1908, Soewarno, on behalf of STOVIA students, explained: "In the last few days some newspapers have featured interesting articles on the activities of the three Raden Ajengs of Jepara and the Regents of Jepara, Temanggoeng, Karanganjar and Koetoarjo.... We have immediately informed the three Raden Ajengs of Jepara about our association and its objectives and we have requested them to establish a local branch, while at the same time we made it known that we also supported their own efforts." Penders, *Indonesia,* 225–27.

198. All this indicates a very modern and fashionable young man, typical of many of the idealists who supported an ethical policy and became enamored of Javanese mysticism and culture. Later, Mühlenfeld became an influential member of the Java Institute and the Javanese cultural reawakening movement. Key colonial supporters of reform, European as well as Javanese, were theosophists.

199. Roekmini continues to indicate that she believed it was Rosita who was preparing Kartini's letters for publication. The archive indicates that her husband conducted negotiations with contributors and the publisher. Her stepdaughter Marie wrote in 1911, after receiving a copy of the book, "What a pity that the time is not yet ripe to publish the intimate letters of Kartini. Now much of her inner struggle must remain a mystery to us." Marie Abendanon to Abendanon, 11 June 1911, KITLV Archive, H 1200, no. 259.

200. The connection would seem strange were it not for the link via Nicolaus Adriani. Adriani and his missionary colleague Albert Kruyt worked closely with, and strongly influenced, the assistant resident of Central Celebes, A. J. N. Engelenberg, in the economic development of the Pamona people of this region. Engelenberg, although later a leading member of the conservative Eurasian political party, the IEV, was regarded at the time as a leading progressive colonial official. J. Coté, "The Colonisation and Schooling of the To Pamona of Central Sulawesi, 1895–1925," Master's thesis, Monash University, 1980.

201. Nellie Stokvis-Cohen Stuart.

202. Roekmini here specifically distinguishes Inlandsche (Native) people from inhabitants of the Dutch East Indies in general (Indische).

203. The Tehupeiory brothers, Johan E. and W. K. Tehupeiory, were from Ambon and were both STOVIA graduates. They had gone to the Netherlands in 1907 to continue their medical studies, accompanied by their sister, who studied for pharmacy. In August 1907, Johan presented a much publicized paper, "The Native before and after the Establishment of the *Algemeen Nederlandsch Verbond* [Dutch language society]," on the importance of widespread access by Indonesians to Dutch-language education. The theme was similar to that of Kartono's speech in 1899 and would have had special interest to Roekmini. The brothers edited a short-lived biweekly Malay-language paper, *Bandera Wolanda,* published in Amsterdam, which, like the more successful multilingual

paper *Bintang Hindia*, was designed for a "modern" Indies readership. They were also involved in the establishment of the Indonesian student association Indische Vereeniging (Indies Association) and presented formal papers on medical and other issues to the Indisch Genootschap, a Dutch learned association. Poeze, *In het Land van de Overheerser,* 58–61.

204. Asmaoen was one of the first three STOVIA graduates who went to the Netherlands to continue their studies (the first being Abdul Rivai). He completed his medical degree there in 1908. Thereafter he became the first Indonesian to be appointed medical officer to the KNIL, the colonial army. However, Dutch officers refused to accept him as an equal and he returned to the Netherlands, where he died in 1916. Poeze, *In het Land van de Overheerser,* 57.

205. It is not clear whether this eventuated. As in the case of the aforementioned Asmaoen, and increasingly in the case of other Netherlands-educated Indonesians, such as Soematri's husband, Sosrohadikoesoemo, the issue for the colonial government became whether and how to incorporate Indonesians of equivalent education into the colonial administration and how such appointees would be received by white colleagues.

206. Santoso was officially referred to in the *Colonial Almanac* as Mas Santoso. All other relatives and most Javanese officials carried at least the title and rank of "raden."

207. Here Roekmini continues the complaint against R. M. A. Adiningrat, regent of Demak, whom Kartini had also consistently castigated as the major obstacle to their plans because of his conservative attitude and his influence within the colonial bureaucracy and within his extended family.

208. Roekmini had earlier commented on his views toward women, and generally on the conservatism of the so-called progressive, Western-educated Javanese male elite.

209. The term "Jong Java" was at the time gaining popular usage to designate the new generation, the *kaum muda,* of Western-educated progressive Indonesians. The term had first been used by Abdul Rivai in 1903, who had also called for the young progressives to join together. In 1905, Tirto Adhisoeryo had advocated a similar idea in his paper, *Soenda Berita.* Adam, *Vernacular Press.* In the Netherlands, the Indische Vereeniging was established in 1908 by Indonesian students, including Roekmini's brother Kartono. Poeze, *In het Land van de Overheerser,* 71–81.

210. Roekmini and Santoso married on 17 August 1908.

211. This suggests an allusion to the three sisters' stance against arranged marriage and polygamy; only Roekmini succeeded in not having an arranged marriage.

212. Sosro Boesono, regent of Ngawi since 1905.

213. Abendanon's niece, Dr. Nellie Stokvis-Cohen Stuart, lived in Semarang, where she established an organization to support the training of Javanese nurses. See also below, Soematri to Rosita, April–May 1918.

214. This describes what was effectively the beginning of the Indische Vereeniging, which Abendanon and Conrad van Deventer, together with Noto Soeroto, were instrumental in establishing. It was later transformed into the influential nationalist organization Perhimpunan Indonesia.

215. There is no indication in the extant correspondence of her sisters Kartinah and Soematri that this school was continued.

216. Roekmini continues to refer to Budi Utomo as a "Young Javanese" organization. The first Budi Utomo congress was held on 5–18 October 1908. Opposition to its limited agenda was already voiced at that meeting. Nagazumi, *Dawn of Indonesian Nationalism,* 44–50; *"Soembangsih" Gedenkboek Boedi-Oetomo,* 1918.

217. This can be considered important evidence of the early participation of women in the nationalist movement.

218. The reference is to the students of the Batavia-based medical school STOVIA, who established the organization. Nagazumi, *Dawn of Indonesian Nationalism,* 40–43. Kartini, in her memorandum on education, had emphasized the importance of communication between male and female intellectuals, and may have been in correspondence with them. In refusing her scholarship, Kartini had urged this be given to a young male student, Agus Salim. However, Kartini herself had never gone as far as Roekmini in making a public call to such a circle.

219. This confirms the important role Abendanon played in establishing the Indische Vereeniging in the Netherlands. He became its patron.

220. Six months after the previous reference to the "Union of the Young Javanese," Roekmini now incorporates the correct name, Budi Utomo, into a Dutch construction: Vereeniging Boedi Oetomo. The initials here reflect the old spelling, "Oetomo."

221. This was apparently the Regentenbond (Union of Regents), known as Sedio Moeljo; it was not officially established, however, until 1911, and not legally constituted until 1913. Based in Semarang, it was founded by R. M. A. A. Koesoemo Oetoyo, regent of Jepara, together with the regent of Temangueng. It was generally seen as having been specifically aimed to protect the position of the priyayi against criticism from the young modern progressives. Van de Doel, *De Stille Macht,* 270–71.

222. According to Bloembergen's account, in the year after the Budi Utomo first met (May 1908), "just about every student of secondary schools, and the administrative and teacher training schools in Java joined." Bloembergen (1931), 1987: 20.

223. Johan Tehupeiory died the day after graduating, from gas poisoning after leaving open a gas valve in his Utrecht rooms. Poeze, *In het Land van de Overheerser,* 6.

224. This seems to have been Raden Ambia Poerbo Soedibio, who was studying at Delft. He was a founding member of the Indische Vereeniging and was still in the Netherlands in 1916.

225. Raden Kamil was the Inspector of Native Education in Semarang. A STOVIA graduate, he completed further medical studies in the Netherlands. Kartini cited him in 1901 as one of four male students who had studied in the Netherlands at government expense, when arguing that the government might also provide financial assistance for her and her sisters to study in the Netherlands. See Kartini to Rosita Abendanon, 29 November 1901.

226. Dr. G. A. J. Hazeu was Adviseur voor Inlandsche Zaken (colonial adviser for native affairs) from 1904 to 1912 and again from 1916 to 1920.

227. The Rechtsschool (native law school) was established in 1909.

228. This was not correct. Henri van Kol was undertaking one of his regular tours of inspection as Socialist MP and party spokesman for colonial affairs. Roekmini last spoke with him in 1902, during his previous visit to Java, when she detailed for the first time her desire to study drawing in the Netherlands. The visit also occasioned a minor scandal when the women's plans were published in *De Locomotief* by a journalist accompanying the parliamentarian on his tour. Anten, "De ontbrekende brief van Kartini."

229. Roekmini is evidently demonstrating her awareness of colonial politics. The new minister of colonies, De Waal Malefijt (1909–13), and his successor, Pleijte (1913–18), were indeed considered relatively progressive, as were the next two governors general, Idenburg (1909–16) and van Limburg Stirum (1916–21). Van den Doel, *De Stille Macht,* 245–66. They marked the high point and end of what Locher-Scholten, *Ethiek in Fragmenten,* defines as the extent of the ethical period.

230. This is a reference to the regular meetings of the new Indische Vereeniging. Jacques Abendanon was a key instigator of the organization, whose meetings he regularly attended and participated in, as did Conrad van Deventer. Its meetings and discussions were published in *Voordrachten en Mededeelingen* from 1911.

231. The congress was attended by three hundred men and women of all nationalities. The influential Dutch liberal politician van Deventer praised it as a useful, moderate force in dismantling feudal power. Nagazumi, *Dawn of Indonesian Nationalism,* 55–65.

232. See Roekmini's earlier criticisms of R. M. A. A. Koesoemo Oetoyo. Roekmini to Rosita, 28 October 1906.

233. Like many others, Roekmini and her sisters were disillusioned by its domination by Javanese officials and aristocracy. Roekmini's sharp criticism of Budi Utomo was echoed in very similar terms later by Soewardi Soerjaningrat (1918) in an article in the commemorative volume of that organization. He saw its value merely in its having been a cultural revival movement. "Het Javaansch Nationalisme in de Indische Beweging," in *Gedenkboek Boedi-Oetomo 1908–18* (Amsterdam: Nederlandsch Indië Oud and Nieuw), 27–48.

234. Dr. Hazeu's official tasks included advising on and supervising the education of the children of the Javanese elite, as well as making arrangements for

their study in the Netherlands. A committee in Batavia had been established to arrange the studies and accommodation for the many students from elsewhere in Java and the islands beyond. Poeze, *In het Land van de Overheerser,* 82.

235. This was Roekmini's first return to Batavia, where, with Kartini and her family, she had stayed with the Abendanons in 1900, following the Abendanons' visit to Jepara. Piet Sijthoff, the former resident of Semarang, was the colonial official through whom all requests to the government had to be channeled. He had consequently been closely involved with Kartini over the three years during which she had spearheaded the attempt to gain further education for the sisters. As revealed in Kartini's correspondence, he took a very close personal interest in her and at times had, according to Kartini, been quite "familiar."

236. Roekmini seems to be commenting nostalgically on the impact of modernity—and intentionally avoiding a more direct train route via the urban centers.

237. Abendanon had arranged Annie's appointment to the Jepara school in order to coach the sisters for the teacher examination. She had soon transferred to Batavia, where she had since married.

238. Later, Annie refused to provide any of her letters from Kartini to be included in Abendanon's 1911 publication, although Roekmini here indicates she was aware of the project. Perhaps Roekmini's careful comment here indicates that Annie had already expressed her misgivings during their meeting. Interviewed in her old age in the early 1950s, she again specifically refused to make public her letters. According to Bouman, her daughter believed that Annie Glaser had been sworn to secrecy by the Tjondronegara family and had burned the letters. Bouman to Nieuwenhuis, 21/9/59 KITLV Archive, H 897, no. 4.

239. Ten named Indonesians from various parts of the archipelago worked under the supervision of this Javanese official, Raden Brata di Widaya. Bloembergen, *De Koloniale Vertoningen,* 259. Abendanon and Mrs. van Zuylen-Tromp were on the Dutch planning committee for the World Exhibition held in Brussels in 1910, and J. E. Jasper contributed from the Indies. The Dutch exhibit emphasized native arts and crafts, including a "live" exhibit which attracted "packed audiences every afternoon for four months" (233–69). Roekmini had become the key link in the Javanese end of the practice via her involvement with Jasper.

240. The advisers of the exhibition, Abendanon, van Zuylen-Tromp, and van Deventer, had insisted that it maintain a serious focus on the cultural and economic importance of indigenous arts and crafts and explicitly not be made into an entertainment with displays of "musicians and dancing girls" as in the past.

241. Jasper, then living in The Hague, was commissioned to write a series of reports on native arts and crafts, the first volumes of which appeared in 1912. He was also listed as a patron of the Indische Vereeniging.

242. Indeed, she was the last. Letters thanking the Abendanons for the gift of *Door Duisternis tot Licht* were also written by the other three sisters in July;

by her oldest brother, Sosroningrat (at the time retired assistant wedono of Pecangan), and younger bother Sosro Moeljono (assistant wedono of Dolopo, Madiun), also in July; by Soelastri's husband, Tjokrohadikoesoemo, in August; and the youngest brother, Rawito, in November. All wrote in Dutch, except for Tjokrohadikoesoemo, who wrote in Malay. The archive does not contain a similar letter from Boesono.

243. This is evidently a modest self-representation, which contrasts with the image of herself presented in her letter to Etty, in which Roekmini emphasized the extent to which she participated in the many hours of reading and discussion that led to the articulation of Kartini's ideas in letters to Dutch friends.

244. Mayong was an important sugar-producing center.

245. Her older brother Sosroningrat—to whom there is no direct reference in any of the sisters' correspondence—responded more formally, but in similar terms adding, rather inappropriately, that having read the book several times, he would now "put it away for my daughter who on 13 July 1911 just turned one, until she has become an adult." Sosroningrat to Abendanon, 14 July 1911.

246. That is, Roekmini's stepdaughter, who was already sixteen when Roekmini married her father.

247. This may be the girls' school established in Rembang in 1910, referred to in Toer, *Sang Pemula,* 84n9. See also Soematri's concern that initial plans for a Kartini School in Semarang also did not accord with Kartini's views. Soematri to Rosita, 16 July 1912.

248. Van Deventer was still recognized as the most authoritative voice on progressive colonial policy, and his lengthy account of Kartini's life, published in the nation's leading journal, *De Gids,* ensured that Kartini became a familiar name in all Dutch households that had any connection with Java. It also ensured financial support for the Kartini Vereeniging and Fonds. Colenbrander and Stokvis, *Leven en Arbeid,* 310–34. The colonial paper *De Locomotief* as well as the Indische Vereeniging–linked paper *Bintang Hindia* also strongly promoted the book (see Soematri to Rosita, 14 July 1914). According to Abendanon's niece, Nellie, commenting at the time of its first appearance, "The Indies public in general has little interest [in the issue] and if it is not strongly promoted it will have little effect." Nellie to Abendanon, 11 June 1911, KITLV archive, H 1200, no. 259.

249. Abendanon spent the rest of his life in the Indies.

250. Hazeu was acting director of education between 1912 and 1916, specifically charged with overseeing the restructuring of native education.

251. Noto Soeroto, founding president of the Indische Vereeniging and already an influential figure for the growing community of Indonesian students studying in the Netherlands, remained an advocate of "cultural nationalism," which emphasized cooperative association with progressive colonial policies. He published his cultural commentary and poetry widely. In his speech to

the Indische Vereeniging on 24 December 1911, which appeared in the first number of its publication *Voordrachten en Mededelingen* (Speeches and Announcements), he argued that Kartini's proposals and ideals perfectly matched those of the Indische Vereeniging. Abendanon and van Deventer also addressed the same meeting on the same subject. Poeze, *In het Land van de Overheerser,* 75–76.

252. Roekmini first met Hilda de Booy-Boissevain in 1900. Kartini corresponded with her thereafter, and a selection of letters to her were included in *Door Duisternis tot Licht.* The exhibition referred to is the women's exhibition De Vrouw 1813–1913, which celebrated the centenary of Dutch independence from France and honored the Dutch Queen Wilhelmina. The exhibition focused on domestic economy, home hygiene, and women's domestic education, and, like earlier exhibitions, included a colonial exhibit, Het Indisch Huis (the Indies home), featuring the interior of a "modern" Javanese home. Hilda de Booy arranged with Abendanon to develop a "Kartini corner" in the exhibition, using photographs and personal items lent by him. Hilda de Booy to Abendanon 9 May, 6 June, 14 and 17 November, 1913 Kartini Archive, H 1200, no. 267. She had also approached the other sisters for contributions. Roekmini proposed to send a large carved frame (Roekmini to Hilda, 19 December 1912, KITLV Archive, H 897, no. 4), and Kardinah eventually sent two dolls representing a bridal couple in traditional costume. Kardinah to Hilda, 6 February 1913, KITLV Archive, H 897, no. 4.

253. Hilda had also requested Roekmini to prepare a biography of Kartini. This was incorporated without significant change into an address that Hilda and others presented several times, between June 1913 and October 1915, beginning first with Hilda's address at the opening of the Indisch Huis exhibition. KITLV Archive, H 897, no. 7. The exhibition in the Netherlands coincided with the opening of the first Kartini School in Semarang. Kartini was again the focus at the women's exhibit at the International Colonial Exhibition in Semarang held the following year. The exhibition also included some of the exhibits from the earlier Dutch exhibition. Poeze, *In het Land van de Overheerser,* 88; M. G. van Heel, ed., *Gedenkboek van de Koloniale Tentoonstelling Semarang 20 Augustus–22 November 1914* (Batavia: Mercurius, 1916), 305–14.

254. An initial meeting of an interim committee in February 1912 recommended that before establishing and publicizing a plan a representative needed to investigate the situation in Java. Van Deventer's 1912 trip was to "gather information and undertake negotiations" for the planned school project. The Kartini Vereeniging was established on 26 February 1913 on his return. His report to the committee indicated the thoroughness of his investigation into the state of girls' education. *Jubileum-Verslag: Uitgegeven ter gelegenheid van het 25-jarig bestaan der vereeniging Kartinifonds te 's-Gravenhage, 1913–1938* ('s-Gravenhage, 1939), 6–9. The Semarang Kartini School committee included both Europeans and prominent Indonesian officials.

255. This was preliminary to the official opening of the school, which did not take place until 15 September 1913; classes were delayed further while the "necessary teaching assistants" were engaged. KITLV Archive, H 897, no. 6.

256. M. C. Brandes was inspector of cultures (commercial crops, specifically sugar and tobacco) grown in the semiautonomous regions of the Yogyakarta and Solo royal and princely houses. Brandes had previously discussed with Kartini the possibility of Oost en West establishing a commercial outlet in Semarang for Jepara craft, for which she would arrange the supply of craftwork. J. Brandes, an academic linguist, researched old Javanese language and archaeology.

257. In a letter to Hilda, she described the frame as featuring Javanese women kneeling positioned so that they would appear to be kneeling before the photograph of Kartini and honoring her with flowers as "a holy ancestor who however still lives on in our spirit." It is not clear if this was the same or whether Roekmini was arranging two frames. Roekmini to Hilda, 19 December 1912, KITLV Archive, H 897, no. 4

258. Abendanon met Rosita in Barcelona in 1883, and this may well have been the first return visit for her.

259. The fund was the Steun voor de Opleiding tot Vrouwelijke Inlandsche Artsen (SOVIA), established by Charlotte Jacobs, sister of the Dutch feminist Aletta Jacobs. I. de Wilde, "Uit de schommelstoelen: Charlotte Jacobs en haar kring in Batavia," in Esther Captain, Marieke Hellevoort, and Marian van der Klein, eds., *Vertrouwd en vreemd: Ontmoetingen tussen Nederland, Indië en Indonesië* (Hiversum: Verloren, 2000), 187–94. See also Kardinah to Rosita, 25 December 1912.

260. It was Hilda de Booy who had originally requested a frame for a photograph that Abendanon had offered for the exhibition. In May she had expressed her impatience to Abendanon at not having received the frame. Later she proposed to reproduce and sell photos of Kartini at the exhibition at five cents each to raise money for the Kartini school. Hilda de Booy-Boissevain to Abendanon, 9 May, 6 June 1913, Kartini Archive, H 1200, no. 267.

261. The continued correspondence with the Abendanons was motivated in part by the possibility of Jacques Abendanon being useful in negotiating with the colonial bureaucracy. While the archive provides no evidence of Boesono, the regent, having sought Abendanon's support, each of the other family members do so in one form or other. At the same time, it is clear that the Abendanons remained committed to the family and any help, financial or otherwise, was clearly freely and gladly given.

262. This situation was highly ironic. On the one hand, Hadiningrat had come to prominence as a progressive member of the Javanese colonial civil service. On the other hand, he had consistently attempted to thwart the attempts by Kartini and her sisters to gain further education. Roekmini to Rosita, 23 June 1902. It now appeared that he had neglected to ensure that his sons—who

in the past would automatically have succeeded to his post—had kept up with newer demands of the changing times.

263. In his account of the native civil service regulations, Santoso reveals the source of the irritation and anger that drove many Javanese officials to join nationalist organizations. Ostensibly, all officers of whatever racial background were, as a result of the 1913 "unification principle," to receive the same pay for the same work. This decision was intended to remove the traditional racial separation between the two arms of the civil service, increasingly accentuated by the growing number of Javanese officials with relevant educational qualifications. This intention was largely canceled out by reclassification of positions and salary scales into categories (A, B, and C), which largely coincided with the race predominantly employed in that category (respectively native, Indo, and European). Van den Doel, *De Stille Macht,* 559. Santoso reveals a further, and more fundamental, issue that would effectively continue to disadvantage and downgrade the Javanese candidate. See also correspondence from Sosrohadikoesoemo to Abendanon, below, on the same issue.

264. *Ondercollector* was a rank between patih and wedono, so in fact this was a promotion, but not to the position of patih, which would have been seen as some compensation for not having been appointed regent. Roekmini quite correctly notes that this was a dead-end position and would not lead to the next rung, that of patih.

265. Sosrohadikoesoemo also refers to the problem and the difficulties experienced of working under a fellow Javanese official, compared to working for a European one, in a letter to Abendanon. See Achmad Sosrohadikoesoemo to Abendanon, 18 February 1914.

266. Roekmini here illustrates the process by which increasing numbers of Indonesian students came to study in the Netherlands after careful selection and under supervision. In 1921, more than seventy-two students arrived in the Netherlands to study. Poeze, *In het Land van de Overheerser,* 163.

267. Siti Soendari Darmabrata founded and edited the women's journal *Wanita Soeworo* (Women's Voice) in 1913 after having first worked as journalist for *Poetri Hindia,* the first Indonesian women's paper, established by Tirto Adhi Soeryo. She had published numerous articles in Javanese, Malay, and Dutch, including some on the position of women in the Middle East. Toer, *Sang Pemula,* 90. See also below, Kardinah to Rosita Abendanon, 7 August 1917. In 1914, the welfare enquiry the *Mindere Welvaart Onderzoek* included her lengthy and ethnographically detailed, if ultimately rather conservative, statement on the need for girls' education. *Verheffing van de Inlandsche Vrouw,* App. 9, 26–38.

268. In fact, she was attending the First Colonial Education Conference in August 1916, organized by Abendanon in The Hague. She presented her paper on women's education in the Malay language but returned to Java shortly thereafter. Poeze, *In het Land van de Overheerser,* 112. Toer states that she traveled on her own resources. *Sang Pemula,* 90.

269. See below, Kardinah's letters to Rosita Abendanon.

270. This comment on Jepara also seems to confirm the dead-end nature of Santosa's appointment.

271. The Van Deventer School, established in Semarang, provided teacher training for Javanese women. See further the correspondence by Kardinah.

272. Roekmini's husband died in 1919, leaving her with five children: two stepsons and her own three, including the child born in February 1917.

273. Tegal was where her sister Kardinah and her husband, the regent, lived.

274. Soematri and her husband lived for some time in Semarang.

275. Kardinah writes in 1958 that the choice of Kudus was motivated by the fact "that she wanted to be nearer the Sedamukti Cemetery, the cemetery of the Tjondronegoro family." Kardinah, "The Three Sisters," 16.

276. Sardjono was the first Javanese to be admitted to (and to graduate from) the Dutch military college, the Koninklijke Militaire Academie in Breda, in 1918. Poeze, *In het Land van de Overheerser*, 145.

277. This is a reference to her son Srigati and to Jacques and Rosita Abendanon.

278. This comment can be compared to Roekmini's account of Djojo Adiningrat in her letter to Rosita in August 1903. The saga of Kartini's son is also reported in Soematri's correspondence.

279. This is Roekmini's second stepson.

280. Evidently Roekmini had received reports from the most recent conference, in 1919. Abendanon organized two major conferences, in 1916 and 1919, on colonial education policy. Of interest to Roekmini was Abendanon's strong argument for separate girls' schools and against coeducation. See also below, on the issue of language and girls' education, the correspondence of Kardinah and of Achmad Sosrohadikoesoemo.

281. Noto Soeroto had published extensively by this time, including three volumes of poetry that had first appeared in various periodicals: *Melatiknoppen* [Buds of the Melati Flower] (1915), *Fluisteringen van den Avondwind* [Whispers of the Evening Wind] (1917), and *Bloeme-ketenen* [Flower Chains] (1918).

282. The end of the war meant a return to regular travel between the Netherlands and the Indies. Thomas B. Pleijte, a liberal democrat minister of colonies during the war, was a friend and colleague of Conrad van Deventer, also a liberal democrat. He had worked in van Deventer's law office in Semarang between 1892 and 1909. His progressive stance was reflected in his advocacy of expanding indigenous administration as part of a policy for greater administrative decentralization and autonomy. Perhaps Roekmini and colonial progressives believed he would become the next governor general after his term as minister. After three "progressive" governors general, however, the postwar period saw the appointment of two conservatives. Van den Doel, *De Stille Macht*, 251ff.

283. Kartini's child, Singgih, had been renamed Soesalip.

284. Wife of the resident of Rembang.

285. Dutch higher elementary school.

286. Deeply embarrassed by having apparently and unintentionally misled the sympathetic resident, Roekmini also seems to be expressing both personal and national pride, which was challenged by this dependence on charity, no matter how well intentioned.

287. Evidently Sardjono's enrolment in military academy in Breda was arranged via the colonial office.

288. Adriani had worked with Abendanon on the second Colonial Education Congress while in Holland, and in 1920 returned to Central Sulawesi via Java.

289. Against the many accounts of successful Indonesian students, the account of Soedjono in the correspondence, together with those of Soesalip and Kartono, represent the dark side of modern life for the new generation of Javanese, bringing much psychological suffering.

290. A Hollandsch-Inlandsche school was the Dutch medium elementary school type for Indonesians, established in 1912 to meet the increasing demand for Dutch-language education. It was also intended as a way of reducing the pressure of increasing Indonesian enrolment in the European school system, in response, particularly, to Eurasian opposition. See correspondence of Kardinah and Soematri below.

291. Under the influence of progressive Dutch educational pedagogy, Fröbelian kindergarten and educative play methods were being introduced into colonial native schools as well. Kartini and Roekmini had experimented with these in their own school in Jepara. See Roekmini to Rosita Abendanon, 28 January 1904; also below, Soematri to Rosita Abendanon 22 July 1904.

292. This may have been arranged by Roekmini's younger brother Rawito, who had joined the railway service, or her brother, who was regent in the Madiun district colonial administration.

293. Kardinah wrote later that Roekmini, apart from teaching and looking after her mother and her own children and later grandchildren, spent much time in welfare work in the villages around Kudus: "Almost every day she went to the villages to visit and to give advice to whoever was in need of it. Such activity made her very happy." In later life she also took up painting again. She died in 1951 after a short illness. Kardinah, "The Three Sisters," 17–18.

294. Strangely, this is the last extant letter by Roekmini in the archive. For some later details on Roekmini's life, see the later correspondence of Soematri, who did provide Rosita with regular reports of her sisters and her mothers' whereabouts and well-being till 1936.

295. The report was published in vol. 3, no. 4, February 1929. Roekmini's later involvement with the women's movement as member of the Vereeniging voor Vrouwenkiesrecht, and possibly Javanese women's organizations, is not referred to in the correspondence. This published report provides some evidence of her later involvement in public affairs, but also represented for her the culmination of the aims she had espoused for more than a quarter of a century.

Chapter 2

1. In fact, the *Regeerings Almanak* indicates that while European officials in the Gewestelijk Bestuur were regularly transferred and/or promoted every three years, appointments of Javanese officials lasted for years and promotions were slow. Roekmini's husband, Santoso, complained of this, having failed, as he believed, to be adequately compensated for eighteen years of service as wedono, and Kardinah's husband, possibly of similar social rank, was left in his position for fourteen years. The position of regent effectively remained a lifetime appointment, despite the fact that in the twentieth century an increasing range of criteria was imposed and family connections were no longer the determinant in making appointments. Kardinah's husband, Rekso Negoro, was regent of Tegal from 1908 to 1930, and Boesono was regent of Ngawi from 1905 to 1938.

2. Three prior extant letters by Kardinah to Rosita (17 October, 30 December 1900, and 23 August 1901), basically "thank you" letters for presents received, have not been included here but were previously published in Coté, *Letters from Kartini*. This letter and the next three, while also previously published, relate to Kardinah's marriage and mark the beginning of her adult life.

3. The three girls had stayed with the Abendanons in Batavia in August 1900.

4. This is an intimation of the impending marriage. Rather than expressing happiness, Kardinah is already alluding to how it would bring to an end their determination to work toward women's emancipation, and specifically their own further education.

5. The marriage was to her cousin, Rekso Harjono, patih of Pemalang. Kartini and Roekmini describe the tearful Kardinah in a letter of the same day (Roekmini to Rosita, 2 December 1901). In a long letter, Kartini describes the events and feelings experienced by the women following the announcement of the arranged marriage, including having ultimately to give "my blessing for sister" when asked by the raden ayu "shortly after 2nd December." She notes that Kardinah specifically asked for the date of the wedding to be brought forward—"then it will be over"—and that she was under doctor's care because of her physical reaction on hearing a marriage had been arranged. See Kartini to Rosita 29 November–2 December.

6. This cri de coeur, while possibly an exaggeration of feeling in acknowledgment of the fact that the marriage represented a retreat from her and Rosita's declared convictions, also reveals the extent to which Kardinah felt torn between traditional and personal feelings toward her parents and the commitment to the modern and public ideals the three women had discussed over many years privately.

7. See also Roekmini to Rosita, 2 December 1901.

8. Nicknamed Kleintje (little one), Kardinah (born 1 March 1881) was only one year younger than her stepsister Roekmini and three years younger than

her sister Kartini. She was an integral member of what Kartini referred to as the "cloverleaf" or "trio."

9. Kartini writes of Kardinah's husband: "He had a governess, his pronunciation of Dutch is good but he speaks less well. He is interested in music, plays almost every instrument, especially the piano, which he has learnt very well." Kardinah also inherited three stepchildren. See Kartini to Rosita, 18 February 1902.

Within a decade her husband succeeded his father as regent of Tegal, taking the title and name of Raden Mas Tumenggung Adipati Rekso Negoro. Kartini was also married to a regent, and their brother Boesono became a regent after the death of their father in 1905. The other members of the family, however, joined the "modern" generation, the kaum muda, becoming or marrying lower officials who were part of the modernized colonial administration.

10. In fact, the archive suggests that after her marriage, Kardinah did not write (perhaps did not dare to write) to Rosita (except for the brief note of 29 January that follows thanking Rosita for the wedding present) until, in 1911, she was sent a copy of Kartini's book, *Door Duisternis tot Licht*.

11. The marriage took place on 24 January 1901, soon after Lebaran, and was attended by the resident of Semarang, Piet Sijthoff, who took a very personal interest in the Jepara sisters. Kartini describes Kardinah as "a beautiful bride. She married in a *wayang* costume and looked very fine; in the evening at the reception she appeared as a fairytale princess from the thousand-and-one-nights." In the same letter Kartini describes Kardinah's journey, during which she met significant family members after the wedding: "From here [Jepara] to Tegal and Pemalang they travelled as though on a tour of honour—at each place where they stopped to visit family they were feted." Kartini comments further: "Papa-in-law thinks of her not as a human being but as a supernatural one." Kartini notes that Kardinah was admired for her Western education and was immediately asked to take responsibility for the education of her stepchildren, thus enabling her to continue part of the sisters' project. See Kartini to Rosita, 18 February 1902.

12. Kardinah wrote later in her memoir that "the communication between herself and her two sisters left in Jepara continued unbroken by means of letters. A younger brother-in-law [not named] . . . also took part in the letter-writing." See Kardinah, "The Three Sisters," 13.

13. This is the next (extant) letter Kardinah wrote to Rosita—a break of ten years. Kardinah had moved to Tegal in 1908 after her husband was promoted from patih of Pemalang to regent of Tegal.

14. Kardinah is using the phrase "Jong Javanen," which by now had specific political connotations. Her comments on education below indicate her familiarity with the emerging nationalist discourse, suggesting an intentional use of the term to denote a political stance.

15. Kardinah writes in her memoir of 1958 that she had in fact been teaching informally in Pemalang, before moving to Tegal, where "the atmosphere was still

very conservative and feudalistic as it was also in other places. In spite of all this I continued to think of and to be devoted to the ideals and aspirations of the Three Sisters and therefore constantly sought for ways whereby I could gradually carry on the work, even if it were only in and around the residence of the Patih itself. After I had been in this new situation several months, I began to teach. At first there were only my own two [step] daughters.... Then several of the older families of Pemalang sent their children to me for their education. Classes were given in writing and sewing." Kardinah, "The Three Sisters," 19–20. This can be compared to Roekmini's attempts and her frustrations with similar "conservative and feudalistic" attitudes. Roekmini to Rosita, 1 November 1911.

16. Kardinah here defines a key issue generating anticolonial sentiment among the Javanese elite: persistent exclusion from Western education and the opportunities it provided. This can also be related to the complaint expressed by Santoso regarding career prospects for this social class. See Santoso to Abendanon, November 1915.

17. This is possibly the most explicit expression of anticolonial sentiment by any of the sisters, apart from that expressed by Kartini earlier. However, guarded anticolonial feeling can also be found in Roekmini's correspondence around this time.

18. Tegal, like all north coast cities, had a significant and long-established Chinese population. The anti-Chinese sentiment expressed here also underpinned the establishment of Sarekat Islam in Solo the following year. This was ostensibly aimed at protecting the indigenous batik manufacturers, as was its predecessor, Sarekat Dagang Islamiyah.

19. Tegal was effectively halfway between Batavia and Semarang.

20. Kartini had always referred to the "cloverleaf," the trio of sisters (Roekmini, Kardinah, and herself) who would change the world of Javanese women. Kardinah is here claiming her entitlement to that legacy. Kardinah's request to administer a Kartini School would seem to have had much merit and justification. The fact it was established in Semarang, apart from this being a more important city, indicates the extent to which this was to be a European project. Soematri's husband's later involvement in that project was unrelated to his connection to the family.

21. One paal (originally expressing the distance between mileposts) was equivalent to 1,500 meters.

22. This was expressed as an English measurement.

23. The informal "Nota" drawn up by van Deventer in consultation with Abendanon and attached with a letter of 27 January 1912 on the eve of van Deventer's departure for Java notes this request for the first Kartini school to be located in Slawie under the patronage of the regent and raden ayu of Tegal. It suggests that Kardinah's request had been taken seriously and that the decision about the school's location was still open at this stage. Van Deventer to Abendanon, 27 January 1912.

24. Kardinah conveys this news as it related both to her sister and to her position as the wife of a fellow regent.

25. The new regent of Rembang, R. M. T. Iskander Abdoel Karen, writing to Abendanon on 3 August 1912 in reply to a letter congratulating him on his appointment, makes no mention of his stepbrother, Kartini's son, other than to say he would ensure that all his brothers and sisters continued with their education and "as regent [would] endeavor to tread in the path of my father in as far as I am able." R. M. T. Iskander Abdoel Karen to Abendanon, 3 August 1912, Kartini Archive, H 1200, no. 316.

26. See Roekmini to Rosita, 17 March 1913, and Soematri to Rosita, 16 July 1912. Van Deventer was in Semarang making arrangements for the establishment of the Kartini School. It was during these discussions that the decision to locate the school in Semarang was finalized.

27. Evidently van Deventer had convinced Kardinah of the appropriateness of the Semarang location for the first Kartini School. Perhaps it was in response to her disappointment that she decided to establish her own school in Tegal, which was set up more in line with the principles Soematri had also implied were more consistent with the ideas of Kartini. See Soematri to Rosita, 16 July 1912. Concurrently her sister Roekmini discussed similar plans to establish a girls' school in Jepara, "the land of Kartini." Roekmini to Rosita, 16 December 1916. All three, therefore, could be said to have held somewhat critical views about the Kartini School, although obviously pleased that the need for girls' education was being considered and that the name of Kartini was being recognized.

28. SOVIA, the Steun voor de Opleiding tot Vrouwlijke Inlandsche Artsen (study fund to support the education of female native doctors), was established by Charlotte Jacobs (van Heel, *Gedenkboek*, chap. 7). Charlotte's sister was the famous Dutch feminist Aletta Jacobs, who visited the Indies in 1911. Jacobs, *Reisbrieven uit Africa en Azië, Benevens eenige brieven uit Zweden en Noorwegen*, vol. 1 (Almelo: H. W. Hilarius, 1913). See also Roekmini to Rosita, 17 March 1913.

29. The implication is that most non-European medical officers would be employed in government and private colonial enterprises such as servicing indentured plantation labor and Indonesian members of the colonial army, rather than in private practice.

30. There is a suggestion that Kardinah had been planning to establish a school since 1911. Apart from the impetus that the establishment of the Kartini School provided, new subsidy regulations introduced in 1914 now made it possible for individuals (as distinct from organizations, typically missionary societies) to apply for subsidies to establish a school. The timing was also opportune, as the government had just begun to reorganize and coordinate facilities for more extended elementary native education and to encourage the establishment of private schools.

31. Kardinah's use of the word "us" here may be a reference to Kartini and her family or to emancipation of Javanese women, but more likely, given her earlier comments, it implies her sense of Javanese nationalism.

32. Kardinah later believes they were lost. See below, Kardinah to Rosita, 16 July 1916.

33. Since 1907 the colonial government had promoted the establishment of three-year village schools, which provided very basic elementary schooling conducted in the regional language and were largely maintained by the village. Teachers at village schools were graduates from the five-year, vernacular second-class native elementary schools to be found in larger towns. Teachers at second-class schools were graduates of first-class native elementary schools, which were found only in provincial towns and offered some Dutch-language education. Kardinah's point is that these school types did not provide practical or vocational education and were merely a pale imitation of European elementary education.

34. One was a cookbook and the other a book on batik-making. They were published in 1918 in Batavia by Albrecht and Sons in four volumes and cost four guilders. "Pupils graduating from Wisma Pranawa were given both these two books as a remembrance." Kardinah, "The Three Sisters," 23.

35. Kardinah later wrote: "They were also used in government schools. From the sale of these books, and later from government subsidy, Wisma Pranawa became quite prosperous." Kardinah, "The Three Sisters," 23.

36. Moresco was director of education.

37. Copies of the positive responses to these applications were sent to Abendanon later.

38. The fact that *all* the city's Indonesian elementary school girls applied was evidence of Kardinah's assessment of education needs (or preferences) but also suggests that her school may have been regarded as a threat to the established native education system.

39. Kardinah does not refer here to the more critical argument that her brother-in-law Sorohadikoesoemo referred to, that Javanese parents generally opposed the coeducational nature of government schools.

40. Kardinah is here indirectly criticizing the colonial assumption that private girls' schools, such as the Kartini School, should be of a "superior" kind and thus offer Dutch-language education. There is also implicitly here a dispute about Kartini's actual intention and whose school—Kardinah's or the Kartini Vereeniging's Kartini School—best represented it.

41. Abendanon became chairman of the Kartini Fonds following the death of van Deventer in 1915. The proposal was to also establish the Van Deventer School in Semarang, with funds collected in honor of the recently deceased van Deventer. Given this new initiative, the need for which she had also already recognized, Kardinah again appeals for recognition as part of the Kartini legacy. Advocating a similar institution to be supported in Tegal, she supplies

the further, practical argument about regional language, again underlining the importance of the issue of language medium in the debate about native education.

42. Abendanon recognized Kardinah's initiative in an article in the first issue of a new Dutch-language journal published by Indonesian students in the Netherlands and edited by Soewardi Soerjaningrat. "Wismo Pranowo (Het huis dat den Blik verruimt)," *Hindia Poetra* 1 (March 1916): 115–17. ("Wismo pranowo" means "the house that broadens one's horizons.")

43. Wartime had made the mail unreliable. A marginal note on the letter states, "It was received later." It is not clear whether the documents attached to the letter by her husband dated 30 March 1916 are a copy re-sent later, as they contain updated figures as well as copies of official documents approving the school subsidy dated December 1916. The letter and the documents are reproduced in the appendix to this volume.

44. This was an undated unofficial memo from the controleur of Tegal reporting the response of the director of education and religion to Kardinah's questions about the subsidy regulations.

45. It was quite common for well-to-do, high-status Javanese families to adopt poor or orphaned children or children of poorer relatives into their families.

46. It is not clear whether Kardinah means that in practice the category of girls who were admitted fitted the requirement or that, given that the school was already up and running, she was prepared to set aside her principles to ensure that subsidies would be forthcoming to keep the school going. However, on the matter of appointing a head teacher (see below), she persisted in her principles, consequently forgoing the subsidy for the time being.

47. The wife of Baron van Hogendorp, Jonkvrouwe Anna van Hogendorp (1841–1915), was the founding chairperson of the Kartini Vereeniging and a leading conservative figure in the Dutch women's movement. She had an expressed interest in the moral condition of women in the colonies. Kartini Vereeniging, *Jubileum Verslag;* Grever and Waaldijk, *Feministische Openbaarheid,* 199; M. C. Kooy-van Zeggelen, "Van Vrouwenleven 1813–1913," in *Ons Huis in Indië,* edited by Indische Commissie der Tentoonstelling "De Vrouw 1813–1913" (Batavia, 1913). The assistant resident, Jonkheer L. de Stuers, a titled member of the aristocracy, was also a colonial progressive and a supporter of the ethical policy. Subsequently resident of the Preanger region, he prepared a proposal in 1918 allowing greater autonomy for native rulers. Together with proposals for the establishment of the consultative assembly, the Volksraad, this was an indication of an accelerated preparation for eventual autonomy. These (limited) initiatives were quickly subverted by more conservative policies after World War I. Van den Doel, *De Stille Macht,* 334–42.

48. Abendanon was active on various committees of Oost en West, a key member of the Van Deventer Fund headed by van Deventer's widow, and chair of the Kartini Fonds.

49. Kardinah gives the impression here that she was defending herself against Abendanon's possible questions about the teaching of the Dutch language.

50. Kardinah wrote in 1958: "Each year during the Muslim fasting month (*Puasa*) many Javanese and Dutch teachers from normal schools and from the HIS visited the Wisma Pranawa. Afterwards they would gather in the kabupaten to discuss the teaching they had observed—some they disapproved of, but there was also much they later imitated." Among her visitors was "Mrs Dewi Sartika and her younger sister Sari Pamerat" (generally reputed to have established the first formal school for girls), who "not only studied but also taught at the school. During their stay in Tegal they were guests of the kabupaten." Kardinah, "The Three Sisters," 23.

51. Kardinah's argument here corresponds directly with that of her brother-in-law, Sosrohadikoesoemo (see his letter of 26 February 1916).

52. Copies of the official decisions dated 8 and 20 December 1916 are included in the archive.

53. There is a hint here that Abendanon, to get Kardinah the subsidy that she refused to accept, may have intervened to convince Batavia to set aside a key principle for eligibility.

54. As noted above, Abendanon's article was published in March 1916 in the new journal *Hindia Poetra*.

55. The informal advice from the director of education was that she should arrange to have her unqualified teachers sit the pupil teacher exams as soon as possible.

56. A *pasar malam* (night market) was a traditional fair, as much an entertainment as it was a *pasar* (market).

57. This is a reference to Soematri.

58. A further indirect reference to the European war.

59. Siti Soendari came to prominence as the founder and editor of the women's journal *Wanito Sworo* (Women's Voice) after being a contributor to the first Indonesian women's journal, *Poetri Hindia* (Women of the Indies), founded by Tirto Adhi Soeryo and his wife. She had moved to Tegal in June 1914, where, she reported, "there was a women's association and I was asked to give a speech." Siti Soendari to Raden Mas Soeryosoeparto (n.d.), cited in Toer, *Sang Pemula*, 99. This was at about the same time that, together with Kardinah's sister Soematri, she provided her contribution to the *Mindere Welvaart Onderzoek* on the condition of Javanese women. *Mindere Welvaart Onderzoek*, 26–38. In August 1916, she had been one of a group of Indonesians invited to contribute to the First Colonial Education Congress, arranged by Abendanon, where she gave a speech on the need for girls' education (translated by Soewardi Soerjaningrat). While in the Netherlands she had evidently met the Abendanons on a personal basis. She returned to Java soon after. Poeze, *In het Land van de Overheerser*, 112.

60. This is a curious opening. While the last extant letter is from six years earlier, Kardinah had written to the Abendanons at length concerning her school and in 1911 had expressly written to thank them for sending her a copy of this book. The break in correspondence can in part be explained by the disruption caused by World War I, but the lapse of memory would seem to reflect the seriousness and length of time of her illness. Soematri also received a copy of this edition. See Soematri to Rosita, 3 November 1923.

61. See Soematri to Rosita, 3 November 1923.

62. This letter evidently did not arrive, as it is not included in the archive.

63. In 1958, Kardinah wrote of the school's demise: "When the Wisma Pranawa had reached its eighth year, I was not very well because I had to teach every day. As there was no one willing to take over my place, the Wisma Pranawa declined until it was finally taken over by the government and made into the first School for Home Economics for Girls (elementary level) in Java. This action naturally disappointed the people, especially since I was forced to cease work there due to my poor health." Kardinah, "The Three Sisters," 24.

64. The hospital became know as the Kardinah Ziekenhuis, and the foundation stone was laid by Soematri (then living in Tegal), "who represented me as I was sick in hospital in Semarang at the time." It later became the Gewestelijk Ziekenhuis (government regional hospital). Later she also opened an "armen tehuis" (home for poor people). Kardinah, "The Three Sisters," 25.

65. Kardinah wrote in 1958: "There were two craftsmen who were well-known for their work. They worked for a Chinese. When I had given them money to pay off their debts they had incurred with their employer, they came to work at the *kabupaten*. Then I bought bars of silver from the bank, gave them to the craftsmen and had them make small bowls with lids and bowls with handles to be used for cakes; these bowls were decorated with inlay.... I would sell the finished bowls to Javanese or Dutch. As time went on there were more and more orders for silver work, especially after I had sent some of the products to fairs in several different towns." Kardinah, "The Three Sisters," 25–26.

66. Throughout the body of correspondence, one is able to gain a sense of the continued expansion and modernization of traditional crafts, an activity with which the sisters continued to be actively engaged.

67. This is the last extant letter from Kardinah. In 1930, her husband retired as regent and they moved to Salatiga. Kardinah lived to 1971. Soematri's later correspondence provides further details about Kardinah.

Chapter 3

1. Ultimately, mobility remained limited for single women in Java, and although Roekmini claims it was a "love match," circumstantial evidence suggests that she would only have found someone within the circuits of local institutions, in her case probably via the controleur and his links with the local Credit Bank administration.

2. Kartinah to Rosita, 20 January 1935.

3. Kartinah to Lien, 20 September 1909. Soematri reports that her mother spent her last years with Roekmini, her other daughter, in Salatiga.

4. Kartinah to Rosita, 10 May 1909.

5. In a remark excised from a published letter to Stella Zeehandelaar, Kartini had written of Javanese men of her class: "I despise them all, married or unmarried; there is not one for whom I have some regard, all of them I reject." Kartini to Stella Zeehandelaar, 6 November 1899.

6. This is the first letter written to Rosita by Kartinah, who was then eighteen years old. As is apparent from the following letter, Kartinah had not joined the family in their visit to the Abendanons in Batavia in 1900 but had met Rosita when the Abendanons stayed at the kabupaten. It became the practice for Rosita to send the sisters presents for Sinterklaas, and later for Lebaran. See also Soematri to Rosita, 3 December 1901.

7. Kartini adds this comment to Kartinah's letter. Presumably Kartini had arranged this set of letters by the sisters to thank Rosita.

8. Kartinah had come to know Annie Glaser when she lived in the kabupaten for some time when first appointed as teacher in Jepara.

9. In pointing to her own modest ambitions and the opposition she too would receive from her parents, Kartinah is concerned with demonstrating her credentials.

10. The Priangan, the cool mountainous region of West Java (Sunda), had become a traditional mountain retreat for colonial officials from the administrative capital, such as Abendanon.

11. The letter is written to Rosita in the role as St. Nicholas. Kartinah demonstrates here how thoroughly she understands the Dutch traditional celebration of this day, which focuses very much on children's presents supposedly delivered by Sinterklaas.

12. At nineteen, a Javanese girl of noble birth would more typically already have been married with children. Kartinah's presentation of herself as "a young girl" may well indicate an appropriation of European literary styling.

13. Possibly a reference to the two younger boys, Moeljono, aged fourteen, and Rawito, aged nine.

14. Their father, following the precedent set by his own father, ensured that both his sons and all his daughters received some Western education. Where Kartini, Roekmini, and Kardinah had to make do with informal arrangements after their elementary schooling, the younger sisters were able to benefit from the improved educational facilities available locally later, in part as the result of Abendanon's educational policies.

15. See also Soematri to Rosita, December 1902.

16. Kartinah appears to have been the first to mention that the Abendanons were leaving the Indies. It was not clear till much later that this would be a permanent departure, following Abendanon's retirement.

17. As Kartini had revealed, the sisters were obliged to learn to live in two quite separate worlds and thus to maintain strict control of their emotional lives.

18. This letter ends a significant gap of five years. Her recent involvement in the events around Budi Utomo, and the departure of Roekmini, had no doubt created for her a significant role as spokesperson for her mother and remaining family, particularly in relation to Kartono. See also Roekmini's correspondence regarding Kartono.

19. Abendanon's speech at an exposition on children's education (Tentoonstelling: Opvoeding van het Kind) in 1909, "De opvoeding van inlandsche meisjes in Ned. Indië," was republished in the first edition of the new journal *Oedajana Para Prajitna,* of which 1,000 copies were sold in the colony. Van Miert, *Bevlogenheid,* 153–63; Poeze, *In het Land van de Overheerser,* 68–69.

20. See also Roekmini to Rosita, 28 March 1909.

21. This was the Indische Vereeniging, established in 1908 by Indonesian students studying in the Netherlands, including her brother Kartono. It provided an opportunity for Indonesian students to meet and discuss regularly—often, it seems, at the Abendanons' house. Jacques had encouraged this idea and remained a major patron. In 1909, it had twenty-three members. Poeze, *In het Land van de Overheerser,* 71–75.

22. Kartinah's letters to Lien van den Berge-Kelder form a separate file in the KITLV Archive, DH 1255. Lien was the wife of the former teacher in Jepara.

23. Dr. Terburgh was the regional medical officer who had introduced radical reforms for eradicating the causes of malaria, typhoid, and cholera epidemics in Semarang. The reorganization of fishponds and the shoreline around the town of Jepara formed part of his malaria-eradication program. J. Coté, "Towards an Architecture of Association: H. F. Tillema, Semarang and the Construction of Colonial Modernity," in P. Nas, ed., *The Indonesian Town Revisited* (Singapore: LIT Verlag/ ISEAS, 2000), 328.

24. H. J. Monod de Froideville was a first lieutenant stationed at military headquarters in Semarang between 1906 and 1910.

25. Casten was assistant resident of Jepara.

26. See Soematri to Lien, 4 November 1912.

27. Blom was a teacher at the European elementary school.

28. Kartinah refers to *Hilda van Suylenburg,* the famous feminist novel that had also impressed Kartini.

29. See also Soematri's gossip about the local Eurasian community, written on the same day.

30. Guus is August Mühlenfeld. See references to him by Roekmini.

31. See Soematri to Lien, September 1911.

32. The Malay term simply means "group or community," but Kartinah may be using it in the then new, politically loaded sense as applied to the new, Western-educated progressive generation of Javanese, usually in the form *kaum muda.*

33. "Blommetjes" is a nice play on words. The reference is to the children of the schoolteacher Mr. Blom. The diminutive form of "Blom" (the little Bloms) becomes the colloquial form for "flowers," a cute description of his daughters.

34. See the parallel letter by Soematri.

35. Kartinah, like each of her sisters, was greatly impressed by the feminist novel *Hilda van Suylenburg*.

36. Evidently this refers to Rosita's responses to Roekmini's letter of 10 August 1910.

37. In 1911, Jasper was listed as a member of the Indische Vereeniging along with most other well-known retired colonial civil servants in the Netherlands as well as actively employed colonial progressives in the Indies.

38. The monthly journal was edited by a Javanese medical graduate, Boenjamin, and its Dutch subtitle meant "Journal for Progressive Javanese." The publication, which covered political and social and economic issues related to Java, appeared in five volumes until it ceased in 1910. Poeze, *In het Land van de Overheerser*, 68–69.

39. Noto Soeroto studied law in the Netherlands after graduating from the Semarang HBS in 1906. He stayed there for many years, writing on colonial politics and Javanese culture, from the perspective of his moderate Indonesian nationalist agenda, and publishing original poetry. Poeze, *In het Land van de Overheerser*, 66; Djajadiningrat-Nieuwenhuis, "Noto-Soeroto."

40. In May 1912, the Dutch feminist Aletta Jacobs describes meeting these same women, who, in contrast to the 70 children and 153 grandchildren of the sultan of Yogyakarta, were exceptionally "modern": "Not only the prince and his uncle, but also all the princesses, sister and nieces of the prince were able to speak perfect Dutch as well as several foreign languages. . . . In these young princesses I met the modern Javanese woman, girls in the style of Kartini who wanted nothing more than to educate themselves and to dedicate their education to the development of their Javanese sisters." Four of the princesses subsequently attended Jacobs's address to the Indies Women's Suffrage meeting in Yogyakarta. Jacobs, *Reisbrieven uit Afrika en Azië*, 485–86.

41. This seems to have been Raden Ambia Poerbo Soedibio, who was studying at Delft. He was a founding member of the Indische Vereeniging.

42. This was the book *Door Duisternis tot Licht*.

43. Hari Raya (the special day) is Lebaran, the day celebrating the end of the fasting month.

44. Soematri and Achmad Sosrohadikoesoemo were married on 7 March 1911. Soematri mentions her intention to celebrate Lebaran in Jepara in her letter of September 1911.

45. Kardinah is indirectly making reference to the behavior and relations of European men towards Javanese women. Similar indirect criticism of the behavior of European men toward Javanese women is also found in Kartini's correspondence. See also Soematri to Lien, 20 December 1909.

46. In Semarang, H. F. Tillema had documented mortality rates from a series of cholera epidemics in the city. The city recorded 3,163 deaths in 1910 and 1,169 in 1911, and mortality in Semarang in the first decade averaged 50–60 per 1,000. J. Coté, "Reading Kartini 1899–1999," 324.

47. Lekkerkerker was an agricultural instructor (with the rank of controleur) working with the Department of Agriculture and Industry.

48. It is not clear what Kartinah intended, although evidently it was an attempt to establish a network of progressive young women. Dutch, by implication, was the language of communication between these women, as it was for their male counterparts. Kartinah highlights the significance of the letter in linking people of like minds, unknown to each other physically. This highlights the significance of Benedict Anderson's famous definition of nation as an "imagined political community."

49. These two people cannot be identified.

50. Evidently this is the same Marietje Mühlenfeld referred to previously, who has reverted to using her maiden name.

51. This is the last extant letter from Kartinah. See the last letters from Soematri for further details on Kartinah's life.

52. See the correspondence of Roekmini's husband, Santoso, at this time.

Chapter 4

1. This is made clear in Kartini's references to her father's work, and later the history behind her husband's appointment to Rembang.

2. Soematri to Rosita, 24 November 1932.

3. Soematri to Rosita, 20 January 1935.

4. Soematri to Rosita, 18 January 1936.

5. Soematri to Rosita, 20 January 1935.

6. Roekmini's last undated letter is probably from 1921. Kardinah writes two more letters after 1917, but only in response to prompting from Rosita. Kartinah writes no letters after her marriage in 1915.

7. Soematri would have been twelve when she met Rosita during her visit to the Jepara kabupaten. This is her first extant letter. See also the letter by Kartinah written on the same occasion. The letters written by her prior to September 1904 have been previously published in Coté, *Letters from Kartini*.

8. This was Raden Mas Sosro Moeljono, then sixteen. His older brother, Kartono, studied at the Semarang HBS between 1890 and 1896, after which he went to the Netherlands. After HBS, Moeljono undertook further studies in Batavia in the Agricultural Institute.

9. While Soematri's account reads as though it was quite natural to be attending school, it was of course an exception, both for Javanese girls to be attending a European elementary school (or any school) and for Javanese boys to be attending the European secondary school. It is not clear when she commenced school. She was still attending classes in Jepara in 1905, according to Roekmini, and thereafter continued with private lessons.

10. Evidently Soematri was not aware of the impending marriage—or believed it was not her place, or the occasion, to mention it. And because she was much younger and not part of the trio who had shared their innermost desires with Rosita, this relationship was of an entirely different order.

11. There had been many references to the rear veranda in Kartini's correspondence too, indicating that it was the place around which family life was centered. See also Kartinah's letter on the same occasion.

12. This was Mr. C. J. R. Both. See also references to him in letters by Roekmini and Kartinah. In 1921, Soematri writes to thank Both for his defence of Kartini when accusations were made in the newspaper *De Locomotief* that Kartini could not possibly have written the letters, citing school records that her marks in the Dutch language were only average. In her letter to Both, she describes the attack as "an expression of jealousy" and could "definitely not be [the work of] an educated, upstanding Westerner [*Westerling*].... What a despicable person he presents himself as with his mean-spirited rooting around in old school archives for information that is totally incorrect." On a happier note, in thanking Mr Both for responding so forcefully, Soematri recalls: "How clearly I can still recall to my mind our French lessons at your house and together with this, the many other happy memories of my youth. I hardly dared suspect that you would still remember your Javanese pupils.... [T]hese memories of so much that is dear and good are what motivate us to strive to provide this also for our children."

13. The reference is to Annie Glaser, with whom she was clearly less familiar than Kartinah was. "Juffrouw" or "Miss" was (and remains) the usual Dutch term of address for a female teacher.

14. In fact, it was Kardinah who was seriously ill. In a letter of 4 August, Roekmini informs Rosita that Kardinah had been receiving specialist treatment for the previous three weeks for "something wrong internally.... [I]t is something that would have forced her to give up the possibility of realizing her dearest wish, to one day become a mother." Roekmini to Rosita, 4 August 1904; not included in this collection.

15. See Kartinah's letter of the same date.

16. As Roekmini's letters at this time make apparent, with the departure of Kartini and with Roekmini responsible for arranging woodcraft orders for Oost en West and other clients, Soematri and Kartinah took on much of the responsibility for the running of their little school.

17. This is not mentioned by Roekmini in her parallel letter of 6 November.

18. Abendanon had been one of a number of "Indies friends" featured in Abdul Rivai's Indies-focused paper *Bintang Hindia* (Star of the Indies), which had been established in 1902. Adam, *Vernacular Press*.

19. The reference is to Kartini's child, Singgih.

20. This was in fact the last letter (extant) until 1910. Because Rosita's departure more or less coincided with Kartini's death, it is apparent that Kartini

formed, or was regarded as, the main link. Only Roekmini retained an unbroken correspondence with Rosita during this period.

21. Caroline's husband was A. L. van den Berge, a teacher in Jepara for a number of years before his appointment to Padang. Soematri and Kartinah's letters to Lien van den Berge-Kelder form a separate file in the KITLV Archive, DH 1255.

22. Soematri had clearly been seriously ill, but there is no indication of the nature of her illness.

23. The book in which Reverend Moisette features is *Hilda van Suylenburg*, by Cecile Goekoop-de Jong van Beek en Donk (1896). Soematri's reaction is the same as that expressed by Kartini about the book in 1899 in letters to her pen friend Stella Zeehandelaar. Kartini also considers the impact the book might have were it translated into Javanese. See Kartini to Stella, 25 May 1899.

24. Soematri later married Raden Ngabehi—Achmad (Mad)—Sosrohadikoesoemo. See below.

25. Evidently a member of the European community in Jepara. Unlike Soematri, Kartinah, in her parallel letters to Lien, provides the complete name of the subjects of her gossip. See Kartinah to Lien, 20 September and 20 December 1909.

26. This contrast between modern-urban and traditional-rural Java is a constant theme in Soematri's correspondence.

27. See also Kartinah's account of the same vacation. Kartinah to Rosita, 20 December 1909.

28. This was with her older brother, Boesono, the regent of Ngawi.

29. See above, Roekmini's reference to Mühlenfeld (Roekmini to Rosita, 17 June 1908). He had been transferred to Boja in 1909.

30. This seems not to have transpired. Mühlenfeld is listed as controleur in Wonogiri in 1912, was on leave in 1914, and entered the Bestuursakademie for further training in 1916 before embarking on a successful career. He continued to be heavily involved in Javanese cultural affairs.

31. The "Soos" was typically the center of local colonial urban society. It was the location where formal and informal community festivities took place and thus represented a bulwark for European colonial communal life and culture. Soematri's gossip here provides some indication of the pettiness of such communities.

32. While providing good insight into the nature of the parochial colonial community, in presenting herself to her friend Lien, she herself reflects the language and attitudes of the same community.

33. This is controleur A. Rzoux Kühr (1908–10), who replaced the similarly behaved Mühlenfeld. Soematri is presumably making reference to the behavior of single European men toward young Javanese women. See also Kartinah to Lien, 20 October 1911.

34. Soematri provides an ironic reflection of colonial attitudes of European solidarity and superiority vis-à-vis the "natives."

35. See also Kartinah to Rosita, 20 September 1909.

36. The news regarding this child bride (and mothers) is passed on without comment but can be assumed to imply the critical views in previous discussions between the two women. Soematri makes an issue of child marriage in her later report to the Mindere Welvaart Onderzoek (see below).

37. All the sisters commend the Abendanons for the attempts they made to assist their brother despite his apparent waywardness. After Kartini's highly optimistic reference to Kartono's progress in July 1903, ongoing reports on Kartono in Roekmini's correspondence from 1904 recount the problems Kartono was experiencing both personally and in relation to his studies.

38. It is not clear why the fact that Kardinah did not write to Rosita after her marriage was self-evident to Soematri.

39. Perhaps because of her own experience of extended hospitalization, Kardinah had evidently developed further the interest in medical advances that she discussed with Kartini and Roekmini prior to her marriage. Later she established a hospital.

40. The publication of *Door Duisternis tot Licht* was intended to raise funds for the support of girls' education. Presumably Roekmini had already told Soematri about this.

41. Jasper was to formulate his ideas in a report that led to the establishment of technical schools. See also Roekmini's association with Jasper in relation to the annual Surabaya craft exhibition.

42. Like her sister Roekmini, from whom she took over supervision of the Jepara woodwork orders, Soematri was involved in and aware of the state of the local wood and handicraft industry. The sisters similarly expressed their antagonism toward Chinese entrepreneurs, reflecting a wider concern that eventually found expression around this time in the formation of Sarekat Islam and its predecessor, Sarekat Dagang Islam, which were aimed initially at protecting the traditional industry against Chinese entrepreneurs and resisting Chinese exploitation.

43. Soematri is alluding to the dramatic events surrounding the arranged marriages of Kardinah and Kartini to emphasize the difference in her situation.

44. Any reference to "the Indies" at this time is ambiguous. However, here it can be taken to indicate the ideals defined by the Javanese organization Budi Utomo, which Soematri had joined in 1909 (see Roekmini to Rosita, 17 June 1908).

45. There is no reference to Achmad Sosrohadikoesoemo in Poeze's account of Indonesian students studying in the Netherlands. Poeze, *In het Land van de Overheerser*.

46. Soematri is indicating that the prejudice still common in Europe at the time against "bluestockings" was also developing in Java as more Javanese women were undertaking Western-style education.

47. A *jaksa* was the chief law officer in the Javanese regency administration.

48. The term "printah aloes" (gentle commands) had become symbolic of the "ethical policy." It could be found in colonial directives of the day reminding colonial officials to exercise their authority through more indirect hints and suggestions, rather than commands. The fact that this usually amounted to the same thing—or at least was intended to produce the same result—ensured that "printah aloes" became an ironic term. Kartini had made reference to similar criticisms by her father and brother. Roekmini's husband, Santoso, also criticized the colonial civil service. As a result of the ethical policy, a number of new departments were established directly or indirectly related to the promotion of indigenous welfare.

49. Soematri uses the then fashionable English term "boy."

50. See also the correspondence of Roekmini at this time.

51. The reference is to J. E. Stokvis, a moderate socialist and progressive and a supporter of the ethical policy and of moderate Javanese nationalism. He was editor of the influential colonial daily *De Locomotief* from 1910 to 1917.

52. Soematri's initial excitement about living in the city soon fades, as she complains about the noise and pace of the urban life.

53. In Poeze's account of Indonesian students studying in the Netherlands, a R. M. A. Soorjopoetro is listed as member of the Indische Vereeniging and active in cultural activities in the Netherlands. Poeze, *In het Land van de Overheerser,* 109. There is no reference to Soegiarto.

54. Henri van Kol, a social democrat and leading critic of colonial policy, rejected the views of the emerging radical Indies Party, the Eurasian political movement of Douwes Dekker, and later radical Indonesian nationalist demands for autonomy. He was nevertheless to the left of the colonial establishment, supportive of progressive colonial reform and shown here to be an attractive figure for a young Javanese generation demanding such reform.

55. This was Governor General A. W. F. Idenburg (1909–16), appointee of the Dutch religious party, the Anti-Revolutionaire Partij, which introduced the so-called ethical policy in 1901. The policy referred to here was part of the broader restructuring of the administration to enable the appointment of indigenous officers to staff the expanded, archipelago-wide administration, and simultaneously to limit the expansion in costs. See also Santoso's criticism of aspects of the restructure. Santoso to Abendanon, 8 November 1915.

56. Achmad Sosrohadikoesoemo was a prominent member of the native civil servants' association Mangoenhardjo, which was preoccupied with the question of equity between European and native officers doing the same work during this period of restructuring.

57. This is a telling description in which Soematri voices her criticism of the impact of modernity. Not only does she describe village women as wearing the less expensive *loerik* cloth (*kain*) rather than the more expensive (especially if hand-printed) and more intricately patterned batik, but they are also crudely dressed, with the material probably hoisted, rather than cut, to their knees.

This can be contrasted with the traditional Javanese female etiquette of wearing tightly fitting batik kain intended to restrict movement at the ankle and requiring a woman of social position to take short and demure steps.

58. This and the later letter to Nellie van Kol are held at the archive of the International Institute for Women's History (IIAV), Amsterdam, Nellie van Kol Archive.

59. Soematri would have first heard of Nellie van Kol (Jacoba Porreij) from Kartini and presumably had read some of her writings. As she reports to Rosita, she had just met her husband, Henri.

60. Kartini wrote numerous letters to Nellie van Kol after meeting her husband, Henri, in 1902. Until 1900 she had been editor of the women's journal *De Vrouw*, but thereafter became involved in spiritualism and the movement for "pure living"—vegetarianism and sexual reform. She withdrew from the socialist movement and joined the Salvation Army. Nellie appeared to have introduced Kartini to several of these interests. She continued writing children's stories and preparing collections of myths and legends suitable for children, for which she had requested contributions from Kartini and Roekmini. *Biografisch Woordenboek*, s.v. "Porreij, Jacoba Maria Petronella."

61. Sosrohadikoesoemo was one of the first Javanese to have been successfully placed in what had been an exclusively European-staffed area of the colonial administration. The "problem" of suitably educated indigenous applicants and the possibility of integrating Western-educated native civil servants into the European division of the colonial civil service had been under discussion for some time but had been regularly undermined by entrenched conservative attitudes among the rank-and-file European (and particularly Eurasian) civil servants.

62. Lily was Nellie's daughter. It has not been possible to identify the article referred to.

63. Soematri and Achmad were married in March of that year.

64. The wedding formalities that would traditionally take place are outlined in descriptions of Kardinah's and Kartini's weddings by Kartini and Roekmini respectively.

65. Soematri implies that, as was increasingly common among the growing community of Western-educated young men, Achmad had been sent to live in the large town (in this case Semarang) in order to undertake a complete European elementary and secondary education. Such students also underwent an informal cultural education in a Dutch household. This arrangement was formalized in Batavia, as described in Roekmini to Rosita, 10 August 1910.

66. The address contains a double term of address for her husband: De Heer (Dutch) and Raden (Javanese), indicating Achmad's privileged (or novel and ambiguous) position as a Javanese in the colonial service. He was in fact one of only three Indonesians appointed to the taxation office, formally an exclusively European branch of the colonial civil service. Reflecting on this appointment,

Dr. Hazeu, the advisor for native affairs, wrote in 1909 that this did not represent a policy change, but rather a response to the embarrassing question of where to place an "out-of-the-ordinary Inlander." He continued: "The more intelligent inlanders—and not least those involved—have understood this and one can hardly overestimate the unfortunate impression that has been created by all this.... [A feeling of mistrust regarding the intentions of the government has arisen] in the hearts of the young men, leaders of the new generation of European educated and well-developed inlanders who through diligence and perseverance have worked themselves up to the level of development of the average European official." Cited in van den Doel, *De Stille Macht,* 192–93.

67. Although the letter of 14 July 1911 includes Achmad's name, it is obviously Soematri who wrote it and added his name to it.

68. Achmad, who had not met the former senior colonial official, writes in an awkward, semiformal (colonial office) style, unlike his wife, who was evidently much more experienced in writing social letters in Dutch.

69. Writing a month earlier, Roekmini makes the same request to Rosita to encourage Kartono to answer her letters. It appears that the mothers (Raden Ayu Moeryam and Ibu Ngasarih) moved between their children, although it remains unclear whether separately or together.

70. The tone of Achmad's request suggests a combination of deference to the former colonial official, a haughtiness reflecting his own social position and his being the male head of household (speaking on behalf of Soematri on a family matter), and a certain disparagement of his errant brother-in-law.

71. Roekmini uses the term "Jong Java" in 1908 as synonymous with the group who established Budi Utomo. Sosrohadikoesoemo also uses uppercase "J," indicating a specific reference to the Young Javanese as a movement rather than a generic reference to younger Javanese; he may here also be referring to Budi Utomo. The association bearing the name was formally established in 1918.

72. Soematri is expressing the continued optimism of her social class in the cooperation and support that could be achieved from association. While Abendanon never reached the political heights of policy making occupied by the recognized promoters of the ethical policy, such as Conrad van Deventer and Henri van Kol, it is evident that after his return to the Netherlands, he worked tirelessly to promote an associationist perspective, particularly through his work on education with Indonesians studying in the Netherlands.

73. Nellie Stokvis-Cohen Stuart, a doctor in Semarang, was the daughter of Abendanon's sister.

74. The reference is to Kartini's husband, R. M. A Djojo Adiningrat, who had been widowed again after remarrying. See also Kardinah to Rosita, 24 May 1912.

75. See also Roekmini to Rosita, 25 December 1912.

76. This was van Deventer's visit to establish the Kartini school in Semarang. See also Kardinah to Rosita, 25 December 1912. It appears that Roekmini did

not meet van Deventer or become involved in a discussion about the proposed school, although he did send her (together with the other sisters) a copy of his article about Kartini. See Roekmini to Rosita, 17 March 1913.

77. Soematri is the only one of the sisters who is expressly critical of the Kartini School proposal, although Kardinah is implicitly critical in her description of her own school. Soematri's husband, although on the Kartini School committee, also expresses his reservations (see below).

78. The Dutch proverb is used to describe those who cannot bear others being happier than themselves or benefitting from something along with them.

79. In contrast, her younger brother, like her husband, was in total support. Moeljono, who was assistant wedono in Madiun, wrote that he would do everything in his power to advance the cause: "As soon as the preliminary regulations have been clarified could you please inform me so that I can promote the idea amongst my colleagues and compatriots. I have even been so bold as to mention your plans recently at a meeting of colonial officials and they received at lot of support." Moeljono to Abendanon, 28 July 1911.

80. That was Kardinah, who was seven years older than she and married in January 1902.

81. The reference is to Lien's child, Jan. The name she uses was a typical Dutch affectionate diminutive form of the name.

82. Soematri had evidently forgotten that she had written about this a year previously in a letter of September 1911.

83. J. C. Donkers was a junior teacher at the Jepara European elementary school between 1904 and 1907.

84. Roekmini had been similarly gladdened by a letter from Kartono earlier that year. See Roekmini to Rosita, 1 February 1912.

85. Regarding the involvement of the sisters in the exhibition De Vrouw, see also Roekmini to Rosita, 17 March 1913. Nellie van Kol was involved in the organization of the exhibition, but it was Hilda de Booy-Boissevain who approached the sisters for contributions.

86. There was evidently a resolution of the major reservation that Soematri seems to have had about the Kartini School. Van Deventer's draft plan for the school, outlined in a *Nota* that he sent to Abendanon, stated: "In the first place it is the daughters of the higher officials who must be qualified themselves for the important task that awaits them." However, it is evident from Kardinah's discussion of her own school that the impression that the Kartini School was a "superior establishment" remained. Van Deventer to Abendanon, 27 January 1912.

87. The comment reveals the major rift developing within the Javanese nationalist movement. Apart from Kardinah, the other sisters emphasize they had married "self-made men." The issue is particularly pertinent in the case of Roekmini, who could be seen to have had an unconditional claim to high priyayi status, if not aristocratic descent, given her mother's and her father's ancestry.

88. Soematri is making reference to Nellie's evangelicalism, as evidently she had broached the question of religion in her reply.

89. Kardinah describes in a memoir of 1958 that she and her two older sisters received traditional Qu'ranic instruction, but it is not clear if this was continued for the younger sisters. Kartini avoids any reference to her own religious instruction, as does Roekmini.

90. This nineteenth-century Dutch poet was also often quoted by Kartini and her other sisters.

91. Soematri, as her previous letters indicate, is obviously better informed about the school than she is prepared to admit to Nellie van Kol. Although Nellie would by this time have been planning the exhibition De Vrouw, this appears not to have been mentioned in her correspondence.

92. Soematri here reflects a more general outcome of the increased mobility at this time: the greater self-awareness due to encountering other Indonesian ethnic groups—here the Betawi, the natives of Batavia—which, at the same time, continued to strengthen a sense of her own (Javanese) nationalism.

93. Soematri recognizes here that the term "priyayi," originally referring to aristocratic lineage, was taking on a modern meaning, referring to those with Western education and colonial positions.

94. The original text and spelling have been retained here. The advice is: "If you don't behave like that the Betawi people won't respect you."

95. As with her earlier sharp criticism of Semarang's residents, here Soematri gives a strongly critical picture of emerging Javanese modernity. The criticism, however, appears specifically directed at the superficial imitation of European lifestyles, rather than Javanese progressivism, which she prides herself in representing.

96. Adriani was in West Java between the end of 1911 and November 1913 before returning to the Netherlands until 1920 for health reasons. Before leaving, he arranged the publication of his major ethnographic work, the third volume of *De Bare'e sprekende Toradjas van Midden-Celebes* [The Bare'e-Speaking Toradja of Central Celebes], which appeared in 1914. The first two volumes, largely written by his missionary colleague Albert Kruyt, appeared in 1912. Published by the government, this was the first major work of modern ethnographic and linguistic research on the eastern archipelago. It significantly stimulated the development of colonial ethnographic research.

97. This is her youngest brother (b. 1892). The Semarang-Cheribon line was a major route for the export of sugar, linking twenty-eight sugar factories to the Semarang port. The railway line was being updated at this time. Krisprantono et al., "The Influence of Economic Development on the Planning and Architecture of Semarang," prepared for Soegijapranata Catholic University (typeset, n.d.).

98. Hazeu was the director of education.

99. This was another initiative of Governor General Idenburg. See above, Soematri to Rosita, 11 November 1910.

100. This is Soematri's response to the Welfare Commission's enquiry into the position of Javanese women. It was published in their report, *Verheffing van de Inlandsche Vrouw* (Raising the Position of the Native Woman), as one of nine papers by Javanese women, including Dewi Sartika and Siti Soendari. The tone and style of Soematri's published submission indicates that it was provided in the form of a letter; the report's editors note only that reference to the addressee was omitted from the original. The letter addresses a specific question posed by the Mindere Welvaart Onderzoek commission, vocational training for women, but covers a number of its other questions as well, particularly regarding the effects of polygamy and child marriage.

101. This was one of the formal questions posed by the Commission.

102. Soematri had reflected this sentiment in an earlier letter to Rosita. There is no indication that Soematri "worked" or sought to do so, and her statement perhaps consciously incorporates an option for "modern" women. The statement, suggesting that women might be financially independent, appears therefore more dramatic than it was. Later she argued that her generation was not yet able to do so, but that the work it undertook made it possible for her daughter's generation to do so.

103. Soematri herself was the child of Sosroningrat's *selir*, who, however, was a significant person in her own right, being a daughter of a prominent Jepara *kiyayi*. It is apparent from the correspondence, however, that no distinction was made between the daughters of the raden ayu (Roekmini and Kartinah) and those of the selir (Kartini, Kardinah, and Soematri). Bouman, a Kartini researcher, writes in 1961, quoting Mrs. Mien Immink, a friend of the family from Mayong days: "The relationship [between the two mothers] was very good. The Raden Ayu ruled in the main building and the secondary wife in the [outside] kitchen. If the children wanted something nice to eat the Raden Ayu would direct them to the kitchen, that is to say, to the secondary wife. While out visiting in Mayong . . . the Raden and the Raden Ayu would sit on chairs and the secondary wife on a mat on the front veranda. Kartini would then play with the Immink girls." Bouman to Nieuwenhuys, 23/10/1961, KITLV Archive. H 897, no. 20.

104. Like the letters of Santoso and Rekso Negoro, those of Sosrohadikoesoemo, directed to Jacques Abendanon, remain formal and have noticeable traces of an official colonial bureaucratic style.

105. F. W. P. Nittel was appointed head of the Pandhuisdienst in 1915.

106. A tradition had developed over time for Javanese to be taken on as unpaid apprentices, usually as copyists, in colonial regional offices. Here Achmad seems to use the term loosely to mean "trainee."

107. J. J. B. Ostmeier was appointed technical instructor in 1907.

108. Like Santoso, Achmad here sets out the key cause of friction and ill feeling within the ranks of the Javanese colonial service: the refusal, despite some official government initiatives, to accept Western-educated Javanese into the mainstream colonial administration, and, in consequence, the disparity in

salaries. Both conditions made it plain that they were being discriminated against on racial grounds, making this new middle class, despite its closeness to the colonial administration, a major source of articulate nationalist feelings.

109. These were Javanese leaders of the Indische Partij, Soewardi Soerjaningrat and Tjipto Mangoenkoesoemo, who, together with E. F. E. Douwes Dekker (D.D.), were exiled to the Netherlands after the banning of their party. The Indische Partij, the first political party in Indonesia, had called for Indies autonomy. As later correspondence indicates, Achmad was a virulent opponent of Indo-European and radical (nationalist or Marxist) policies.

110. This criticism represents a generalization reflecting his own work situation and is also reminiscent of Soematri's criticism of private modern Javanese families. Apart from the professional irritation experienced by his class, this also indicates the deep divisions within the emerging nationalist movement: between conservative nationalists, intent on achieving equality with European colleagues and modernization of Javanese society to a level comparable with Europeans, and radical nationalists, demanding political emancipation.

111. Social Democrat Labor Party.

112. As made clear in a previous letter by Soematri, Achmad had met and presumably discussed his position with van Kol. Tichelman notes the enmity between the local Semarang-based Social Democrat party and van Kol, the Dutch parliamentary leader of the Social Democrats. F. Tichelman, *Socialisme in Indonesië* (Dordrecht: Foris, 1985), 114–15.

113. The English proverb given in this translation has a harsher connotation than the Dutch one Achmad uses, which translates literally as "You can't break steel with your hands," suggesting that since Kartono has made up his mind there will be no changing it—not, as the English proverb might suggest, that Kartono was a good-for-nothing and could not be reformed.

114. See Roekmini to Rosita Abdendanon-Mandri, 17 March 1913.

115. The reference is to her brother Kartono.

116. Sosrohadikoesoemo was appointed to the position of technical instructor at the Semarang branch of the department in May of that year.

117. Freemasonry provided an important platform for colonial progressives and Western-educated Javanese intellectuals to exchange ideas. T. Stevens, *Vrijmetselarij en samenleving in Nederlands-Indië en Indonesië, 1764–1962* (Hilversum: Verloren, 1994).

118. Abendanon, who had advocated girls' schools since 1900, published articles on girls' education in 1909, 1911, 1913, 1914, and 1916. He reiterated these arguments in a paper presented on this subject at the First Colonial Education Conference in August 1916. Achmad is clearly here responding to Abendanon's views on the subject. Poeze, *In het Land van de Overheerser*, 111–13; J. H. Abendanon, *Prae-adviezen van het Eerste Koloniaal Onderwijscongress: te houden te 's-Gravenhage op 28, 29 en 30 Augustus 1916* ('s-Gravenhage: Korthuis, 1916): 292–300; see also Kartinah to Rosita, 10 May 1909.

119. The headquarters of the ISDV (Indische Sociaal-Democratische Vereeniging; Indies Social Democratic Party) was in Semarang. The party was actively attempting to recruit from the Western-educated Javanese elite as well as within the Semarang branch of the Indonesian nationalist association Sarekat Islam. Its strong emphasis on Marxist doctrine alienated moderate progressives, both European and Javanese. At the time, the editor of *De Locomotief,* J. E. Stokvis (with whom Achmad and Soematri were on personal terms), was writing strident articles against Henk Sneevliet, leader of the ISDV. Mühlenfeld, another "progressive socialist" close to the family, was also an anti-Marxist. Both colonial progressives argued that the ISDV was more concerned with Marxism than with the real interests of the Javanese.

120. Achmad is touching on a major argument dividing moderate and more radical nationalists at the time. Briefly, advocates of more Dutch education could be reckoned among the "associationists," those who counted on cooperative relations with progressive colonial authorities to achieve increasing autonomy, while more radical voices were demanding autonomy—but not yet necessarily independence—directly. After 1913, the declaration of the Indische Partij for autonomy dramatically raised the temperature of such debates but also introduced further complications: the apparent increased influence and need to take account of Marxist and socialist ideas; the competition between Eurasians and indigenous nationalists for control of the autonomy movement; and the competition between those advocating Javanese nationalism and those advocating Indonesian nationalism.

121. Achmad seems quite ready to use this derogatory term applied to Eurasians, whose political party, Insulinde (established in 1907), was actively claiming political and social rights in protecting the colonially born, largely mixed-race population against growing competition from both migrant Europeans and Western-educated Indonesians. U. Bosma, *Karel Zaalberg: Journalist en strijder voor de Indo* (Leiden: KITLV, 1997).

122. Dr. Dirk J. A. Westerveld, teacher of German at the Semarang HBS from 1904 to 1924, was an active member of the socialist Social Democratic Workers Party (SDAP). He had been active on the Semarang municipal council in improving urban housing and promoting sanitation reform and education. Coté, "Towards an Architecture of Association." Westerveld's views on language echoed those of Soewardi Soerjaningrat, former co-leader of the Indische Partij, of whom Achmad was also critical, in a paper to the First Colonial Education Congress later in 1916. This position—the primacy of the vernacular language medium—became dominant in nationalist discourse only later.

123. Sosrohadikoesoemo and Westerveld were both members of the Semarang Municipal Council. Sosrohadikoesoemo seems to have regarded Westerveld as an advocate of Eurasian political goals; his role as municipal councillor would seem to confirm this, but he is not mentioned in this role in Bosma's account of early-twentieth-century politics. Bosma, *Karel Zaalberg.* Groeneboer

describes Westerveld as the most "extreme spokesman" of the "native language medium" cause (K. Groeneboer, *Weg tot het Westen: Het Nederlands voor Indië 1600–1950* [Leiden: KITLV, 1993], 321) but notes that, at a conference organized in Semarang in preparation for the 1916 First Colonial Education Congress, thirteen leading Javanese and many moderate nationalist Javanese organizations declared themselves in favor of extending Dutch-language education on the same grounds as Sosrohadikoesoemo (329). That Kardinah insisted on the Javanese language medium may have been determined by the fact that she was concerned with women's education, while the "real debate" was about male education.

124. Raden Kamil, the inspector of native education, organized the meeting on the language issue in Semarang, which concluded in support of Dutch-language education. See Roekmini to Rosita, 28 March 1909.

125. The above-mentioned volume of the *Mindere Welvaart Onderzoek* also made the point that the development of girls' schools was almost entirely due to private endeavor, largely European initiated, though the schools were entirely staffed by Javanese. According to that report, in 1912 only 1 Indonesian girl was attending HBS, 635 were enrolled in public European elementary schools, 62 in private European elementary schools, 881 in public native elementary schools, and 5,745 in private native elementary schools. Girls constituted only about 6 percent of enrollments in three-year village schools. *Mindere Welvaart Onderzoek*, 1914, 39.

126. One key issue was the colonial insistence that government schools be coeducational. Although Abendanon argued against this at the Eerste Kolonial-Onderwijscongres, the persistence of this principle, seen by Dutch pedagogues as "progressive," can be ascribed to both the strength of Dutch pedagogical principles within the colonial education bureaucracy and, possibly, the assumption that this arrangement would help undermine "backwards" Islamic traditions. Kardinah specifically criticized it.

127. While Sosrohadikoesoemo was an active member of the Kartini School Committee, his target in this matter clearly remains the colonial government.

128. Sosrohadikoesoemo here introduces a very contemporary argument into what is effectively, as he admits, a rather conservative and traditionalist-sounding position.

129. This outline of Sosrohadikoesoemo's position—presumably essentially the argument of his speech referred to in his previous letter—can be compared with that of his sister-in-law, Kardinah, who expressed an almost identical position.

130. This issue, as Sosrohadikoesoemo would have known, was debated at a meeting of the Indische Vereeniging and reported in *Voordrachten en Mededeelingen* 3, no. 2 (1914): 56–73. In this letter Sosrohadikoesoemo sets out the core nationalist position that lay at the heart of the education debate, both in Java and among Indonesian students in the Netherlands. These issues had also been discussed at length by the Indische Vereeniging. Abendanon (as well as

Soewardi Soerjaningrat and Sosrokartono, but not all Indonesian speakers) argued against mixed marriage in principle, while Sosrohadikoesoemo's more tolerant position reflected that of Ratu Langi. *Voordrachten en Mededeelingen* 3, no. 2 (1914): 56–73; Poeze, *In het Land van de Overheerser,* 105–6. Kartini had also been accused of aiming for a European husband.

131. Mangoenhardjo, of which Sosrohadikoesoemo was a leading member, was a Semarang-based organization aimed at promoting the welfare and conditions of young Javanese colonial officials. It was closely allied to Budi Utomo. Its published minutes for 1912–14 include reports on the provision of native education, girls' education, study in the Netherlands, specific work conditions for Javanese officials, and occasionally political questions. See *"Mangoenhardjo": Vereeniging van Inlandsche Ambtenaren te Semarang,* 1913, 1915.

132. Atmodirono was an architect employed in the Public Works Department and, like Sosrohadikoesoemo, a Javanese member of the Semarang Municipal Council and a member of the Kartini Vereeniging committee in Semarang. He was president of Mangoenhardjo, the Javanese civil servant association.

133. This congress possibly represented the climax in the development of the nationalist movement of this era. Indonesian involvement in the defense of the Indies against a possible attack during World War I was seen by moderate nationalists, particularly Budi Utomo, as a means of demanding political participation. The issue was carefully cultivated by progressive colonial authorities as a means of strengthening an associationist orientation among moderate Indonesian intellectuals. The 31 August conference in Batavia brought together representatives of all the nationalist groups (Budi Utomo, Sarekat Islam, Regentenbond, Insulinde), produced a resolution supporting Dutch interests in return for greater political rights, and elected a representative deputation to present its demands to the Dutch Crown and parliament. In Semarang, where Sosrohadikoesoemo spoke, the meeting attracted 3,000 people and, under the influence of the more radical local Sarekat Islam and ISDV branches, voted "anti-Indië Weerbaar." Other, more radical Indonesian nationalists such as Soewardi Soerjaningrat similarly refused to support Dutch interests. Tichelman, *Socialisme in Indonesië,* 21–24; Poeze, *In het Land van de Overheerser,* 112–16.

134. Henk Sneevliet, a Dutch unionist, arrived in Semarang in 1913 and founded the Indisch Sociaal-Democratische Vereeniging, the forerunner of the Indonesian Communist Party (PKI). He also founded the first Indonesian labor union in Semarang. Asser Baars arrived in Surabaya in 1915 and taught at the HBS until he was fired for his views. Both men were eventually deported back to the Netherlands because of their radical Marxist views and political agitation. Through the ISDV, originally European in membership but gradually attracting radical Indonesian and Eurasian nationalists, they were able to exercise significant influence in both the Indonesian Sarekat Islam and the Eurasian association Insulinde. Tichelman, *Socialisme in Indonesië.* They and

their supporters were thus at the opposite pole from the Kartini sisters and their colonial associates.

135. The Sarekat Islam president was Raden Haji Oemar Said Tjokroaminoto. In April 1916, the SI and ISDV in Semarang organized a large public meeting to address public housing needs. By the time of its second congress in 1917, the SI was adopting increasingly more radical language, and the following year it appointed ISDV members to its local branch. In 1921, however, Tjokroaminoto rejected radical Marxist influence by forcing a split between SI and the PKI. Tichelman, *Socialisme in Indonesië*, 381–86.

136. Soematri is apparently reflecting her husband's active political opposition to the influence of the declared Marxist leaders and founders of the ISDV, who had succeeded in radicalizing the local Sarekat Islam branch and more generally were attempting to influence the attitude of Indonesian intellectuals. A Colonial Secret Intelligence report in 1917 concluded, from consultations with Sosrohadikoesoemo and like-minded Javanese intellectuals, that in their view "The revolutionary socialist would never gain an influence on Javanese." Tichelman, *Socialisme in Indonesië*, 632–33.

137. A sash or shawl worn by Javanese women and traditionally used to carry infants but also worn as a decorative item with formal attire.

138. Soematri is reiterating a feminist/nationalist position against continuing colonial opposition and, no doubt, in advance of the majority of her male compatriots.

139. It has not been possible to identify this person.

140. Dr. Nellie Stokvis-Cohen Stuart headed the Vereeniging tot Bevordering der Inlandsche Ziekenverpleging (Organization for the Promotion of Native Nursing), established in Semarang.

141. Hazeu was director of education. His responsibility also included the care and supervision of the further education of children of the Indonesian elite. See also Roekmini to Rosita and Mr. Abendanon, 10 August 1910.

142. After the war, heated debate surrounded the formation of political groupings within the Volksraad, the colonial consultative assembly. Inside the assembly, new demands for political autonomy expressed by formerly moderate leaders such as Tjipto Mangoenkoesoemo and Tjokroaminoto were resisted by increasingly reactionary Eurasian and European members and by the colonial and Dutch governments. The earlier generation of associationists became increasingly sidelined. Van den Doel, *De Stille Macht*, 350–57. Outside the Volksraad, more strident nationalist demands were being made. Soematri appears to be excusing "these excesses" by her compatriots in the light of this Dutch reaction.

143. After World War I, the number of Indonesian students coming to the Netherlands increased with the increasing availability of scholarships. In 1921, seventy-two students arrived, forty-eight of whom were Javanese.

144. Jan Ligthart (1859–1916) was an influential progressive educationist and socialist. Soewardi Soerjaningrat, who later founded of the equally progressive

Taman Siswa education system in Yogyakarta, studied Ligthart's methods while in the Netherlands. Ligthart emphasized the educative importance of parents and teachers working together. N. Bakker, *Kind en Karakter: Nederlandse pedagogen over opvoeding in het gezin 1845–1925* (Amsterdam: Het Spinhuis, 1995): 79–80.

145. See Roekmini's correspondence with Rosita Abendanon.

146. See above.

147. Soematri is evidently referring to the radicalization of Sarekat Islam. In 1919, it was accused of harbouring a secret radical wing, Afdeeling B, that was instigating antigovernment activities. Semarang was the center of much of this radicalism, both in the ideas of its local branch, which was increasingly influential across the SI, and in the branch's apparent involvement in union strike action and mass movements such as riots by Javanese against Chinese businesses in Kudus in 1918.

148. Neither Roekmini's stepson nor the two Javanese students named by Soematri are referred to in Poeze's extensive account of Indonesian students studying in the Netherlands. Poeze, *In het Land van de Overheerser*.

149. As Kartini's letters attest, Mrs. Ovink-Soer had been a major influence on Kartini, Roekmini, and Kardinah, but especially Kartini, when, as wife of the assistant resident of Jepara between 1896 and 1899, she had regularly had the young women in her home and effectively provided them with an extended education in cooking, painting. It is not likely that Soematri experienced this personally.

150. This was the 1923 edition of the book. A deluxe edition was also sent to the influential Prince Mangkunegara VII, the leading figure in the movement for the reawakening of Javanese culture supported by numerous colonial progressive figures who attended the annual cultural congresses held between 1918 and 1923. The prince wrote to Abendanon in June thanking him for the book and its "gentle hints for social advancement presented by this worthy lady." Like Soematri, Mangkunegara was concerned about some of the "excesses" that resulted from such changes, but he concluded: "While at the moment we are living through the earliest stages of development and given that such excesses are usually to be found in just that stage, we should not allow ourselves to be overly concerned by them." Mangkunegara to Abendanon, 23 July 1923, KITLV Archive, H 1200, no. 248.

151. The allusion is to Jules Verne's famous book *Around the World in 80 Days*. Verne and Conan Doyle were very popular in the Indies at this time.

152. This can be taken as a reference to those Javanese who still upheld the notion and prospect of "association," the possibility of gradual development with the support and cooperation of Dutch and colonial progressives and progressive colonial policies.

153. The allusion here is to the spread of communism. On his return to Java, Kartono (who noticeably is not mentioned in Soematri's later letters) was also accused of being a communist.

154. Soematri uses an abbreviation of Soearto's name throughout.

155. The last extant dated letter from Roekmini is from 1921. In 1931, Roekmini attended the All-Asian Women's Conference in Lahore as representative of the Indonesian Women's Congress. Blackburn, "Political Relations among Women," 184. It is remarkable that no extant correspondence mentions this or Roekmini's broader involvement in the women's movement. That this silence might suggest an ideological break with Rosita or Dutch progressives would seem unlikely given the tone and content of the last extant letter.

156. That is, Ngasirah, also Kartini's mother,

157. That is the former raden ayu, Moerjam, the mother of Roekmini, Kartinah, and the oldest sister, Soelastri. She is here referred to respectfully as (H)Ibu. Soelastri (1877–?) receives very little mention throughout the correspondence as she had married and left home in the 1890s and, like Ngasirah's older sons, Slamet (1873–?) and Boesono (1874–?), played no role in the story, although Boesono appears to have been somewhat involved in colonial reforms as regent and was not totally unimpressed by his sisters' efforts.

158. Abendanon died in 1925.

159. Kartini reported on that meeting in a letter of 17 April 1904.

160. If these letters were written, they appear not to have survived, as they are not included in the archive.

161. There is no indication who this person may be.

162. This summary of the contemporary situation matches Ricklefs's concise summary of the period: "After 1930, there is no dispute about the decline in welfare. Education produced some able and loyal officials but it also produced a tiny dissatisfied elite who led the anti-colonial movements. M. Ricklefs, *A History of Modern Indonesia since 1300*, 2nd ed. (Basingstoke: Macmillan, 1993), 152.

163. That visit in August 1900 is described at length in a letter by Kartini to Rosita, 8 August 1901. Coté, *Letters from Kartini*, 1–20.

164. After the death of their father in 1905, Sosro Boesono was appointed regent of Ngawi. While he was traditional in his views, Kartini and Roekmini had noted his sympathy for their cause. As the older brother of Kartono and a regent, he must have felt disappointed with his wayward brother.

165. It is notable that in the roll call of family members Soematri makes no mention of Kartono, who had returned to Java in 1925 and at this time was well established in Bandung, with a national reputation as a mystic and healer. Perhaps this reference to the fallibility of human predictions is a covert reference to him!

166. This is the last letter to Rosita in the correspondence archive of the five sisters. Rosita died in 1944. But see also one further letter by Kardinah to Hilda de Booy-Boissevain written in 1951.

Appendix

1. This letter was a copy, possibly transcribed and re-sent following news that the original had been lost. The attached documents were all copies.

2. In 1958, Kardinah recalled the following names: Mr. Reksowardojo (head teacher), Mrs. Soemjar (cooking), her daughter Soesmini, Mrs. Sostomihardjo and Soertigemi ("a girl from an Outer island"), Mrs. van den Bos (sewing and embroidery), and Mrs. Aisijah (religion), "daughter of the head of the mosque in Tegal." Kardinah, "The Three Sisters," 22.

3. Presumably this indicates the difference between what was budgeted for and the actual costs. Salaries had to be increased. References to "teacher" in this document need not have indicated a qualified teacher, but a distinction is clearly being made in the use of the Dutch term "onderwijzeres" (translated here as "teacher") and the Indonesian term "guru" (also meaning "teacher"). Given the task (teaching cooking and batik-making), it seems that gurus were experienced practitioners but not qualified instructors. The significance of religious education in the school is not clear. While apparently the position was downgraded to "pupil teacher, needlework and religious education," it now attracted a higher salary. The designation "pupil teacher" also indicated that the teacher was being prepared for a trained teacher examination, suggesting an upgrading. Unlike the Semarang Kartini School, which was planned as a "neutral" school, Kardinah's school was designated in government documents as a private Islamic school.

4. This document appears to be a personalized summary prepared by the controleur for the regent and Kardinah. The text in brackets after the title is a note apparently from Kardinah to Abendanon.

5. [Note in original] In connection with the request to this Department for a female government schoolteacher to be provided for the school based on government resolution of 25 August 1914 No. 28 (supplement No. 8195) (which followed representations from the Resident of Pekalongan in his letter of 14 September No. 11061/28, which responded to the Departmental memorandum of 31 May No. 14273, attached herewith), the Inspector of Native Education for District Two has made enquiries which, according to a report just received, have been successful in locating such a teacher.

Glossary

adat	tradition, custom, law
akal	problem
babu	nursemaid
batik	traditionally designed cloth
Budi Utomo	Ennobling Endeavour; first Indonesian national organization, est. 1908
bupati	Javanese regional ruler
controleur (D)	lower European colonial official
des(s)a	village
dokter djawa	graduate of the medical training school for natives
dukun	Javanese spiritualist, mystic, Javanese traditional healer
eerendienst (D)	worship, religion
fonds (D)	fund
Fröbel (work)	"progressive" educational materials based on the pedagogical ideas of Friedrich Fröbel
garuda	eagle
gudang	storage shed
gunting	scissors
guru	teacher
hari raya	special (holy) day
HBS (D)	hogere burger school, academic secondary school
Hibu	(= Ibu, mother), reference to Raden Ayu Moryam, Roekmini's mother
HIS (D)	Hollandsch-Inlandsche School, Dutch-language native elementary school
Indo (D)	Eurasian

Inlandsch (D)	Native
ISDV (ISDP)	Indische Sociaal-Democratische Vereeniging, Indies Social Democratic Partij
jaksa	regional Javanese law officer in Native colonial service
kebaya	traditional women's blouse
kabupaten	official residence of the bupati or regent
kaum muda	young generation
keras	harsh, rough
ketimun	cucumber
Klein Ambtenaar Examen (D)	Junior Civil Service exam
kleintje (D)	little one
Lebaran	end of fasting celebration
magang(s)	Javanese office apprentice
mandur	foreman
mantri	low-ranking native colonial official
mantri guru	elementary school head teacher
Mevrouw (D)	Mrs.
Mindere Welvaart Onderzoek (D)	Declining Welfare Enquiry
Mijnheer (D)	Mister
MULO (D)	meer uitgebreid lager onderwijs, higher elementary school
nijverheid (D)	industry (work)
onderwijs (D)	education
paal (D)	linear measurement, 1506.94 meters
pasangrahan	government guest house
pasar malam	evening market, fair
patih	regent's executive officer
plangi	specially designed silk cloth
priyayi	Javanese aristocrat, upper class
Puasa	fasting month
pusaka(s)	family heirloom(s)
raden ayu	title of (principal) wife of regent, priyayi

raden ajeng	title of unmarried daughter of regent, priyayi
saron	smallest instrument in the gamelan
sarong	item of traditional clothing
sirih	betel nut
Sarekat Islam (SI)	Islamic Brotherhood, early nationalist organization
Sinterklaas (Sint) (D)	St. Nicholas, St. Nicholas's Day, 6 December
Social-Democratische Arbeiders Partij	Social Democratic Labor Party
slendang	cloth worn over the shoulder, used to hold infant
soga	brown coloring
studiefonds (D)	study fund
tandu	litter, sedan chair
tukang	tradesman
vereeniging (D)	organization (modern spelling *vereniging*)
wedel	blue (indigo) coloring
wedono	district official

Bibliography

Abendanon, J. H. "De Opvoeding van Inlandsche Meisjes in Ned-Indië *Oedyana Para Prajitna*, 1, 1909–10, pp. 18–23.
———. Bevordering van het Onderwÿts van Meisjes Behoorende Tot de Inheemsche Bevolking van Ned- Indië, Eerste Koloniale Onderwijs Congres, 1916.
———. *Prae-adviezen van het Eerste Koloniaal Onderwijscongress: te houden te 's-Gravenhage op 28, 29 en 30 Augustus 1916.* 's-Gravenhage: Korthuis, 1916.
———. "Wismo Pranowo (Het Huis Dat Den Blik Verruimt)." *Hindia Poetra*, 1916 I, pp. 115–17.
Adam, A. *The Vernacular Press and the Emergence of Modern Indonesian Consciousness (1855–1913).* Ithaca, NY: Southeast Asia Program, Cornell University, 1995.
Adriani, N., and A. C. Kruyt. *De Bare'e sprekende Toradjas van Midden-Celebes* [The Bare'e-Speaking Toradja of Central Celebes]. 3 vols. Batavia: Landsdrukkerij, 1912–14.
Amin Singgih. "Djiwa Besar." Photocopy, 1967.
Anderson, B. "A Time of Darkness and a Time of Light: Transpositions in Early Nationalist Thought." In A. Reid and D. Marr, eds., *Perceptions of the Past in Southeast Asia.* Singapore: Heinemann, 1980.
Anten, J. "De ontbrekende brief van Kartini." *Indische Letteren* 20 (2005): 24–32.
Bachtiar, H. "Pahlawan nasional dan R.A. Kartini." *Kompas*, 8/12/87.
Bakker, N. *Kind en Karakter: Nederlandse pedagogen over opvoeding in het gezin 1845–1925.* Amsterdam: Het Spinhuis, 1995.
Bel, J. *Nederlandse Literatuur in het Fin de Siècle.* Amsterdam: Amsterdam University Press, 1993.
Biografisch Woordenboek van het Socialisme en de Arbeidersbeweging in Nederland. http://www.iisg.nl/bwsa.
Biografisch Woordenboek van Nederland, s.v. "Abendanon, Jacque Henrij."
Blackburn, S. "Political Relations among Women in a Multi-cultural City." In K. Grijns and P. Nas, eds., *Jakarta-Batavia: Socio-cultural Essays*, 175–98. Leiden: KITLV Press, 2000.

———. *Women and the State in Modern Indonesia.* Cambridge: Cambridge University Press, 2004.

Bloembergen, M. *De Koloniale Vertoningen: De verbeelding van Nederlands-Indië op de Wereldtentoonstellingen (1880–1931).* Amsterdam: Wereldbibliotheek, 2002.

Bosma, U. *Karel Zaalberg: Journalist en strijder voor de Indo.* Leiden: KITLV, 1997.

Bouman, H. *Meer Licht over Kartini.* Haarlem: H. F. Paris, 1954.

Chatterjee, P. *The Nation and Its Fragments: Colonial and Postcolonial Histories.* Princeton: Princeton University Press, 1993.

———. "The Nation and Its Women." In Chatterjee, *The Nation and Its Fragments,* 135–57.

Colenbrander, H. T., and J. E. Stokvis, eds. *Leven en Arbeid van Mr. C. Th. van Deventer.* 3 vols. Amsterdam: P. N. van Kampen, 1916–17.

Coté, J. "The Colonisation and Schooling of the To Pamona of Central Sulawesi, 1895–1925." Master's thesis, Monash University, 1980.

———. "The Correspondence of Kartini's Sisters: Annotations on the Indonesian Nationalist Movement, 1905–1925." *Archipel* 55 (1998): 61–82.

———. "Exhibiting Women's Labour: R. A. Kartini and the Dutch Women Exhibition of 1898." In M. Waarbeek and F. Dieteren, eds., *Een Vaderland voor Vrouwen/A Fatherland for Women,* 119–35. Amsterdam: IISG/IIVA, 2000.

———. *Letters from Kartini: An Indonesian Feminist, 1900–1904.* Clayton: Monash Asia Institute; Melbourne: Hyland House, 1992.

———. *On Feminism and Nationalism: Kartini's Letters to Stella Zeehandelaar.* Clayton: Monash Asia Institute, 2005.

———. "'Our Indies Colony': Reading First Wave Dutch Feminism from the Periphery." *European Journal of Women's Studies* 6 (1999): 463–84.

———. "Reading Kartini 1899–1999: Education and the Colonial Experience in Java." In Joyce Goodman and Jane Martin, eds., *Gender Politics and the Experience of Education: An International Perspective,* 199–224. London: Woburn Press, 2002.

———. "Tirto Adhi Soerjo and the Narration of Indonesian Modernity, 1909–1912." *Review of Indonesian and Malaysian Affairs* 32 (1998): 1–41.

———. "Towards an Architecture of Association: H. F. Tillema, Semarang and the Construction of Colonial Modernity." In P. Nas, ed., *The Indonesian Town Revisited,* 319–47. Singapore: LIT Verlag/ ISEAS, 2002.

Dewantara, Ki Hadjar. "Welke plaats behooren bij het onderwijs te nemen, eensdeels de inheemsche talen (ook Chineesch en Arabisch), anderzijds het Nederlandsch." In *Kebudajaan.* Vol. 2a of *Karja Ki Hadjar Dewantara.* Yogyakarta: Taman Siswa, 1967.

Djajadiningrat-Nieuwenhuis, M. "Noto Soeroto: His Ideas and the Late Colonial Intellectual Climate." *Indonesia* 55 (April 1993): 41–72.
Djoko Suryo. "Social and Economic Life in Rural Semarang under Colonial rule in the Later Nineteenth Century." PhD dissertation, Monash University, 1982.
Doel, H. W. van den. "Indianisatie en ambtenarensalarissen." *Tijdschrift voor Geschiedenis* 100 (1987): 556–79.
———. *De Stille Macht: Het Europese binnenlands bestuur op Java en Madoera, 1806–1942.* Amsterdam: Bert Bakker, 1994.
Fanon, F. *Black Skin, White Mask.* New York: Grove Press, 1967.
Geertz, H., ed. *Letters of a Javanese Princess.* Translated by A. L. Symmers. New York: Norton, 1964.
Grever, M., and B. Waaldijk. *Feministische Openbaarheid: De Nationale Tentoonstelling van Vrouwenarbeid in 1898.* Amsterdam: Stichting, 1998.
Groeneboer, K. *Weg tot het Westen: Het Nederlands voor Indië 1600–1950.* Leiden: KITLV, 1993.
Heel, M. G. van, ed. *Gedenkboek van de Koloniale Tentoonstelling Semarang 20 Augustus–22 November 1914.* Batavia: Mercurius, 1916.
Hoop, L. de. "Ethicus in een Koloniaal Conflict: Een studie naar Dr G. A. J. Hazeu in de onderwijs en bestuurs-verhoudingen in Nederlands-Indië (1900–1920)." Master's thesis, University of Groningen, 1984.
Indische Vereeniging. *Voordrachten en Medeelingen.* Delft: M. van Waltman Beeks, 1911–15.
Jacobs, A. *Reisbrieven uit Africa en Azië, Benevens eenige brieven uit Zweden en Noorwegen.* Vol. 1. Almelo: H. W. Hilarius, 1913.
Jaquet, Frits G. P., ed. *Brieven: aan Mevrouw R. M. Abendanon-Mandri en haar echtgenoot.* Dordrecht: Foris, 1987.
———. "Introduction: Archief Oost en West." KITLV. Typescript, n.d.
Jubileum-Verslag: Uitgegeven ter gelegenheid van het 25-jarig bestaan der vereeniging Kartinifonds te 's-Gravenhage, 1913–1938. 's-Gravenhage, 1939.
Kardinah, Reksonegoro. "The Three Sisters." Translated by A. King. Typescript, 1958.
Kartini, Raden Adjeng. *Door Duisternis tot Licht: Gedachten over en voor het Javaansche volk.* Edited by E. Allard. Amsterdam: Nabrink, 1976.
Kooy-van Zeggelen, M. C. "Van Vrouwenleven 1813–1913." In *Ons Huis in Indië,* edited by Indische Commissie der Tentoonstelling "De Vrouw 1813–1913." Batavia, 1913.
Krisprantono. "Conservation of the Tuntang Railway Heritage." Soegyapranata Catholic University, Semarang. Typescript, n.d.
Krisprantono et al. "The Influence of Economic Development on the Planning and Architecture of Semarang." Typeset, n.d.

Laffan, M. *Islamic Nationhood and Colonial Indonesia: The Umma below the Winds.* London: RoutledgeCurzon, 2003.
Langeveld, H. *Dit Leven van Krachtig Handelen: Hendrikus Colijn, 1869–1944.* Vol. 1, *1869–1933.* Amsterdam: Balans, 1998.
Locher-Scholten, E. *Ethiek in Fragmenten: Vijf studies over kolonial denken en doen van Nederlanders in de Indonesische Archipel, 1877–1942.* Utrecht: HES, 1981.
Maandblad Vanwege de Vereeniging voor Vrouwenkiesrecht. Vol. 3 (1928) to vol. 6 (1931).
"Mangoenhardjo": Vereeniging van Inlandsche Ambtenaren te Semarang. 1911–16.
Miert, H. van. *Bevlogenheid en Onvermogen: Mr J. H. Abendanon en de Ethische Richting in het Nederlandse Kolonialisme.* Leiden: KITLV, 1991.
Mrazek, R. *Engineers of Happy Land: Technology and Nationalism in a Colony.* Princeton: Princeton University Press, 2002.
Nagazumi, A. *The Dawn of Indonesian Nationalism: The Early Years of Budi Utomo.* Tokyo: Institute of Developing Economies, 1972.
Official Tourist Bureau. *Illustrated Tourist Guide to Buitenzorg, the Preanger and Central Java.* Batavia: Official Tourist Bureau, 1913.
Onderzoek naar de Mindere Welvaart der Inlandsche Bevolking op Java en Madoera. Vol. 7, Pt. ixb3, *Verheffing van de Inlandsche Vrouw.* Batavia: Landsdrukkerij, 1914.
Otterspeer, W. *Leiden Oriental Connections, 1850–1940.* Leiden: Brill, 1989.
Penders, C. *Indonesia: Selected Documents.* St. Lucia: Queensland University Press, 1977.
Poeze, H. *In Het Land van de Overheerser.* Vol. 1, Indonesiërsin Nederland, 1600–1950. Dordrecht: Foris, 1986.
Prae-Adviezen en Stenografisch Verslag. *Eerste Koloniaal Onderwijs Congress, s'Gravenhage, 28, 29 en 30 Augustus, 1916.* 's-Gravenhage: Korthuis, 1916.
Purbopranoto, Koentjoro. "Ter Nagedachtenis van Drs RMP Sosro Kartono." *Bijdragen tot de Taal-, Land- en Volkenkunde* 129, nos. 2–3 (1973): 287–301.
Quinn, G. *The Novel in Javanese.* Leiden: KITLV Press, 1992.
Ricklefs, M. *A History of Modern Indonesia since 1300.* 2nd ed. Basingstoke: Macmillan, 1993.
———. *A History of Modern Indonesia since 1200.* 3rd ed. London: Palgrave, 2001.
Sears, L. *Shadows of Empire: Colonial Discourse and Javanese Tales.* Durham, NC: Duke University Press, 1996.
Semarangsche Jaarmarkttentoonstelling. *Verslag van de Eerste Semarangsche Jaarmarkt-Tenoonstelling, 1908.* Batavia: Landsdrukkerij, 1911.

Shiraishi, T. *An Age in Motion: Popular Radicalism in Java, 1912–1926.* Ithaca: Cornell University Press, 1990.
Singgih, Amin. "Djiwa Besar." Typescript, 1967.
"Soembangsih": Gedenkboek Boedi-Oetomo, 1908–1918. Amsterdam: Nederlandsch Indië Oud En Nieuw, 1919.
Soeroto, Noto. *Van Overheersching naar Zelfregeering* [From Colonization to Self-Rule]. 's-Gravenhage: Adi-Poestaka, 1931.
Stevens, T. "Semarang, Central Java and the World, 1870–1900." In *The Indonesian City,* edited by P. Nas. Dordrecht: Foris, 1986.
———. *Vrijmetselarij en Samenleving in Nederlands-Indië en Indonesië, 1764–1962.* Hilversum: Verloren, 1994.
Stuurman, S. *"Wacht op onze daden': Het Liberalisme en de Vernieuwing van de Nederlandse Staat.* Amsterdam: Bert Bakker, 1992.
Surya Ningrat. "Het Javaansch Nationalisme in de Indische beweging." In *"Soembangsih," Gedenkboek Boedi-Oetomo, 1908–1918,* 27–48. Amsterdam, 1918.
Sutherland, Heather. *The Making of the Bureaucratic Elite: The Colonial Transformation of the Javanese Priyayi.* Singapore: Heinemann Educational Books, 1979.
———. "Notes on Java's Regent Families. Part One." *Indonesia* 16 (1973): 113–47.
Taselaar, A. *De Nederlandse Koloniale Lobby: Ondernemers en de Indische Politiek, 1914–1940.* Leiden: Research School CNWS, 1998.
Taylor, J., ed. *Women Creating Indonesia: The First Fifty Years.* Clayton: Monash Asia Institute, 1997.
Tichelman, F. *Socialisme in Indonesië.* Dordrecht: Foris, 1985.
Tjitrosomo, A. S. "Dr Sosro Kartono." Typescript, 1967.
Toer, Pramoedya Ananta. *Sang Pemula.* Jakarta: Hasta Mitra, 1985.
Verslag van de Eerste Semarangsche Jaarmarkt-Tenoonstelling, 1908. 1911.
Vreede-De Stuers, C. "Augustine Magdalena Wawu Runtu." *Archipel* 38 (1988).
Wal, S. L. van der. *Het Onderwijsbeleid in Nederlands-Indië, 1900–1940: Een Bronnenpublikatie.* Groningen: J. B. Wolters, 1963.
Wertheim, W. *The Indonesian Town: Studies in Urban Sociology.* The Hague: W. van Hoeve, 1958.
Wilde, I. de. "Uit de schommelstoelen: Charlotte Jacobs en haar kring in Batavia." In *Vertouwd en vreemd: Ontmoetingen tussen Nederland, Indië en Indonesië,* edited by Esther Captain, Marieke Hellevoort, and Marian van der Klein, 187–94. Hiversum: Verloren, 2000.

Index

Abendanon, Eduard (Didi/Edi), 26, 62, 65–66, 69, 87, 113, 121, 122, 126, 127, 131, 184, 324, 325, 326, 330
Abendanon, Gandolph (Doppie, Dolf), x, 26, 69, 295, 301, 326, 335
Abendanon, Jacques Henri: attendance at Universal Races Congress, 29; background and career, 26–30; death, 297, 379; financial support for Roekmini, 168, 171, 173, 177; influence on development of moderate nationalism, 23, 27, 144, 145, 146, 343; letters to, 2–3; mentor to visiting Indonesian students, 27, 28, 29, 31, 361; opposition to Kartini and Roekmini studying in Europe, 7; role in debates on colonial policy, 16, 26–30, 337; support for Kartini and Roekmini to study in Batavia, 7–9; support for Kartono, 27, 121, 142–43, 144–45, 149, 157, 224–25, 230, 232, 251, 267
Abendanon, John, 26, 119, 156–57, 335, 346
Abendanon-Mandri, Rosita, 2, 7; background, 24–25; preparing Kartini's letters for publication, 134, 137, 139, 151, 153, 251, 340, 341, 366; public-political significance of relationship with sisters, 17; sketches in *Door Duisternis tot Licht*, 323
Adiningrat, Raden Ario Djojo (Kartini's husband): arranged marriage to Kartini, 73–74, 76, 79–80, 327; birth of son Singgih, 96–97, 169; death, 195; widowed, 97, 137, 369. *See also* Soesalip (Singgih)
Adriani, Nicolaus, 22, 51, 76, 92, 129, 270, 330, 338, 341, 371
agricultural credit banks, 131–32, 339
All Asian Women's Conference (Lahore, 1931), 322, 379
Aminah, Njai Haji Siti, 4
anticolonial movement, 379
anticolonial sentiment, 193, 354

arts and crafts. *See* native arts and crafts
Asmaoen, 140, 342
associationism, 30–31, 33, 35, 37, 185, 186, 369, 376, 377, 378
Atmodirono (architect), 23, 283, 284, 292, 376
Australia, 111

Baars, Asser, 285, 376
Bachtiar, Harsya, 33
Bali, 38, 41, 255, 259, 333
Bandera Wolanda (newspaper), 341
Batavia: colonial administration, 22, 206, 207, 212, 298; craftsmen transferred to, 329; modernization of, 38, 70, 85, 218; native arts and crafts, 122, 322, 331, 332, 336; plans of Kartini and Roekmini to train as teachers, 6, 7–9, 32, 60, 66, 69, 73, 76, 81, 325, 326, 327, 328; posting of Jacques Abendanon, 17, 31, 84; posting of Soematri's husband, 51, 269–70, 298, 299; schooling of Srigati (Roekmini's son), 166; training of Soedjono (Roekmini's stepson), 175–76; visit by Roekmini, 150–51, 345; visits by sisters, 41, 218
batik work, 131
Berge, A. L. van den, 365
Berge-Kelder, Johanna Wilhelmina Caroline van den (Lien), 226, 258, 361
Bervoets, H., 22, 53, 84, 101, 142, 329, 332
Bintang Hindia (newspaper), 245, 342, 346
Birkenhouwer, H. R., 284
Boeatan, 122, 136, 336, 340
Boenjamin, 362
Boesono (brother of Kartini), 76, 116, 120, 130, 150, 214, 327, 334, 338, 348, 352, 379
Booy-Boissevan, Hilda de, 158, 186, 347, 348
Borel, Henri, 115, 333
Both, C. J. R., 220, 243, 324, 364
Brandes, M. C., 22, 159, 276
Brooshooft, Pieter, 316, 319

Budi Utomo, 20–21, 23, 34, 39, 53, 143–44, 145, 148, 206, 225, 340–41, 343, 344, 369, 376

Castens, Phie, 226, 227, 229, 361
Central Celebes, 139
child marriage, 54, 250, 366, 372
child welfare, 54
Chinese: appropriation of Javanese culture, 93, 131, 331, 335, 366; batik, 131; domination of indigenous economy, 132, 339; Kartini's view of, 319, 331; nationalist antagonism against, 30, 37–38, 193, 339, 354; population in Java, 15, 314; riots against businesses in Kudus, 378; in Tegal, 319, 354
cholera, 234, 363
colonial attitudes, to natives, 250, 365
colonial bureaucracy, 55–56, 186
colonial civil service: causes of friction, 275, 367, 368, 372–73; frustration at regulations, 348–49, 161–64, 352; intrigues and corruption, 186; Javanese hierarchies within, 329; unification principle, 349
colonial education policy, 192, 192–93, 198, 202, 206–7, 278, 280–82, 290–91, 350, 356, 357
colonial ethnographic research, 371
colonial government (in Batavia) 22, 206, 207, 212, 298
colonial investments, 316
colonial lobby, 27, 316
colonial policy, 16, 27–28, 185. *See also* ethical policy
colonial politics, 30–32, 344
colonial progressivism, 31, 32, 185, 350, 367, 378
Comité voor het Javaansch Nationalisme (Committee for Javanese Nationalism), 34
Comité voor Javaansche Cultuurontwikkeling, 337
communism, 45, 153, 294
crafts. *See* native arts and crafts
cultural change, 14
cultural exhibitions, 336
cultural nationalism, 48, 346–47
cultural nationalist consciousness, 29

Damesweekblad van Indië, Het (journal), 127, 134, 337
Darsito, Raden Mas, 291
Delden, A. J. W. van, 4
Demak, 4
demography, 15–16, 314
desa schools, 198, 356

Deventer, Conrad van, 22, 27, 28, 30, 37, 137, 155, 158, 196, 263, 277, 319, 343, 344, 346, 347, 354, 355, 356, 369–70. *See also* Van Deventer Teacher Training School
Deventer Fonds, 168, 204
Didi. *See* Abendanon, Eduard
Dirdjoprawiro, Raden, 214–15, 236
Dokter Djawa school. *See* STOVIA
domestic science, 61, 132, 138, 198, 200, 324
Donkers, J. C., 266, 370
Door Duisternis tot Licht (Kartini), 15, 16, 30, 38, 115, 134, 137, 139, 151, 153, 154–55, 158, 190, 210, 233, 254, 260, 261–62, 264, 278, 295, 314, 319, 323, 333, 345–46, 347
Doppie. *See* Abendanon, Gandolph
Douwes Dekker, E. F. E., 23, 367, 373
Ducroo, Piet, 136, 340
Duero (Mr.). *See* Ducroo, Piet
Dutch East Indies Company (VOC), 3
Dutch-language education, 28, 35, 36, 192, 200, 204, 278, 318, 335, 341, 351, 356, 358, 375
Dutch Protestant Missionary Society, 22
Dutch women's movement, 5, 16, 18

Echo, De (journal), 63, 88
Edi. *See* Abendanon, Eduard
education: focus of progressive colonialists, 32–33; of girls (*see* women's education); and nationalism, 34–38, 278–79, 374; for native population, 346; and opposition to coeducational schools, 280, 281, 375; results of, 298–99, 379; studying in the Netherlands, 166–67, 255, 291, 293, 349, 377. *See also* domestic science; women's education
Eereschuld, Een (pamphlet), 22, 37
Eerste Koloniaal-Onderwijs Congres. *See* First Colonial Education Conference
Eigen Haard (journal), 130, 338
Elizabeth, Queen of Romania, 334
Engelenberg, A. J. N., 341
ethical period, 344
ethical policy, 16, 28, 316, 319, 335, 339, 341, 357, 367
ethici, 28
Eurasians, 20, 31, 361, 374
European schools, 12, 84, 156, 192, 313

feminist/nationalist view, 286, 377
First Colonial Education Conference (The Hague), 36, 349, 358, 375
freemasonry, 277–78, 373
Fröbel pedagogy and equipment, 51, 54, 83, 86, 93, 177, 292, 329, 331, 351

gamelan, 37, 79, 93
Gazan de la Meuse, Mrs., 204
Genestet, P. A. de, 82, 269, 328, 371
Gezelle, Guido, 122
Gids, De (journal), 346
"Give the Javanese Education," 312
Glaser, Annie, 23, 57, 61–62, 64, 151, 218, 312, 322–23, 324, 345, 360, 364
Gonggrijp, G. L., 74, 76, 97, 134, 327, 332, 339
Great Depression, 296, 298

Hadiningrat, R. M. A. A., 32, 35, 136, 140, 161, 317, 334, 340, 348–49
hari raya, 234, 362
Hazeu, G. A. J., 22, 28, 146, 150–51, 157, 271, 344–45, 346, 369, 377
Hilda van Suylenburg (novel), 34, 227, 229–30, 246–47, 250–51, 361, 365
Hindia Poetra (journal), 358
Hogendorp, Baron van, 203, 357
Hogendorp, Jonkvrouwe Anna van, 357
Holland: Indonesian students, 166–67, 172, 255, 290, 291, 293, 295, 349, 377; demand for native arts and crafts, 6, 32, 85, 128, 336; Kartini and Roekmini's travel and study plans, 7, 59, 60, 63–64, 67
Hollandsch-Inlandsche schools (HIS), 177, 351

Idenburg, A. W. F., 255, 367, 371
Immink, Mien, 372
Indië Weerbaar, 284, 376
Indische culture, 31
Indische Gids, 311
Indische Partij (IP), 21, 23, 217, 276, 373, 374
Indische Sociaal-Democratische Vereeniging (ISDV) (Indies Social Democratic Party), 23, 278, 367, 374, 376
Indische Vereeniging (Netherlands), 23, 29, 45, 140, 143, 144, 148, 225, 313, 342, 343, 344, 347, 361, 362, 367, 375
Indisch Genootschap, 342
Indisch Huis exhibition, 158, 347
"Indo" movement, 23
Indonesia, establishment of new nation, 186
Indonesian Communist Party (PKI), 321, 376
Indonesian identity, 38, 336
Indonesian language, 36
Indonesian nationalist movement, 2, 241
Indonesian student movement (Netherlands), 23, 33, 313
Indonesian Women's Congress, 55, 182–83, 351
"Inlander/Inlandsch," use of term, 323
Insulinde, 374, 376
internal furlough, 41

International Colonial Institute, 29
international women's movement, 16
Islam, 311, 328, 338
Islamic nationalist movement, 9, 34

Jacobs, Aletta, 355, 362
Jacobs, Charles, 348
Jacobs, Charlotte, 22, 355
Japan, 115, 126
Jasper, J. E., 22, 104, 122, 125, 128, 132, 153, 231, 252, 332, 336–37, 345, 362, 366
Java Institute, 341
Javanese cultural revival movement, 22, 23, 34, 318, 337, 341, 344
Javanese etiquette, 323, 368
Javanese fairy tales, 337
Javanese-language education, 278–79, 374–75
Javanese nationalism, 20–23, 34, 38, 141–42, 185, 205, 216–17, 239, 240, 336, 356
Javanese nationalist movement, 376; conservatives and radicals in, 185–86, 238–89, 267, 284–85, 290, 370, 373, 376–77
Javanese traditional culture and customs, 6, 76, 79, 101, 108, 137–38, 258–59, 327, 332, 368
Jepara, 3–4, 42, 311
Jepara woodworking industry, 6, 37, 95, 122–23, 139–40, 329, 331, 336
Joekes, A. M., 283
Jong Java (Young Java), 53, 141, 261, 342, 353, 369

kabupaten schools, 185, 285, 321
Kalinyamat, Ratu, 311
Kamil, Raden, 146, 279, 283, 344, 375
Kardinah (Kleintje): anticolonial sentiment, 193, 354; application for subsidy for school, 199, 356; arranged marriage, 6, 7, 12, 14, 43, 50, 51, 56–57, 184, 187–90, 352, 353; bond with her sisters, 10–14, 352–53; death, 186, 359; education, 12; educational publications, 198, 356; introduction to Dutch feminist literature, 5; lifespan, 1; married life, 191; mother, 4; national consciousness, 185; personal battle between tradition and modernity, 12–13; proposal to administer a Kartini School, 193–94, 354; reaction to publication of Kartini's letters, 191–94; support of father, 5; teaching in Javanese, 36, 204, 205, 353–54; Wismo Pranowo girls' school, 185, 197–206, 207, 208–9, 211–12, 359
Kardina Ziekenhuis (hospital), 212, 359

Index 393

Kartinah: benefits brought by older sisters, 13–14; correspondents, 39–40, 216, 236, 363; education, 118, 127, 136, 220, 334, 360; lifespan, 1; marriage, 214, 215, 236–37; mother, 4; national consciousness, 185; personality, 215; relationship with sisters, 215, 222, 223

Kartini, Raden Ajeng: arranged marriage, 6, 9, 13, 14, 43–44, 51, 72–75, 77–80, 328; bond with her sisters, 10–14; death, 2, 3, 10, 95–98, 223, 331–32; education, 12; introduction to Dutch feminist literature, 5; internal conflicts, 12–13; marriage ceremony, 79; maternal lineage, 4; mother, 4; paternal lineage, 3–4; personality, 50–51; place in history of international feminism, 1; place in Indonesian history, 1, 2; plan to study in Europe, 6–7; plan to train as teacher in Batavia, 6, 7–9; recognized as national hero, 15, 213, 314; relationship with siblings, 1–2; school, 102, 117; support of father, 5

Kartini Fonds, 27, 29, 36, 197, 204, 280, 281, 315, 346, 356

Kartini Schools, 22, 32, 33, 155, 185, 186, 193–94, 199, 272, 285, 340, 346, 354, 356; in Semarang, 158, 196, 263, 265, 267, 269, 347, 354, 355, 369–70, 370, 371

Kartini Vereeniging, 36–37, 158, 346, 347, 356, 357

Kartono: death, 321; as healer and mystic, 340, 379; involvement in establishment of Oost en West, 31, 324; shared ideas with Kartini, 10, 119, 313; speech on Dutch-language education for Javanese, 35, 318, 326; study in the Netherlands, 5–6, 55–61, 30–31, 104, 105, 124, 130–31, 133, 135, 136–37, 144–45, 148, 149–50, 152, 157, 315, 338, 339, 340; support from Abendanon family, 27, 121, 142–43, 144–45, 149, 157, 224–25, 230, 232, 251, 267

kaum generation, 229, 361

Kebon Sirih, 25, 151

kemajuan (progress), 32–34

Kenjo Pinardi, 204

Kern, Professor, 137, 340

Kesteren, C. E. van, 4, 311

Kleintje. *See* Kardinah

Kol, Henri van, 22, 27, 28, 30, 37, 58, 60, 63, 148, 152, 255–56, 257, 276, 312, 323, 344, 367, 373

Kol, Nellie van, 63, 64, 74, 82, 95, 256–58, 268–69, 331, 337, 368, 371

Kolonial Instituut, 316

Krefeld Arts and Crafts Exhibition, 126, 337

Kruyt, Albert, 341, 371

Kudus, 4, 311, 378

Kunst Oud en Nieuw (journal), 153

Lange, Anna Elisabeth de, 24, 26

Lawick van Pabst, J. W., 22, 128, 338

Lebaran, 81, 328, 332

Lekkerkerker, C., 235, 363

letters: and role and possibilities of letter writing, 17–18, 39–40, 363; shift in tone of the sisters' letters, 18–20

Lien. *See* Berge-Kelder, Johanna Wilhelmina Caroline van den

Ligthart, Jan, 291, 377–78

literary style, 19–20

Locomotief, De (newspaper), 7, 58–59, 141, 311, 346

Maandblad Vereeniging voor Vrouwenkiesrecht (magazine), 54, 321

Madura, 4

Majapahit empire, 3

malaria, 361

Malay language, 36, 319

Mangkunegara VII, Royal Prince, 34, 38

Mangoenhardjo (native civil servants' association), 283, 367, 376

Mangoenkoesoemo, Surwedo, 293

Mangoenkoesoemo, Tjipto, 373, 377

Mangoenwikromo, Ibu, 336

Mardi Kamoeljan (Striving for Progress), 54–55

marriage, 55, 59, 117–18, 282–23, 323, 335–36, 375–76. *See also* child marriage; polygamy

measles, 71, 327

Mensinga, A. L., 104, 333

Mindere velvaart Onderzoek commission, 271, 372

mixed marriages, 282–83, 375–76

mobility, 40–42, 269–70, 371

modernity, 338; cultural revolution of, 2, 14; impact of, 256, 270, 367–78, 371; in Java, 38–40, 42–44; victims of, 44–47

Moeljono (brother of Kartini), 104, 239, 241–42, 333, 335, 363, 370

Moeryam, Raden Ayu, 4, 108–9, 296, 333, 369, 379

Moresco, E. (Director of Education), 198, 207, 356

Mühlenfeld, August (Guus), 22, 127, 134, 135–36, 138–39, 227, 228–29, 249, 260, 266, 337, 339, 341

394 Index

Mühlenfeld, Marietje, 22, 46, 227, 228–29, 236, 248, 249, 260, 266, 339, 363

National Exhibition of Women's Work (The Hague), 5–6, 11, 18, 324, 335
nationalism, and education, 34–38
nationalist consciousness, 89, 185, 331
"native," use of the term, xi–xii, 59
native arts and crafts, 32; appropriation by Chinese, 93, 131, 331, 335, 366; Batavia exhibition, 122, 322, 331, 336; Brussels exhibition, 153, 345; Cheribon exhibition, 212; craft school, 52, 337; Krefeld exhibition, 125–26, 128, 337; Paris exhibition, 120, 336; Pekalongan exhibition, 212; popularity and demand for, 212, 329, 336, 359; promotion by Oost en West, 31, 32, 81, 85, 87, 127, 328, 331, 332, 336; Semarang exhibition (annual market), 131, 317, 338, 347; Surabaya exhibition, 104, 122, 125, 128, 131, 132, 139, 322, 339, 366; Tegal exhibition, 212. *See also* Jasper, J. E.; Jepara woodworking industry; National Exhibition of Women's Work (The Hague)
native education, 211–12, 346, 357
Native Law School, 146, 344
native schools, 12, 192, 193, 313–14
native welfare, 121, 335
Negoro, Rekso (Kardinah's husband), 185, 186, 352, 353
Ngasirah, Ibu, 4, 296, 369, 379
Nittel, F. W. P., 274–75, 372
Noto Soeroto, 23, 29, 33, 38, 157, 171, 231, 317, 318, 343, 346–47, 350, 362

Oedayana Para Prayitna (monthly journal), 231, 362
Oetoyo, R. M. A. A. Koesoemo, 23, 116, 117–18, 125–26, 140, 148, 334, 337, 344
Onderwijs, Eeredienst en Nijverheid (OEN), 157, 192, 193
Oost en West, 52; advocacy of colonial reform, 31, 203; establishment of, 324, 332; promotion of native arts and crafts, 31, 32, 81, 85, 87, 127, 328, 331, 332, 336; support for Indonesian students in the Netherlands, 31, 63, 295, 338
"Oproep aan Jong Java," 2, 141
Ostmeier, J. J. B., 275, 276, 372
Overveldt-Biekart, Mrs. van, 54
Ovink-Soer, Marie, 5, 293, 323, 378

Padang, 41, 226, 246, 249, 259, 365
padmi, 4, 12

pasar malam, 207, 208, 358
Perhimpunan Indonesia, 29, 343
plague, 153
Pleijte, Thomas B., 172, 350
Poetri Hindia (Women of the Indies—journal), 349, 358
political autonomy, 377
polygamy, 273–74, 372
practical education philosophy, 83, 329
Prianger, 218–19
"printah aloes," 253, 367
priyayi, 16, 214, 270, 371
Puasa, 102, 328

Quartero, W. P. (controleur of Jepara), 60

Rangi, Ratu, 376
Rawito (brother of Kartini), 105, 116, 271, 333, 334, 335, 371
Razoux Kürh, A., 365
Rechtsschool (native law school), 146, 344
reformist colonial politics, 22, 27–28
Regentenbond (Union of Regents), 343, 376
Regentes (ship), 70
religious instruction, 268, 371
Rivai, Abdul, 38, 342
Roekmini, Raden Ajeng, 1, 4; artistic ability and aspirations, 51, 60–61, 127, 132–33, 326; birth of first child (Ori), 147–48, 151; birth of second child (Kayati), 152; birth of third child (Srigati), 160; bond with her sisters, 10–14, 89–90; "A Call to Young Java," 138, 14–42; close relationship with Kartini, 13–14, 50–51, 68, 73, 75, 78, 99–100, 154; death, 213, 351; death of first child, 164–65; desires and future plans, 52–53, 76–77, 90–91, 118–19, 139; educational ideas, 135, 138; employment, 125, 132, 138, 143, 177–78, 179, 181, 296; engagement and marriage, 12–13, 43, 55, 137–39, 142–43, 214, 340, 359; intellectual and nationalist development, 53–54; introduction to Dutch feminist literature, 5; nationalist consciousness, 89, 101, 138, 143–44, 145, 147–48, 331; nursing training, 67–68, 325–26; opposition from family, 117, 119, 136, 137, 140, 143; pension, 168, 173–75, 177; personal battle between tradition and modernity, 12–13; personal life, 55–56; personality, 51, 335; plan to study in Europe, 6–7, 58–62, 63–64, 324–25; plan to train as teacher in Batavia, 6, 7–9, 66, 325, 327; poetry, 122–24; publications, 127, 134, 337; public life, 54–55;

Index 395

Roekmini, Raden Ajeng *(cont.)*
  relationship with Rosita Abendanon-Mandri, 50; support of father, 5; and woodcraft, 131, 139
Royal Netherlands Institute of Southeast Asian and Caribbean Studies, ix–x, 2

St. Nicholas Day (*Sinterklaas*), 56, 219, 322, 332, 360
Salatiga, 116, 334
Salim, Agus, 9
Santoso (Roekmini's husband), 55–56, 137–38, 143, 162–64, 165–66, 186, 340, 349, 350, 352
Sarekat Dagang Islamiyah, 319, 354
Sarekat Islam, 21, 23, 38, 44, 284–85, 292, 319, 354, 376, 377, 378
Sarjono (Roekmini's stepson), 150, 166–67, 173, 174–75, 176, 177, 178, 181
Sartika, Dewi, 23, 33, 372
school subsidy, 84, 85, 329
Sedio Moeljo, 343
Sekola Derma, 204
selir, 4, 12
Semarang: as a center for public activity, 49, 55; establishment of first Kartini School, 27, 36, 37, 158, 196, 263, 265, 267, 269, 347, 354, 355, 369–70, 370, 371; as a major urban administrative and business center, 4, 40, 41; native arts and crafts exhibition (annual market), 131, 317, 338, 347; posting of Soematri's husband, 37, 41, 153; Roekmini's plan for nursing training, 77
Semarang-Batavia railway, 193
Semarang Municipal Council, 374
Sijthoff, P. (resident of Semarang), 8, 151, 312, 326, 345, 353
Singgih. *See* Soesalip
Singgo (Singowirio), 109, 333
smallpox, 71, 72, 327
Sneevliet, Henk, 285, 376
Snouck Hurgronje, C., 30
Social Democratic Party, 323
Social Democratic Workers Party (SDAP), 276, 373, 374
Soearto (Arto) (Soematri's son), 295, 296–98, 300, 379
Soedibio, Raden Ambia Poerbo, 343, 362
Soedjono (Roekmini's stepson), 169–71, 172–73, 175–76, 179–80
Soekarno, President (Indonesia), 314
Soelastri, 4
Soematri: benefits brought by older sisters, 13–14; birth of first child (Soearto),
262–63, 265, 300; birth of second child (Soemiani), 279; education, 118, 127, 136, 242, 243, 334, 363; engagement and marriage, 153, 232, 238, 247, 249, 252, 253, 254–55, 258–59, 362, 365; lifespan, 1; mother, 4; national consciousness, 185; personality and character, 215, 238, 259; relationship with sisters, 297–98; on religion, 268–69
Soemiani (Soematri's daughter) 279, 298, 299, 301
Soemoto, R. M., 231
Soendari, Siti, 23, 209, 358, 372
Soeriosoeparto, 34, 318
Soerjaningrat, Soewardi, 21, 34, 36, 38–39, 315, 344, 373, 374, 376, 377
Soesalip (Singgih) (Kartini's son), 98, 121–22, 134, 137, 169, 172, 195, 196, 223–24, 231, 245–46, 287, 288–89, 300, 320, 332, 333, 336, 350, 363
Soetino (son of Boesono), 300
Soewarno, 21, 341
Soorjopoetro, R. M. A., 255, 367
Soos, 250, 365
Sosrohadikoesoemo, Raden Ngabehi (Achmad) (Soematri's husband): background and education, 239, 366; career, 40, 55–56, 186, 239, 252, 257, 261, 274–75, 276, 293, 342, 349, 367, 368–69, 372; correspondence with Abendanon family, 186, 261–62, 274–84, 358, 369, 372; education, 35, 259, 368; marriage to Soematri, 362; opposition to radical nationalist and Marxist policies, 275–76, 373; political views, 23, 35–37, 55–56, 216, 239, 342, 356
Sosrokartono. *See* Kartono
Sosroningrat, Raden Mas Adipati Ario, 3, 4, 35, 43; death, 52, 105–8, 107, 333; liberal attitude toward daughters, 5, 12, 335; support for daughters, 5
Srigati (Roekmini's son), 167, 180, 181, 182, 321, 350
Steun voor de Opleiding tot Vrouwelijke Inlandsche Artsen (SOVIA), 196–97, 348, 355
Stokvis, J. E. 319, 346, 386
Stokvis, Z., 142, 254–55, 319, 367, 374
Stokvis-Cohen Stuart, Nellie, 22, 122, 140, 142, 146, 180, 287, 336, 341, 342, 377
Stork, An, x
STOVIA, 20–21, 192, 196, 328, 338
Stuers, Mrs. de, 203
Stuers, Jonkheer L. de, 357

Surabaya, native arts and craft exhibition, 104, 122, 125, 128, 131, 132, 139, 322, 339, 366
Susunan/Susuhunan of Solo, 41, 69–70
Sylva, Carmen, 117, 334

Taman Siswa education system, 39, 378
Tegal, 36, 37, 41, 69, 193–94, 209, 210, 212, 236, 276, 293, 294, 295, 319, 350, 352, 353, 354, 358, 359. *See also* Van Deventer Teacher Training School; Wisma Pranowo (Kardinah's school)
Tehupeiory, Johan E., 140, 145, 341, 343
Tehupeiory, W. K., 140, 341
Terburgh, J. T., 226, 361
Tirto Adhi Soerjo, 34, 38, 349, 358
Tjokroaminoto, Raden Haji Oemar Said, 377
Tjokrohadisosro (Soelastri's husband), 55, 88, 330
Tjondronegoro, Pangeran Ario, 4, 32
Tjondronegoro family, 3, 4, 15, 345
tourism, 40, 41
traditional feudal honorifics, 10–11
transnational capitalism, 28, 31

unification principle (civil service), 349
Universal Races Congress, 29

Van Deventer Teacher Training School, 36, 168, 208, 283, 350, 356
Vereeniging tot Bevordering der Inlandsche Ziekenverpleging (Organization for the Promotion of Nursing), 287, 377
Vereeniging voor Vrouwenkiesrecht (VVV), 54–55, 204, 322, 351
Versteegh, Marietje, 236
Volksraad, 377

Wanita Soeworo (Women's Voice—journal), 349, 358
Wawo Runtu, Etti, 50, 88, 321, 330
Wederopbouw, 34, 38
Weekblad voor Indie, Het, 141
Westerveld, Dirk J. A., 23, 279, 374, 375
Wijoto Kenjo Deso, 204

Wilhelmina, queen of the Netherlands, 6, 130, 327, 329, 347
Wilhelmina Room, 85
Wisma Pranowo (Kardinah's school), 185, 197–206, 293, 303–10, 355, 356, 357, 358, 379–80
women: behavior of European men toward Javanese women, 362, 365; as carriers of tradition, 35; financial independence for, 272, 372; improvement of conditions for, 11, 54, 90–91, 358; role in nationalist movement, 343; Welfare Commission's enquiry into position of Javanese women, 271–74, 372
women's education, 54, 168, 171, 192–93, 216, 350; achievements, 299; admission to native medical school, 196–97; advocacy for, 23, 136, 225, 278, 285, 349, 361, 373; classroom established by Kartini, 73, 75, 78, 83–84, 85–86, 91–92, 102, 117, 329, 334; establishment of girls' schools, 204–5, 317; first "native" women to gain financial support to study, 9; funds to assist students, 159, 348; further study in Europe, 312; girls' school in Jepara, 138, 143, 340, 343; girls' school in Rembang, 155, 346; girls' school in Tegal, 185; opposition to, 251–22, 253, 366; and opposition to coeducational schools, 280–21, 375; opposition to establishing girls' schools, 140, 335; rejection of Europeanization of native girls, 205; support for establishment of girls' schools, 28, 36, 138, 335; teacher training schools, 209, 280–82, 375; vocational training, 272–74, 372. *See also* domestic science; Kartini Schools; Wisma Pranowo
women's health, 22, 54
women's suffrage movement, 54, 362

Zeehandelaar, Stella, 10, 317
Zeilinga, E. A., 85, 329
Zuylen-Tromp, N. van, 120, 122, 127, 131, 136, 335, 345

Index 397

www.ingramcontent.com/pod-product-compliance
Lightning Source LLC
Chambersburg PA
CBHW031228290426
44109CB00012B/209